S·O·U·R·C·E·S

NOTABLE
SELECTIONS IN

Multicultural Education

About the Editor

JANA NOEL is an associate professor of educational foundations at Montana State University, Bozeman. She received her Ph.D. in philosophy of education from the University of California, Los Angeles, in 1991. Her research focuses on multicultural, social, and philosophical issues in education. In particular, much of her work has been in the areas of multicultural teacher education and Aristotelian practical reasoning. She is the author of the textbook *Developing Multicultural Educators* (Longman, 1999), and she has published in such journals as *Journal of Teacher Education, Teaching Education, Educational Theory,* and *Studies in Philosophy and Education.* Noel is past president of the Philosophical Studies of Education group within the American Educational Research Association, and she serves as secretary-treasurer of the International Network of Philosophers of Education.

S·O·U·R·C·E·S

NOTABLE SELECTIONS IN
Multicultural Education

EDITED BY

JANA NOEL
Montana State University

Dushkin/McGraw-Hill

A Division of The McGraw·Hill Companies

Manufactured in the United States of America

First Edition

    5 6 7 8 9 10   QPF/QPF   0 5 4 3

Library of Congress Cataloging-in-Publication Data
  Main entry under title:
    Sources: notable selections in multicultural education/edited by Jana Noel.—1st ed.
    Includes bibliographical references and index.
    1. Multicultural education. I. Noel, Jana, *comp.*

                                                                    370.19
  0-07-233330-8   ISSN: 1525-3724

 Printed on Recycled Paper

Preface

Multicultural education as a field has developed within a set of historical, philosophical, political, economic, and social contexts. There are a number of differing perspectives on the importance or role of multicultural education in today's society, and there are numerous ideas for the practice of multicultural education in classrooms and schools. This volume is intended to provide a broad and accessible layout of the field of multicultural education. It is a collection of the important and notable readings and authors that have helped to shape the field of multicultural education and that will continue to shape the field in years to come. It is intended to fill a void by including selections in the areas of the theoretical bases for multicultural education, which lay the framework that enables K–12 and college/university educators and administrators to create multicultural classrooms and schools. Through these readings, multicultural educators can set their current practices within the comprehensive set of ideas found within the selections presented here.

This book is intended for both undergraduate and graduate courses in the areas of multicultural education and social foundations of education. Course titles that are commonly seen in these areas include Multicultural Education; Pluralism in Education; Cultural Diversity in Education; Race, Class, and Gender in Education; Social Equity in Education; Social Foundations of Education; and Foundations of Education. These types of courses are offered in most universities nationwide. In many states, the certification of teachers requires that they have taken at least one course dealing with multicultural education, thus making the multicultural education course a required one. In addition, at the graduate level, many universities offer these types of courses within their programs to help future teachers, administrators, researchers, and professors to better understand multicultural issues within society and within the schools. This volume is intended to allow for more effective use of multicultural education in such courses. For teachers and professors, the lack of availability of the notable articles in the field of multicultural education makes it difficult to prepare for a course, develop a syllabus, and create a reading list. For students, who would frequently be asked to read a number of the selections in this book, this book gathers the selections in a way that makes them readily available. And for researchers, a collection such as this one allows for a broad and accessible examination of the field.

Finally, this collection will enable educators to create multicultural classrooms and overall school environments with a better understanding of the important ideas that have shaped the field. The selections in this book give recommendations for the practice of multicultural education in several settings: in the classroom, when selecting the curriculum, and when planning and administering school environments to make them multicultural.

ORGANIZATION OF THE BOOK.   This book begins with two sections that focus on the foundations and key concepts that are integral to the field of multicultural education. Part 1 provides the basis for the remainder of the book by putting multicultural education into historical, philosophical, and social contexts. This section of the book helps teachers, researchers, and students to understand how current practices in multicultural education have been conceived and developed within a set of societal contexts. Part 2 presents selections from past and present that have clarified the key concepts in multicultural education. These concepts are crucial to the understanding of important concepts within society, such a prejudice and racism, and how these help to frame what multicultural education means and how it is practiced.

The next section shifts the focus to the study of multicultural education as a field. Part 3 presents selections that critically discuss studying the field of multicultural education. This section begins with selections that are critical of the very idea of multicultural education and that posit a return to a more conservative view of society. It ends with selections that remind readers of the importance of using multicultural education as a way to address the most important social issues within school and society, asking us to recognize the important political and ethical implications of multicultural education.

This book concludes with two sections that address the practices of multicultural education. Part 4 includes selections on providing multicultural education for all students. This section applies the principles of multicultural education to the question of how to best educate students from many diverse groups. And finally, Part 5 ties together all of the ideas in this book into sections on multicultural practices in the schools. This section's selections give recommendations of how to make classrooms and curriculum more multicultural and how to make multicultural education part of an entire schoolwide effort.

SELECTION OF MATERIALS FOR THE BOOK.   Part of the very nature of the field of multicultural education is that there are multiple perspectives on the theories and practices involved in it. This can sometimes leave an educator feeling confused or overwhelmed about how to study multicultural education or how to practice it. Throughout this book, it can be seen that there are multiple—and sometimes competing—perspectives on multicultural education. But, importantly, each perspective presented provides additional ways of understanding multicultural education.

The sections give a broad inclusion of areas, ideas, and concepts that have actually forged the field of multicultural education. The selections have been chosen based on their high level of use or reference within courses and materials in the field of multicultural education. In some cases, the selection itself is critical to the study of multicultural education, as it is included in many courses and works on multicultural education. In other cases, the author has been recognized among multicultural educators as providing crucial advances in the understanding or framing of multicultural education. Each selection is preceded by a brief introductory headnote that lays out the importance of the selection and its author to the development of the field of multicultural education. A short summary of the selection can also be found in the headnote.

Many possible selections and authors have been left out of this collection. This is unavoidable in a volume such as this one. My hope is that the selections included will provide a broad spectrum of topics and sample approaches to the field so that educators will be able to get a feeling for the field as a whole.

ON THE INTERNET.   Each part in this book is preceded by an *On the Internet* page. This page provides a list of Internet site addresses that are relevant to the part as well as a description of each site.

A WORD TO THE INSTRUCTOR.   An *Instructor's Manual With Test Questions* (multiple-choice and essay) is available through the publisher for instructors using *Sources: Notable Selections in Multicultural Education* in the classroom.

ACKNOWLEDGMENTS.   I want to thank several people from Dushkin/ McGraw-Hill who helped me in the process of pulling together this book. Theodore Knight, list manager for the Sources series, has been especially helpful from the start of the project. David Dean, the previous list manager for the Sources series, was involved at the beginning. David Brackley, senior developmental editor, has helped in the final stages of the process. And thanks to all the other staff at Dushkin/McGraw-Hill who helped to put this book into production.

And on a personal note, I want to give special thanks to David Powell and to my parents Jim and Jan Noel, who have all given me love, support, and encouragement not only in this book but in all of my personal and professional endeavors.

Jana Noel
Montana State University

Contents

PART ONE

Foundations of Multicultural Education

On the Internet . . .

Sites appropriate to Part One

The American Educational Studies Association (AESA) is an educational organization comprised of teachers, researchers, and students who focus on the foundations of education fields of history, philosophy, sociology, anthropology, politics, economics, and comparative/international studies.

> http://ericir.syr.edu/AESA/

The Philosophy of Education Society (PES) is the national organization of philosophers of education in the United States. This Web site offers links to articles, issues, and resources of interest to those studying philosophy of education and other foundations of education fields.

> http://www.ed.uiuc.edu/EPS/PES/

This Web site gives access to *Sociology of Education Abstracts,* a set of abstracts of articles from across the world covering the social and cultural context of schooling and society.

> http://www.carfax.co.uk/sea-ad.htm

CHAPTER 1

Historical Perspectives on Multicultural Education

1.1 RONALD T. TAKAKI

A Different Mirror

Ronald T. Takaki is a leading scholar of ethnic studies, with a particular focus on multicultural history. He examines original historical documents in his efforts to provide an understanding of the common experiences of immigrants, the working class, and women throughout history. He writes of the conditions of countries, old and new, and of immigrants, and he records the words of songs sung by workers throughout history. Through his words, we can see our history and our future as a multicultural nation. Takaki encourages us to examine the historical context that lies behind our multicultural society. Without it, he says, we are left confused by ethnic and racial changes and violence in America today. We need to learn about each other's cultures, histories, and economic situations, he urges, and to hear the stories told by the people of all races, classes, and genders. "Their stories are worthy. Through their stories, the people who have lived America's history can help all of us understand that Americans originated from many shores, and that all of us are entitled to dignity."

Takaki is a professor of ethnic studies at the University of California, Berkeley. His studies of the multicultural history of the United States include the book from which the following selection is excerpted, *A Different Mirror: A History of Multicultural America* (Little, Brown, 1993). Although Takaki looks at multicultural history through the experiences of many groups, his main focus is on Asian Americans. His other books include *Strangers from a Different Shore: A History of Asian Americans* (Little, Brown, 1989) and *Iron Cages: Race and Culture in 19th-Century America* (Oxford University Press, 1990).

Key Concept: shared struggles in multicultural history

I had flown from San Francisco to Norfolk and was riding in a taxi to my hotel to attend a conference on multiculturalism. Hundreds of educators from across the country were meeting to discuss the need for greater cultural diversity in the curriculum. My driver and I chatted about the weather and the tourists. The sky was cloudy, and Virginia Beach was twenty minutes away. The rearview mirror reflected a white man in his forties. "How long have you been in this country?" he asked. "All my life," I replied, wincing. "I was born in the United States." With a strong southern drawl, he remarked: "I was wondering because your English is excellent!" Then, as I had many times before, I explained: "My grandfather came here from Japan in the 1880s. My family has been here, in America, for over a hundred years." He glanced at me in the mirror. Somehow I did not look "American" to him; my eyes and complexion looked foreign.

Suddenly, we both became uncomfortably conscious of a racial divide separating us. An awkward silence turned my gaze from the mirror to the passing landscape, the shore where the English and the Powhatan Indians first encountered each other. Our highway was on land that Sir Walter Raleigh had renamed "Virginia" in honor of Elizabeth I, the Virgin Queen. In the English cultural appropriation of America, the indigenous peoples themselves would become outsiders in their native land. Here, at the eastern edge of the continent, I mused, was the site of the beginning of multicultural America. Jamestown, the English settlement founded in 1607, was nearby: the first twenty Africans were brought here a year before the Pilgrims arrived at Plymouth Rock. Several hundred miles offshore was Bermuda, the "Bermoothes" where William Shakespeare's Prospero had landed and met the native Caliban in *The Tempest*. Earlier, another voyager had made an Atlantic crossing and unexpectedly bumped into some islands to the south. Thinking he had reached Asia, Christopher Columbus mistakenly identified one of the islands as "Cipango" (Japan). In the wake of the admiral, many peoples would come to America from different shores, not only from Europe but also Africa and Asia. One of them would be my grandfather. My mental wandering across terrain and time ended abruptly as we arrived at my destination. I said good-bye to my driver and went into the hotel, carrying a vivid reminder of why I was attending this conference.

Questions like the one my taxi driver asked me are always jarring, but I can understand why he could not see me as American. He had a narrow but widely shared sense of the past—a history that has viewed American as European in ancestry. "Race," [novelist] Toni Morrison explained, has functioned as a "metaphor" necessary to the "construction of Americanness": in the creation of our national identity, "American" has been defined as "white."

Ronald T. Takaki

But America has been racially diverse since our very beginning on the Virginia shore, and this reality is increasingly becoming visible and ubiquitous. Currently, one-third of the American people do not trace their origins to Europe; in California, minorities are fast becoming a majority. They already predominate in major cities across the country—New York, Chicago, Atlanta, Detroit, Philadelphia, San Francisco, and Los Angeles.

This emerging demographic diversity has raised fundamental questions about America's identity and culture. In 1990, *Time* published a cover story on "America's Changing Colors." "Someday soon," the magazine announced, "white Americans will become a minority group." How soon? By 2056, most Americans will trace their descent to "Africa, Asia, the Hispanic world, the Pacific Islands, Arabia—almost anywhere but white Europe." This dramatic change in our nation's ethnic composition is altering the way we think about ourselves. "The deeper significance of America's becoming a majority nonwhite society is what it means to the national psyche, to individuals' sense of themselves and their nation—their idea of what it is to be American." ...

African Americans have been the central minority throughout our country's history. They were initially brought here on a slave ship in 1619. Actually, these first twenty Africans might not have been slaves; rather, like most of the white laborers, they were probably indentured servants. The transformation of Africans into slaves is the story of the "hidden" origins of slavery. How and when was it decided to institute a system of bonded black labor? What happened, while freighted with racial significance, was actually conditioned by class conflicts within white society. Once established, the "peculiar institution" would have consequences for centuries to come. During the nineteenth century, the political storm over slavery almost destroyed the nation. Since the Civil War and emancipation, race has continued to be largely defined in relation to African Americans—segregation, civil rights, the underclass, and affirmative action. Constituting the largest minority group in our society, they have been at the cutting edge of the Civil Rights Movement. Indeed, their struggle has been a constant reminder of America's moral vision as a country committed to the principle of liberty. Martin Luther King clearly understood this truth when he wrote from a jail cell: "We will reach the goal of freedom in Birmingham and all over the nation, because the goal of America is freedom. Abused and scorned though we may be, our destiny is tied up with America's destiny."

Asian Americans have been here for over one hundred and fifty years, before many European immigrant groups. But as "strangers" coming from a "different shore," they have been stereotyped as "heathen," exotic, and unassimilable. Seeking "Gold Mountain," the Chinese arrived first, and what happened to them influenced the reception of the Japanese, Koreans, Filipinos, and Asian Indians as well as the Southeast Asian refugees like the Vietnamese and the Hmong. The 1882 Chinese Exclusion Act was the first law that prohibited the entry of immigrants on the basis of nationality. The Chinese condemned this restriction as racist and tyrannical. "They call us 'Chink,'" complained a Chinese immigrant, cursing the "white demons." "They think we no good! America cuts us off. No more come now, too bad!" This precedent later provided a basis for the restriction of European immigrant groups such as Italians, Russians, Poles, and Greeks. The Japanese painfully discovered that their accomplishments in America did not lead to acceptance, for during World War II, unlike Italian Americans and German Americans, they were placed in internment camps. Two-thirds of them were citizens by birth. "How could I as a 6-month-old child born in this country," asked Congressman Robert Matsui years later, "be declared by my own Government to be an enemy alien?" Today, Asian Americans represent the fastest-growing ethnic group. They have also become the focus of much mass media attention as "the Model Minority" not only for blacks and Chicanos, but also for whites on welfare and even middle-class whites experiencing economic difficulties.

Chicanos represent the largest group among the Hispanic population, which is projected to outnumber African Americans. They have been in the United States for a long time, initially incorporated by the war against Mexico. The treaty had moved the border between the two countries, and the people of "occupied" Mexico suddenly found themselves "foreigners" in their "native land." As historian Albert Camarillo pointed out, the Chicano past is an integral part of America's westward expansion, also known as "manifest destiny." But while the early Chicanos were a colonized people, most of them today have immigrant roots. Many began the trek to El Norte in the early twentieth century. "As I had heard a lot about the United States," Jesus Garza recalled, "it was my dream to come here." "We came to know families from Chihuahua, Sonora, Jalisco, and Durango," stated Ernesto Galarza. "Like ourselves, our Mexican neighbors had come this far moving step by step, working and waiting, as if they were feeling their way up a ladder." Nevertheless, the Chicano experience has been unique, for most of them have lived close to their homeland—a proximity that has helped reinforce their language, identity, and culture. This migration to El Norte has continued to the present. Los Angeles has more people of Mexican origin than any other city in the world, except Mexico City. A mostly mestizo people of Indian as well as African and Spanish ancestries, Chicanos currently represent the largest minority group in the Southwest, where they have been visibly transforming culture and society.

The Irish came here in greater numbers than most immigrant groups. Their history has been tied to America's past from the very beginning. Ireland represented the earliest English frontier: the conquest of Ireland occurred before the colonization of America, and the Irish were the first group that the English called "savages." In this context, the Irish past foreshadowed the Indian future. During the nineteenth century, the Irish, like the Chinese, were victims of British colonialism. While the Chinese fled from the ravages of the Opium Wars, the Irish were pushed from their homeland by "English tyranny." Here they become construction workers and factory operatives as well as the "maids" of America. Representing a Catholic group seeking to settle in a fiercely Protestant society, the Irish immigrants were targets of American nativist hostility. They were also what historian Lawrence J. McCaffrey called "the pioneers of the American urban ghetto," "previewing" experiences that would later be shared by the Italians, Poles, and other groups from southern and eastern Europe. Furthermore, they offer contrast to the immigrants from Asia. The Irish came about the same time as the Chinese, but they had a distinct advantage: the Naturalization Law of 1790 had reserved citizenship for "whites" only. Their compatible complexion allowed them to assimilate by blending into American Society. In making their journey successfully into the mainstream, however, these immigrants from Erin pursued an Irish "ethnic" strategy: they promoted "Irish" solidarity in order to gain political power and also to dominate the skilled blue-collar occupations, often at the expense of the Chinese and blacks.

Fleeing pogroms and religious persecution in Russia, the Jews were driven from what John Cuddihy described as the "Middle Ages into the Anglo-American world of the *goyim* 'beyond the pale.' " To them, America represented the Promised Land. This vision led Jews to struggle not only for themselves but also for other oppressed groups, especially blacks. After the 1917 East St. Louis race riot, the Yiddish *Forward* of New York compared this anti-black violence to a 1903 pogrom in Russia: "Kishinev and St. Louis—the same soil, the same people." Jews cheered when Jackie Robinson broke into the Brooklyn Dodgers in 1947. "He was adopted as the surrogate hero by many of us growing up at the time," recalled Jack Greenberg of the NAACP Legal Defense Fund. "He was the way we saw ourselves triumphing against the forces of bigotry and ignorance." Jews stood shoulder to shoulder with blacks in the Civil Rights Movement: two-thirds of the white volunteers who went south during the 1964 Freedom Summer were Jewish. Today Jews are considered a highly successful "ethnic" group. How did they make such great socioeconomic strides? This question is often reframed by neoconservative intellectuals like Irving Kristol and Nathan Glazer to read: if Jewish immigrants were able to lift themselves from poverty into the mainstream through self-help and education without welfare and affirmative action, why can't blacks? But what this thinking overlooks is the unique history of Jewish immigrants, especially the initial advantages of many of them as literate and skilled. Moreover, it minimizes the virulence of racial prejudice rooted in American slavery.

Indians represent a critical contrast, for theirs was not an immigrant experience. The Wampanoags were on the shore as the first English strangers arrived in what would be called "New England." The encounters between Indians and whites not only shaped the course of race relations, but also influenced the very culture and identity of the general society. The architect of Indian removal, President Andrew Jackson told Congress: "Our conduct toward these people is deeply interesting to the national character." Frederick Jackson Turner understood the meaning of this observation when he identified the frontier as our transforming crucible. At first, the European newcomers had to wear Indian moccasins and shout the war cry. "Little by little," as they subdued the wilderness, the pioneers became "a new product" that was "American." But Indians have had a different view of this entire process. "The white man," Luther Standing Bear of the Sioux explained, "does not understand the Indian for the reason that he does not understand America." Continuing to be "troubled with primitive fears," he has "in his consciousness the perils of this frontier continent. . . . The man from Europe is still a foreigner and an alien. And he still hates the man who questioned his path across the continent." Indians questioned what Jackson and Turner trumpeted as "progress." For them, the frontier had a different "significance": their history was how the West was lost. But their story has also been one of resistance. As Vine Deloria [a writer and one of today's leading Indian spokesmen] declared, "Custer died for your sins."

By looking at these groups from a multicultural perspective, we can comparatively analyze their experiences in order to develop an understanding of their differences and similarities. Race, we will see, has been a social construction that has historically set apart racial minorities from European immigrant groups. Contrary to the notions of scholars like Nathan Glazer and Thomas Sowell, race in America has not been the same as ethnicity. A broad comparative focus also allows us to see how the varied experiences of different racial and ethnic groups occurred within shared contexts.

During the nineteenth century, for example, the Market Revolution employed Irish immigrant laborers in New England factories as it expanded cotton fields worked by enslaved blacks across Indian lands toward Mexico. Like blacks, the Irish newcomers were stereotyped as "savages," ruled by passions rather than "civilized" virtues such as self-control and hard work. The Irish saw themselves as the "slaves" of British oppressors, and during a visit to Ireland in the 1840s, Frederick Douglass found that the "wailing notes" of the Irish ballards reminded him of the "wild notes" of slave songs. The United States annexation of California, while incorporating Mexicans, led to trade with Asia and the migration of "strangers" from Pacific shores. In 1870, Chinese immigrant laborers were transported to Massachusetts as scabs to break an Irish immigrant strike; in response, the Irish recognized the need for interethnic working-class solidarity and tried to organize a Chinese lodge of the Knights of St. Crispin. After the Civil War, Mississippi planters recruited Chinese immigrants to discipline the newly freed blacks. During the debate over an immigration exclusion bill in 1882, a senator asked: If Indians could be located on reservations, why not the Chinese?

Other instances of our connectedness abound. In 1903, Mexican and Japanese farm laborers went on strike together in California: their union officers had names like Yamaguchi and Lizarras, and strike meetings were conducted in Japanese and Spanish. The Mexican strikers declared that they were standing in solidarity with their "Japanese brothers" because the two groups had toiled together in the fields and were now fighting together for a fair wage. Speaking in impassioned Yiddish during the 1909 "uprising of twenty thousand" strikers in New York, the charismatic Clara Lemlich compared the abuse of Jewish female garment workers to the experience of blacks: "[The bosses] yell at the girls and 'call them down' even worse than I imagine the Negro slaves were in the South." During the 1920s, elite universities like Harvard worried about the increasing numbers of Jewish students, and new admissions criteria were instituted to curb their enrollment. Jewish students were scorned for their studiousness and criticized for their "clannishness." Recently, Asian-American students have been the targets of similar complaints: they have been called "nerds" and told there are "too many" of them on campus.

Indians were already here, while blacks were forcibly transported to America, and Mexicans were initially enclosed by America's expanding border. The other groups came here as immigrants: for them, America represented liminality—a new world where they could pursue extravagant urges and do things they had thought beyond their capabilities. Like the land itself, they found themselves "betwixt and between all fixed points of classification." No longer fastened as fiercely to their old countries, they felt a stirring to become new people in a society still being defined and formed.

Ronald T. Takaki

These immigrants made bold and dangerous crossings, pushed by political events and economic hardships in their homelands and pulled by America's demand for labor as well as by their own dreams for a better life. "By all means let me go to America," a young man in Japan begged his parents. He had calculated that in one year as a laborer here he could save almost a thousand yen—an amount equal to the income of a governor in Japan. "My dear Father," wrote an immigrant Irish girl living in New York, "Any man or woman without a family are fools that would not venture and come to this plentyful Country where no man or woman ever hungered." In the shtetls of Russia, the cry "To America!" roared like "wild-fire." "America was in everybody's mouth," a Jewish immigrant recalled. "Businessmen talked [about] it over their accounts; the market women made up their quarrels that they might discuss it from stall to stall; people who had relatives in the famous land went around reading their letters." Similarly, for Mexican immigrants crossing the border in the early twentieth century, El Norte became the stuff of overblown hopes. "If only you could see how nice the United States is," they said, "that is why the Mexicans are crazy about it."

The signs of America's ethnic diversity can be discerned across the continent—Ellis Island, Angel Island, Chinatown, Harlem, South Boston, the Lower East Side, places with Spanish names like Los Angeles and San Antonio or Indian names like Massachusetts and Iowa. Much of what is familiar in America's cultural landscape actually has ethnic origins. The Bing cherry was developed by an early Chinese immigrant named Ah Bing. American Indians were cultivating corn, tomatoes, and tobacco long before the arrival of Columbus. The term *okay* was derived from the Choctaw word *oke*, meaning "it is so." There is evidence indicating that the name *Yankee* came from Indian terms for the English—from *eankke* in Cherokee and *Yankwis* in Delaware. Jazz and blues as well as rock and roll have African-American origins. The "Forty-Niners" of the Gold Rush learned mining techniques from the Mexicans; American cowboys acquired herding skills from Mexican *vaqueros* and adopted their range terms—such as *lariat* from *la reata*, *lasso* from *lazo*, and *stampede* from *estampida*. Songs like "God Bless America," "Easter Parade," and "White Christmas" were written by a Russian-Jewish immigrant named Israel Baline, more popularly known as Irving Berlin.

... Carlos Fuentes points out that mirrors have been found in the tombs of ancient Mexico, placed there to guide the dead through the underworld. He also tells us about the legend of Quetzalcoatl, the Plumed Serpent: when this god was given a mirror by the Toltec deity Tezcatlipoca, he saw a man's face in the mirror and realized his own humanity. For us, the "mirror" of history can guide the living and also help us recognize who we have been and hence are. In *A Distant Mirror*, Barbara W. Tuchman finds "phenomenal parallels" between the "calamitous 14th century" of European society and our own era. We can, she observes, have "greater fellow-feeling for a distraught age" as we painfully recognize the "similar disarray," "collapsing assumptions," and "unusual discomfort."

But what is needed in our own perplexing times is not so much a "distant" mirror, as one that is "different." While the study of the past can provide collective self-knowledge, it often reflects the scholar's particular perspective or view of the world. What happens when historians leave out many of America's peoples? What happens, to borrow the words of Adrienne Rich, "when someone with the authority of a teacher" describes our society, and "you are not in it"? Such an experience can be disorienting—"a moment of psychic disequilibrium, as if you looked into a mirror and saw nothing."

Through their narratives about their lives and circumstances, the people of America's diverse groups are able to see themselves and each other in our common past. They celebrate what Ishmael Reed has described as a society "unique" in the world because "the world is here"—a place "where the cultures of the world crisscross." Much of America's past, they point out, has been riddled with racism. At the same time, these people offer hope, affirming the struggle for equality as a central theme in our country's history. At its conception, our nation was dedicated to the proposition of equality. What has given concreteness to this powerful national principle has been our coming together in the creation of a new society. "Stuck here" together, workers of different backgrounds have attempted to get along with each other.

> People harvesting
>
> Work together unaware
>
> Of racial problems,

wrote a Japanese immigrant describing a lesson learned by Mexican and Asian farm laborers in California.

Finally, how do we see our prospects for "working out" America's racial crisis? Do we see it as through a glass darkly? Do the televised images of racial hatred and violence that riveted us in 1992 during the days of rage in Los Angeles frame a future of divisive race relations—what Arthur Schlesinger, Jr., has fearfully denounced as the "disuniting of America"? Or will Americans of diverse races and ethnicities be able to connect themselves to a larger narrative? Whatever happens, we can be certain that much of our society's future will be influenced by which "mirror" we choose to see ourselves. America does not belong to one race or one group, the people in this study remind us, and Americans have been constantly redefining their national identity from the moment of first contact on the Virginia shore. By sharing their stories, they invite us to see ourselves in a different mirror.

1.2 JOEL SPRING

The Great Civil Rights Movement and the New Culture Wars

Joel Spring has written about the multifaceted nature of America's multicultural history. His early work in the 1970s and 1980s focused attention on the influence that the factory and corporate models of production had on the purposes and functions of schools throughout the twentieth century. He infuses his work with the political nature of American education, and he points out the political agendas for education through its history. Spring has also focused on policies that serve to separate students based on test scores and on race. His current work is on multicultural educational history, as it has been infused with the sometimes conflicting values of the cultures and communities and the politics and bureaucracy.

In the following selection from the book *Deculturalization and the Struggle for Equality: A Brief History of the Education of Dominated Cultures in the United States,* 2d ed. (McGraw-Hill, 1997), Spring describes the efforts of a number of minority groups to gain civil and educational equality. In discussing the period from the 1940s to the 1990s, he describes the civil rights movement as the protesting of the generations of domination of Anglo-American culture. Spring has included sections on African American efforts, Native American education efforts, and Mexican American efforts. He focuses especially on school desegregation efforts and on the call for recognition of the cultures of all students. He describes many of the legal cases and court decisions, the groups and individuals involved in the efforts, and the types of activities undertaken, such as nonviolent protests. He introduces and describes Martin Luther King, Jr., the Southern Christian Leadership Conference, the American Indian Movement, and the Mexican American Legal Defense and Education Fund, among others, as leading the efforts to gain civil and educational rights for all.

Key Concept: efforts toward civil and educational rights

*E*xtending from the 1940s into the 1990s, the great civil rights movement was a continuation of the culture wars initiated by English colonists when they invaded Native American lands in North America. From the time of the invasion to the 1990s, many citizens tried to assure that Protestant Anglo-American culture would be the dominant culture of the United States. For instance, in the 1990s, historian Arthur Schlesinger, who opposed multicultural education in public schools and advocated the teaching of Protestant Anglo-American culture, wrote, "For better or worse, the white Anglo-Saxon Protestant tradition was for two centuries—and in crucial respects still is—the dominant influence on American culture and society."[1]

In the nineteenth and twentieth centuries, those believing the United States should be united by a Protestant Anglo-American culture advocated the "civilization" and deculturalization of Native Americans, Mexican Americans, Puerto Ricans, and Jewish and Catholic immigrants from southern and eastern Europe. Some citizens believed in the racial superiority of whites that resulted in the segregation of African Americans, Native Americans, Mexican Americans, and Asian Americans. In the early twentieth century, believers in the racial superiority of whites, particularly whites from England and Germany, used standardized testing to provide validity to their views.

The great civil rights movement was composed of dominated groups who protested the domination of Protestant Anglo-American culture. Activists among Native Americans, African Americans, Mexican Americans, Asian Americans, and Puerto Ricans demanded restoration and recognition of their cultures. Many of these activists rejected the idea of a single dominating culture for the idea of a pluralistic society with many cultures given recognition in the public schools. Besides demands for cultural pluralism, activists demanded the end of school segregation and racism in educational practices.

Leading the way in the great civil rights movement were members of the National Association for the Advancement of Colored People (NAACP), who fought the continuation of segregation in schools and public facilities, and the lack of opportunity to participate in the American economic system. In addition, they demanded recognition for African-American culture in the public schools. The actions of African Americans contributed to the militancy of other groups in demanding equality of educational opportunity and recognition of their cultures in public schools.

Native Americans campaigned for self-determination and cultural recognition. Mexican Americans continued their struggles against segregation and they sought preservation of Mexican culture and the Spanish language in the schools. By the 1960s, Puerto Ricans joined Mexican Americans in supporting bilingual education.

Also, the great civil rights movement opened the door to demands that the public schools reflect minority cultures. African Americans, Native Americans, Mexican Americans, Asian Americans, and Puerto Ricans demanded that their unique cultures be recognized and be given a place in the school curriculum. These demands gave impetus to the movement for multicultural education in the 1980s and 1990s.

The desegregation of American schools was the result of over a half century of struggle by the black community. Since its founding in the early part of the twentieth century, the NAACP had struggled to end discriminatory practices against minority groups. The school desegregation issue was finally decided by the U.S. Supreme Court in 1954 in *Brown v. Board of Education of Topeka*. The decision did not bring immediate results, because resistance to court-ordered desegregation arose. The frustration caused by the slow pace of school integration and the continuation of other forms of discrimination contributed to the growth of a massive civil rights movement in the late 1950s and early 1960s. The response of national political leaders to the civil rights movement was the enactment of strong civil rights legislation.

It is important to remember that school desegregation and civil rights legislation were not the products of a benign government but were the result of tremendous struggle and public demonstrations. Politically, African Americans were forced by their lack of power at local and state levels to seek redress for their grievances from the federal government. National leaders tried to avoid dealing with civil rights issues but were finally forced by public demonstrations to take action. With regard to schooling, federal action resulted in greater federal control of local schools and a feeling among school board members that local control of education was rapidly disappearing.

The key legal issue in the struggle for desegregation was the interpretation of the Fourteenth Amendment to the Constitution. This constitutional amendment was ratified in 1868, shortly after the close of the Civil War. One of its purposes was to extend the basic guarantees of the Bill of Rights into the areas under state and local government control. The most important and controversial section of the Fourteenth Amendment states, "No State shall make or enforce any law which shall abridge the privileges or immunities of citizens...nor...deprive any person of life, liberty, or property, without due process of law; nor deny to any person within its jurisdiction the equal protection of the laws."

A major test of the meaning of the Fourteenth Amendment with regard to segregation occurred in 1895 in a Supreme Court case involving Homer Plessy, who was one-eighth black and seven-eighths white and had been arrested for refusing to ride in the "colored" coach of a train, as required by Louisiana law. The Supreme Court ruled that segregation did not create a badge of inferiority if segregated facilities were equal and the law was reasonable. In establishing the "separate but equal doctrine," the Supreme Court failed to clearly define what constitutes equal facilities and what is reasonable.

The overturning of the separate but equal doctrine and a broader application of the Fourteenth Amendment came in 1954 in the historic and controversial Supreme Court decision *Brown v. Board of Education of Topeka*. In 1953, *Brown* was one of the five school segregation suits to reach the Supreme Court. It became the first case simply because the five cases were heard in alphabetical order. The Brown case began in 1951, when Oliver Brown and twelve other parents represented by NAACP lawyers brought suit to void a Kansas law that permitted but did not require local segregation of the schools. In this particular

13

case, Oliver Brown's daughter was denied the right to attend a white elementary school within five blocks of her home and forced to cross railroad tracks and travel twenty-one blocks to attend an all-black school. The federal district court in Kansas ruled against Oliver Brown, using the argument that the segregated schools named in the suit were substantially equal and thus fell within the separate but equal doctrine.

In preparing its brief for the Supreme Court, the NAACP defined two important objectives: (1) to show that the climate of the times required an end to segregation laws and (2) to show that the separate but equal doctrine contained a contradiction in terms—that is, that separate facilities were inherently unequal. Evidence from recent findings in the social sciences presented by the NAACP to prove that separate facilities were inherently unequal provided the basis for overturning the separate but equal doctrine. It also caused a storm of protest alleging that the Supreme Court was basing decisions on nonlegal arguments. Throughout the South, it was widely believed that the Court was being persuaded by communist-oriented social scientists. Billboards appeared on highways demanding the impeachment of Chief Justice Earl Warren for his role in subverting the Constitution.

The Supreme Court argued in the Brown decision, "In the field of public education the doctrine of 'separate but equal' has no place. Separate educational facilities are inherently unequal." To support this argument, the Supreme Court wrote one of the most controversial single sentences ever to appear in a Court decision: "Whatever may have been the extent of psychological knowledge at the time of *Plessy* v. *Ferguson* this finding is amply supported by modern authority."[2]

In 1955 the Supreme Court issued its enforcement decree for the desegregation of schools. One problem facing the Court was the lack of machinery for supervising and ensuring the desegregation of vast numbers of segregated school districts. The Court resolved this problem by relying on federal district courts to determine the equitable principles for desegregation. Federal judges were often part of the social fabric of their local communities and resisted attempts at speedy desegregation. Consequently, integration occurred at a slow pace until additional civil rights legislation was passed in the 1960s and the mounting frustrations in the black community fed the flames of a militant civil rights movement.[3]

The evolution of the mass media in the 1950s was an important factor in the civil rights movement because it became possible to turn local problems into national issues. Thus, even though presidents had traditionally shown a great deal of deference to the important white southern political structure, the emergence of the mass media as a powerful force allowed both the federal government and civil rights groups to put unprecedented pressure on southern political leaders, forcing them to comply with national civil rights legislation. In fact, enforcement of the Supreme Court school desegregation ruling depended in large part on civil rights groups making effective use of television. In one sense, the struggle that took place was a struggle between public images. Concern over America's international image grew as pictures of racial injustice flashed around the world, and the president's public image was often threatened when examples of racial injustice were shown to millions of television viewers and the question was asked, What is our president doing about this situation?

The most dramatic technique used by civil rights groups was nonviolent confrontation. The massive nonviolent response of black people in the South confronted with an array of cattle prods, clubs, and fire hoses wielded by cursing southern law enforcement units provided dramatic and shocking television viewing for the nation. The Congress on Racial Equality (CORE), the Student Nonviolent Coordinating Committee (SNCC), and the Southern Christian Leadership Conference (SCLC), led by the Reverend Martin Luther King, Jr., provided the national drama and the final push for national civil rights legislation....

NATIVE AMERICANS

As African Americans were leading the fight against segregated schooling, Native Americans were attempting to gain control of the education of their children and restore their cultural heritage and languages to the curriculum. Native Americans shared a common interest with Mexican Americans and Puerto Ricans in supporting bilingual and multicultural education....

INDIAN EDUCATION: A NATIONAL TRAGEDY

Throughout the 1960s and 1970s, federal administrators gave support to Indian demands for self-determination. During his election campaign in 1968, Richard M. Nixon declared, "The right of self-determination of the Indian people will be respected and their participation in planning their own destiny will actively be encouraged."[4]

It was in this climate of civil rights activism and political support for Indian self-determination that the U.S. Senate Committee on Labor and Public Welfare issued in 1969 the report *Indian Education: A National Tragedy—A National Challenge.* The report opened with a statement condemning previous educational policies of the federal government: "A careful review of the historical literature reveals that the dominant policy of the Federal Government toward the American Indian has been one of forced assimilation ... [because of] a desire to divest the Indian of his land."[5]

After a lengthy review of the failure of past educational policies, the report's first recommendation was "maximum participation and control by Indians in establishing Indian education programs."[6] In its second recommendation, the report called for maximum Indian participation in the development of educational programs in federal schools and local public schools. These educational programs were to include early childhood education, vocational education, work-study, and adult literacy education. Of special importance was the recommendation to create bilingual and bicultural education programs.

Native American demands for bilingual and bicultural education were aided by the passage of Title VII of the Elementary and Secondary Education Act of 1968 or, as it was also called, the Bilingual Education Act. This was...a product of political activism by Mexican-American groups. Native Americans used funds provided under this legislation to support bilingual programs in Indian languages and English. For instance, the Bilingual Education Act provided support for bilingual programs in Navajo and English at the...Rough Rock Demonstration School.[7]

The congressional debates resulting from the criticism leveled at Indian education in the report *Indian Education: A National Tragedy—A National Challenge* eventually culminated in the passage of the Indian Education Act in 1972. The declared policy of the legislation was to provide financial assistance to local schools to develop programs to meet the "special" educational needs of Native American students. In addition, the legislation created a federal Office of Indian Education.[8]

In 1974, the Bureau of Indian Affairs issued a set of procedures for protecting student rights and due process. In contrast to the brutal and dictatorial treatment of Indian students in the boarding schools of the late nineteenth and early twentieth centuries, each Indian student was extended the right "to make his or her own decisions where applicable."[9] And, in striking contrast to earlier deculturalization policies, Indian students were granted "the right to freedom of religion and culture."[10]

The most important piece of legislation supporting self-determination was the 1975 Indian Self-Determination and Education Assistance Act, which gave tribes the power to contract with the federal government to run their own education and health programs. The legislation opened with the declaration that it was "An Act to provide maximum Indian participation in the Government and education of Indian people; to provide for the full participation of Indian tribes in programs and services conducted by the federal government."[11]

The Indian Self-Determination and Education Assistance Act strengthened Indian participation in the control of education programs. The legislation provided that, in a local school district receiving funds for the education of Indian students that did not have a school board having a majority of Indians, the district had to establish a separate local committee composed of parents of Indian students in the school. This committee was given the authority over any Indian education programs contracted with the federal government.

The principles embodied in the Indian Self-Determination and Education Assistance Act were expanded upon in 1988 with the passage of the Tribally Controlled Schools Act. In addition to the right to operate schools under federal contract as provided in the 1975 legislation, the Tribally Controlled Schools Act provided for outright grants to tribes to support the operation of their own schools.[12] ...

Similar to African Americans, Mexican Americans turned to the courts to seek redress for their grievances. In Ontario, California, in 1945, Mexican-American parents demanded that the school board grant all requests for transfer out of the Mexican schools. When the board refused this request, Gonzalo Mendez and William Guzman brought suit for violation of the Fourteenth Amendment to the Constitution. The school board responded to this suit by claiming that segregation was not based on race or national origins but on the necessity of providing special instruction.[13]

In 1946 a U.S. District Court ruled in *Mendez et al.* v. *Westminster School District of Orange County* that Mexicans were not Indians as claimed under the 1935 California law. The judge argued that the only possible argument for segregation was the special educational needs of Mexican-American children. These needs centered around the issue of learning English. Completely reversing the educational justification for segregation, the judge argued that "evidence clearly shows that Spanish-speaking children are retarded in learning English by lack of exposure to its use by segregation."[14] Therefore, the court ruled that segregation was illegal because it was not required by state law and because there was no valid educational justification for segregation.[15]

Heartened by the Mendez decision, the League of United Latin American Citizens (LULAC), the Mexican-American equivalent of the NAACP, forged ahead in its legal attack on segregation in Texas. With support from LULAC, a group of parents in 1948 brought suit against the Bastrop Independent School District, charging that local school authorities had no legal right to segregate children of Mexican descent and that this segregation was solely because the children were of Mexican descent. In *Delgado* v. *Bastrop Independent School District*, the court ruled that segregating Mexican-American children was illegal and discriminatory. The ruling required that the local school district end all segregation. The court did give local school districts the right to separate some children in the first grade only if scientific tests showed that they needed special instruction in English and the separation took place on the same campus.[16]

In general, LULAC was pleased with the decision. The one point they were dissatisfied with was the provision for the separation of children in the first grade. This allowed local schools to practice what was referred to in the latter part of the twentieth century as "second-generation segregation." Second-generation segregation refers to the practice of using educational justifications for segregating children within a single school building. In fact, many local Texas school districts did use the proviso for that purpose.[17]

While the Mendez and Delgado decisions did hold out the promise of ending segregation of Mexican Americans, local school districts used many tactics to avoid integration, including manipulation of school district lines, choice plans, and different forms of second-generation segregation. For instance, the California State Department of Education reported in 1966 that 57 percent of the children with Spanish surnames were still attending schools that were predominantly Mexican American. In 1973, a civil rights activist, John Caughey, estimated that two-thirds of the Mexican-American children in Los Angeles attended segregated schools. In *All Deliberate Speed: Segregation and Exclusion in California Schools, 1855–1975,* Charles Wollenberg estimates that in California by 1973 more Mexican and Mexican-American children attended segregated schools than in 1947.[18]

The continuation of de facto forms of segregation resulted in the formation in 1967 of the Mexican American Legal Defense and Education Fund (MALDEF). Initially, MALDEF focused on cases dealing with students who were punished for participating in civil rights activities. In 1968, MALDEF focused its attention on the inequitable funding of school districts in Texas that primarily served Mexican Americans. Not only were Mexican-American children facing de facto segregation, but the schools they were attending were also receiving less funding than schools attended by Anglos.[19]

The case brought by MALDEF, *Rodriguez* v. *San Antonio Independent School District,* had major implications for financing of schools across the country. In the case, a group of Mexican-American parents brought a class action suit against the state of Texas for the inequitable funding of school districts. In 1971, a federal district court ruled that the Texas school finance system was unconstitutional. In its decision, the federal district court applied—as the U.S. Supreme Court had in the 1954 school desegregation case—the equal protection clause of the Fourteenth Amendment. The inequality in financing of school districts was considered a denial of equal opportunity for Mexican-American children to receive an education. The U.S. Supreme Court overturned the decision on March 12, 1973, with the argument that school finance was not a constitutional issue. This Supreme Court decision meant that all school finance cases would have to be dealt with in state courts. Since 1973, numerous cases involving inequality in the financing of public schools have been argued in state courts.[20]

In 1970, Mexican Americans were officially recognized by the federal courts as an identifiable dominated group in the public schools in a MALDEF case, *Cisneros* v. *Corpus Christi Independent School District.* A central issue in the case was whether or not the 1954 school desegregation decision could be applied to Mexican Americans. The original Brown decision had dealt specifically with African Americans who were segregated by state and local laws. In his final decision, Judge Owen Cox ruled that blacks and Mexican Americans were segregated in the Corpus Christi school system law and that Mexican Americans were an identifiable dominated group because of their language, culture, religion, and Spanish surnames.[21] ...

The culture wars of the late twentieth century reflect the centuries-old effort to make English and Anglo-American Protestant culture the unifying language and culture of the United States. Originating in the sense of cultural superiority brought to North America by English colonists and emerging during cultural wars throughout U.S. history, the attempt to make Anglo-American culture the dominant culture of the United States was seriously challenged by the great civil rights movement and the new immigration.

NOTES

1. Arthur M. Schlesinger Jr., *The Disuniting of America* (Knoxville, TN: Whittle Direct Books, 1991), p. 8.

2. *Brown et al.* v. *Board of Education of Topeka et al.* (1954), reprinted in Albert P. Blaustein and Clarence C. Ferguson, Jr., *Desegregation and the Law* (New Brunswick, NJ: Rutgers University Press, 1957), pp. 273–282.

3. "The Effects of Segregation and the Consequences of Desegregation: A Social Science Statement," appendix to Appellants' Brief filed in the *School Segregation Cases* in the Supreme Court of the United States, October term, 1952, in John Bracey, August Meier, and Elliott Rudwick, eds., *The Afro-Americans: Selected Documents* (Boston: Allyn & Bacon, 1972), pp. 661–671.

4. Francis Paul Prucha, *The Indians in American Society: From Revolutionary War to the Present* (Berkeley: University of California Press, 1985), p. 82.

5. U.S. Congress, Senate Committee on Labor and Public Welfare, *Indian Education: A National Tragedy—A National Challenge*, 91st Cong., 1st Sess. (Washington, D.C.: U.S. Government Printing Office, 1969), p. 9.

6. Ibid., p. 106.

7. Jon Reyhner and Jeanne Eder, *A History of Indian Education* (Billings: Eastern Montana College, 1989), pp. 132–135.

8. "Indian Education Act, June 23, 1972," in Francis Paul Prucha, ed., *Documents of United States Indian Policy* (Lincoln: University of Nebraska Press, 1990), pp. 263–264.

9. "Student Rights and Due Process Procedures, October 11, 1974," in Prucha, *Documents*, p. 271.

10. Ibid.

11. "Indian Self-Determination and Education Assistance Act, January 4, 1975," in Prucha, *Documents*, p. 274.

12. "Tribally Controlled Schools Act of 1988," in Prucha, *Documents*, pp. 314–315.

13. Reyhner and Eder, *History of Indian Education*, p. 126.

14. Quoted in Ibid., p. 128.

15. Ibid., pp. 127–129. Also see Gilbert G. Gonzalez, *Chicano Education in the Era of Segregation* (Philadelphia: Balch Institute Press, 1990), pp. 147–156.

16. Guadelupe San Miguel, Jr., *"Let All of Them Take Heed": Mexican Americans and the Campaign for Educational Equality in Texas, 1910–1981* (Austin: University of Texas Press, 1987), pp. 123–124.

17. Ibid., p. 125.

18. Charles Wollenberg, *All Deliberate Speed: Segregation and Exclusion in California Schools, 1855–1975* (Berkeley: University of California Press, 1976), p. 134.

19. San Miguel, *"Let All of Them Take Heed,"* pp. 169–173.

20. Ibid., pp. 173–174.

21. Ibid., pp. 177–179.

CHAPTER 2 Early Writings on Multicultural Education

2.1 BOOKER T. WASHINGTON

The Atlanta Exposition Address, September 18, 1895

Booker T. Washington (1856–1915) was born into slavery, and he spent his life offering ideas and creating practices to attempt to reconcile whites and blacks after slavery. In the postslavery South, Washington founded the Tuskegee Normal and Industrial Institute in Alabama in 1881 and the National Negro Business League in 1900. He was invited to speak to a number of conventions dealing with changing conditions in the South, including the Atlanta Exposition in Atlanta, Georgia, on September 18, 1895; that speech is presented in the following selection.

Washington believed that African Americans (termed "Negroes" during his time) would have the most success entering into the mainstream economic life of the United States by growing slowly into positions of economic capabilities through positions of labor. He told blacks that instead of aiming for the top levels of life right away, they should grow slowly into mainstream life by serving in labor positions. To put these beliefs into practice, his Tuskegee Institute emphasized industrial education, skilled trades, agriculture, and domestic service. He asked southern white leaders to put faith in blacks to help the South grow stronger through their labors. Many people criticized Washington for encouraging the same feeling of submission that had been placed onto blacks during slavery. Washington has also been condemned for moving too slowly and not taking a strong enough stand toward freedom. However, blacks and whites widely supported his ideas of slow progression out of slavery and into economic life through the development of labor skills.

Key Concept: bringing blacks into economic life through positions of labor

"Cast down your bucket where you are...."

One-third of the population of the South is of the Negro race. No enterprise seeking the material, civil, or moral welfare of this section can disregard this element of our population and reach the highest success. I but convey to you, Mr. President and Directors, the sentiment of the masses of my race when I say that in no way have the value and manhood of the American Negro been more fittingly and generously recognized than by the managers of this magnificent Exposition at every stage of its progress. It is a recognition that will do more to cement the friendship of the two races than any occurrence since the dawn of freedom.

Not only this, but the opportunity here afforded will awaken among us a new era of industrial progress. Ignorant and inexperienced, it is not strange that in the first years of our new life we began at the top instead of at the bottom; that a seat in Congress or the State Legislature was more sought than real estate or industrial skill; that the political convention or stump speaking had more attractions than starting a dairy farm or truck garden.

A ship lost at sea for many days suddenly sighted a friendly vessel. From the mast of the unfortunate vessel was seen a signal: "Water, water, we die of thirst." The answer from the friendly vessel at once came back, "Cast down your bucket where you are." A second time the signal, "Water, water, send us water," ran up from the distressed vessel and was answered, "Cast down your bucket where you are." And a third and fourth signal for water was answered "Cast down your bucket where you are." The captain of the distressed vessel, at last heeding the injunction, cast down his bucket and it came up full of fresh, sparkling water from the mouth of the Amazon River.

To those of my race who depend on bettering their condition in a foreign land, or who underestimate the importance of cultivating friendly relations with the Southern white man who is their next-door neighbor, I would say: Cast down your bucket where you are; cast it down in making friends, in every manly way, of the people of all races by whom we are surrounded. Cast it down in agriculture, mechanics, in commerce, in domestic service, and in the professions. And in this connection it is well to bear in mind that whatever other sins the South may be called upon to bear, when it comes to business pure and simple, it is in the South that the Negro is given a man's chance in the commercial world, and in nothing is this Exposition more eloquent than in emphasizing this chance. Our greatest danger is that, in the great leap from slavery to freedom, we may overlook the fact that the masses of us are to live by the productions of our hands and fail to keep in mind that we shall prosper in the proportion as we learn to dignify and glorify common labor, and put brains and skill into the common occupations of life; shall prosper in proportion as we learn to draw the line between the superficial and the substantial, the ornamental gewgaws of life and the useful. No race can prosper till it learns that there is as much dignity in tilling a field as in writing a poem. It is at the bottom of life we must begin, and not at the top. Nor should we permit our grievances to overshadow our opportunities.

To those of the white race who look to the incoming of those of foreign birth and strange tongue and habits for the prosperity of the South, were I permitted I would repeat what I say to my own race, "Cast down your bucket where you are." Cast it down among the 8,000,000 Negroes whose habits you know, whose fidelity and love you have tested in days when to have proved treacherous meant the ruin of your firesides. Cast down your bucket among these people who have, without strikes and labor wars, tilled your fields, cleared your forests, builded your railroads and cities, and brought forth treasures from the bowels of the earth and helped make possible this magnificent representation of the progress of the South. Casting down your bucket among my people, helping and encouraging them as you are doing on these grounds, and, with education of head, hand and heart, you will find that they will buy your surplus land, make blossom the waste places in your fields, and run your factories.

While doing this, you can be sure in the future, as in the past, that you and your families will be surrounded by the most patient, faithful, law-abiding, and unresentful people that the world has seen. As we have proved our loyalty to you in the past, in nursing your children, watching by the sickbed of your mothers and fathers, and often following them with tear-dimmed eyes to their graves, so in the future, in our humble way, we shall stand by you with a devotion that no foreigner can approach, ready to lay down our lives, if need be, in defense of yours; interlacing our industrial, commercial, civil, and religious life with yours in a way that shall make the interests of both races one. In all things that are purely social we can be as separate as the fingers, yet one as the hand in all things essential to mutual progress.

There is no defense or security for any of us except in the highest intelligence and development of all. If anywhere there are efforts tending to curtail the fullest growth of the Negro, let these efforts be turned into stimulating, encouraging and making him the most useful and intelligent citizen. Effort or means so invested will pay a thousand percent interest. These efforts will be twice blessed—"blessing him that gives and him that takes."

There is no escape, through law of man or God, from the inevitable:

The laws of changeless justice bind
Oppressor with oppressed,
And close as sin and suffering joined
We march to fate abreast.

Nearly sixteen million hands will aid you in pulling the load upward, or they will pull against you the load downward. We shall constitute one-third and more of the ignorance and crime of the South, or one-third its intelligence and progress; we shall contribute one-third to the business and industrial prosperity of the South, or we shall prove a veritable body of death, stagnating, depressing, retarding every effort to advance the body politic.

Gentlemen of the Exposition: As we present to you our humble effort at an exhibition of our progress, you must not expect overmuch. Starting thirty years ago with ownership here and there in a few quilts and pumpkins and chickens (gathered from miscellaneous sources), remember: the path that has led us from these to the invention and production of agricultural implements, buggies, steam engines, newspapers, books, statuary, carving, paintings, the management of drugstores and banks, has not been trodden without contact with thorns and thistles. While we take pride in what we exhibit as a result of our independent efforts, we do not for a moment forget that our part in this exhibition would fall far short of your expectations but for the constant help that has come to our educational life, not only from the Southern states, but especially from Northern philanthropists who have made their gifts a constant stream of blessing and encouragement.

The wisest among my race understand that the agitation of questions of social equality is the extremest folly, and that progress in the enjoyment of all the privileges that will come to us must be the result of severe and constant struggle rather than of artificial forcing. No race that has anything to contribute to the markets of the world is long in any degree ostracized. It is important and right that all privileges of the laws be ours, but it is vastly more important that we be prepared for the exercise of those privileges. The opportunity to earn a dollar in a factory just now is worth infinitely more than the opportunity to spend a dollar in an opera house.

In conclusion, may I repeat that nothing in thirty years has given us more hope and encouragement and drawn us so near to you of the white race as this opportunity offered by the Exposition; and here bending, as it were, over the altar that represents the results of the struggles of your race and mine, both starting practically empty-handed three decades ago, I pledge that, in your effort to work out the great and intricate problem which God has laid at the doors of the South, you shall have at all times the patient, sympathetic help of my race. Only let this be constantly in mind that, while from representations in these buildings of the product of field, of forest, of mine, of factory, letters and art, much good will come—yet by far above and beyond material benefits, will be that higher good, that let us pray God will come, in a blotting out of sectional differences and racial animosities and suspicions, in a determination to administer absolute justice, in a willing obedience among all classes to the mandates of law. This, coupled with material prosperity, will bring into our beloved South a new heaven and a new earth.

2.2 W. E. B. DU BOIS

Of Mr. Booker T. Washington and Others

The writings of educators Booker T. Washington and W. E. B. (William Edward Burghardt) Du Bois (1868–1963) illustrate the essential differences of opinion among leading scholars as to the necessary approaches to gain group and individual respect. While Washington encouraged accommodation—the slow progression toward full participation in society by fitting into already existing society—Du Bois urged taking steps toward liberation. He also urged the taking of active steps toward gaining legal and civil rights. These conflicting themes of accommodation and liberation can be seen in the writings of scholars from many diverse groups throughout history.

Du Bois was the first African American to receive a Ph.D. from Harvard University, and he cofounded the National Association for the Advancement of Colored People (NAACP) in 1909. His focus in his life's work was on the intellectual and political advancement of blacks. He has many political, scholarly, and literary achievements, including *The Souls of Black Folk* (Vintage Books, 1990), from which the following selection has been excerpted.

Du Bois criticizes Washington's plan as giving the perception that blacks had given up on attempts to gain civil and political equality and personal self-esteem. He raises the question, Isn't the gaining of self-respect worth more than land or houses? He argues that by submitting themselves to lower levels of status just to receive economic benefits, blacks are giving up their self-respect. Du Bois urges insistence on the equal rights of blacks, that the right to vote and to an education must be stated plainly and unequivocably. If this is not done, he concludes, then blacks are shirking their responsibility to make the world a better place for all.

Key Concept: insistence on equal political and civil rights for African Americans

From birth till death enslaved; in word, in deed, unmanned!
Hereditary bondsmen! Know ye not
Who would be free themselves must strike the blow?

—Byron.

*E*asily the most striking thing in the history of the American Negro since 1876 is the ascendancy of Mr. Booker T. Washington. It began at the time when war memories and ideals were rapidly passing; a day of astonishing commercial development was dawning; a sense of doubt and hesitation overtook the freedmen's sons,—then it was that his leading began. Mr. Washington came, with a simple definite programme, at the psychological moment when the nation was a little ashamed of having bestowed so much sentiment on Negroes, and was concentrating its energies on Dollars. His programme of industrial education, conciliation of the South, and submission and silence as to civil and political rights, was not wholly original; the Free Negroes from 1830 up to wartime had striven to build industrial schools, and the American Missionary Association had from the first taught various trades; and Price and others had sought a way of honorable alliance with the best of the Southerners. But Mr. Washington first indissolubly linked these things; he put enthusiam, unlimited energy, and perfect faith into this programme, and changed it from a by-path into a veritable Way of Life. And the tale of the methods by which he did this is a fascinating study of human life.

It startled the nation to hear a Negro advocating such a programme after many decades of bitter complaint; it startled and won the applause of the South, it interested and won the admiration of the North; and after a confused murmur of protest, it silenced if it did not convert the Negroes themselves.

To gain the sympathy and coöperation of the various elements comprising the white South was Mr. Washington's first task; and this, at the time Tuskegee was founded, seemed, for a black man, well-nigh impossible. And yet ten years later it was done in the word spoken at Atlanta: "In all things purely social we can be as separate as the five fingers, and yet one as the hand in all things essential to mutual progress." This "Atlanta Compromise" is by all odds the most notable thing in Mr. Washington's career. The South interpreted it in different ways: the radicals received it as a complete surrender of the demand for civil and political equality; the conservatives, as a generously conceived working basis for mutual understanding. So both approved it, and to-day its author is certainly the most distinguished Southerner since Jefferson Davis, and the one with the largest personal following.

Next to this achievement comes Mr. Washington's work in gaining place and consideration in the North. Others less shrewd and tactful had formerly essayed to sit on these two stools and had fallen between them; but as Mr. Washington knew the heart of the South from birth and training, so by singular insight he intuitively grasped the spirit of the age which was dominating the North. And so thoroughly did he learn the speech and thought of triumphant commercialism, and the ideas of material prosperity, that the picture of a lone black boy poring over a French grammar amid the weeds and dirt of a neglected home soon seemed to him the acme of absurdities. One wonders that Socrates and St. Francis of Assisi would say to this.

And yet this very singleness of vision and thorough oneness with his age is a mark of the successful man. It is as though Nature must needs make men narrow in order to give them force. So Mr. Washington's cult has gained unquestioning followers, his work has wonderfully prospered, his friends are legion, and his enemies are confounded. To-day he stands as the one recognized spokesman of his ten million fellows, and one of the most notable figures in a nation of seventy millions. One hesitates, therefore, to criticise a life which, beginning with so little, has done so much. And yet the time is come when one may speak in all sincerity and utter courtesy of the mistakes and shortcomings of Mr. Washington's career, as well as of his triumphs, without being thought captious or envious, and without forgetting that it is easier to do ill than well in the world.

The criticism that has hitherto met Mr. Washington has not always been of this broad character. In the South especially has he had to walk warily to avoid the harshest judgments,—and naturally so, for he is dealing with the one subject of deepest sensitiveness to that section. Twice—once when at the Chicago celebration of the Spanish-American War he alluded to the color-prejudice that is "eating away the vitals of the South," and once when he dined with President Roosevelt—has the resulting Southern criticism been violent enough to threaten seriously his popularity. In the North the feeling has several times forced itself into words, that Mr. Washington's counsels of submission overlooked certain elements of true manhood, and that his educational programme was unnecessarily narrow. Usually, however, such criticism has not found open expression, although, too, the spiritual sons of the Abolitionists have not been prepared to acknowledge that the schools founded before Tuskegee, by men of broad ideals and self-sacrificing spirit, were wholly failures or worthy of ridicule. While, then, criticism has not failed to follow Mr. Washington, yet the prevailing public opinion of the land has been but too willing to deliver the solution of a wearisome problem into his hands, and say, "If that is all you and your race ask, take it."

Among his own people, however, Mr. Washington has encountered the strongest and most lasting opposition, amounting at times to bitterness, and even to-day continuing strong and insistent even though largely silenced in outward expression by the public opinion of the nation. Some of this opposition is, of course, mere envy; the disappointment of displaced demagogues and the spite of narrow minds. But aside from this, there is among educated and thoughtful colored men in all parts of the land a feeling of deep regret, sorrow, and apprehension at the wide currency and ascendancy which some of Mr. Washington's theories have gained. These same men admire his sincerity of purpose, and are willing to forgive much to honest endeavor which is doing something worth the doing. They coöperate with Mr. Washington as far as they conscientiously can; and, indeed, it is no ordinary tribute to this man's tact and power that, steering as he must between so many diverse interests and opinions, he so largely retains the respect of all. . . .

Mr. Washington represents in Negro thought the old attitude of adjustment and submission; but adjustment at such a peculiar time as to make his programme unique. This is an age of unusual economic development, and Mr. Washington's programme naturally takes an economic cast, becoming a gospel of Work and Money to such an extent as apparently almost completely to overshadow the higher aims of life. Moreover, this is an age when the more advanced races are coming in closer contact with the less developed races, and the race-feeling is therefore intensified; and Mr. Washington's programme practically accepts the alleged inferiority of the Negro races. Again, in our own land, the reaction from the sentiment of war time has given impetus to race-prejudice against Negroes, and Mr. Washington withdraws many of the high demands of Negroes as men and American citizens. In other periods of intensified prejudice all the Negro's tendency to self-assertion has been called forth; at this period a policy of submission is advocated. In the history of nearly all other races and peoples the doctrine preached at such crises has been that manly self-respect is worth more than lands and houses, and that a people who voluntarily surrender such respect, or cease striving for it, are not worth civilizing.

In answer to this, it has been claimed that the Negro can survive only through submission. Mr. Washington distinctly asks that black people give up, at least for the present, three things,—

- First, political power,
- Second, insistence on civil rights,
- Third, higher education of Negro youth,—

and concentrate all their energies on industrial education, the accumulation of wealth, and the conciliation of the South. This policy has been courageously and insistently advocated for over fifteen years, and has been triumphant for perhaps ten years. As a result of this tender of the palm-branch, what has been the return? In these years there have occurred:

1. The disfranchisement of the Negro.
2. The legal creation of a distinct status of civil inferiority for the Negro.
3. The steady withdrawal of aid from institutions for the higher training of the Negro.

These movements are not, to be sure, direct results of Mr. Washington's teachings; but his propaganda has, without a shadow of doubt, helped their speedier accomplishment. The question then comes: Is it possible, and probable, that nine millions of men can make effective progress in economic lines if they are deprived of political rights, made of servile caste, and allowed only the most meagre chance for developing their exceptional men? If history and reason give any distinct answer to these questions, it is an emphatic *No.* And Mr. Washington thus faces the triple paradox of his career:

1. He is striving nobly to make Negro artisans business men and property-owners; but it is utterly impossible, under modern competitive methods, for workingmen and property-owners to defend their rights and exist without the right of suffrage.
2. He insists on thrift and self-respect, but at the same time counsels a silent submission to civic inferiority such as is bound to sap the manhood of any race in the long run.
3. He advocates common-school and industrial training, and depreciates institutions of higher-learning; but neither the Negro common-schools, nor Tuskegee itself, could remain open a day were it not for teachers trained in Negro colleges, or trained by their graduates.

This triple paradox in Mr. Washington's position is the object of criticism by two classes of colored Americans. One class is spiritually descended from Toussaint the Savior, through Gabriel, Vesey, and Turner, and they represent the attitude of revolt and revenge; they hate the white South blindly and distrust the white race generally, and so far as they agree on definite action, think that the Negro's only hope lies in emigration beyond the borders of the United States. And yet, by the irony of fate, nothing has more effectually made this programme seem hopeless than the recent course of the United States toward weaker and darker peoples in the West Indies, Hawaii, and the Philippines,— for where in the world may we go and be safe from lying and brute force?

The other class of Negroes who cannot agree with Mr. Washington has hitherto said little aloud. They deprecate the sight of scattered counsels, of internal disagreement; and especially they dislike making their just criticism of a useful and earnest man an excuse for a general discharge of venom from small-minded opponents. Nevertheless, the questions involved are so fundamental and serious that it is difficult to see how men like the Grimkes, Kelly Miller, J. W. E. Bowen, and other representatives of this group, can much longer be silent. Such men feel in conscience bound to ask of this nation three things:

1. The right to vote.
2. Civic equality.
3. The education of youth according to ability.

They acknowledge Mr. Washington's invaluable service in counselling patience and courtesy in such demands; they do not ask that ignorant black men vote when ignorant whites are debarred, or that any reasonable restrictions in the suffrage should not be applied; they know that the low social level of the mass of the race is responsible for much discrimination against it, but they also know, and the nation knows, that relentless color-prejudice is more often a cause than a result of the Negro's degradation; they seek the abatement of this relic of barbarism, and not its systematic encouragement and pampering by all agencies of social power from the Associated Press to the Church of Christ. They advocate, with Mr. Washington, a broad system of Negro common schools supplemented by thorough industrial training; but they are surprised that a man of Mr. Washington's insight cannot see that no such educational system ever has rested or can rest on any other basis than that of the well-equipped college and university, and they insist that there is a demand for a few such institutions throughout the South to train the best of the Negro youth as teachers, professional men, and leaders.

This group of men honor Mr. Washington for his attitude of conciliation toward the white South; they accept the "Atlanta Compromise" in its broadest interpretation; they recognize, with him, many signs of promise, many men of high purpose and fair judgment, in this section; they know that no easy task has been laid upon a region already tottering under heavy burdens. But, nevertheless, they insist that the way to truth and right lies in straightforward honesty, not in indiscriminate flattery; in praising those of the South who do well and criticising uncompromisingly those who do ill; in taking advantage of the opportunities at hand and urging their fellows to do the same, but at the same time in remembering that only a firm adherence to their higher ideals and aspirations will ever keep those ideals within the realm of possibility. They do not expect that the free right to vote, to enjoy civic rights, and to be educated, will come in a moment; they do not expect to see the bias and prejudices of years disappear at the blast of a trumpet; but they are absolutely certain that the way for a people to gain their reasonable rights is not by voluntarily throwing them away and insisting that they do not want them; that the way for a people to gain respect is not by continually belittling and ridiculing themselves; that, on the contrary, Negroes must insist continually, in season and out of season, that voting is necessary to modern manhood, that color discrimination is barbarism, and that black boys need education as well as white boys....

The South ought to be led, by candid and honest criticism, to assert her better self and do her full duty to the race she has cruelly wronged and is still wronging. The North—her co-partner in guilt—cannot salve her conscience by plastering it with gold. We cannot settle this problem by diplomacy and suaveness, by "policy" alone. If worse come to worst, can the moral fibre of this country survive the slow throttling and murder of nine millions of men?

The black men of America have a duty to perform, a duty stern and delicate,—a forward movement to oppose a part of the work of their greatest leader. So far as Mr. Washington preaches Thrift, Patience, and Industrial Training for the masses, we must hold up his hands and strive with him, rejoicing in his honors and glorying in the strength of this Joshua called of God and of man to lead the headless host. But so far as Mr. Washington apologizes for injustice, North or South, does not rightly value the privilege and duty of voting, belittles the emasculating effects of caste distinctions, and opposes the higher training and ambition of our brighter minds,—so far as he, the South, or the Nation, does this,—we must unceasingly and firmly oppose them. By every civilized and peaceful method we must strive for the rights which the world accords to men, clinging unwaveringly to those great words which the sons of the Fathers would fain forget: "We hold these truths to be self-evident: That all men are created equal; that they are endowed by their Creator with certain unalienable rights; that among these are life, liberty, and the pursuit of happiness."

CHAPTER 3 Philosophical Perspectives on Multicultural Education

3.1 KENNETH R. HOWE

Liberal Democracy, Equal Educational Opportunity, and the Challenge of Multiculturalism

Kenneth R. Howe is a philosopher of education who works in the areas of equality of educational opportunity and professional ethics. His most recent book is *Understanding Equal Educational Opportunity: Social Justice, Democracy, and Schooling* (Teachers College Press, 1997). His work in this area was initiated by the recognition that the concept of *equal educational opportunity* is understood differently by different people. Among the meanings attached to the concept are equality of access, compensatory measures, equality of results, and equal treatment for everyone. Howe's approach to the topic is to try to more clearly illuminate what the concept means and then to discuss what it means in practice.

In the following selection from "Liberal Democracy, Equal Educational Opportunity, and the Challenge of Multiculturalism," *American Educational Research Journal* (Fall 1992), Howe discusses some of the philosophical concepts involved in equal educational opportunity. He discusses several main issues: deliberation, freedom worth wanting, and equal educational opportunity as enabling. Howe emphasizes the importance of education as helping individuals to be able to deliberate effectively in order to make choices and to control their own lives. For freedom to be worth wanting, he believes, the individual must truly be able to understand the options and to deliberate about those choices. For example, Howe asks, if a student is counseled into vocational training when neither he nor his parents know the implications of such a direction in the child's education, is that really a choice? Is that freedom to choose? In connecting to multicultural education, then, minority students must not be given choices that are not really choices within that child's culture.

Key Concept: educational opportunities worth wanting

A GENERAL CHARACTERIZATION OF EQUAL EDUCATIONAL OPPORTUNITY

Questions about the aims of schooling and nature of the curriculum can only be answered from within a political theory that adumbrates the more general sociopolitical functions of public education. I will set aside broader questions of political theory and presuppose a liberal democratic theory[1]—the kind of political theory in which the principle of equal educational opportunity finds its home. My task [here] will be to show how the liberal democratic tradition in general and the principle of equal educational opportunity in particular are robust enough to accommodate the peculiar challenge posed by multicultural education.

The principle of equal educational opportunity serves to justify demanding of public education something short of full equality: it demands only equality of opportunities, which it is then the responsibility of school children or their parents to act on. In this way, the concept of freedom is built into the concept of equal educational opportunity. As Onora O'Neil remarks, "The concept of equal educational opportunity cannot be rid of its libertarian birthmark, even after radical surgery."[2]

At least since Coleman's reflections,[3] a controversy has existed regarding whether the criterion of equality of educational opportunity should be equality of access or equality of results; and both criteria have proven problematic. Although guaranteeing equality of access is an advance over such practices as *de jure* segregation, it can be quite hollow if it merely amounts to removing formal barriers to the choices students and their parents might make, as *de facto* segregation aptly illustrates. On the other hand, guaranteeing equality of results seems to demand too much, both in terms of the capabilities of schools and in terms of how it threatens to block the freedom that students and their parents might otherwise wish to exercise.

This way of framing the problem seems to leave open two ways of responding: abandoning freedom and choice, on the grounds that they are ideological shams that merely serve to justify vast inequality, or abandoning equality of results, on the grounds that freedom is a cherished value that ought not to be sacrificed and that results cannot be equalized in any case. There is a third response, however, that merits careful examination: abandoning the quest for tidy solutions to clashes among fundamental principles, on the grounds that uncertainty, tentativeness, and tensions among political principles are permanent features of the project of democracy. I will briefly describe and defend this third approach, which, borrowing from Walzer, I shall call "interpretive."[4]

The interpretive approach has two methodological features that exist in tension. First, social criticism is construed as immanent, which is to say it must gain a foothold in the vocabulary and accepted principles of a given political community if it is to have anything to say to the members of such a community and to have any chance of constructively influencing them. In this vein, Walzer encourages social critics "to interpret to one's fellow citizens the world of meanings that we share" and warns against abstract philosophizing:

> Justice and equality can conceivably be worked out as philosophical artifacts, but a just or an egalitarian society cannot be. If such a society isn't already here—hidden, as it were, in our concepts and categories—we will never know it concretely or realize it in fact.[5]

Given the prominence of the principle of equal educational opportunity in the conversation about a just system of education, the immanent feature of the interpretive approach argues against abandoning it as mere ideological sham or as hopelessly muddled. Rather, the aim should be to devise philosophically defensible interpretations that have some chance of winning broad acceptance.

Working in the other direction, however, is the second feature of the interpretive approach: conceptual revisionism. This feature requires that political argument be progressive and dynamic, and not merely a lexicographical or historical account of what political principles mean or have meant. Instead, political argument must investigate shared principles and their implications, point to conflicts and inconsistencies, and respond to changing circumstances and knowledge. This feature of the interpretive approach argues in favor of revising the concept of equal educational opportunity as necessary so that it best accommodates competing principles and their implications—the principles of equality and freedom in particular—in light of current circumstances.

The approach just described has been adopted in one shape or another by various thinkers, most notably Gutmann.[6] In particular, Gutmann begins with the assumption that equality of educational opportunity is a serviceable principle, then entertains and rejects several conceptions, and finally reaches the somewhat counterintuitive conclusion that equality of educational opportunity requires equalizing certain educational results (namely, those that go into the "democratic threshold").[7] It will be sufficient for present purposes to set the intricacies of such arguments aside and to note three pivotal issues that any adequate interpretation of equality of educational opportunity must accommodate.

1. Freedom and opportunities worth wanting. The concept of freedom has different senses. The weakest sense requires only voluntariness and intent—a kind of freedom possessed even by young children. A stronger sense requires these features plus the ability to identify and weigh alternatives and their consequences and to choose the one judged best from among them—a kind of freedom attributed to normal adults.[8] It should require no argument to establish that these senses of freedom are not equally worth wanting. The first sense is simply too weak; in order to be free in even a minimal sense of being in control of one's life, the second sense is required.

A necessary condition of freedom sufficiently worth wanting, then, is the ability to deliberate effectively, but this is clearly not a sufficient condition. For, to make use of the ability to deliberate effectively, an individual must also have the opportunity to exercise it. The opportunity to exercise it, in turn, requires (1) that information necessary for deliberation is available and (2) that social conditions do not impose a burden for acting on the results of deliberation that is disproportionate to the burden of other deliberators.

As an illustration of condition (1), consider Dennett's distinction between "bare" and "real" opportunities.[9] He gives the example of a group of prisoners who have their prison doors unlocked by the prison guards while they are asleep and locked again before they awaken. According to Dennett, because the prisoners do not have the information they need to deliberate, they have only a "bare" opportunity to escape. As an illustration of condition (2), imagine a family that displays its disapproval of U.S. military involvement in the Persian Gulf and receives threats to its safety and property as a result. Here, although the requisite information for deliberation is available, acting on the results of deliberation entails a burden that is disproportionate to the burden of those who wish to express their support for military involvement. The principle of freedom of expression in this case is blunted, and therefore resembles only a "bare" opportunity.

The point is that neither the prisoners nor the dissenting family enjoy kinds of opportunities worth wanting, and similar examples are easy to find in education. For example, imagine a ninth-grade student who is being "counseled" into a vocational track and who, along with his or her parents, lacks knowledge about the consequences of such a decision. Also imagine that the family's cultural makeup leads it to be intimidated by and deferential to school authorities. First, the knowledge required for effective deliberation is missing. Second, the family is pressured by social conditions that are implicitly hostile to making a different decision. In general, something more is required in the name of equalizing educational opportunity than equalizing these kinds of "bare" opportunities.

2. Equal educational opportunity as enabling. Education is, no doubt, valuable in its own right, but it also is *enabling* in the sense that it serves (however imperfectly) as the gateway for obtaining other societal goods, such as desirable employment, adequate income, and political power. For this reason, equal *educational* opportunity is related to equal opportunity more generally because it serves as an important link in what might be termed an opportunity chain. Accordingly, the strength of the educational link determines the overall strength of the opportunity chain in the sense that the array of opportunities open to an individual is (again, imperfectly) determined by the quality of his or her education.

The opportunity chain is complicated by the fact that educational opportunity itself has this same chain-like character. That is, taking advantage of early educational opportunities is related to having later ones. For example, children who fail to learn to read early on have their curricular options progressively narrowed as they proceed through the K–12 curriculum, as compared to their counterparts who do learn to read. Consequently, their educational opportunities will be likewise narrowed such that they will be incapable of enjoying equality of educational opportunity and equality of opportunity more generally as they approach adulthood.

Several lessons may be drawn from this observation. First, what at one point in time serves as an educational end (like reading) later serves as a means to other ends (like reading textbooks for content). Thus, certain educational ends (or results) must be accomplished in order for certain other educational opportunities to exist. Second, and as a consequence of this, the concept of equal educational opportunity needs to be conceived in terms of *educational careers* rather than specific episodes within such careers, lest educational opportunities become merely "bare" and not worth wanting.

Working out the details of this claim outstrips the aims of this article.[10] By way of a brief illustration, however, consider how far a free adult literacy program goes toward equalizing educational opportunity. The argument that such programs promote equality of educational opportunity gains its force by isolating particular choices from the broader social scheme that determines the scope and kinds of opportunities that individuals possess, and by glossing over the fact that adults who are free to undertake or pass up literacy programs suffer from a restricted range of opportunities. It seems quite reasonable to suggest that the need for adult literacy programs signals a failure of earlier education, a failure to produce earlier results required to expand the scope of adult opportunity—educational and otherwise. It also seems quite reasonable to suggest that to be put in the position of being an adult having the choice of whether to become literate hardly seems a choice worth wanting. (Compare a compensatory program like having the choice of whether to receive free medical treatment for work-related lung disease.)

3. Equal educational opportunity and children.   Children raise a very special problem with respect to the concept of equal educational opportunity: Because children (especially young ones) lack the capacity for effective deliberation, this capacity must be instilled in them before questions regarding the other two requisites for freedom and opportunity worth wanting—adequate information and social support—even arise. Up to a certain age, then, children cannot possess freedom and opportunities genuinely worth wanting. Thus, it is up to someone else—schools, parents, or both—to act on children's behalf to ensure that they one day are able to possess these things. In other words, paternalistic interference in children's freedom (in the weak sense) is justified in the name of preparing them to enjoy freedom (in the strong sense) later on in life.

Involving paternalistic interference in the name of children's best educational interests raises a number of potential (as well as real) conflicts—between schools and children, parents and children, parents and parents, schools and parents, and so forth—insofar as what educational opportunities are indeed worth wanting often can be (and is) in dispute. This is a large and complex issue, and much of it lies beyond the scope of this article. . . .

In summary, when applied to children,[11] a defensible interpretation of the principle of equal educational opportunity is required to take into account the observation that (1) education should be enabling, (2) the concept of equal educational opportunity is best applied to educational careers rather than isolated incidents, and (3) children are not in a position to exercise freedom and opportunities (worth wanting) until they gain the capacity to deliberate effectively. . . .

The principle of equal educational opportunity can only be realized for cultural minorities by rendering educational opportunities worth wanting, and rendering educational opportunities worth wanting requires that minorities not be required to give up their identities in order to enjoy them. For minorities who can live with the liberal educational ideal—and I think most can—some "cultural elbow room"[12] must be provided within the area it circumscribes. To . . . paraphrase [Will] Kymlicka:

> It only makes sense to invite people to participate in *schooling* (or for people to accept that invitation) if they will be treated as equals. And that is incompatible with defining people in terms of roles they did not shape or endorse.

NOTES

1. In this context, by "liberal" I mean a general tradition in political theory. *Within* this tradition, there are liberals and conservatives in the more popular sense that would distinguish, for example, Ted Kennedy from William F. Buckley.

2. Onora O'Neill, "Opportunities, Equalities, and Education," *Theory and Decision* 7, no. 4 (1976): 275–295. I, for one, have attempted to perform such surgery. See my "In Defense of Outcomes-Based Conceptions of Equal Educational Opportunity."

3. James Coleman, "The Concept of Equality of Educational Opportunity," *Harvard Educational Review* 38, no. 1 (1968): 7–22.

4. Michael Walzer, *Interpretation and Social Criticism* (Cambridge, Mass.: Harvard University Press, 1987).

5. Michael Walzer, *Spheres of Justice: A Defense of Pluralism and Equality* (New York: Basic Books, 1983), xiv.

6. Amy Gutmann, *Democratic Education* (Princeton, NJ.: Princeton University Press, 1987).

7. Gutmann denies that she requires inputs or outcomes to be equalized. I think she is simply mistaken about this. For although she clearly denies that *all* educational outcomes must be equalized, in the end she nonetheless holds that *some* must be, namely, those that are required by the "democratic threshold."

8. A still stronger kind requires the features of the first two kinds plus the ability to reflect about one's basic value commitments and way of life—a kind of freedom attributed to especially reflective adults. As it turns out, the second level is all that schools should be required (or permitted) to foster, because the third level entails having questioned one's most fundamental commitments (e.g., one's religious commitments) to qualify as free. Although this is what philosophical types strive for, it is inappropriate to demand this of the population in general. See, for example, Stephen Macedo, *Liberal Virtues* (New York: Oxford University Press, 1990).

9. Daniel Dennett, *Elbow Room: The Varieties of Free Will Worth Wanting* (Cambridge, Mass: MIT Press, 1984).

10. I am currently developing a more elaborate analysis and defense of this point in a paper tentatively entitled "Equal Educational Opportunity as Educational Opportunities Worth Wanting."

11. I include the conditional because some thinkers believe that children's lack of autonomy and the associated authority to represent their own interests requires a different moral perspective and vocabulary. Onora O'Neill, "Children's Rights and Children's Lives," *Ethics* 98 (1988): 445–463, for example, is willing to (proposes to) forgo rights language in the case of children. A similar move could be made with respect to equal educational opportunity, namely, it could be judged as having no defensible application to children. For a response, see my "In Defense of Outcomes-Based Conceptions of Equal Education Opportunity."

12. The concept of "elbow room" is borrowed from Dennett's book by that name.

The Passions of Pluralism: Multiculturalism and the Expanding Community

Maxine Greene's approach to multicultural education is to see the diverse nation as a community. She uses literary works and ethnographies to bring out the voices of people who have been unintentionally overlooked and purposefully silenced. She calls these omissions of diverse voices as "gaps in our understandings." Greene would like for us to engage with others in explorations and discussions of what it means to be a person. From dialogue we learn about the many perspectives on life by the young and the old, the excluded and the powerless, and those in poverty. Her hope is that by helping students to look through multiple perspectives on life, to hear and read a wide range of human stories, those young people will want to transform society into a place where all voices are heard.

Greene is a professor emeritus at Teachers College, Columbia University in New York City, where she was for many years the William F. Russell Professor of Foundations of Education. Her life prior to academia involved actively fighting for people's rights to be heard. She became involved in antifascist activities in Spain, and she served as legislative director of the American Labor Party in Brooklyn, New York. Thus her concern for bringing diverse voices to readers and teachers arises out of her own life experiences. Greene's aesthetic and literary approach to the study and practice of education has resulted in bringing the diverse stories of people to the attention and emotions of readers and teachers. Several of her well-known books include *Landscapes of Learning* (Teachers College Press, 1978), *Teacher as Stranger* (Wadsworth Publishing, 1973), and *The Dialectic of Freedom* (Teachers College Press, 1988). The following selection is from her article "The Passions of Pluralism: Multiculturalism and the Expanding Community," *Educational Researcher* (January–February 1993).

Key Concept: engaging in dialogue to gain multiple perspectives on life

*T*here have always been newcomers in this country; there have always been strangers. There have always been young persons in our classrooms we did not, could not see or hear. In recent years, however, invisibility has been refused on many sides. Old silences have been shattered; long-repressed voices are making themselves heard. Yes, we are in search of what John Dewey called "the Great Community" (1954, pp. 143ff), but, at once, we are challenged as never before to confront plurality and multiplicity. Unable to deny or obscure the facts of pluralism, we are asked to choose ourselves with respect to unimaginable diversities. To speak of passions in such a context is not to refer to the strong feelings aroused by what strikes many as a confusion and a cacophony. Rather, it is to have in mind the central sphere for the operation of the passions: "the realm of face-to-face relationships" (Unger, 1984, p. 107). It seems clear that the more continuous and authentic personal encounters can be, the less likely it will be that categorizing and distancing will take place. People are less likely to be treated instrumentally, to be made "other" by those around. I want to speak of pluralism and multiculturalism with concrete engagements in mind, actual and imagined: engagements with persons, young persons and older persons, some suffering from exclusion, some from powerlessness, some from poverty, some from ignorance, some from boredom. Also, I want to speak with imagination in mind, and metaphor, and art, Cynthia Ozick writes:

> Through metaphor, the past has the capacity to imagine us, and we it. Through metaphorical concentration, doctors can imagine what it is to be their patients. Those who have no pain can imagine those who suffer. Those at the center can imagine what it is to be outside. The strong can imagine the weak. Illuminated lives can imagine the dark. Poets in their twilight can imagine the borders of stellar fire. We strangers can imagine the familiar hearts of strangers. (1989, p. 283)

TOWARDS A COMMUNITY OF PERSONS

Passions, then, engagements, and imagining: I want to find a way of speaking of community, an expanding community, taking shape when diverse people, speaking as *who* and not *what* they are, come together in speech and action, as [historian] Hannah Arendt puts it, to constitute something in common among themselves. She writes: "Plurality is the condition of human action because we are all the same, that is, human, in such a way that nobody is ever the same as anyone else who ever lived, lives, or will live" (1958, p. 57). For her, those present on a common ground have different locations on that ground; and each one "sees or hears from a different position." An object—a classroom, a neighborhood street, a field of flowers—shows itself differently when encountered by a variety of spectators. The reality of that object (or classroom, or neighborhood, or field of flowers) arises out of the sum total of its appearances. Thinking of those spectators as participants in an ongoing dialogue, each one speaking out of a distinct perspective and yet open to those around, I find a kind of paradigm for what I have in mind. I discover another in the work of Henry Louis Gates, Jr., who writes about the fact that "the challenge facing America in the next century will be the shaping, at long last, of a truly common public culture, one responsive to the long-silenced cultures of color" (1991, p. 712). (It is not long, it will be remembered, since the same Professor Gates asked in a *New York Times* article, "Whose canon is it anyway?" See Gates, 1992.) More recently, he has evoked the philosopher Michael Oakeshott and his notion of a conversation with different voices. Education, Gates suggests, might be "an invitation into the art of this conversation in which we learn to recognize the voices, each conditioned by a different perception of the world." Then Gates adds: "Common sense says that you don't bracket out 90% of the world's cultural heritage if you really want to learn about the world" (1991, p. 712).

For many, what is common sense for Gates represents an attack on the coherence of what we think of as our heritage, our canon. The notion of different voices conditioned by different perspectives summons up the spectre of relativism; and relativism, according to Clifford Geertz, is the "intellectualist Grande Peur." It makes people uneasy, because it appears to subvert authority; it eats away at what is conceived of as objectively real. "If thought is so much out in the world as this," Geertz asks, as the uneasy might ask, "what is to guarantee its generality, its objectivity, its efficacy, or its truth?" (1983, p. 153). There is irony in Geertz's voice, since he knows and has said: "For our time and forward, the image of a general orientation, perspective, *Weltanschauung*, growing out of humanistic studies (or, for that matter, out of scientific ones) and shaping the direction of the culture is a chimera." He speaks of the "radical variousness of the way we think now" and suggests that the problem of integrating cultural life becomes one of "making it possible for people inhabiting different worlds to have a genuine, and reciprocal, impact upon one another" (p. 161). This is troubling for people seeking assurances, seeking certainties. And yet they, like the rest of us, keep experiencing attacks on what is familiar, what James Clifford calls "the irruption of otherness, the unexpected" (1988, p. 13). It may well be that our ability to tolerate the unexpected relates to our tolerance for multiculturalism, for the very idea of expansion and the notion of plurality....

The seer of the life of communion, according to Dewey, was Walt Whitman. Whitman wrote about the many shapes arising in the country in his time, "the shapes of doors giving many exits and entrances" and "shapes of democracy... ever projecting other shapes." In "Song of Myself" (in total contradiction to the fundamentalist version of the "American way") he wrote:

Through me many long dumb voices,

Voices of the interminable generations of prisoners and slaves,

Voices of the diseas'd and despairing and of thieves and dwarfs,

Voices of cycles of preparation and accretion,

And of the threads that connect the stars, and of wombs and of the
     father-stuff,

And of the rights of them the others are down upon....

Through me forbidden voices....

—(Whitman, 1931, p. 53)

He was, from all appearances, the seer of a communion arising out of "many shapes," out of multiplicity. There is no suggestion of a melting pot here, nor is there a dread of plurality.

SILENCE AND INVISIBILITY: THE NEED TO REPAIR

For some of us, just beginning to feel our own stories are worth telling, the reminders of the "long dumb voices," the talk of "the rights of them the others are down upon" cannot but draw attention to the absences and silences that are as much a part of our history as the articulate voices, the shimmering faces, the images of emergence and success. Bartleby, the clerk who "prefers not to" in Herman Melville's story [Billy Budd] (1986), may suddenly become exemplary. What of those who said no, who found no place, who made no mark? Do they not say something about a society that closed too many doors, that allowed people to be abandoned like "wreckage in the mid-Atlantic" (Melville, 1986, p. 121)? What of those like Tod Clifton in Ralph Ellison's *Invisible Man*? A former youth leader in the so-called Brotherhood, he ends up selling Sambo dolls in front of the public library. When the police try to dislodge him, he protests; and they kill him. The narrator, watching, wonders:

> Why did he choose to plunge into nothingness, into the void of faceless faces, or soundless voices, lying outside history? . . . All things, it is said, are duly recorded —all things of importance, that is. But not quite; for actually it is only the known, the seen, the heard, and only those events that the recorder regards as important are put down. . . . But the cop would be Clifton's historian, his judge, his witness, his executioner, and I was the only brother in the watching crowd. (1952, p. 379)

The many who ended up "lying outside history" diminished the community, left an empty space on the common ground, left undefined an aspect of reality.

It is true that we cannot know all the absent ones, but they must be present somehow in their absence. Absence, after all, suggests an emptiness, a void to be filled, a wound to be healed, a flaw to be repaired. I think of E. L. Doctorow painting a landscape of denial at the beginning of *Ragtime*, appealing to both wonder and indignation, demanding a kind of repair. He is writing about New Rochelle in 1906 but he is presenting a past that reaches into the present, into *our* present, whether or not we ride trolleys anymore.

> Teddy Roosevelt was President. The population customarily gathered in great numbers either out of doors for parades, public concerts, fish fries, political picnics, social outings, or indoors in meeting halls, vaudeville theatres, operas, ballrooms. There seemed to be no entertainment that did not involve great swarms of people. Trains and steamers and trolleys moved them from one place to another. That was the style; that was the way people lived. Women were stouter then. They visited the fleet carrying white parasols. Everyone wore white in summer. There was alot of sexual fainting. There were no Negroes. There were no immigrants. (1975, pp. 3–4)

The story has focally to do with a decent, intelligent Black man named Coalhouse Walker, who is cheated, never acknowledged, never understood, scarcely *seen*, and who begins his own fated strategy of vengeance which ends when promises are broken and he is shot down in cold blood. Why is he unseen? Why were there no Negroes, no immigrants? More than likely because of the condition of the minds of those in power, those in charge. Ellison may explain it when he attributes invisibility to "a peculiar disposition of the eyes of those with whom I come in contact. A matter of the construction of their inner eyes, those eyes with which they look through their physical eyes upon reality" (1952, p. 7). But that disposition must itself have been partly due to the play of power in discourse as well as in social arrangements. We may wonder even now what the assimilation or initiation sought by so many educators signified when there were so many blanked out spaces—"no Negroes . . . no immigrants," oftentimes no full-grown women.

Looking back at the gaps in our own lived experiences, we might think of silences like those Tillie Olsen had in mind when she spoke of literary history "dark with silences," of the "unnatural silences" of women who worked too hard or were too embarrassed to express themselves (1978, p. 6), of others who did not have the words or had not mastered the proper "ways of knowing" (Belenky, Clinchy, Goldberger, & Tarule, 1986). We might ponder the plight of young island women, like Jamaica Kincaid's Lucy from Antigua, forced to be "two-faced" in a post-colonial school: "Outside, I seemed one way, inside I was another; outside false, inside true" (1990, p. 18). For years we knew no more about people like her (who saw "sorrow and bitterness" in the face of daffodils because of the Wordsworth poem she had been forced to learn) than we did about the Barbadians Paule Marshall has described, people living their fragmented lives in Brooklyn. There was little consciousness of what Gloria Anzaldua calls *Borderlands/La Frontera* on which so many Latinos live (1987), or of the Cuban immigrants like the musicians in Oscar Hijuelos's *The Mambo Kings Sing Songs of Love* (1989). Who of us truly wondered about the builders of the railroads, those Maxine Hong Kingston calls "China Men," chopping trees in the Sandalwood and Sierra Nevada Mountains? Who of us could fill the gaps left by such a person as Ah Goong, whose "existence was outlawed by the Chinese Exclusion Acts"? His family, writes Kingston,

> did not understand his accomplishments as an American ancestor, a holding, homing ancestor of this place. He'd gotten the legal or illegal papers burned in the San Francisco earthquake and fire; he appeared in America in time to be a citizen and to father citizens. He had also been seen carrying a child out of the fire, a child of his own in spite of the laws against marrying. He had built a railroad out of sweat, why not have an American child out of longing? (1989, p. 151)

Did we pay heed to a person like Michelle Clift, an Afro-Caribbean woman who felt that speaking in words that were not her own was a form of speechlessness? Or to a child like Pecola Breedlove in Toni Morrison's (1972) *The Bluest Eye*, the unloved Black child who wanted to look like Shirley Temple so she could be included in the human reality? Or to a Mary Crow Dog, who finds her own way of saying in the autobiography, *Lakota Woman?* How many of us have been willing to suffer the experiences most recently rendered in Art Spiegelman's two-volume comic book called *Maus*? He tells about his father, the ill-tempered Vladek, a survivor of Auschwitz, and his resentful sharing of his Holocaust memories with his son. Every character in the book is an animal: the Jews, mice; the Germans, cats; the Poles, pigs. It is a reminder, not simply of a particular culture's dissolution. ("Anja's parents, the grandparents, her big sister Tosha, little Bibi, and our Richieu.... All what is left, it's the photos"; 1991, p. 115). It is a reminder of the need to recognize that everything is possible, something normal people (including school people) either do not know or do not want to know.

To open up our experience (and, yes, our curricula) to existential possibilities of multiple kinds is to extend and deepen what we think of when we speak of a community. If we break through and even disrupt surface equilibrium and uniformity, this does not mean that particular ethnic or racial traditions ought to replace our own. Toni Morrison writes of pursuing her freedom as a writer in a "genderized, sexualized, wholly racialized world," but this does not keep her from developing a critical project "unencumbered by dreams of subversion or rallying gestures at fortress walls" (1992, pp. 4–5). In her case, the project involves exploring the ways in which what we think of as our Americanness is in many ways a response to an Africanist presence far too long denied. She is not interested in replacing one domination by another; she is interested in showing us what she sees from her own perspective—and, in showing us, enriching our understanding not only of our own culture, but of ourselves....

As Charles Taylor and Alasdair MacIntyre have written, we understand our lives in narrative form, as a quest. Taylor writes: "because we have to determine our place in relation to the good, therefore we cannot be without an orientation to it, and hence must see our life in stories" (1989, p. 51). Clearly, there are different stories connected by the same need to make sense, to make meaning, to find a direction.

To help ... the diverse students we know articulate their stories is not only to help them pursue the meanings of their lives to find out *how* things are happening, to keep posing questions about the why. It is to move them to learn the "new things" [Paulo] Freire spoke of, to reach out for the proficiencies and capacities, the craft required to be fully participant in this society, and to do so without losing the consciousness of who they are. That is not all. Stories... must break through into what we think of as our tradition or our heritage. They should with what Cornel West has in mind when he speaks about the importance of acknowledging the "distinctive cultural and political practices of oppressed people" without highlighting their marginality in such a way as to further marginalize them. Not only does he call attention to the resistance of Afro-Americans and that of other long-silenced people. He writes of the need to look at Afro-Americans' multiple contributions to the culture over the generations. We might think of the music, Gospel, jazz, ragtime; we might think of the Black churches; we might summon up the Civil Rights movement and the philosophies, the dreams that informed it; we might ponder—looking back, looking around—the images of courage, the images of survival. West goes on to say:

> Black cultural practices emerge out of a reality they cannot *not* know—the ragged edges of the real, of necessity; a reality historically constructed by white supremacist practices in North America.... These ragged edges—of not being able to eat, not to have shelter, not to have health care—all this is infused into the strategies and styles of black cultural practices." (1989, p. 23)

Viewed in connection with the idea of multiculturalism, this does not mean that Afro-American culture in all its variousness can be defined mainly in terms of oppression and discrimination. One of the many reasons for opening spaces in which Afro-Americans can tell their own stories is that they, far more than those from other cultures, can explain the ways in which poverty and exclusion have mediated their own sense of the past. It is true that experiences of pain and abandonment have led to a search for roots and, on occasion, for a revision of recorded history. What is crucial is the provision of opportunities for telling all the diverse stories, for interpreting membership as well as ethnicity, for making inescapable the braids of experience woven into the fabric of America's plurality....

CONCLUSION

Learning to look through multiple perspectives, young people may be helped to build bridges among themselves; attending to a range of human stories, they may be provoked to heal and to transform. Of course there will be difficulties in affirming plurality and difference and, at once, working to create community. Since the days of [Alexis] De Tocqueville, Americans have wondered how to deal with the conflicts between individualism and the drive to conform. They have wondered how to reconcile the impassioned voices of cultures not yet part of the whole with the requirements of conformity, how not to lose the integrity of those voices in the process, how not to allow the drive to conformity determine what happens at the end. But the community many of us hope for now is not to be identified with conformity. As in Whitman's way of saying, it is a community attentive to difference, open to the idea of plurality. Something life-affirming in diversity must be discovered and rediscovered, as what is held in common becomes always more many-faceted—open and inclusive, drawn to untapped possibility.

No one can predict precisely the common world of possibility, nor can we absolutely justify one kind of community over another. Many of us, however, for all the tensions and disagreements around us, would reaffirm the value of principles like justice and equality and freedom and commitment to human rights since, without these, we cannot even argue for the decency of welcoming. Only if more and more persons incarnate such principles, we might say, and choose to live by them and engage in dialogue in accord with them, are we likely to bring about a democratic pluralism and not fly apart in violence and disorder. Unable to provide an objective ground for such hopes and claims, all we can do is speak with others as eloquently and passionately as we can about justice and caring and love and trust. Like Richard Rorty and those he calls pragmatists, we can only articulate our desire for as much intersubjective agreement as possible, "the desire to extend the reference of 'us' as far as we can" (1991, p. 23). But, as we do so, we have to remain aware of the distinctive members of the plurality, appearing before one another with their own perspectives on the common, their own stories entering the culture's story, altering it as it moves through time. We want our classrooms to be just and caring, full of various conceptions of the good. We want them to be articulate, with the dialogue involving as many persons as possible, opening to one another, opening to the world. And we want them to be concerned for one another, as we learn to be concerned for them. We want them to achieve friendships among one another, as each one moves to a heightened sense of craft and wide-awakeness, to a renewed consciousness of worth and possibility.

With voices in mind and the need for visibility, I want to end with a call for human solidarity by Muriel Rukeyser, who—like many of us—wanted to "widen the lens and see/standing over the land myths of identity, new signals, processes." And then:

> Carry abroad the urgent need, the scene,
>
> to photograph and to extend the voice,
>
> to speak this meaning.
>
> Voices to speak to us directly. As we move.
>
> As we enrich, growing in larger motion,
>
> this word, this power.
>
> —(Rukeyser, 1938, p. 71)

This power, yes, the unexplored power of pluralism, and the wonder of an expanding community.

REFERENCES

Anzaldua, G. (1987). *Borderlands/La Frontera: The new mestiza.* San Francisco: Spinsters/Aunt Lute.

Arendt, H. (1958). *The human condition.* Chicago: University of Chicago Press.

Belenky, M. F., Clinchy, B., Goldberger, N., & Tarule, J. (1986). *Women's ways of knowing.* New York: Basic Books.

Clifford, J. (1988). *The predicament of culture.* Cambridge, MA: Harvard University Press.

Dewey, J. (1954). *The public and its problems.* Athens, OH: Swallow Press.

Doctorow, E. L. (1975). *Ragtime*. New York: Random House.

Ellison, R. (1952). *Invisible Man*. New York: Signet.

Gates, Jr., H. L. (1992). The master's pieces: On canon formation and the African-American tradition. In Gates, *Loose Canons* (pp. 17–42). New York: Oxford University Press.

Gates, Jr., H. L. (1991). Goodbye, Columbus? Notes on the culture of criticism. *American Literacy History*, 3(4), 711–727.

Geertz, C. (1983). *Local knowledge*. New York: Basic Books.

Hijuelos, O. (1989). *The mambo kings sing songs of love*. New York: Farrar, Straus, & Giroux.

Hughes, R. (1992, April 23). Art, morality & Mapplethorpe. *The New York Review of Books*, pp. 21–27.

Kincaid, J. (1990). *Lucy*. New York: Farrar, Straus, & Giroux.

Kingston, M. H. (1989). *China men*. New York: Vintage.

Melville, H. (1986). Bartleby. In H. Melville, *Billy Budd, sailor and other stories* (pp. 95–130). New York: Bantam Books.

Morrison, T. (1972). *The bluest eye*. New York: Pocket Books.

Morrison, T. (1992). *Playing in the dark: Whiteness and the literary imagination*. Cambridge, MA: Harvard University Press.

Olsen, T. (1978). *Silences*. New York: Delacorte.

Ozick, C. (1989). *Metaphor and memory*. New York: Knopf.

Rorty, R. (1991). Solidarity or objectivity? In Rorty, *Objectivity, relativism, and truth*. Cambridge, England: Cambridge University Press.

Rukeyser, M. (1983). *The book of the dead*. New York: Covici-Friede.

Schlesinger, Jr., A. M. (1992). *The disuniting of America: Reflections on a multicultural society*. New York: Norton.

Spiegelman, A. (1991). *Maus II*. New York: Pantheon Books.

Taylor, C. (1989). *Sources of the self*. Cambridge, MA: Harvard University Press.

Unger, R. M. (1984). *Passion: An essay on personality*. New York: Free Press.

Walker, A. (1982). *The color purple*. New York: Washington Square Press.

West, C. (1989). Black culture and postmodernism. In B. Kruger & P. Mariani (Eds.), *Remaking history*. Seattle: Bay Press.

Whitman, W. (1931). *Leaves of grass*. New York: Aventine Press.

Sociological and Anthropological Perspectives on Multicultural Education

4.1 SAMUEL BOWLES

Unequal Education and the Reproduction of the Social Division of Labor

Samuel Bowles has applied his knowledge in the fields of sociology and economics to the study of education. Most of his work is on understanding capitalism within a democracy, with a focus on the structure of labor, the organization of work, and the resulting inequities in society and schools. He is cohead of the MacArthur Foundation research group on the costs of inequality. Although Bowles is not first and foremost an educational scholar, his explanations of class distinctions and the role of schools to reproduce those class divisions have been widely studied and accepted within the fields of education and multicultural education. The following selection is from a

48

Chapter 4
Sociological and
Anthropological
Perspectives on
Multicultural
Education

chapter titled "Unequal Education and the Reproduction of the Social Division of Labor" in a book edited by Martin Carnoy, *Schooling in a Corporate Society: The Political Economy of Education in America,* 2d ed. (McKay, 1975).

Bowles writes that unequal education is part of the capitalist society of the United States and is inherent within the class distinctions created by capitalism. He further contends that inequalities in the school system serve to reproduce the existing class structure, benefiting the upper strata of society. Schools have evolved in the way that they have, he believes, as a response to the needs of corporate society, producing a social division of labor with differences in rules, opportunities, and expectations of different classes of students. In discussing reform efforts in schools, Bowles asserts that reform efforts have failed because they have not challenged the basic class distinctions of capitalism.

Key Concept: education as the reproduction of class inequalities

*T*he ideological defense of modern capitalist society rests heavily on the assertion that the equalizing effects of education can counter the disequalizing forces inherent in the free-market system. That educational systems in capitalist societies have been highly unequal is generally admitted and widely condemned. Yet educational inequalities are taken as passing phenomena, holdovers from an earlier, less enlightened era, which are rapidly being eliminated.

The record of educational history in the United States, and scrutiny of the present state of our colleges and schools, lend little support to this comforting optimism. Rather, the available data suggest an alternative interpretation. In what follows I argue (1) that schools have evolved in the United States not as part of a pursuit of equality, but rather to meet the needs of capitalist employers for a disciplined and skilled labor force, and to provide a mechanism for social control in the interests of political stability; (2) that as the economic importance of skilled and well-educated labor has grown, inequalities in the school system have become increasingly important in reproducing the class structure from one generation to the next; (3) that the U.S. school system is pervaded by class inequalities, which have shown little sign of diminishing over the last half century; and (4) that the evidently unequal control over school boards and other decision-making bodies in education does not provide a sufficient explanation of the persistence and pervasiveness of inequalities in the school system. Although the unequal distribution of political power serves to maintain inequalities in education, the origins of these inequalities are to be found outside the political sphere, in the class structure itself and in the class subcultures typical of capitalist societies. Thus, unequal education has its roots in the very class structure which it serves to legitimize and reproduce. Inequalities in education are part of the web of capitalist society, and are likely to persist as long as capitalism survives....

Unequal schooling reproduces the social division of labor. Children whose parents occupy positions at the top of the occupational hierarchy receive more years of schooling than working-class children. Both the amount and the content of their education greatly facilitates their movement into positions similar to those of their parents.

Because of the relative ease of measurement, inequalities in years of schooling are particularly evident. If we define social-class standing by the income, occupation, and educational level of the parents, a child from the 90th percentile in the class distribution may expect on the average to achieve over four and a half more years of schooling than a child from the 10th percentile.[1] ... [S]ocial-class inequalities in the number of years of schooling received arise in part because a disproportionate number of children from poorer families do not complete high school.[2] ... [T]hese inequalities are exacerbated by social-class inequalities in college attendance among those children who did graduate from high school: even among those who had graduated from high school, children of families earning less than $3,000 per year were over six times as likely *not* to attend college as were the children of families earning over $15,000.[3]

Because schooling, especially at the college level, is heavily subsidized by the general taxpayer, those children who attend school longer have access for this reason alone to a far larger amount of public resources than those who are forced out of school or who drop out early.[4] But social-class inequalities in public expenditure on education are far more severe than the degree of inequality in years of schooling would suggest. In the first place, per-student public expenditure in four-year colleges greatly exceeds that in elementary schools; those who stay in school longer receive an increasingly large *annual* public subsidy.[5] Second, even at the elementary level, schools attended by children of the poor tend to be less well endowed with equipment, books, teachers, and other inputs into the educational process. Evidence on the relationship between the level of school inputs and the income of the neighborhoods that the schools serve ... indicate[s] that both school expenditures and more direct measures of school quality vary directly with the income levels of the communities in which the school is located.

Inequalities in schooling are not simply a matter of differences in years of schooling attained or in resources devoted to each student per year of schooling. Differences in the internal structure of schools themselves and in the content of schooling reflect the differences in the social-class compositions of the student bodies. The social relations of the educational process ordinarily mirror the social relations of the work roles into which most students are likely to move. Differences in rules, expected modes of behavior, and opportunities for choice are most glaring when we compare levels of schooling. Note the wide range of choice over curriculum, life style, and allocation of time afforded to college students, compared with the obedience and respect for authority expected in high school. Differentiation occurs also within each level of schooling. One needs only to compare the social relations of a junior college with those of an elite four-year college,[7] or those of a working-class high school with those of a wealthy suburban high school, for verification of this point.[8]

Chapter 4
Sociological and
Anthropological
Perspectives on
Multicultural
Education

The various socialization patterns in schools attended by students of different social classes do not arise by accident. Rather, they stem from the fact that the educational objectives and expectations of both parents and teachers, and the responsiveness of students to various patterns of teaching and control, differ for students of different social classes.[9] Further, class inequalities in school socialization patterns are reinforced by the inequalities in financial resources documented above. The paucity of financial support for the education of children from working-class families not only leaves more resources to be devoted to the children of those with commanding roles in the economy; it forces upon the teachers and school administrators in the working-class schools a type of social relations which fairly closely mirrors that of the factory. Thus, financial considerations in poorly supported working-class schools militate against small intimate classes, against a multiplicity of elective courses and specialized teachers (except disciplinary personnel), and preclude the amounts of free time for the teachers and free space required for a more open, flexible educational environment. The lack of financial support all but requires that students be treated as raw materials on a production line; it places a high premium on obedience and punctuality; there are few opportunities for independent, creative work or individualized attention by teachers. The well-financed schools attended by the children of the rich can offer much greater opportunities for the development of the capacity for sustained independent work and the other characteristics required for adequate job performance in the upper levels of the occupational hierarchy.

Much of the inequality in American education exists between schools, but even within a given school different children receive different educations. Class stratification within schools is achieved through tracking, differential participation in extracurricular activities, and in the attitudes of teachers and guidance personnel who expect working-class children to do poorly, to terminate schooling early, and to end up in jobs similar to those of their parents.[10]

Not surprisingly, the results of schooling differ greatly for children of different social classes. The differing educational objectives implicit in the social relations of schools attended by children of different social classes has already been mentioned. Less important but more easily measured are differences in scholastic achievement. If we measure the output of schooling by scores on nationally standardized achievement tests, children whose parents were themselves highly educated outperform children of parents with less education by a wide margin. A recent study revealed, for example, that among white high school seniors, those whose parents were in the top education decile were on the average well over three grade levels ahead of those whose parents were in the bottom decile.[11] Although a good part of this discrepancy is the result of unequal treatment in school and unequal educational resources, much of it is related to differences in the early socialization and home environment of the children.

Given the great social-class differences in scholastic achievement, class inequalities in college attendance are to be expected. Thus one might be tempted to argue that the data ... are simply a reflection of unequal scholastic achievement in high school and do not reflect any *additional* social-class inequalities peculiar to the process of college admission. This view, so comforting to the admissions personnel in our elite universities, is unsupported by the available data.... Access to a college education is highly unequal, even for children of the same measured "academic ability."

The social-class inequalities in our school system and the role they play in the reproduction of the social division of labor are too evident to be denied. Defenders of the educational system are forced back on the assertion that things are getting better, that inequalities of the past were far worse. And, indeed, some of the inequalities of the past have undoubtedly been mitigated. Yet, new inequalities have apparently developed to take their place, for the available historical evidence lends little support to the idea that our schools are on the road to equality of educational opportunity. For example, data from a recent U.S. Census survey...indicate that graduation from college has become increasingly dependent on one's class background. This is true despite the fact that the probability of high school graduation is becoming increasingly equal across social classes. On balance, the available data suggest that the number of years of schooling attained by a child depends upon the social-class standing of his father at least as much in the recent period as it did fifty years ago.[12]

The argument that our "egalitarian" education compensates for inequalities generated elsewhere in the capitalist system is so patently fallacious that few persist in maintaining it. But the discrepancy between the ideology and the reality of the U.S. school system is far greater than would appear from a passing glance at the...data. In the first place, if education is to compensate for the social-class immobility caused by the inheritance of wealth and privilege, education must be structured so as to yield a negative correlation between social-class background of the child and the quantity and quality of his schooling. Thus the assertion that education compensates for inequalities in inherited wealth and privilege is falsified not so much by the extent of the social-class inequalities in the school system as by their very existence, or, more correctly, by the absence of compensatory inequalities.

Moreover, if we turn from the problem of intergenerational immobility to the problem of inequality of income at a given moment, a similar argument applies. In a capitalist economy, the increasing importance of schooling in the economy exercises a disequalizing tendency on the distribution of income even in the absence of social-class inequalities in quality and quantity of schooling. To see why this is so, consider a simple capitalist economy in which only two factors are used in production: uneducated and undifferentiated labor, and capital, the ownership of which is unequally distributed among the population. The only source of income inequality in this society is the unequal distribution of capital. As the labor force becomes differentiated by type of skill or schooling, inequalities in labor earnings contribute to total income inequality, augmenting the inequalities inherent in the concentration of capital. This will be the case even if education and skills are distributed randomly among the population. The disequalizing tendency will of course be intensified if the owners of capital also acquire a disproportionate amount of those types of education and training which confer access to high-paying jobs.[13] A substantial negative correlation between the ownership of capital and the quality and quantity of schooling received would have been required merely to neutralize the disequalizing effect of the rise of schooling as an economic phenomenon. And while some research

52

*Chapter 4
Sociological and
Anthropological
Perspectives on
Multicultural
Education*

has minimized the importance of social-class biases in schooling,[14] nobody has yet suggested that class and schooling were inversely related!

NOTES

1. The data for this calculation refer to white males who were aged 25–34 in 1962. See S. Bowles, "Schooling and Inequality from Generation to Generation" (Paper presented at the Far Eastern Meetings of the Econometric Society, Tokyo, 1970).

2. [Data] understate the degree of social-class inequality in school attendance because a substantial portion of upper-income children not enrolled in public schools attend private schools. Private schools provide a parallel educational system for the upper class. I have not given much attention to these institutions as they are not quantitatively very significant in the total picture. Moreover, to deal extensively with them might detract attention from the task of explaining class inequalities in the ostensibly egalitarian portion of our school system.

3. For recent evidence on these points, see U.S. Bureau of the Census, *Current Population Reports* (Series P–20), nos. 183 and 185.

4. W. L. Hansen and B. Weisbrod, "The Distribution of Costs and Direct Benefits of Public Higher Education: the Case of California," *Journal of Human Resources* 5, no. 3 (Summer 1970): 361–370.

5. In the school year 1969–70, per-pupil expenditures of federal, state, and local funds were $1,490 for colleges and universities and $747 for primary and secondary schools. U.S. Office of Education, *Digest of Educational Statistics, 1969* (Washington, D.C.: Government Printing Office, 1969).

6. See also P. C. Sexton, *Education and Income* (New York: Viking Press, 1961).

7. See J. Binstock, *"Survival in the American College Industry"* mimeograph, 1971.

8. E. Z. Friedenberg, *Coming of Age in America* (New York: Random House, 1965). It is consistent with this pattern that the play-oriented, child-centered pedagogy of the progressive movement found little acceptance outside of private schools and public schools in wealthy communities. See Cohen and Lazerson, "Education and the Industrial Order."

9. That working-class parents seem to favor more authoritarian educational methods is perhaps a reflection of their own work experiences which have demonstrated that submission to authority is an essential ingredient in one's ability to get and hold a steady, well-paying job.

10. See, for example, A. B. Hollingshead, *Elmtown's Youth* (New York: John Wiley, 1949); W. L. Warner and P. S. Lunt, *The Social Life of a Modern Community* (New Haven: Yale University Press, 1941); R. Rosenthal and L. Jacobson, *Pygmalion in the Classroom* (New York: Holt, Rinehart, and Winston, 1968); and W. E. Schafer, C. Olexa, and K. Polk, "Programmed for Social Class: Tracking in High School," *Trans-action* 7, no. 12 (October 1970): pp. 39–46.

11. Calculation based on data in James S. Coleman et al. *Equality of Educational Opportunity*, vol. 2 (Washington, D.C.: U.S. Office of Education, 1966), and methods described in S. Bowles, "Schooling and Inequality from Generation to Generation."

12. See P. M. Blau and O. D. Duncan, *The American Occupational Structure* (New York: Wiley, 1967). More recent data do not contradict the evidence of no trend toward

equality. A 1967 Census survey, the most recent available, shows that among high school graduates in 1965, the probability of college attendance for those whose parents had attended college has continued to rise relative to the probability of college attendance for those whose parents had attended less than eight years of school. See U.S. Bureau of the Census, *Current Population Reports* (Series P–20), no. 185, 11 July 1969.

13. A simple statistical model will elucidate the main relationships involved.

Let y (individual or family income) be the sum of w (earnings from labor, including embodied education and skills, L) and k (earnings from capital, K), related according to the equation $y = w + k = aK^A L^B$. The coefficients A and B represent the relative importance of capital and labor as sources of income. The variance of the logarithm of income (a common measure of inequality) can then be represented by the following expression:

$$\text{var} \log y = A^2 \text{var} \log K + B^2 \text{var} \log L + 2AB \text{ covar } (\log L, \log K).$$

The first term on the right represents the contribution of inequalities in capital ownership to total inequality, the second measures that part of total income inequality due to inequalities of education and skills embodied in labor, and the third represents the contribution to income inequality of social class inequalities in the supply of skills and schooling. Prior to the educational differentiation of the labor force, the variance of labor was zero. All workers were effectively equal. The variance of the logarithm of income would then be owed entirely to capital inequality and would be exactly equal to $A^2 \text{var} \log K$. The rise of education as a source of income and labor differentiation will increase the variance of the logarithm of embodied labor unless all workers receive identical education and training. This is true even if the third term is zero, indicating no social class inequalities in the provision of skills and education.

To assert the conventional faith in the egalitarian influence of the rising economic importance of education, one would have to argue that the rise of education is likely to be associated with either (1) a fall in A, the relative importance of capital as a source of earnings; (2) a decrease in the size of the covariance of the logarithms of capital and labor; (3) a decrease in the inequality of capital ownerships; or (4) an increase in equality in the supply of education. While each is possible, I see no compelling reason why education should *produce* these results.

14. See, for example, Robert Hauser, "Educational Stratification in the United States," *Sociological Inquiry* 40 (Spring 1970): 102–29.

Adaptation to Minority Status and Impact on School Success

John U. Ogbu, one of the world's leading educational anthropologists, specializes in the comparative study of minority education. He does research on the identities, experiences, and education of students, with a focus on minority status and class status. He makes a distinction between voluntary and involuntary minorities, comparing the experiences, identity, and education of each. Ogbu's work has been recognized by numerous organizations and foundations. He was named Distinguished Scholar/Research on minority education by the American Educational Research Association. He has received grants to further his research from a number of foundations, including the MacArthur Foundation, the Rockefeller Foundation, and the National Institute of Education. He is Alumni Distinguished Professor of Anthropology at the University of California, Berkeley.

In the following selection, which has been taken from "Adaptation to Minority Status and Impact on School Success," *Theory Into Practice* (Autumn 1992), Ogbu explains why some minority groups, as groups, are more successful in school than other minority groups. He distinguishes between what he calls immigrant, or voluntary, minorities and nonimmigrant, or involuntary, minorities, and he goes on to discuss the community forces within these groups that differ both historically and currently. According to Ogbu, voluntary and involuntary minorities differ in terms of how they were initially incorporated into American society. Ogbu examines the degree of trust in whites that these minorities have developed over time, models of how to get ahead in U.S. society, and the strategies that the groups and individuals use in order to have a sense of self-esteem and group identity. The community forces that affect students differently across different groups include historical experiences, cultural models, cultural frames of reference, degrees of trust, and educational strategies that are developed and used in schools.

Key Concept: community factors impacting minority student school performance

From my comparative research both in the United States and internationally, I suggest that an essential key to understanding the differences in the school adjustment and academic performance of minority groups is understanding of (a) the *cultural models* a minority group has with regard to the U.S. society and schooling, (b) the *cultural and language frame of reference* of a minority group, (c) the *degree of trust or acquiescence* the minorities have for White Americans and the societal institutions they control, and (d) the *educational strategies* that result from the above elements. These four factors are dependent in part on the group's history, its present situation, and its future expectations. They are combined in the term *community forces*.

Cultural model is used to mean peoples' understandings of their world, which guide their interpretations of events in that world and their own actions in it. (Folk theory or folk model is a comparable term.) (See Ogbu, 1974; also, Bohannan, 1957; Holland & Quinn, 1987; Holy & Stuchlik, 1981.)

Cultural/language frames of reference are either ambivalent/oppositional or non-oppositional. Non-oppositional cultural/language frames of reference are due to *primary* cultural/language differences. These are differences that existed *before* a group became a minority, such as before immigrants from China, India, or Latin America arrived in the United States.

For example, before Punjabi Indians in Valleyside, California, arrived in the United States, they spoke Punjabi, practiced Sikh, Hindu, or Moslem religion, had arranged marriages, and the males wore turbans. The Punjabis also brought to America their own way of raising children. For example, they differ from White Americans in training children to make decisions and manage money (Gibson, 1988). The Punjabis continue to some extent these beliefs and practices in America.

Primary cultural differences result in a cultural frame of reference that is merely different, not oppositional. This frame of reference leads the bearers of primary cultural/language differences to interpret the cultural/language differences they encounter in school and workplace as *barriers to overcome* in order to achieve their goals.

Oppositional or ambivalent cultural frames of reference are due to *secondary* cultural/language differences. The latter are differences that arose *after* a group has become a minority, such as after Blacks were brought to America as slaves, or after an American Indian tribe was conquered, moved, and placed on a "reservation."

This type of cultural difference is thus the product of reactions to a contact situation, especially one that involves the subordination of one group by another. At the beginning of the contact, both the dominant group and the minority group are characterized by primary cultural differences. But subsequently, the minorities develop new cultural features and reinterpret old ones in order to cope with their subordination or oppression.

African Americans, for instance, spoke numerous African languages and practiced a variety of primary African cultural patterns at the time of their arrival in America as chattels of the dominant Whites. However, due to the subordination and oppressive conditions of the slavery period, the indigenous

56

*Chapter 4
Sociological and
Anthropological
Perspectives on
Multicultural
Education*

languages and cultural patterns eventually were mostly lost, reinterpreted, or replaced by new cultural and language forms.

These new cultural and language forms, behaviors, and meanings became the minorities' cultural frame of reference or ideal ways guiding behaviors. They became oppositional partly because the minorities were not rewarded for behaving like White Americans, were not permitted to behave like Whites, were punished for behaving like Whites, or, because under such circumstances the ideal way of behaving or cultural frame of reference symbolized their shared or collective sense of identity and self-worth.

Minorities with oppositional cultural/language frames of reference do not define cultural or language differences they encounter in society and school as barriers to overcome, but as markers of *identity to be maintained.* For these minorities, there is "a White way" and "a minority way" of talking and behaving. These minorities feel strongly that their way of talking, walking, etc., is an expression of their group identity; and that the "White way" is an expression of White identity (Ogbu, 1991a).

Degree of trust or acquiescence in a relationship with White Americans and their institutions is important. Some minorities have experienced many episodes in their relationship with Whites that have led them to believe that Whites and the institutions they control cannot be trusted; their comparative frame of reference is the education in White suburbs and they usually conclude that they are given different and inferior education.

Educational strategies encompass the attitudes, plans, and actions minorities use or do not use in their pursuit of formal education. Educational strategies are very much influenced by the minorities' cultural models, degree of trust or acquiescence, and cultural/language frames of reference.

An essential point of these community forces—i.e., cultural models, degree of trust or acquiescence, cultural/language frames of reference, and educational strategies—is that they are group or collective phenomena. Although they may be manifested at an individual level, they are characteristic of the group *qua* group. In other words, to understand minority students' (as well as minority parents') behaviors, decisions, or attitudes toward schooling, we need to understand the cultural models, degree of trust, cultural frames of reference, and educational strategies of the minority group from which they come.

GROUP DIFFERENCES

All minority groups face certain similar barriers in school, including inferior curriculum, denigrating treatment, and cultural and language barriers, as well as social and economic barriers in the wider society. Yet some minorities are more able than others to adjust socially and do well academically in school.

As discussed above, factors that contribute to the differences in social adjustment and academic performance are the groups' differing cultural models, degree of trust, cultural frames of reference, and educational strategies, i.e., differing community forces. (See Fordham & Ogbu, 1986; Gibson, 1986, 1988; Gibson & Bhachu, 1991; Gibson & Ogbu, 1991; Lee, 1984; Schofield, 1982;

Suarez-Orozco, 1987; Weis, 1985.) A major factor in these community forces appears to be the groups' histories and self-perceptions *vis-à-vis* the dominant group. To understand how history and self-perception shape these community forces, minority groups can be classified into the following: (a) autonomous; (b) immigrant or voluntary; and (c) non-immigrant or involuntary.

Autonomous minorities are minority groups that may be culturally or linguistically distinct but are not politically, socially, or economically subordinated to major degrees. These groups have relatively high rates of school success. White examples in the United States include Jews and Mormons; there are no non-White examples in the United States. Autonomous minorities are not discussed further in this article.

Immigrant or voluntary minorities are people who have moved more or less voluntarily to the United States because they believe that this would result in more economic well-being, better overall opportunities, and/or greater political freedom. Even though they experience subordination once here, the positive expectations they bring with them influence their perceptions of the U.S. society and schools controlled by Whites. Their children do not usually experience disproportionate and persistent problems in social adjustment and academic achievement. Examples in California are Chinese and Punjabi immigrants.

Refugees are not immigrant or voluntary minorities and are not the subject of this article. Yet I must note that there is a good deal of misunderstanding about refugees in the United States, especially Southeast Asian refugees, some of whom are doing well in school; others poorly. I have tried to explain elsewhere the distinction between refugees and immigrant minorities (Ogbu, 1991b). The point to stress here is that refugees are not synonymous with immigrants.

The third type is *non-immigrant or involuntary minorities.* Involuntary minorities are those groups that are a part of the United States society because of slavery, conquest, or colonization, rather than by choice because of expectations of a better future. They usually have no other "homeland" to which to return if their experiences in the United States become unbearable. It is these involuntary minorities that have the most difficulties with school adjustment and academic achievement. Examples of involuntary minorities include African Americans, Mexican Americans, Native Americans, and Native Hawaiians. (For the Mexican Americans, I consider those of Southwest origins, rather than immigrants from Mexico, see Ogbu, 1978; Ogbu & Matute-Bianchi, 1986.)[1]

Comparative research suggests that voluntary minorities, such as Chinese, Punjabi, and South American immigrants, have cultural models, degree of trust, cultural/language frames of reference, and educational strategies that differ from those of involuntary minorities, such as African Americans, Mexican Americans, Native Americans, and Native Hawaiians.

Voluntary minorities have cultural models that lead them to accept uncritically mainstream folk theory and strategies of getting ahead in the United States and to interpret their economic hardships as temporary problems they can and will overcome through education and hard work. Additionally they tend to acquiesce in their relationship with school personnel and White authorities controlling other societal institutions. Their cultural/language frames of reference enable them to interpret cultural and language barriers in school as

58

*Chapter 4
Sociological and
Anthropological
Perspectives on
Multicultural
Education*

barriers to be overcome in order to achieve their immigration goals. Finally, these voluntary minorities do make concerted efforts to overcome the cultural and language barriers they experience in school and mainstream society.

Under these circumstances, one finds in voluntary minority communities an educational climate or orientation that strongly endorses academic success as a means of getting ahead in the United States. Equally important, one also finds culturally sanctioned high and persistence academic efforts. In these communities, social, peer, and psychological pressures not only encourage students to perform like Whites but also to surpass Whites in academic achievement.

In contrast, one finds in the communities of involuntary minorities cultural models that make them skeptical that they can get ahead merely through mainstream beliefs and strategies, even though they verbally endorse education as a means of getting ahead. Their cultural models lead them to attribute their economic and other difficulties to *institutionalized discrimination*, which, in their opinion, will not necessarily be eliminated by hard work and education alone.

Involuntary minorities tend to distrust school personnel and White people (or their minority representatives) who control other societal institutions. Their cultural/language frames of reference lead them to interpret the cultural and language differences they encounter in school as symbols of their group identity to be maintained, and to consciously and/or unconsciously avoid crossing cultural and language boundaries (see Fordham & Ogbu, 1986; Ogbu, 1982, 1985, 1991a; Ogbu & Matute-Bianchi, 1986). Unlike voluntary minorities, involuntary minorities are the groups likely to demand or need culturally compatible curriculum, teaching and learning styles, communication style, and interactional style, rather than accept the school counterparts or, as Gibson puts it, "play by the rules" (Au, 1981; Moll & Diaz, 1987; Erickson & Mohatt, 1982; Gibson, 1988; Philips, 1983)....

IMPACT ON SCHOOL OUTCOMES

These differing elements of the community forces of the minority groups work in combination with societal factors to ultimately produce educational strategies that either enhance or discourage school success. This process occurs in a step-wise fashion as follows: Initially, a minority group's understanding of its place in United States society is partially determined by its initial terms of incorporation (voluntary or involuntary) and subsequent subordination; these understandings, in turn, determine the group's cultural model of schooling. Its cultural model also determines the group members' coping responses to the U.S. society as a whole, as well as in a given locality. These coping responses, expressed in the forms of folk theories about making it, and alternative or survival strategies, tend to require and promote adaptational attitudes, skills, and role models that may or may not be compatible with the pursuit of academic success. The initial terms of incorporation and subsequent treatment also determine the degree of trust the minorities have for the schools and Whites (or their minority representatives) who control the schools.

Additionally a minority group's cultural frame of reference and collective identity may lead its members to interpret the cultural and language differences they encounter as barriers to be overcome or as markers of group identity to be maintained. Those who interpret the cultural and language differences as barriers to be overcome will usually make concerted efforts and, with appropriate assistance from the schools, acquire the standard language and behavioral norms of the school. Those who interpret these differences as identity symbols and boundary-maintaining may consciously or unconsciously perceive learning the standard English language and cultural behaviors of the school as detrimental to their language and cultural identity and make little or no effort to cross cultural and language boundaries. . . .

CONCLUSION

Many who study literacy problems among African-American children and similar minorities focus on what goes on within the school, classroom, or family. This is probably due to the American cultural orientation of explaining educational behavior in terms of what takes place in these settings. It is also because of emphasis on remediation or improvement research, rather than research to understand the nature and scope of the problem, especially in comparative perspective. The assumption of this article is that in order to understand the disproportion and persistence of the literacy problems of African Americans and similar minorities, we must go beyond the events and situations in the school, classroom, and home. We must examine the historical and structural contexts of these events and situations in a comparative framework.

Voluntary and involuntary minorities differ not only in initial terms of incorporation into American society but also in their cultural models of what it means to be a minority, how to get ahead, and the role of education in getting ahead in the United States. They differ in the degree to which they trust White Americans and the institutions, such as schools, that are controlled by Whites; and they differ in collective identity and cultural frame of reference for judging appropriate behavior and affirmation of group membership and solidarity.

These distinguishing beliefs and practices affect the cultural knowledge, attitudes, and behaviors that minority parents employ in preparing their children for school and minority children bring to school. The latter interact with school factors and together they influence the children's social adjustment and academic performance.

NOTES

1. We classify Mexican Americans as an involuntary minority group because they were initially incorporated by conquest: The "Anglos" conquered and annexed the Mexican territory where Chicanos were living in the southwest, acts that were completed

60

Chapter 4
Sociological and
Anthropological
Perspectives on
Multicultural
Education

by the Treaty of Quadalupe Hildago in 1948 (see Acuna, 1981; Ogbu & Matute-Bianchi, 1986). Mexicans coming to the United States from Mexico are immigrants and may be properly designated as *Mexicanos* until they assume the identity or sense of peoplehood of the conquered group.

We also classify Puerto Ricans on the mainland United States as an involuntary minority group because they are more or less a "colonized group." The United States conquered or colonized Cuba, Puerto Rico, and the Philippines in 1898. Both Cuba and the Philippines later gained independence; for this reason Cubans and Filipinos coming to the United States come more or less as immigrants or refugees. The status of Puerto Rico is ambiguous: It is neither a state within the U.S. policy nor an independent nation in the real sense. Many Puerto Ricans feel that their "country" is still a colony of the United States (see Ogbu, 1978, 1990).

In summary, we classify a minority group as "voluntary" if its members have chosen to come to the United States and have not been forced by White Americans to become a part of the country through conquest, slavery, or colonization. That people are "forced" to flee their country by war, famine, political upheaval, etc., is not relevant to our classification. What matters is that members of the minority group do not interpret their presence in the United States as forced on them by White Americans. The distinction between the groups usually shows up in ethnographic studies focusing on the minority groups themselves.

REFERENCES

Acuna, R. (1981). *Occupied America: The Chicano's struggle toward liberation*. San Francisco: Canfield Press.

Au, K. H. (1981). Participant structure in a reading lesson with Hawaiian children: Analysis of a culturally appropriate instructional event. *Anthropology and Education Quarterly, 10*, 91–115.

Bohannan, P. (1957). *Justice and judgment among the Tiv*. London: Oxford University Press.

Erickson, F., & Mohatt, J. (1982). Cultural organization of participant structure in two classrooms of Indian students. In G. D. Spindler (Ed.), *Doing the ethnography of schooling: Educational anthropology in action* (pp. 132–175). New York: Holt, Rinehart & Winston.

Fordham, S., & Ogbu, J. U. (1986). Black students' school success: Coping with the burden of "acting White." *Urban Review, 18*(3), 1–31.

Gibson, M. A. (1986). Playing by the rules. In G. Spindler (Ed.), *Education and cultural process* (2nd ed., pp. 274–281). Prospect Heights, IL: Waveland Press.

Gibson, M. A. (1988). *Accommodation without assimilation: Sikh immigrants in an American high school and community*. Ithaca, NY: Cornell University Press.

Gibson, M. A., & Bhachu, P. (1991). The dynamics of educational decision making. In M. A. Gibson & J. U. Ogbu (Eds.), *Minority status and schooling: A comparative study of immigrant vs. involuntary minorities* (pp. 63–95). New York: Garland.

Gibson, M. A., & Ogbu, J. U. (1991). *Minority status and schooling: A comparative study of immigrant vs. involuntary minorities*. New York: Garland.

Holland, D. C., & Quinn, N. (1987). Introduction. In N. Quinn & D. C. Holland (Eds.), *Cultural models in language and thought* (pp. 3–40). New York: Cambridge University Press.

Holy, L., & Stuchlik, M. (1981). The structure of folk models. In L. Holy & M. Stuchlik (Eds.), *The structure of folk models* (pp. 1–34). New York: Academic Press.

Lee, Y. (1984). *A comparative study of East Asian American and Anglo American academic achievement: An ethnographic study.* Unpublished doctoral dissertation, Department of Anthropology, Northwestern University.

Moll, L. C., & Diaz, S. (1987). Change as the goal of educational research. *Anthropology and Education Quarterly, 18,* 300–311.

Ogbu, J. U. (1974). *The next generation: An ethnography of education in an urban neighborhood.* New York: Academic Press.

Ogbu, J. U. (1978). *Minority education and caste: The American system in cross-cultural perspective.* New York: Academic Press.

Ogbu, J. U. (1982). Cultural discontinuities and schooling. *Anthropology and Education Quarterly, 13,* 290–307.

Ogbu, J. U. (1985). Research currents: Cultural-ecological influences on minority school learning. *Language Arts, 62,* 860–869.

Ogbu, J. U. (1990). Minority status and literacy in comparative perspective. *Daedalus, 119,* 141–168.

Ogbu, J. U. (1991a). Cultural diversity and school experience. In C. E. Walsh (Ed.), *Literacy as praxis: Culture, language, and pedagogy* (pp. 25–50). Norwood, NJ: Ablex.

Ogbu, J. U. (1991b). *Understanding cultural diversity and school learning.* Invited presentation at the annual meeting of the American Educational Research Association (Division D), Chicago.

Ogbu, J. U., & Matute-Bianchi, M. E. (1986). Understanding sociocultural factors in education: Knowledge, identity, and adjustment in schooling. In *Beyond language: Social and cultural factors in schooling language minority students* (pp. 73–142). Sacramento: California State Department of Education, Bilingual Education Office.

Philips, S. U. (1983). *The invisible culture: Communication in classroom and community on the Warm Springs Indian Reservation.* New York: Longman.

Schofield, J. W. (1982). *Black and White in school: Trust, tension, or tolerance.* New York: Praeger.

Suarez-Orozco, M. M. (1987). Becoming somebody: Central American immigrants in U.S. inner-city schools. *Anthropology and Education Quarterly, 18,* 287–299.

Weis, L. (1985). *Between two worlds: Black students in an urban community college.* Boston: Routledge & Kegan Paul.

CHAPTER 5 Ethnographic Perspectives on Multicultural Education

Savage Inequalities: Children in America's Schools

Through his numerous books on the conditions of schools and communities, especially those of poverty, Jonathan Kozol brings to our attention the struggles and hopes of overlooked children within U.S. society. He is concerned with the extreme racial segregation in U.S. schools and the corresponding disparaging differences in funding, safety, and quality of schools. He employs an ethnographic approach, in which he spends time within the communities that he is studying. His work directly addresses such concerns as poverty, homelessness, and educational inequality. Kozol has received several awards for his work, including the Robert F. Kennedy Book Award and the Conscience in Media Award.

In the following selection, drawn from the book *Savage Inequalities: Children in America's Schools* (Crown Publishers, 1991), Kozol applies his ethnographic approach to the schools and communities of several cities throughout the United States. He gives not only the details about the physical makeup of the schools and communities but also the words of the children who are impacted by these conditions. Kozol describes conditions ranging from the raw sewage contaminating the streets and schools in East St. Louis to the lack of medical and dental care. In describing the latter's impact on children, he writes, "Children live for months with pain that grown-ups would find unendurable." Using these details and descriptions, Kozol argues for more equitable funding for schools across the country and urges legislators and educators to stop ignoring the needs of the millions of children who live in poverty in the United States.

Key Concept: ethnography of inequalities among U.S. schools and communities

*I*t was a long time since I'd been with children in the public schools.

I had begun to teach in 1964 in Boston in a segregated school so crowded and so poor that it could not provide my fourth grade children with a classroom. We shared an auditorium with another fourth grade and the choir and a group that was rehearsing, starting in October, for a Christmas play that, somehow, never was produced. In the spring I was shifted to another fourth grade that had had a string of substitutes all year. The 35 children in the class hadn't had a permanent teacher since they entered kindergarten. That year, I was their thirteenth teacher.

The results were seen in the first tests I gave. In April, most were reading at the second grade level. Their math ability was at the first grade level.

In an effort to resuscitate their interest, I began to read them poetry I liked. They were drawn especially to poems of Robert Frost and Langston Hughes. One of the most embittered children in the class began to cry when she first heard the words of Langston Hughes.

> *What happens to a dream deferred?*
> *Does it dry up*
> *like a raisin in the sun?*

She went home and memorized the lines.

The next day, I was fired. There was, it turned out, a list of "fourth grade poems" that teachers were obliged to follow but which, like most first-year teachers, I had never seen. According to school officials, Robert Frost and Langston Hughes were "too advanced" for children of this age. Hughes, moreover, was regarded as "inflammatory."

I was soon recruited to teach in a suburban system west of Boston. The shock of going from one of the poorest schools to one of the wealthiest cannot be overstated. I now had 21 children in a cheerful building with a principal who welcomed innovation.

After teaching for several years, I became involved with other interests —the health and education of farmworkers in New Mexico and Arizona, the problems of adult illiterates in several states, the lives of homeless families in

New York. It wasn't until 1988, when I returned to Massachusetts after a long stay in New York City, that I realized how far I'd been drawn away from my original concerns. I found that I missed being with schoolchildren, and I felt a longing to spend time in public schools again. So, in the fall of 1988, I set off on another journey.

During the next two years I visited schools and spoke with children in approximately 30 neighborhoods from Illinois to Washington, D.C., and from New York to San Antonio. Wherever possible, I also met with children in their homes. There was no special logic in the choice of cities that I visited. I went where I was welcomed or knew teachers or school principals or ministers of churches.

What startled me most—although it puzzles me that I was not prepared for this—was the remarkable degree of racial segregation that persisted almost everywhere. Like most Americans, I knew that segregation was still common in the public schools, but I did not know how much it had intensified. The Supreme Court decision in *Brown v. Board of Education* 37 years ago, in which the court had found that segregated education was unconstitutional because it was "inherently unequal," did not seem to have changed very much for children in the schools I saw, not, at least, outside of the Deep South. Most of the urban schools I visited were 95 to 99 percent nonwhite. In no school that I saw anywhere in the United States were nonwhite children in large numbers truly intermingled with white children.

Moreover, in most cities, influential people that I met showed little inclination to address this matter and were sometimes even puzzled when I brought it up. Many people seemed to view the segregation issue as "a past injustice" that had been sufficiently addressed. Others took it as an unresolved injustice that no longer held sufficient national attention to be worth contesting. In all cases, I was given the distinct impression that my inquiries about this matter were not welcome.

None of the national reports I saw made even passing references to inequality or segregation. Low reading scores, high dropout rates, poor motivation—symptomatic matters—seemed to dominate discussion. In three cities —Baltimore, Milwaukee and Detroit—separate schools or separate classes for black males had been proposed. Other cities—Washington, D.C., New York and Philadelphia among them—were considering the same approach. Black parents or black school officials sometimes seemed to favor this idea. Booker T. Washington was cited with increasing frequency, [W. E. B.] Du Bois never, and Martin Luther King only with cautious selectivity. He was treated as an icon, but his vision of a nation in which black and white kids went to school together seemed to be effaced almost entirely. Dutiful references to "The Dream" were often seen in school brochures and on wall posters during February, when "Black History" was celebrated in the public schools, but the content of the dream was treated as a closed box that could not be opened without ruining the celebration.

For anyone who came of age during the years from 1954 to 1968, these revelations could not fail to be disheartening. What seems unmistakable, but, oddly enough, is rarely said in public settings nowadays, is that the nation, for all practice and intent, has turned its back upon the moral implications, if not yet the legal ramifications, of the *Brown* decision. The struggle being waged to-day, where there is any struggle being waged at all, is closer to the one that was addressed in 1896 in *Plessy v. Ferguson,* in which the court accepted segregated institutions for black people, stipulating only that they must be equal to those open to white people. The dual society, at least in public education, seems in general to be unquestioned.

To the extent that school reforms such as "restructuring" are advocated for the inner cities, few of these reforms have reached the schools that I have seen. In each of the larger cities there is usually one school or one subdistrict which is highly publicized as an example of "restructured" education; but the changes rarely reach beyond this one example. Even in those schools where some "restructuring" has taken place, the fact of racial segregation has been, and continues to be, largely uncontested. In many cities, what is termed "re-structuring" struck me as very little more than moving around the same old furniture within the house of poverty. The perceived objective was a more "effi-cient" ghetto school or one with greater "input" from the ghetto parents or more "choices" for the ghetto children. The fact of ghetto education as a permanent American reality appeared to be accepted.

Liberal critics of the Reagan era sometimes note that social policy in the United States, to the extent that it concerns black children and poor children, has been turned back several decades. But this assertion, which is accurate as a description of some setbacks in the areas of housing, health and welfare, is not adequate to speak about the present-day reality in public education. In public schooling, social policy has been turned back almost one hundred years.

These, then, are a few of the impressions that remained with me after re-visiting the public schools from which I had been absent for a quarter-century. My deepest impression, however, was less theoretical and more immediate. It was simply the impression that these urban schools were, by and large, extraor-dinarily unhappy places. With few exceptions, they reminded me of "garrisons" or "outposts" in a foreign nation. Housing projects, bleak and tall, surrounded by perimeter walls lined with barbed wire, often stood adjacent to the schools I visited. The schools were surrounded frequently by signs that indicated DRUG-FREE ZONE. Their doors were guarded. Police sometimes patrolled the halls. The windows of the schools were often covered with steel grates. Taxi drivers flatly refused to take me to some of these schools and would deposit me a dozen blocks away, in border areas beyond which they refused to go. I'd walk the last half-mile on my own. Once, in the Bronx, a woman stopped her car, told me I should not be walking there, insisted I get in, and drove me to the school. I was dismayed to walk or ride for blocks and blocks through neighborhoods where every face was black, where there were simply *no white people anywhere.*

In Boston, the press referred to areas like these as "death zones"—a spe-cific reference to the rate of infant death in ghetto neighborhoods—but the feeling of the "death zone" often seemed to permeate the schools themselves. Looking around some of these inner-city schools, where filth and disrepair were worse than anything I'd seen in 1964, I often wondered why we would agree to let our children go to school in places where no politician, school board pres-ident, or business CEO would dream of working. Children seemed to wrestle with these kinds of questions too. Some of their observations were, indeed, so trenchant that a teacher sometimes would step back and raise her eyebrows and then nod to me across the children's heads, as if to say, "Well, there it is! They know what's going on around them, don't they?"

It occurred to me that we had not been listening much to children in these recent years of "summit conferences" on education, of severe reports and ominous prescriptions. The voices of children, frankly, had been missing from the whole discussion.

This seems especially unfortunate because the children often are more interesting and perceptive than the grown-ups are about the day-to-day realities of life in school. For this reason, I decided, early in my journey, to attempt to listen very carefully to children and, whenever possible, to let their voices and their judgments and their longings find a place within [my] book—and maybe, too, within the nation's dialogue about their destinies. I hope that, in this effort, I have done them justice.

East St. Louis—which the local press refers to as "an inner city without an outer city"—has some of the sickest children in America. Of 66 cities in Illinois, East St. Louis ranks first in fetal death, first in premature birth, and third in infant death. Among the negative factors listed by the city's health director are the sewage running in the streets, air that has been fouled by the local plants, the high lead levels noted in the soil, poverty, lack of education, crime, dilapidated housing, insufficient health care, unemployment. Hospital care is deficient too. There is no place to have a baby in East St. Louis. The maternity ward at the city's Catholic hospital, a 100-year-old structure, was shut down some years ago. The only other hospital in town was forced by lack of funds to close in 1990. The closest obstetrics service open to the women here is seven miles away. The infant death rate is still rising.

As in New York City's poorest neighborhoods, dental problems also plague the children here. Although dental problems don't command the instant fears associated with low birth weight, fetal death or cholera, they do have the consequence of wearing down the stamina of children and defeating their ambitions. Bleeding gums, impacted teeth and rotting teeth are routine matters for the children I have interviewed in the South Bronx. Children get used to feeling constant pain. They go to sleep with it. They go to school with it. Sometimes their teachers are alarmed and try to get them to a clinic. But it's all so slow and heavily encumbered with red tape and waiting lists and missing, lost or canceled welfare cards, that dental care is often long delayed. Children live for months with pain that grown-ups would find unendurable. The gradual attrition of accepted pain erodes their energy and aspiration. I have seen children in New York with teeth that look like brownish, broken sticks. I have also seen teen-agers who were missing half their teeth. But, to me, most shocking is to see a child with an abscess that has been inflamed for weeks and that he has simply lived with and accepts as part of the routine of life. Many teachers in the urban schools have seen this. It is almost commonplace.

Compounding these problems is the poor nutrition of the children here —average daily food expenditure in East St. Louis is $2.40 for one child—and the underimmunization of young children. Of every 100 children recently surveyed in East St. Louis, 55 were incompletely immunized for polio, diphtheria, measles and whooping cough. In this context, health officials look with all the more uneasiness at those lagoons of sewage outside public housing. . . .

A 16-year-old student in the South Bronx tells me that he went to English class for two months in the fall of 1989 before the school supplied him with a textbook. He spent the entire year without a science text. "My mother offered to help me with my science, which was hard for me," he says, "but I could not bring home a book."

In May of 1990 he is facing final exams, but, because the school requires students to pass in their textbooks one week prior to the end of the semester, he is forced to study without math and English texts.

He wants to go to college and he knows that math and English are important, but he's feeling overwhelmed, especially in math. He asked his teacher if he could come in for extra help, but she informed him that she didn't have the time. He asked if he could come to school an hour early, when she might have time to help him, but security precautions at the school made this impossible.

Sitting in his kitchen, I attempt to help him with his math and English. In math, according to a practice test he has been given, he is asked to solve the following equation: "$2x - 2 = 14$. What is x?" He finds this baffling. In English, he is told he'll have to know the parts of speech. In the sentence "Jack walks to the store," he is unable to identify the verb.

He is in a dark mood, worried about this and other problems. His mother has recently been diagnosed as having cancer. We leave the apartment and walk downstairs to the street. He's a full-grown young man, tall and quiet and strong-looking; but out on the street, when it is time to say good-bye, his eyes fill up with tears.

In the fall of the year, he phones me at my home. "There are 42 students in my science class, 40 in my English class—45 in my home room. When all the kids show up, five of us have to stand in back."

A first-year English teacher at another high school in the Bronx calls me two nights later: "I've got five classes—42 in each! We have no textbooks yet. I'm using my old textbook from the seventh grade. They're doing construction all around me so the noise is quite amazing. They're actually *drilling* in the hall outside my room. I have more kids than desks in all five classes.

"A student came in today whom I had never seen. I said, 'We'll have to wait and see if someone doesn't come so you can have a chair.' She looked at me and said, 'I'm leaving.'"

The other teachers tell her that the problem will resolve itself. "Half the students will be gone by Christmastime, they say. It's awful when you realize that the school is *counting* on the failure of one half my class. If they didn't count on it, perhaps it wouldn't happen. If I *began* with 20 students in a class, I'd have lots more time to spend with each of them. I'd have a chance to track them down, go to their homes, see them on the weekends. . . . I don't understand why people in New York permit this."

One of the students in her class, she says, wrote this two-line poem for Martin Luther King:

He tried to help the white and black.
Now that he's dead he can't do jack.

Another student wrote these lines:

America the beautiful,
Who are you beautiful for?

"Frequently," says a teacher at another crowded high school in New York, "a student may be in the wrong class for a term and never know it." With only one counselor to 700 students system-wide in New York City, there is little help available to those who feel confused. It is not surprising, says the teacher, "that many find the experience so cold, impersonal and disheartening that they decide to stay home by the sad warmth of the TV set."

... Surely there is enough for everyone within this country. It is a tragedy that ... good things are not more widely shared. All our children ought to be allowed a stake in the enormous richness of America. Whether they were born to poor white Appalachians or to wealthy Texans, to poor black people in the Bronx or to rich people in Manhasset or Winnetka, they are all quite wonderful and innocent when they are small. We soil them needlessly.

5.2 PENELOPE ECKERT

Jocks and Burnouts

Penelope Eckert is a professor of linguistics at Stanford University and a senior research scientist at the Institute for Research on Learning. In her work, Eckert focuses on the relation between social identity and linguistic variation. Through her extensive ethnographic work with adolescents, she has detailed how language conveys local social meaning. She has discovered that there are local dynamics within linguistic patterns, and that these dynamics relate to such social constructs as class, gender, age, race, ethnicity, social networks, social categories, and communities of linguistic practice.

In her ethnographic study *Jocks and Burnouts: Social Categories and Identity in the High School* (Teachers College Press, 1989), Eckert provides insights into the lives, thoughts, and words of students as the students define and label each other as "jocks" and "burnouts." In addition to quoting the students, she helps to construct the socioeconomic patterns of the community and school as well. In the following selection from *Jocks and Burnouts*, Eckert describes how many aspects of school and community life help to reinforce the labels given to each other by students. Economic status can be laid directly over the jock-burnout distinction, with jocks generally coming from middle-class families and burnouts coming from the working classes. Eckert provides an analysis of not only how the housing patterns within the community differentiate jocks and burnouts but also the way in which the different students make use of the physical aspects of the neighborhoods. Even the different parts of the school serve various functions for the students of different labels. This ethnographic study has much to say to educators today about students' perceptions of the "haves" and "have-nots" amidst a growing split and increasing violence among students.

Key Concept: conditions related to student-created labels for each other

INTRODUCTION

So what is a jock then?

Someone who gets into school, who does her homework, who, uh, goes to all the activities, who's in Concert Choir, who has her whole day surrounded by school. You know, "tonight I'm gonna go to concert choir practice and today maybe I'll go watch track, and then early this morning maybe, oh, I'll go help a teacher or something." You know....

69

Although Jocks and Burnouts take their names from athletics and drugs, respectively, these are neither necessary nor sufficient criteria for category membership. The term *Jock* originated in sports, which are so central to the high school culture. Indeed, varsity athletes are seen as serving the interests of the school and the community, representing the school in the most visible arena, and symbolizing all that is thought to be healthy and vigorous in American culture.... Most important school activities center around sports events, and in common usage the term *Jock* has extended beyond athletes to all students who make those activities run. Although Jock is a common term for "athlete" in our culture, it is generally applied to people for whom athletics is a way of life. A Jock may be simply a person who engages regularly in some sport, but in general usage the term is used for someone whose life-style embraces a broader ideal associated in American culture with sports. The ideal Jock is good at more than one sport, trains regularly, follows the "clean" life-style considered necessary for maintaining physical fitness, and generally embraces American ideals of athletic fair play and competition. In the high school, this ideal of the squeaky-clean, all-American individual is given an even broader interpretation. The high school Jock embodies an attitude—an acceptance of the school and its institutions as an all-encompassing social context, and an unflagging enthusiasm and energy for working within those institutions. An individual who never plays sports, but who participates enthusiastically in activities associated with student government, unquestioningly may be referred to by all in the school as a Jock.

Another name in Belten High for Burnouts is "Jells," shortened from "Jello Brains" and alluding to the degenerative effects of drugs. But just as there are Jocks who are not athletes, there are Burnouts who do not do drugs. Drugs are this generation's most frightening form of rebellion, and as such they are taken as a symbol by and for the school's alienated category. One might more properly consider that these alienated adolescents are "burned out" from long years of frustration encountered in an institution that rejects and stigmatizes them as it fails to recognize and meet their needs. The complexity of the connotations of the category names is reflected in their use. Although the terms *Jock* and *Burnout* are used in certain unambiguous contexts to refer to an athlete or a "druggie," they frequently must be disambiguated through compounding. Thus, such terms as "Jock-Jock," "Sports-Jock," and "Burned-out Burnout" are commonly used to refer to an athlete or a habitual drug user.

The names, and even the stereotypes, of the Jock and Burnout categories belie a broader distinction and a profound cultural split, which reflects in turn the split between the adult middle and working classes. This does not mean that category membership is strictly determined by class, or that all differences between the categories arise directly from class differences. However, the considerable extent to which class is salient to these categories conspires to elevate the category stereotypes to class stereotypes, to produce a polarization of attitudes toward class characteristics associated with either category within the value-laden atmosphere of the school, and hence to force a corresponding polarization of behavioral choice. In this way, the Jock and Burnout categories come to mediate adult social class within the adolescent context....

> I guess the thing about the different schools that—only thing different I guess is that Casper thinks of Belten as a punk rock school, and Simmons I guess they have —they're all Beatlemaniacs over there. Belten thinks that Casper people are stuck up . . . stuff like that. Other than that, the people are the same, really, the ones that I know.

Opened in the 1950s, Belten is the oldest of several high schools in Neartown, a suburb of Detroit. Belten's approximately 2000 students come from families ranging from solid working class through upper middle class. Part of Detroit's urban sprawl, Neartown is one section of a vast geographic and socioeconomic continuum. In the Detroit suburban area, geography and class are clearly tied along the north–south and east–west axes. With the notable exception of some wealthy waterfront areas east of the city, socioeconomic status rises as one moves north and west from the primarily black and poor inner city. Neartown's northwest corner, the farthest from Detroit, is the most rural, most recently developed, and wealthiest. This pattern is repeated by and large within the sections of the town served by its several high schools.

The students of Belten High generally point to the less affluent eastern end of Neartown as "Burnout" neighborhoods, particularly those at the more densely populated southeast end. In fact, these neighborhoods yield Jocks, Burnouts, and In-betweens, but there are certain factors that make them "Burnout" neighborhoods. First, there is somewhat of a concentration of Burnouts living in the southeast corner of town. In addition, the main local Burnout hangouts are in the eastern neighborhoods, particularly in the southeast: the parks and school yards where many Burnouts organize pickup games or hang out in good weather. The socioeconomic makeup of each category is not homogeneous, but the socioeconomic balance of the categories reflects clear differentiation. Table 1 shows the percentages of members of the central Jock and Burnout clusters, as well as of a range of In-between clusters, from three socioeconomic strata. These percentages are based on students' reports, in the 118 tape-recorded interviews of Belten students, of their parents' education and occupation. It should be noted that the percentages did not change significantly when the determination of class was based on information about a working mother, a working father, or both. The percentages show a clear difference in the overall socioeconomic makeup of the polarized categories and suggest an intermediate status for the In-Betweens.

The Jock and Burnout categories are more than a simple reflection of parents' socioeconomic identity; they are pivotal in the transition from childhood to adult status, and both upward and downward mobility are achieved through the mediation of these categories. Of course there will be changes once a cohort has graduated from high school, but the current aspirations of the members of each category are more closely related to class than to actual origins. While almost all of the Jocks intend to go on to college, only 10 percent of the Burnouts expressed interest in college, and a number of them were not enrolled in college preparatory curricula. As Table 2 shows, the balance of choice of curriculum reflects these differences in aspiration. This table is based on school records of

TABLE 1

Socioeconomic Class Makeup (in Percentages) of Each Social Category

	JOCKS	IN-BETWEENS	BURNOUTS
Working class	16	16	50
Lower middle class	34	42	22
Upper middle class	50	42	23

second semester junior year enrollments for 102 students clearly belonging to Jock and Burnout network clusters.

The Local Environment

Neartown itself is a continuum: There is no town center, only interspersed industrial, commercial, and residential areas, with scattered shopping centers. Hangouts are fast-food restaurants and shopping centers, parks, and roller-skating rinks. Some of the most salient differences between social categories in Belten are closely involved with differences in geographic orientation and in the exploitation of local resources. The adolescent population must carve a relatively uninteresting geographic continuum into a world with significant areas, and they do this as part of the expression of their social identities.

... [O]ne of the important differences between Jocks and Burnouts is geographic orientation. Both categories use restaurants and particularly fast-food restaurants. But while the Burnouts make regular use of other local public space—parks, streets, skating rinks, pool halls—the Jocks confine their activities largely to movie theatres, homes, and the school. To a great extent, the Jocks' small use of local geography is a function of their intense involvement in school, which serves as the center of most of their leisure activities. Mobility beyond Neartown is equally telling. Most middle class Neartowners have turned their backs on Detroit and discourage their children from visiting or taking an interest in the city. The parental upward mobility that brought people from Detroit to Neartown dictates the abandonment of urban orientation and ties. To a great extent, Jocks visit other towns only in connection with sports events and to go to shopping malls and restaurants. The latter two take them not east to Detroit, but generally to more affluent suburban areas. Most Jocks rarely go to Detroit; of those who do, most limit their use of their city to public facilities, particularly sports arenas. A few go to museums and concerts, Greektown, and the Renaissance Center. Burnouts, on the other hand, cautiously extend their activities beyond Neartown toward Detroit. As they get older and more mobile, Burnouts expand their use of public space into the suburbs closer to Detroit, and into Detroit itself, gravitating to areas that provide contact with people from other towns.

This difference in geographic orientation stems from a variety of factors. Perhaps the clearest of these is the large number of Burnouts that have moved recently to the suburbs from Detroit. Some of them still have friends in Detroit

TABLE 2

Course Enrollments (in Percentages) Within Each Social Category

Penelope Eckert

| | ACADEMIC COURSES | | | | VOCATIONAL COURSES | | | |
	AP	A-B	C	R	M-A	VOC	BUS	F-L
Male Jocks	5	71	12	0	4	5	3	0
Male Burnouts	0	36	14	9	6	33	3	0
Female Jocks	11	70	7	0	7	0	2	4
Female Burnouts	0	19	28	7	11	9	5	21

AP   Advanced placement courses
A-B-C   Letters refer, in descending order, to the level of difficulty as listed in the school catalog
R   Remedial
M-A   Music and art
BUS   Business courses
F-L   Family life (traditional home economics courses and courses in child care)
VOC   Other vocational courses

and still visit their old neighborhoods. The urban migration that creates suburban populations plays a clear role in the Jock–Burnout split, even in schools such as Belten, much of whose population moved there at one time or another from Detroit or its closer suburbs. More than half of Belten's students were born outside of Neartown, most of them in Detroit. Based on the reports of 94 students, 40 percent began school before coming to Neartown, and about 24 percent moved to Neartown after the fifth grade. These numbers are not evenly distributed between the social categories: 17 percent of the Jocks, 23 percent of the In-Betweens, and 36 percent of the Burnouts moved after fifth grade.

A further aspect of the differential geographic orientation of Jocks and Burnouts is adaptive. While most of the Jocks' next life stage will be in an isolated and specialized institution similar to the high school, most Burnouts will leave school and directly begin to compete with adults in the workplace. While the high school negotiates the next life stage for its Jocks, it is of little use to Burnouts in finding a place in the job market. Participation in school activities is an important qualification for college admission, but it does little to enhance an individual's qualification for a blue-collar job, and while the school plays an active role in advising about college admission, it does little toward placing students in blue-collar jobs. In finding employment, most Burnouts expect to rely on contacts outside of school, particularly on relatives and friends already in the work force. Therefore, it is not in a Burnout's interests to pursue social activities in school; it is in his or her interests to pursue activities and contacts that provide access to the local work force. This work force is centered not in the affluent suburbs, but in the urban center and the closer, more urban suburbs. A work force orientation, therefore, is in many ways an urban orientation.

Finally, the Burnouts look at Detroit as a source of personal autonomy. While the Jocks seek autonomy in the occupation of institutional roles, the Burnouts seek it in the personal freedoms associated with adult status and in an independent relation with the larger environment. To some extent this can be linked to the difference in the salience of the adolescent life stage between those who will remain in educational institutions and those who are emerging into the work force. With adult responsibilities looming in the near future, the Burnouts can see no reason to postpone the pleasures of adult status. Adult status represents both personal freedom and interaction in the "real world," both of which are highly circumscribed in the school. Finally, there is the simple love of freedom, excitement, and, for some, danger. These various factors weigh differently for different Burnouts, but ultimately they all conspire to lead Burnouts into the urban area.

The sociogeographic continuum of the metropolitan area provides adolescents with a clear perspective on their place in the world. Beltsen High School lies squarely in the average socioeconomic range in American society. When individuals compare themselves with those surrounding communities, they develop more of a perspective on their "real-world" social status. Burnouts can look to the relative poverty of friends in Detroit, with their greater problems and lower aspirations; Jocks can look to those in more westerly and northerly suburbs who do not have jobs, who drive fancy cars and wear designer clothes, and who may even plan to go to out of state to college. The local environment polarizes Jocks and Burnouts, but at the same time it protects them from the threat of comparison with those in surrounding communities who represent greater socioeconomic and behavioral extremes. Within the limitations of the local context, Jocks can avoid feeling poor and unsophisticated in comparison with their more affluent neighbors in suburbs to the north and west, and Burnouts can feel independent and rebellious without facing the dangers and insecurities of those living closer to Detroit. During high school, the confrontation with the world outside the community is still mitigated by the familiar and relatively safe context of the school. For this reason, many of those who hate school most are nonetheless loyal to their school. In part, this is a loyalty to what the students see as the school's socioeconomic mean, as reflected in one student's discussion of Neartown's wealthier school:

> They're a lot richer and they're really stuck up and they are better at a lot of things, but I'd rather be worse and proud of Belten than go to Simpson.

Each school seems to pride itself on its socioeconomic characteristics—Belten staff and students alike quote the broad socioeconomic range of its student body as its main advantage and as accounting for what they consider to be the school's very special character....

Daily Routines

Use of the building is closely tied to the daily schedule. The class schedule outlines a routine for each student, organizing encounters with other students as well as movements into and though various parts of the building. The school day is divided into three 54-minute class periods in the morning, a noon period of approximately $1\frac{1}{2}$ hours, and two 54-minute class periods in the afternoon.

Six minutes are allowed between class periods for changing rooms. The fourth (lunch) period is divided into three half-hour segments, two of which are spent in class and one at lunch. Fourth-hour classes are staggered so that some meet during the first two segments, some during the last two, and some during the first and third, with the lunch segment in the middle. Following disturbances in the school parking lot in the late 1970s, the administration imposed a "closed campus" policy, forcing students to remain in the school building during school hours except for authorized travel to curricular programs in other schools. Although students may not leave the building during the lunch hour, they are free to gather in the south wing and the courtyard, and with permission they may go to the library. The intersections between the south wing and the north–south halls are monitored during this time, as are the north, south, and middle (leading to the library) exits from the back hall.

Students work their social routines around their class schedules. They also work their class schedules around their social lives, by trying to get into classes with their friends. Thus classes are not simply part of the educational routine, but strategic points in the students' daily social encounters. Changing classes is punctuated with routine social encounters at designated places—in the hall, in the courtyard, at the lockers. Students know whom they can expect to pass in the hall on the way from one class to the next and can adjust their route or speed to guarantee meeting those they particularly wish to see. Depending on the period, individuals may rush to a designated spot for a quick encounter with a group, a friends, or a boyfriend/girlfriend; or they may do their route slowly, greeting a variety of people on the way. One particular class change might be the highpoint of a student's day. By and large, groups meet at set times and places before and after school, and virtually all students have a lunchtime routine, going to the same place with the same people, sometimes migrating at an appointed time to another place to wait for the bell to ring at the end of the period.

To a great extent, the individual's enjoyment of school routine is a function of the size of his or her social network. Those who have only a small group of friends are limited in their encounters to times of mutual availability. Some students have no group of school friends and must move through their day in isolation. Changing classes is not much of a problem for people with limited networks, since they can move with purpose through a crowd, but lunchtime can be a difficult and painful time. The smaller one's social network, the smaller are one's chances of having the same lunch period as one's friends, and the individual who eats alone or walks in the halls alone during this period of heightened visibility is stigmatized. Those who find themselves alone manage as best they can by making themselves inconspicuous, drifting as an unwelcome guest among established groups, or simply hiding. They do not, however, escape notice:

> We'd make fun of people that walked too close to the wall. We'd always call them "wall huggers." Because they didn't, they wouldn't walk down the middle of the hall. If they were walking by themselves, they walked by the wall, like it was their friend… It just seems like anybody who's alone usually stands right next to the wall. Just a little thing we noticed.

Loners can protect themselves by adopting a philosophical attitude, as the following girl who recognizes that people notice her solitude:

> They always have to be with someone because they're worried about what other people would think if they were walking down the hall alone, which is no big deal. It doesn't hurt.

But it does hurt, as one girl who finds lunch company by imposing on relatively inhospitable groups poignantly described:

> I just have friends that I say "hello" to and are acquaintances, but I don't have any best friends.... I just see them a lot in school, because like they're, they got their own very good friends. I'm just, you know, like to the people I know, I'm just a friend. I'm not a person you'd call up and invite to parties and get stoned with, you know. I wish I was, though. I mean I feel, at weekends I feel so left out, I sit there and, you know, "Ma, I'm so depressed, I want friends," you know. But, you know, there are some times, some times I think, uh, I'm better off not having too many friends because one can get just bogged down with all their "Oh, can you come over to my house today"; "No, I'm coming over her house, sorry." You know, I don't know. They just don't like me for what I am.

Lunch for the first day of the semester is stressful for most high school students, as they worry about whom they're going to eat with. The degree of stress varies inversely with the extensiveness of one's social networks. "Who has the same lunch" is a major preoccupation that can serve as a factor in choosing classes.

> See, this semester I was really bummed out. I wanted to get a change to fourth hour, because there's nobody in my lunch hour that I really know. But I sit, like, at a table with a bunch of girls that I know, but I don't really know. Um, Joan Smith, Judy—I don't know her last name, shows how well I know her. Those are really the only two that I even know that sit there. The rest of them just . . .

How did you start eating with them?

> Well, I don't know. Um, I went in the first day, and I was going to sit with Daphne Brown. But she was hanging around all the people that are on the swimming team. And like, I don't know them, you know.

The contrast between being a longer and being a member of the vast networks that constitute the Jock and Burnout categories can be the difference between social night and day. By virtue of their extensive networks, the Jocks and the Burnouts suffer the least at lunchtime. Intensive consultation lets Jocks know whom they will be eating with before they arrive in the cafeteria. There is always at least one girl Jock and one boy Jock table in each lunch hour, and Jocks find both security and visibility in their ability to sit at that table.

Well see, well you find out, you know, before you go in there. And it's like, Joe Sloan, he played basketball with us, Alan Marsten did, and Peter Brown. And like I know Dan Jones, and Mark Johnson, I knew them already. So you know, Joe and Alan and those guys that play basketball, I knew what they had, you know, what lunch. So I was, I went in there looking for them.... Everyone asks what lunch you eat to find out who they can sit with.

The Burnouts do not even have to find out ahead of time who has the same lunch, since they know that their friends will be in the courtyard.

This [selection] deals more with Jocks and Burnouts than with the people who make up the majority of the student population—the many In-betweens who find their way between and around the categories. It also does not deal with the people who never find their niche in the high school—people who don't fit in and who feel lucky if they can remain sufficiently invisible to escape community ridicule. [There are] social dynamics that make extreme isolation possible. If a Jock is the opposite of a Burnout, a nerd is the opposite of both. While the Jocks and the Burnouts are no more interesting than the rest of the student body, the concentration of social energy in the maintenance of their oppositional identities not only limits their own freedom but that of everyone else in the school.

PART TWO

Key Concepts in Multicultural Education

On the Internet . . .

Sites appropriate to Part Two

The Anti-Defamation League (ADL) was organized for the purpose of helping to secure justice and fair treatment for all people. It gathers information and develops materials that help people learn how to fight prejudice and racism.

```
http://www.adl.org
```

The Southern Poverty Law Center is a nonprofit organization that combats hate, intolerance, and discrimination through education and litigation. The organization provides a number of resources for educators to help teach about these issues.

```
http://www.splcenter.org
```

CHAPTER 6 Culture

6.1 EDWARD T. HALL

What Is Culture?

In his book *The Silent Language* (Doubleday, 1981), from which the follow-ing selection has been taken, anthropologist Edward T. Hall proposes that culture is a form of communication. Culture is the way that adults commu-nicate to their children the important parts of their society. Culture is what we often subconsciously communicate to each other by our actions. In the following selection, Hall emphasizes that the study of culture is the study of our own lives, of our own ways of thinking and living. Because the study of culture is the study of ourselves, he explains, it is difficult to comprehend. It is easier to think of culture as a description of someone else's culture, to see culture as exotic customs. But, says Hall, it is crucial to study our own cul-ture in order to understand ourselves and our society. This study of culture has the purpose of making us self-conscious, of making known to ourselves what it is that makes up everyday life.

Throughout his writings, Hall has focused on the different styles of cultural groups. He has written about proxemics—the study of the space that people surround themselves with and their communication and interaction patterns. In addition to *The Silent Language,* his leading books include *The Hidden Dimension* (Doubleday, 1966) and *Beyond Culture* (Anchor Press, 1976).

Key Concept: the study of one's own culture

Culture is a word that has so many meanings already that one more can do it no harm.... For anthropologists culture has long stood for the way of life of a people, for the sum of their learned behavior patterns, attitudes, and ma-terial things. Though they subscribe to this general view, most anthropologists tend to disagree however, on what the precise substance of culture is. In practice their work often leads some of them to a fascination with a single category of events among the many which make up human life, and they tend to think of this as the essence of all culture. Others, looking for a point of stability in the flux of society, often become preoccupied with identifying a common particle or element which can be found in every aspect of culture. In sum, though the concept of culture was first defined in print in 1871 by E. B. Tylor, after all these years it still lacks the rigorous specificity which characterizes many less revolutionary and useful ideas.

Even more unfortunate is the slowness with which the concept of culture has percolated through the public consciousness. Compared to such notions as the unconscious or repression, to use two examples from psychology, the idea of culture is a strange one even to the informed citizen. The reasons for this are well worth noting, for they suggest some of the difficulties which are inherent in the culture concept itself.

... Culture is not an exotic notion studied by a select group of anthropologists in the South Seas. It is a mold in which we are all cast, and it controls our daily lives in many unsuspected ways. In my discussion of culture I will be describing the part of human behavior which we take for granted—the part we don't think about, since we assume it is universal or regard it as idiosyncratic.

Culture hides much more than it reveals, and strangely enough what it hides, it hides most effectively from its own participants. Years of study have convinced me that the real job is not to understand foreign culture but to understand our own. I am also convinced that all that one ever gets from studying foreign culture is a token understanding. The ultimate reason for such study is to learn more about how one's own system works. The best reason for exposing oneself to foreign ways is to generate a sense of vitality and awareness—an interest in life which can come only when one lives through the shock of contrast and difference.

Simply learning one's own culture is an achievement of gargantuan proportions for anyone. By the age of twenty-five or thirty most of us have finished school, been married, learned to live with another human being, mastered a job, seen the miracle of human birth, and started a new human being well on his way to growing up. Suddenly most of what we have to learn is finished. Life begins to settle down.

Yet our tremendous brain has endowed us with a drive and a capacity for learning which appear to be as strong as the drive for food or sex. This means that when a middle-aged man or woman stops learning he or she is often left with a great drive and highly developed capacities. If this individual goes to live in another culture, the learning process is often reactivated. For most Americans tied down at home this is not possible. To forestall atrophy of their intellectual powers people can begin learning about those areas of their own culture which have been out of awareness. They can explore the new frontier.

The problem which is raised in talking about American culture without reference to other cultures is that an audience tends to take the remarks personally. I once addressed a group of school principals on the subject of culture. We were discussing the need for Americans to progress in their jobs, to get ahead, and to receive some recognition so that they would know in a tangible way that they were actually getting someplace. One of the audience said to me, "Now you are talking about something interesting, you're talking about me." When the man in the audience learned something about himself, the study of culture got lost in the shuffle. He did not seem to realize that a significant proportion of the material which was highly personal to him was also relevant cultural data.

A knowledge of his own culture would have helped this same man in a situation which he subsequently described for the audience. In the middle of a busy day, it seems, his son had kept him waiting for an hour. As a result he was aware that his blood pressure had risen rather dangerously. If both the father and the son had had a cultural perspective on this common and infuriating oc- currence the awkward quarrel which followed might have been avoided. Both father and son would have benefited if the father had understood the cultural basis of his tension and explained, "Now, look here. If you want to keep me waiting, O.K., but you should know it is a real slap in the face to anyone to be kept waiting so long. If that's what you want to communicate, go ahead, but be sure you know that you are communicating an insult and don't act like a startled fawn if people react accordingly."

The best reason for the layperson to spend time studying culture is that he/she can learn something useful and enlightening about himself/herself. This can be an interesting process, at times harrowing but ultimately reward- ing. One of the most effective ways to learn about oneself is by taking seriously the cultures of others. It forces you to pay attention to those details of life which differentiate them from you.

For those who are familiar with the subject the remarks I have just made should be a clear indication that [these ideas are] not simply a rehash of what previous writers on the subject of culture have said. The approach is new. It involves new ways of looking at things. Indians and natives of the South Pa- cific, the hallmarks of most anthropological texts, are used. However, they are introduced solely to clarify points about our own way of life, to make what we take for granted stand out in perspective.... The complete theory of culture as communication is new and has not been presented in one place before.

... The language of culture speaks as clearly as the language of dreams Freud analyzed, but, unlike dreams, it cannot be kept to oneself. When I talk about culture I am not just talking about something in the abstract that is im- posed on mankind and is separate from individuals, but about humans them- selves, about you and me in a highly personal way.

The Dynamics of Cultural Transmission

As Henry T. Trueba describes culture, it is the values and assumptions that guide everyday life. In his article "The Dynamics of Cultural Transmission," in Henry T. Trueba et al., *Healing Multicultural America: Mexican Immigrants Rise to Power in Rural California* (Falmer Press, 1993), a key point is that while we used to think that culture is always shared sets of behaviors, values, and norms, today we realize that culture is always reshaped dynamically by people. While all societies have methods for transmitting their culture, in America it is constantly changing due to an influx of immigrants. So culture needs to be seen as dynamic. Cultural transmission is often done in schools, communities, and families, and it has often been thought of as one-sided. But in reality, says Trueba, culture is constantly reinterpreted, recreated, and reshaped as it is passed on in schools and families.

Trueba was born in Mexico City and lived in Mexico until 1962. He earned his M.A. and his Ph.D. in theology and anthropology. He is the author and editor of many books, and he has served as editor of *Anthropology and Education Quarterly*. Trueba was dean of education at the University of California, Davis, and director of the university's Linguistic Minority Research Project. His work has focused on the social and cultural context of education and the role of culture and language in learning. *Healing Multicultural America,* from which the following selection has been taken, is a historical and anthropological study of the efforts of a Mexican American community to maintain the home language and culture as well as acquire a second language and culture and of the feelings of alienation and discrimination.

Key Concept: culture as constantly reshaped

Cultural values, as transmitted from one generation to another, provide the energy and commitment necessary to act. Whatever we do collectively, we do because, in an effort to enhance a cultural value, we agree upon it. Apple (1990) has noted that liberal educational philosophies ignore fundamental structural issues that determine the overall outcome of schooling (failure of minorities, for example), while at the same time enforcing questionable assumptions about the role of education and the attributes of a liberal education. One of these assumptions is that 'education and the culture it both produces and transmits' are independent and autonomous features of society, and consequently that education is primarily intended to produce 'knowledge and knowledgeable individuals through the sponsoring of academic research and curriculum reform' (Apple, 1990:19). In the context of these questionable assumptions Apple observes:

> In contradistinction to this set of assumptions about education and its relation to a social order, the cultural and educational apparatus are interpreted as elements in a theory of *social control* by those individuals who are concerned with cultural and economic reproduction. Hence, challenges are made to at least three interrelated notions: that the selection processes are neutral; that 'ability' (rather than the socialization of students to socially and economically related norms and values) is what schools actually *do* focus on; and whether the schools *are* actually organized to teach technical curricular skills and information to all students so that each person has an equal chance at economic rewards (Apple, 1990:19).

Culture, as it is transmitted in schools, with the values and assumptions that guide action in everyday life, is one of the most controversial concepts in America. The reason is not only that the concept itself is elusive and difficult, but that the acceptance of a particular concept of culture has implications for the acceptance of American culture, and our own cultural identity as individuals. For several decades the concepts of culture and cultural transmission have been known, and the essential of culture identified: socially shared norms, codes of behavior, values, assumptions, etiquette, and world view. Culture, according to some anthropologists, 'is made up of the concepts, beliefs, and principles of action and organization' (Goodenough, 1976:5). Understanding one's own culture is hard enough, but other peoples' culture is a real challenge. According to anthropologists the test of such understanding is being able to function effectively in other peoples' cultures. Paradoxically, however, it is only in our attempts to understand the culture of others that we come to understand our own culture. Hence, cross-cultural comparisons have been valued as powerful and insightful methodological instruments in anthropology. Being in another culture and observing unfamiliar behaviors forces us to analyze our own motives and meanings as we act. The problem is not so much 'to state what someone did but to specify the conditions under which it is culturally appropriate to anticipate that he, or persons occupying his role, will render an equivalent performance' (Frake, 1964:112). Knowing another culture is being able to anticipate peoples' observed behaviors; this requires cultural knowledge and an understanding of their cultural values. Yet, the understanding of ongoing cultural changes, processes of adaptation in cultural contact, and adaptive strategies (see Trueba, Cheng and Ima, 1993), requires a better understanding of the process of cultural transmission. Making inferences in order to interpret behavior in another culture is one level of understanding; being able to identify appropriate behavior and to anticipate change requires a deeper knowledge of a culture. Obviously, there are differences among the many cultures of the world; not all are equally complex in terms of their technology, social structure and economy; consequently culture change varies from one culture to another. But some of the cultures, such as the American culture, are particularly complex because they tolerate a great deal of variance and a wide range of adaptive strategies on the part of newcomers.

American society is not easy for newcomers to understand. We have incorporated culturally different populations from all around the world, and people belonging to different social strata. Becoming American can mean many things, and it can occur either in a relatively short time or can take generations. To refugees seeking freedom and economic opportunities, as much as to illegal aliens crossing at great personal risk a busy California highway in their attempts to escape the border patrol, the desire to become American is frequently interpreted as the realization of a 'good education' for their children, and a secure economic future for the entire family. It is an escape from the psychological prison of terrorism and poverty. Unfortunately, the very dreams that bring immigrants and refugees to America are shattered in the first years of their children's experience in schools. Much of the effort to reform schools is focused on the need to meet the learning needs of culturally and linguistically different children. As Apple indicates in his critical analysis of some theories advocated by the pragmatic traditions of American education:

> The pragmatic position tends to ignore the possibility that some theories must contradict the present reality and, in fact, must consistently work against it. These critical inquiries *stand in witness* of the negativity involved in all too many current institutional (economic, cultural, educational, political) arrangements and thus can illuminate the possibility of significant change. In this way, the act of criticism contributes to emancipation in that it shows the way linguistic or social institutions have been reified or thingified so that educators and the public at large have forgotten why they evolved, and that people made them and thus can change them (Apple, 1990:133. Emphasis in original).

At the same time that inquiry and disagreement are defended as requirements of democratic institutions and positive elements to maintain such institutions through needed changes in education, Apple insists that the intent of critiquing scholarship and educational institutions is twofold:

> First, it aims at illuminating the tendencies for unwarranted and often unconscious domination, alienation, and repression within certain existing cultural, political, educational, and economic institutions. Second, through exploring the negative effects and contradictions of much that unquestioningly goes on in these institutions, it seeks to 'promote conscious [individual and collective] emancipatory activity' (Apple, 1990:133).

Immigrants and their children search for the cultural values that permit them to function effectively in American democracy. The pace of cultural adaptation is determined by experiences and perceptions in pre-arrival times of immigrants, refugees and other newcomers. The nature of the cultural shock and conflict resulting from rapid social change is a function of newcomers' ability to understand American cultural values, and to reconcile with their own home values. In turn, immigrants and refugees are pressed to selectively retain those values and patterns they consider essential to their own self-identity and their capacity to cope with cultural conflict in the new country.

Newcomers will ask themselves many times: What is American culture? What is the essence of American democracy? How does democracy lead to freedom of religion, freedom of speech, and to economic success? Will future Americans continue to defend with passion democratic values and respect cultural differences? Culture contact and change are inevitable, and continues to affect all modern societies, especially American and European industrial societies who are attracting large numbers of immigrants and refugees. The conflict faces both newcomers and other Americans. The ideal of a multicultural America has some rough realities attached, such as the slow pace of certain groups to function in American society, and their inability to buy into the core values of working ethic and participation in the political process. Consequently, an important issue here is the need to socialize newcomers into the core values of American society, the need to establish the process of cultural transmission in such a way that it does not violate newcomers' basic rights to their language, culture and privacy. Multicultural America can only be successful if, in addition to the diverse cultural resources and traditions, we all can function as a society. Before the concept of cultural transmission is discussed, however, the notion of culture needs to be revisited.

George and Louise Spindler were among the first anthropologists to use and describe the process of cultural transmission as a dynamic transactional process through which culture is reinterpreted and recreated. This means that culture is not merely passed from one generation to another, with some changes and revisions. Culture is continuously reshaped and reinterpreted, precisely in the context of socializing others, especially the young, to the American way of life. The Spindlers' research resulted in descriptions of schools, academic competition, multiethnic settings, cultural conflict, and of relatively harmonious traditional middle-class instructional environments. What all these various settings had in common was the critical function of passing on cultural values unique to American society. The challenge confronted by the Spindlers in their attempt to map out the behavioral responses of immigrant, refugee and minority persons facing culture change led them to three tasks:

1. The redefinition of culture, cultural transmission, and cultural conflict as interlocking concepts;

2. The demystification of ethnographic (cross-cultural) research methods appropriately used to study culture, cultural conflict and cultural transmission;

3. The construction of a new theoretical model ('cultural therapy') to resolve cultural conflict.

REDISCOVERING CULTURE

The process of cultural transmission is readily observable as adult members of a society teach their young to carry on the daily duties necessary for meeting physical and spiritual needs of all members. Different societies have their own ways to carry on the teaching of the young to preserve their life styles and distribution of labor. American Indians were taught to hunt, fish and make pottery; they were also taught to respect nature and protect the environment. Much of their religion and ritual aims at inculcating respect for the natural environment. Many modern societies, who must face war and terrorism on a daily basis, teach their children hatred for the enemy, the use of weapons, and the value of destroying the enemy. Ethnic identity and survival of the ethnic group are inseparable.

Culture, therefore, can be conceived as a dynamic process that is reconstructed in the very activities whose purposes are to transmit survival skills and the rationale for using such skills. The parameters within which a society exists define the nature of the cultural values transmitted. These parameters are linked to macro-social elements, as well as to a number of micro-interactional factors surrounding survival activities. It is here that values generally shared by the entire society have different significance for different peoples, depending on the social context of their upbringing. Hunting, canoeing and physical endurance skills can be highly functional in a riverine culture of the Piraparana, in Matto Grosso, but not very functional in New York or Chicago. While there is a great deal of individual differentiation in ethnic groups (their notion of living in a family, of attending school, and cooperating in a community), there are also similar responses to the new culture (responses to a market economy, a democratic political system, demands for the use of English as a national language or as language of instruction), responses to demands for conformity in behavior, etc. These similar responses reflect a secondary socialization into a new common culture. It is precisely through this process of transmission of American culture (which for newcomers often occurs in schools) that American culture takes new life and becomes a powerful instrument for social cohesiveness. In this sense, American culture is not an abstract concept of new cognitive codes resulting from assimilation of school values through school activities. What we mean is that the acquisition of American culture by individuals from other cultures is not a cumbersome and somewhat amorphous sum total of the home cultural values and traditions plus those of school. It is the result of a selective process of acceptance of some values, rejection of others, integration of others, and a final commitment to adopt a particular life style.

Thus, what culture becomes, if understood as a dynamic force resulting from actual tangible transactions in given multicultural interactional contexts, is a powerful force that has led many different individuals to the pursuit of same values: values of freedom and competitive search for economic prosperity. Culture is revealed to us in what people do, and it is a concept helpful in understanding why people do whatever they do. Thus, there is an intimate relationship between action and culture, as well as between motivation to act and to hold cultural values (Spindler, G., 1959, 1977; Trueba, Spindler and Spindler, 1989). Much effort in our lives is invested in action, but action that is motivated by the need to pursue and protect certain values. When values change, action changes.

All societies have mechanisms to teach their youngsters how to live in a social group and enhance its survival through the transmission of knowledge accumulated over generations. The teaching of fishing, hunting and agricultural techniques is essential to some pre-literate societies; for modern technological and industrial societies, the teaching of literacy and critical thinking skills is essential to survive. What holds societies together is their members' ability to acquire and transmit knowledge. Without the transmission of the knowledge gained in previous centuries in industrial societies, our cities would be paralyzed and our health would decay rapidly. Hence the importance of education and schooling. Education is a transactional (interactive) process that aims at transferring, sharing from one generation to the next the cultural capital (knowledge, traditions and values) stored and enlarged by the efforts of our ancestors. Education is indeed the instrument that permits modern societies to motivate its youngsters to learn what is collectively indispensable to maintain the quality of life known to members of society. The cultural capital of America is highly diversified and continuously changing with the influx of immigrants. Its unique ways to handle cultural conflict, to respect ethnic identities and the dialectical nature of democratic institutions has a long and strong philosophical tradition that finds its way in our daily way of life and our schools.

American philosophers and historians, such as Crevecoeur, Jefferson, Martineau, Toqueville, von Hubner, and Turner deal, in the interpretation of George and Louise Spindler, with the crux of cultural transmission, conflict and accommodation, religious affiliation and of children's socialization into roles to be played at home in the family, as well as in public life. The Spindlers view American culture as a dialogue (Spindler and Spindler with Trueba and Williams, 1990) between individuals and collectivities, but a dialogue that leads people to rediscover and restructure democratic concepts, behaviors, values and the historical interpretation of such concepts. To recognize that cultural transmission does not occur in a historical vacuum, but that it is continuously shaped by the historical present of Americans as they live their collective conflicts, and find appropriate adaptative strategies that lead them to success, is to recognize the dynamics of American democracy.

If conflict is at the essence of democracy, a successful democracy must include the mechanics for conflict resolution. American cultural values, as opposite and polarized as they may seem in history, must be instrumental to resolve conflict. Cultural transmission must reflect the inherent conflicts of democratic processes, the polarization in movements that mirror antagonism, or advocacy for values that are seemingly opposite: conformity or individualism, cooperation or competition, resistance to law and order or submission to the law, continuity or discontinuity, religiousness or secularism, adherence to strict moral codes or liberal social mores. Americans' ability to respect people with opposed views allows them to reach a critical balance of forces; it permits development of cultural movements and cultural discourse in opposite directions. This is American democracy. In the end, cultural continuity or discontinuity, change or resistance to change, conformity or individualism, high moral standards or liberal attitudes, are all emphasized during the cycles of tolerance and intolerance for diversity; cycles that repeat themselves through history, as newcomers arrive with new contrasting characteristics but a new commitment to define (and re-define) democracy. These cycles affect mainstream people's view of newcomers, ethnic cultures and the role of home languages.

Cultural continuities and discontinuities, which are the result of cultural transmission in given historical contexts, can be best understood in a cross-cultural and long-term perspective, because the cycles of recurring similarities and contrasts are observed best over many years. For example, in the comparative studies presented by George Spindler and his colleagues, we can see a remarkable consistency in cultural values and themes (Spindler, G., Ed., *Educational and Cultural Process: Anthropological Approaches*, 1987a, but especially the chapters by Goldman and McDermott, pp. 282–299; Spindler, G. and Spindler, L. (Eds) *Interpretive Ethnography of Education: At Home and Abroad*, 1987a, especially chapters by the Spindlers, pp. 143–67; by Ogbu, J., 1987, pp. 255–78 and by Gibson, M., 1987, pp. 281–310; see also Spindler and Spindler's 'Schoenhausen', 1988:31–43; Gibson, 1988). Early socialization of the Palau, Ulithi, Hano, and Eskimo led George Spindler to discuss the role of schools in the socialization of Americans (1987:303–334).

The belief by some optimists that American society has overcome its racist biases was shattered by the video of LA policemen brutally beating Rodney King, an African American already apprehended and surrounded by fifteen policemen. The comments of some of the policemen in front of nurses, and their reference to the beating as a game, accompanied by an implied satisfaction of having inflicted such serious physical punishment on an African American, brings home the reality of prejudice. African Americans are not seen possessing the human dignity bestowed upon their white counterparts. Yes, American society has moved along with the passing of Civil Rights legislation and the increase of African Americans in professions and careers reserved for whites in previous years. Today's problems in Los Angeles are not different from the problems observed by George and Louise Spindler in their study of 'model teachers', such as 'Roger Harker' (1988:25–31) and by Hanna's 'Public Social Policy and the Children's World' (Hanna, 1988:316–55). Racism is not a simple attitudinal problem, it is an integral part of some segregated European cultures and some American quasi-apartheid practical living arrangements. Attempts at integration show the far-reaching structural changes needed in all our social and cultural institutions.

Cultural pluralism, with its inherent conflict of shock, dissonance, or incongruence as experienced by the various ethnic groups, and with a successful cultural adjustment, congruence, harmony and balance, as experienced by others, lead us to recognize the complexity of American democracy. American democracy, which is cemented in cultural diversity, requires continuity and change. To explain the flexibility of American culture that accommodates continuity and change, George Spindler had discussed two important concepts . . . : the concept of the *enduring self* (the consistent self-perception as being culturally attached to a given cultural setting) and of the *situated self* (the part of ourselves adapting continuously to new settings). The world moves too fast and does not permit us to anchor ourselves and our families in any value system. Long-term ethnographic studies have capitalized on the contributions of the Spindlers and produced important theoretical developments. The cycles of 'compression and decompression' or the variations in emotional intensity experienced by humans in their transition from one status to another, were used by Borish to describe the transitions from childhood to adulthood, from peaceful schooling to training for war activities, and from oppression to emancipation among the Kibbutz (Borish, 1988:181–199). Other researchers, also capitalizing on the work by the Spindlers, have established cross-cultural comparisons to examine cultural characteristics and values. Fujita and Sano (1988:73–97) for example, using the Spindlers' *Reflective Cross-cultural Interviewing* technique, compare and contrast how children were treated in American and Japanese day-care centers, and the basic cultural assumptions of the teachers in these centers; Macias working with the Papago Indian children (1987:363–380) and Anderson-Levitt working with French children (1987:171–92) use cross-cultural approaches pioneered by the Spindlers many years before.

REFERENCES

ANDERSON-LEVITT, K.M. (1987) 'Cultural knowledge for teaching first grade: An example from France', in SPINDLER, G. and SPINDLER, L. (Eds) *Interpretive Ethnography of Education: At Home and Abroad* (1987) Hillsdale, NJ: Lawrence Erlbaum Associates, Publishers, pp. 171–92.

APPLE, M. (1990) *Ideology and Curriculum*, New York, NY: Routledge.

BORISH, S. (1988) 'The winter of their discontent: Cultural compression and decompression in the life cycle of the Kibbutz adolescent', in TRUEBA, H. and DELGADO-GAITAN, C. (Eds) *School and Society: Teaching Content Through Culture*, New York, NY: Praeger, pp. 181–99.

FRAKE, C. (1964) 'Notes on queries in ethnography', *American Anthropologist*, **66**(3), pp. 132–45.

FUJITA, M. and SANO, T. (1988) 'Children in American and Japanese day-care centers: Ethnography and reflective cross-cultural interviewing', in TRUEBA, H. and DELGADO-GAITAN, C. (Eds) *School & Society: Teaching Content Through Culture*, New York, NY: Praeger, pp. 73–97.

GIBSON, M. (1987) 'Punjabi immigrants in an American High School', in SPINDLER, G. and SPINDLER, L. (Eds) *Interpretive Ethnography of Education: At Home and Abroad*, Hillsdale, NJ: Lawrence Erlbaum Assoc., (pp. 281–310).

GIBSON, M. (1988) *Accommodation Without Assimilation: Sikh Immigrants in an American High School*, Ithaca, NY: Cornell University Press.

GOLDMAN, S. and McDERMOTT, R. (1987) 'The culture of competition in American schools', *Education and Cultural Process: Anthropological Approaches*, Second Edition, Prospect Heights, IL: Waveland Press, Inc., pp. 282–89.

GOODENOUGH, W. (1976) 'Multiculturalism as the normal human experience', *Anthropology and Education Quarterly*, **7**(4), pp. 4–7.

HANNA, J.L. (1988) 'Public social policy and the children's world: Implications of ethnographic research for desegregated schooling', in SPINDLER, G. (Ed.) (1988) *Doing* the *Ethnography of Schooling: Educational Anthropology in Action*, Prospect Heights, IL: Waveland Press, Inc., pp. 310–55.

MACIAS, J. (1987) 'The hidden curriculum of Papago teachers: American Indian strategies for mitigating cultural discontinuity in early schooling', in SPINDLER, G. and L., (Eds) *Interpretive ethnography of education: At Home and Abroad*, Hillsdale, NJ: Lawrence Erlbaum Assoc., pp. 363–80.

OGBU, J. (1987) 'Variability in minority school performance: A problem in search of an explanation', *Anthropology and Education Quarterly*, **18**(4), pp. 312–34.

SPINDLER, G. (1959) *Transmission of American Culture*, The Third Burton Lecture, Cambridge, MA: Harvard University Press.

SPINDLER, G. (1977) 'Change and continuity in American core cultural values: An anthropological perspective' in DERENZO, G.D. (Ed.) *We the People: American Character and Social Change*, Westport CT: Greenwood, pp. 20–40.

SPINDLER, G. (Ed.) (1987a). *Education and Cultural Process: Anthropological Approaches*, Second Edition, Prospect Heights, IL: Waveland Press, Inc.

SPINDLER, G. (Ed.) (1988) (second edition) *Doing the Ethnography of Schooling: Educational Anthropology in Action*, Prospect Heights, IL: Waveland Press, Inc.

SPINDLER, G. and SPINDLER, L. (Eds) (1987a) *The Interpretive Ethnography of Education: At Home and Abroad*, Hillsdale, NJ: Lawrence Erlbaum Assoc.

SPINDLER, G. and SPINDLER, L., with TRUEBA, H., and WILLIAMS, M. (1990) *The American Cultural Dialogue and its Transmission*, London, England: Falmer Press.

TREUBA, H.T., CHENG, L. and IMA, K. (1993) *Myth or Reality: Adaptive Strategies of Asian Americans in California*, London, England: Falmer Press.

TRUEBA, H.T., SPINDLER, G. and SPINDLER, L. (Eds) (1989) *What do Anthropologists Have to Say about Dropouts?*, London, England: Falmer Press.

CHAPTER 7 Prejudice

7.1 GORDON W. ALLPORT

Theories of Prejudice

Gordon W. Allport is an influential scholar who helped to formalize the study of and understanding of the concept of prejudice. His writing on the concept, presented in part in the following selection, is still influential in today's scholarship on prejudice. Sometimes called a "personality theorist," Allport focuses on how prejudice can become a part of a person's personality. He has contributed to the knowledge of prejudice through his ideas on the concept and through his contributions to the methodology of studying prejudice—for instance, through his scales that measure the level of a person's prejudice.

In the following selection from *The Nature of Prejudice* (Doubleday, 1958), Allport proposes six theories of how prejudice is formed within individuals and society. These include the historical, psychological, and sociological underpinnings for the development of prejudice. It is important for Allport that all of these six approaches be studied because they each have something to teach us about prejudice. As he says, they cannot be reduced to a single theory about prejudice but rather present us with a multifaceted understanding of the development of prejudice.

Key Concept: factors in the development of prejudice

What do we mean when we speak of a "theory" of prejudice? Do we imply that the theory in question is offered as a complete and sovereign explanation for all human prejudice? Seldom is this the case, even though when we read enthusiastic exponents of the Marxian view, or of the scapegoat theory, or of some other, we sometimes gain the impression that the author feels that he

FIGURE 1

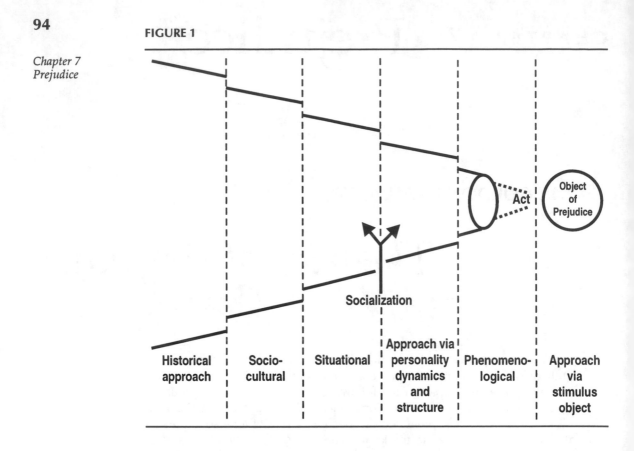

Socialization

Historical
approach

Socio-
cultural

Situational

Approach via
personality
dynamics
and
structure

Phenomeno-
logical

Approach
via
stimulus
object

Act

Object
of
Prejudice

has buttoned up the subject completely. Yet as a rule most "theories" are advanced by their authors to call attention to some one important causal factor, without implying that no other factors are operating. Usually an author selects for emphasis one of the six approaches in [Fig. 1]; he then develops his ideas concerning certain forces that operate within this approach to create prejudice.

Our own approach to the problem is eclectic. There seems to be value in all of the six main approaches, and some truth in virtually all of the resulting theories. It is not possible at the present time to reduce them to a single theory of human action.

It will help the reader to note that causal influences lying toward the right side of Fig. 1 tend to be more immediate in time and more specifiable in operation. A person acts with prejudice in the first instance because he perceives the object of prejudice in a certain way. But he perceives it in a certain way partly because his personality is what it is. And his personality is what it is chiefly because of the way he was socialized (training in family, school, neighborhood). The existing social situation is also a factor in his socialization and may also be a determinant of his perceptions. Behind these forces lie other valid but more remote causal influences. They involve the structure of society in which one lives, long-standing economic and cultural traditions, as well as national and historical influences of long duration. While these factors seem so remote as to be alien to the immediate psychological analysis of prejudiced acts, they are, nonetheless, important causal influences.

Let us look now more closely at some of the characteristic features of each of the six major approaches indicated in Fig. 1.[1]

HISTORICAL EMPHASIS

Impressed by the long history that lies behind each and every present-day ethnic conflict, historians insist that only the total background of a conflict can lead to its understanding. Anti-Negro prejudice in America, for example, is a historical matter, having its roots in slavery, in carpetbagging, and in the failure of reconstruction in the South following the Civil War.

Commenting on recent efforts to establish a purely psychological view of the subject, one historian objects:

> Such studies are enlightening only within narrow limits. For personality is itself conditioned by social forces; in the last analysis, the search for understanding must reach into the broad social context within which personality is shaped.[2]

While admitting the force of this criticism, we may point out that while history provides "the broad social context" it cannot tell why within this context one personality develops prejudice and another does not. And this is precisely the question that the psychologist most wants to answer. Here, then, is an instance of an unprofitable quarrel. Both specialists are indispensable, for they are seeking to answer not identical, but complementary, questions.

Historical studies are markedly diverse in type. Some, but not all, stress the importance of economic determinants. An example of this treatment is the *exploitation theory* of prejudice held by Marxists and others. A brief summary of its argument is given by Cox.

> Race prejudice is a social attitude propagated among the public by an exploiting class for the purpose of stigmatizing some group as inferior so that the exploitation of either the group itself or its resources may both be justified.[3]

This author goes on to argue that race prejudice rose to unprecedented heights in the nineteenth century when European imperial expansion called for some justification. Therefore, poets ([Rudyard] Kipling), racial theorists ([Houston Stewart] Chamberlain), and statesmen proclaimed colonial peoples to be "inferior," "requiring protection," a "lower form of evolution," a "burden" to be borne altruistically. All this pious concern and condescension masked the financial advantage that came from exploitation. Segregation developed as a device for preventing sympathy and sentiments of equality. Sexual and social taboos placed on the colonial peoples prevented them from developing expectations of equality and freedom of choice.

Many considerations make this theory attractive. It explains the rationalizations for economic exploitation that are frequently heard: the Orientals only "need" a handful of rice a day to live on; the Negro shouldn't receive high wages, for he will spend them unwisely trying to rise above his racial station; the Mexicans are so primitive that they would only drink and gamble away their money if they had it; so too the American Indian.

While there is obvious truth in the exploitation theory it is weak in many particulars. It fails to explain why there is not equal prejudice against all exploited people. Many of the immigrant groups coming to America have been exploited without suffering from prejudice to the extent that Negroes and Jews have suffered. Nor is it clear that Jews are, in fact, victims of economic exploitation. The Quakers and Mormons were at one time severely persecuted in America, but certainly not primarily for economic reasons.

Nor is it correct to consider bigotry against even the Negro in America as wholly an economic phenomenon, though it is here that Cox's argument is strongest. While it seems obvious that many white people derive advantage from underpaying Negro workers and rationalizing the injustice through theories concerning their "animal nature," still the story is more complex. White employees in factories, or white tenant farmers, are similarly exploited, but no ritual of discrimination has developed against them. In sociological studies of certain Southern communities, for example, it turns out that on an objective scale of "class," Negroes are no lower than the whites. Their cabins are no smaller, their income is no less, their household facilities are the same. Yet their position socially and psychologically is lower.

We conclude, therefore, that the Marxist theory of prejudice is far too simple, even though it points a sure finger at *one* of the factors involved in prejudice, viz., rationalized self-interest of the upper classes.

The contributions of history to the understanding of prejudice are by no means confined to the economic interpretation. The rise of Hitler in Germany together with his genocide policies cannot be understood except by tracing an ominous sequence of events historically.[4]

Whether this fateful progression can be explained fully by history without the help of psychology is not here the question. We insist only that any pattern of prejudice existing in any part of the world receives marked illumination when it is examined from the historical point of view.

SOCIOCULTURAL EMPHASIS

[I] will deal with some of the multitude of sociocultural factors that help explain group conflict and prejudice. Sociologists and anthropologists place principal weight on this type of theorizing. Like the historian, they are impressed by the total social context in which prejudiced attitudes develop. Within this social context some writers emphasize the traditions that lead to conflict; some the relative upward mobility in out-groups and in-groups; some the density of the populations concerned; some the type of contacts that exist between groups.

For the present, let us cite one example from theories in this class—the phenomenon known as *urbanization* and its possible relation to ethnic prejudice. The case is argued somewhat as follows.

Although people desire peaceful and affiliative relations with others, this striving has been badly blocked by the mechanical culture of our day—especially by the culture of our cities that arouses so much insecurity and uncertainty in men's minds. In the city personal contacts are diminished. Literally or figuratively the assembly line rules us. Central government replaces local and more intimate forms of government. Advertising controls our standards of living and our desires. Giant corporations fill the landscape with monstrous factories, regulating our employment, income, and safety. No longer do personal thrift, private effort, face-to-face adjustments count for much. Fear of the Juggernaut settles upon us. Big city life expresses to us what is inhuman, impersonal, dangerous. We fear and hate our subservience to it.

What has this urban insecurity to do with prejudice? For one thing, as mass-men we follow the conventions of the times. The snob-appeals of advertising affect us deeply. We want more goods, more luxury, more status. The standards forced upon us by advertisers call for contempt of people who are poor, who do not reach the level of material existence that is prescribed. Hence we look down upon groups economically below us—upon Negroes, immigrants and rustics. (Here we note echoes of the Marxian view.)

But while we yield to the materialistic urban values, we also hate the city that engenders them. We hate the domination of finance and shady politics. We despise the traits that develop in response to urban pressures. We dislike those who are sneaky, dishonest, selfish, too clever, too ambitious, vulgar, noisy, and on the fringe of old-fashioned virtues. These urban traits have been personified in the Jew. "The Jews are hated today," writes Arnold Rose, "primarily because they serve as a symbol of city life."[5] They are symbols especially of that monster, all-dominant, much feared City of New York. The city has emasculated us. We will therefore hate the symbol of the city—the Jew.

The merit of this theory is that it has a logic that applies both to anti-Semitism and to feelings of condescension toward other minorities who have not "made the grade." It would have some difficulty, however, in explaining why Japanese-American farmers were so vehemently feared and hated during World War II. It would also be forced to concede that "city hatred" is as intense among rural dwellers as among urbanites, for ethnic prejudice is certainly as acute in the country as in the town.

Blending a historical and a sociocultural emphasis, we have the *community* pattern theory of prejudice. Here the stress is upon the basic ethnocentrism of every group.

In Europe there is an intricate network of historic hostilities. A given city, especially in the eastern sectors, might at various times have been "owned" by Russia, Lithuania, Poland, Sweden, the Ukraine. Descendants of all these assorted conquerors might still reside in the city and with some justification regard all other claimants as pretenders or intruders. A veritable checkerboard of prejudice results. Even should the settlers of disputed territories migrate, say to America, the traditional hostilities may move with them. But unless there is a strong community pattern in the New World as well as in the Old, ancient animosities are likely to die out. Many, perhaps most, immigrants want to start a new life, and have chosen a new community pattern where (to their mind) there is an atmosphere of freedom, equal opportunity, and a sense of dignity available to all.

SITUATIONAL EMPHASIS

If we subtract the historical background from the sociocultural approach we have left a *situational emphasis.* That is to say, emphasis upon past patterns gives way to emphasis upon current forces. Several theories of prejudice are of this order. One might, for example, speak of an *atmosphere* theory. A child grows up surrounded by immediate influences and very soon reflects them all. Lillian Smith, in *Killers of the Dream,* propounds such a theory.[6] The Southern child obviously has no knowledge of historical events, of exploitation, or of urban values as such. All he knows is that he must *conform* to the complex and inconsistent teaching that he receives. His prejudice is thus merely a mirror image of what he now sees around him.

An instance of the subtle impact of atmosphere in shaping attitudes is implied in the following incident.

> An inspector of education in a British African colony wondered why so little progress was made in learning English in a certain native school. Visiting the classroom, he asked the native teacher to put on a demonstration of his method of teaching English. The teacher complied, first making, however, the following preface to the lesson in the vernacular which he did not know the inspector understood: "Come now, children, put away your things, and let us wrestle for an hour with the enemy's language."

Other situational theories may stress the present *employment situation:* and see hostility primarily in terms of prevailing economic competition. Or they may regard prejudice primarily as a phenomenon of upward and downward *social mobility.* Situational theories also may stress the importance of *types of contact* between groups, or the relative *density* of groups....

PSYCHODYNAMIC EMPHASIS

If man is by nature quarrelsome or hostile we must expect conflict to flourish. Theories that stress causation in human nature are inevitably psychological in type in contrast to the historical, economic, sociological, or cultural points of view mentioned above.

In good standing is the *frustration* theory of prejudice. It is a psychological theory rooted in the "nature of man." It can readily admit that affiliative needs seem as basic, or more basic, than protest and hatred, and at the same time hold that when positive and friendly advances toward the environment are thwarted, ugly consequences result.

We can clarify the theory by citing the vehement prejudice of a World War II veteran:

> When asked about possible unemployment and a future depression he replied:
> We'd better not have it. Chicago'll blow wide open. On South Park the niggers are gettin' so smart. We'll have a race riot that'll make Detroit look like a Sunday School picnic. So many are bitter about the part the Negro played in the war. They got all the soft jobs—the quartermasters, engineers. They're no good for anything else. The white got his ass shot off. They're pretty bitter. If both whites and niggers get laid off, that'll be bad. I'm gonna eat. I know how to use a gun.[7]

This case clearly shows the role of frustration in causing, or intensifying, prejudice. Deprivation and frustration lead to hostile impulses, which if not controlled are likely to discharge against ethnic minorities. With emotional provocation, a person's view of his social world becomes constricted and distorted. He sees personal demons (minorities) at work because his normal directed thinking is blocked by the intensity of his feelings. He cannot analyze the evil; he can only personify it.

The frustration theory is sometimes known as the *scapegoat* theory.... All formulations of this theory assume that anger once engendered may be displaced upon a (logically irrelevant) victim.

It has been pointed out that the chief weakness of this theory is that it fails to tell upon what victim the hostility will be discharged. It also fails to explain why in many personalities no such displacement takes place, however great the frustration....

Another type of "nature of man" theory emphasizes the *character structure* of the individual person. Only certain types of people develop prejudice as an important feature in their lives. These seem to be insecure and anxious personalities who take the authoritarian and exclusionist way of life rather than the relaxed and trusting democratic way.

Like the frustration theory, the character structure theory has much evidence to back it up.... These two theories are not, however, all-sufficient, but require supplementation from other theories we are here surveying.

PHENOMENOLOGICAL EMPHASIS

A person's conduct proceeds immediately from his view of the situation confronting him. His response to the world conforms to his definition of the world. He attacks members of one group because he perceives them as repulsive, annoying, or threatening; members of another he derides because to him they are crude, dirty, and stupid. Both visibility and verbal labels ... help define the object in perception so that it can be readily identified.... [H]istorical and cultural forces, and the person's entire character structure, may lie behind his hypotheses and perceptions. Writers who approach the study of prejudice from the phenomenological point of view assume the convergence of all these factors into a final common focus. What the man finally believes and perceives is the important thing. Obviously, the stereotype plays a prominent part in sharpening the perception prior to action.

The phenomenal level, as we have said, is the immediate level of causation, but it is well to combine this approach with others. If we do not do so we are likely to lose sight of the equally important determinants that are to be found in the underlying dynamics of personality as well as in the situational, cultural, and historical contexts of life.

EMPHASIS ON EARNED REPUTATION

Finally we come once again to the problem of the *stimulus object* itself. There may be . . . bona fide differences between groups that provoke dislike and hostility. Enough has been said, however, to show that these differences are much *less* than they are imagined to be. In most cases a reputation is not earned but is gratuitously thrust upon a group.

It would be impossible to find any social scientist today who would subscribe completely to the *earned reputation* theory. At the same time, some warn against assuming that every minority group is always blameless. There may be ethnic or national traits that *are* menacing, and that therefore invite realistic hostility. Or, still more likely, hostility may feed partly on realistic estimates of the stimulus (the true nature of groups) and partly on the many unrealistic factors that comprise prejudice. Some writers, therefore, advocate an *interaction theory.*[8] Hostile attitudes are *in part* determined by the nature of the stimulus (earned reputation) and *in part* by considerations essentially irrelevant to the stimulus (e.g., scapegoating, conforming to tradition, stereotypes, guilt projection, etc.).

There is certainly no objection to such an interaction theory provided proper weight is given to each of the two sets of factors. It says little more than "Let's allow for the simultaneous operation of all scientifically established causes of hostile attitudes, not forgetting to include relevant features of the stimulus object itself." Taken in this broad sense, there can be no possible objection to the theory.

FINAL WORD

By far the best view to take toward this multiplicity of approaches is to admit them all. Each has something to teach us. None possesses a monopoly of insight, nor is any one safe as a solitary guide. We may lay it down as a general law applying to all social phenomena that *multiple causation* is invariably at work and nowhere is the law more clearly applicable than to prejudice.

NOTES

1. The sixfold approach is developed more fully by the author in a paper entitled, "Prejudice: a problem in psychological causation," *Journal of Social Issues,* 1950, Supplement Series No. 4; likewise published in T. PARSONS AND E. SHILS, *Toward a Theory of Social Action,* Part 4, Chapter 1, Cambridge: Harvard Univ. Press, 1951.

2. O. HANDLIN. Prejudice and capitalist exploitation. *Commentary,* 1948, *6,* 79–85. See also by the same author *The Uprooted: The Epic Story of the Great Migrations that Made the American People.* Boston: Little, Brown, 1951.

3. O. C. COX. *Caste, Class, and Race.* New York: Doubleday, 1948, 393.

4. P. W. MASSING. *Rehearsal for Destruction.* New York: Harper, 1949.

5. A. ROSE. Anti-Semitism's root in city-hatred. *Commentary,* 1948, *6,* 374–378; also published in A. ROSE (ED.), *Race Prejudice and Discrimination,* New York: Alfred A. Knopf, 1951, Chapter 49.

6. LILLIAN SMITH. *Killers of the Dream.* New York: W. W. Norton, 1949.

7. B. BETTELHEIM AND M. JANOWITZ. *The Dynamics of Prejudice: A Psychological and Sociological Study of Veterans.* New York: Harper, 1950, 82.

8. *Cf.* B. ZAWADSKI. Limitations of the scapegoat theory of prejudice. *Journal of Abnormal and Social Psychology,* 1948, *43,* 127–141. Also, G. ICHHEISER, Sociopsychological and cultural factors in race relations, *American Journal of Sociology,* 1949, *54,* 395–401.

Research on Prejudice Reduction

Glenn S. Pate presents a summary of some main findings within research about reducing prejudice in the following selection from "Research on Prejudice Reduction," *Educational Leadership.* The key findings relate to intergroup contact, level of self-worth of individuals, and social and informational factors contributing to the reduction of prejudice. Of key importance for Pate is that the contact between individuals of different racial or gender groups is carefully structured. It is important for individuals in both groups to have equal status in the situation that is created. Further, co-operation needs to be encouraged rather than competition. Thus, if contact between members of different racial and gender groups is structured in ways that encourage cooperation among individuals who have equal status in the situation, prejudice may be reduced. However, Pate cautions, the intergroup contact must be structured carefully or else prejudice can sometimes grow to even stronger levels.

Pate is an associate professor at the University of Arizona in Tucson. His research focuses on how schools can help reduce prejudice within society. He has published several articles and book chapters providing summaries and suggestions for prejudice reduction.

Key Concept: conditions for reducing prejudice

Most of the writing on prejudice has described and documented the types and extent of prejudice or prescribed what to do about it. Surprisingly little empirical research has been reported on the subject. Fortunately, however, there have been some productive studies on which we can base generalizations.

1. Facts or information about another group are not sufficient to change attitudes.

The most common approach to combating prejudice is to increase one group's knowledge about another group—on the assumption that if we have accurate information, we will not hold misconceptions and false stereotypes. As long ago as 1946, a few people recognized that this is an ineffective approach. "Perhaps the most glaring defect of intercultural education as it functions at present is that it is geared for the most part only to intellectual values.

It assumes—an assumption yet to be empirically confirmed—that ignorance is the real barrier, that the truth will set men free, that the objective facts about race and race prejudice are sufficient automatically to eliminate bias and suspicion and hatred" (Glicksberg, 1946). Similar conclusions were later reached by Trager and Yarrow (1952) in studying prejudices expressed by children.

Tansik and Driskill (1977) discovered negative changes in racial attitudes held by supervisors at a military base. The supervisors who attended a required training course, viewed the message as manipulative and propagandist. If we require such an experience for students, we need to be careful about how we package and present the program.

"Facts do not speak for themselves; rather they are interpreted through the experience and biases of those hearing them" (Morland, 1963, p. 125). Knowledge *alone* will not reduce prejudice; knowledge is something of a prerequisite to prejudice reduction, not the sole means.

2. Class prejudice may be stronger than racial or religious prejudice.

Perhaps if white people do not like Blacks, it is not because of racial differences, but because Blacks are perceived as being poor and of a lower class. As Clore and his associates (1978) discovered in a study of interracial attitudes and behavior at a summer camp, "One of the most stubborn obstacles to positive changes in racial attitudes is the brute fact of class differences between Blacks and Whites. Blacks as a group do not enjoy the same economic positions as Whites and are, therefore, associated in fact and fantasy with the characteristics of lower class membership" (p. 107).

In an exhaustive study of prejudice among adolescents, class prejudice was an extremely strong factor (Glock and others, 1975). "These results identify a significant element of class prejudice in racial social distance just as the earlier results demonstrated the importance of class prejudice in teenagers' expression of social distance toward Jews" (p. 137). The power of class prejudice presents a tremendous challenge to society and schools. As Glock and others point out, "Unfortunately, it is not possible to sort out what is uniquely racial in racial social distance from what is class-based. The presence of both elements, however, makes it probable that, as the social status of Blacks improves, some reduction in gross prejudice is to be expected" (p. 138). The improvement in the social status of Blacks is slow and in fact is retarded by prejudice. Thus we have a vicious cycle.

3. An individual who has a high degree of self-acceptance will likely have a low degree of prejudice.

This point is in line with the theory that you cannot like other people if you do not like yourself. Research substantiates the relationship between self-concept and prejudicial attitudes. Rubin (1967) verified the correlation between self-acceptance and prejudice in an experimental study. More important, he was able to increase one group's self-acceptance and observed a significant decrease in prejudice.

In a sophisticated laboratory experiment, Cook (1972) compared individuals who changed their attitudes in a positive direction with people who did not change. The primary difference was that those who changed held positive attitudes toward people in general. Those who changed also scored higher on self-esteem measures. Probably the most effective approach schools can take to combat prejudice is to improve students' self-concept.

4. Students who work in interracial learning teams develop positive attitudes and cross-ethnic friendships.

Of great relevance to classroom procedures are the findings of Weigel and others (1975). They studied the impact of two different teaching methods in seventh- and ninth-grade classrooms—the traditional whole-class method and a method designed to foster intragroup cooperation. The latter teaching technique involved the formation of small, ethnically heterogeneous groups that shared goals and rewards. Intergroup competition was used to foster intragroup cooperation. The small-group competition was better evaluated and endorsed by the teachers and resulted in greater cross-ethnic friendship choices. Comparable findings were reported by Cohen (1973) and Slavin (1979).

The implications of the cross-ethnic learning teams must be taken with a caveat, however: it is extremely important that the group experience success. This caution is expressed by Cohen (1973) and Weigel and others (1975), who concluded from reviewing the literature on the success-failure variable that "Greater group attraction occurs under conditions of group success than group failure and that subjects may exhibit increased prejudice if the interracial group is unsuccessful" (p. 773).

5. The cognitive, affective, and behavioral components of prejudice are not necessarily related.

One of the primary shortcomings of prejudice reduction programs in schools is confusion as to the exact nature of the objectives. Are we trying to change what students know and how they think, what attitudes they hold, or how they act? Programs that focus on the cognitive, such as teaching information about ethnic groups, do not necessarily change students' affective and behavior dimensions of prejudice.

We might expect that the way people think, their attitudes, and their behavior would be closely related; research indicates that this is not always true. Studies by Merz and Pearlin (1972) and by Mann (1972) show that one of the three dimensions may change while the other two dimensions remain constant.

A study of the literature also identifies a controversy over cause and effect. Some writers believe that attitudes determine behavior while others feel that attitudes adjust to be consistent with behavior, even though the behavior may have initially been forced. Schools should target their prejudice-reducing efforts toward any of the three dimensions without expecting unrealistic results in the other dimensions. It is important for schools to deliberately focus their objectives and not attempt to reduce prejudice in general with vague and unclear objectives.

Glenn S. Pate

Most teachers are familiar with the power of audiovisual techniques, and the application of these techniques to attitude modification is no exception. I remember the effect on my eighth grade students of the film, "The Autobiography of Miss Jane Pittman."

In addition to the overall effectiveness of film, Kraus (1972) found that an integrated cast had more effect than either an all-white or all-black cast. Kraus also summarized research on changing attitudes (primarily racial) through media (primarily film), and developed certain generalizations. The core of these is that the intended objectives and knowledge of the audience must be clear and specific.

In a study of two experimental groups and a control group, Houser (1978) found that audiovisual media was an effective instructional approach and that the group which had viewed the most films gave significantly fewer prejudicial responses. While most of us are prepared to accept the power of media, no studies are available that accept the long-term effects of these approaches.

7. Social contacts may reduce prejudice under certain conditions.

There is substantial information in the literature to suggest a relationship between social contact and prejudice. Social contact may be one of the essential conditions for reducing prejudice if the contact is positive. However, social contact is not a panacea for eliminating the widespread effects of prejudice. It may be either positive or negative, favorable or unfavorable.

In general, contact between different racial or ethnic groups does indeed reduce prejudice *if* certain conditions of the contact are met. Excellent overviews of the research are given by Amir (1972), Mack (1970), and Selltiz and Cook (1963). According to Selltiz and Cook (p. 159), "It appears that personal association with members of an ethnic group other than one's own generally leads to favorable changes in attitude toward that group—if the following conditions hold:"

- There is an opportunity to get to know one another as individuals.
- The individuals in the two groups have equal status in the situation. This point has been verified using college students (Cook, 1972), merchant seamen (Brophy, 1946), department store employees (Harding and Hogrefe, 1952), housing projects (Deutsch and Collins, 1951), soldiers (Stouffer, 1949; and Mack and Duster, 1964), and was pioneered as a crucial variable by Allport (1954).
- They have common interests and similar characteristics such as age or occupation.
- The social norms are favorable to association between the two groups. The social climate established by the leaders or authority figures in a situation, especially in school settings, is part of and largely determines the social norms. The importance of climate has been established by Fishman and Fishman (1977) in working with Jewish youth on racial

attitudes and by Bennett (1979) in studying friendship patterns. Selltiz and Cook (1963, p. 160) state, "One of the most solidly supported findings about intergroup contact is that the social climate within which it takes place—and especially the standards and the example set by leaders in the situation—strongly influence the outcome."

- The circumstances of the situation favor cooperation or at least do not introduce competition or conflict. This point is reinforced by the findings on the effects of learning teams discussed earlier.

- The presence or the activities of members of the two groups help in the achievement of the individual's goals, or at least do not present an obstacle to them. This principle is supported by the early work of Allport (1954) and more recently by Amir (1972).

Many of the conditions which are thought to reduce prejudice may also serve to *increase* prejudice when misapplied. Conditions that reflect competition, ethnocentrism, differing absolute values and beliefs that are objectionable to others, poor education and socioeconomic class differences (Amir, 1972; Rose, 1974) may also lead to more prejudice.

Obviously there are many contact situations that do not meet the criteria for positive effects, and there is research to support negative results. Kramer (1950) studied housing patterns and found that Whites living close to a black neighborhood had stronger hostile feelings toward Blacks than did Whites who lived a greater distance from the neighborhood. Fairchild and Gurin (1978, p. 763) reviewed research and found, "Studies in privately owned residential areas revealed a sharply contrasting (with public housing) set of outcomes. Despite varying methodologies and locations, the trend of the research during the early 1950s clearly indicated a pattern of initial and continuing hostility on the part of the White residents." Carithers (1970, p. 41) also summarized research and reported, "There is no general agreement about the effects of interracial contact on attitude change. Some studies have found heightened tolerance; some heightened resistance; some no change. There seems to be, however, a general agreement that racial contact per se will not bring about increased tolerance or acceptance." However, these negative findings and opinions do not detract from the contact theory; rather, they underline the need for the essential conditions of contact to be met.

Positive social contact can result in students' becoming less sensitive about their differences and less critical and less judgmental about the differences of others. Teachers can help reduce prejudice in the classroom by minimizing conditions that promote prejudiced feelings and behaviors. Students can be encouraged to work together harmoniously, rather than separately, on various classroom assignments. Criteria for grouping can be based on obvious differences as well as on the attainments and abilities of students. Also, since teachers are critical in influencing student behaviors, teachers should consider further modeling the behaviors and forming the diverse associations that they expect of their students.

In light of the reported research, it appears that we have some substantial knowledge about the reduction of prejudice. In spite of this, several salient questions remain for which we need answers in order to promote a prejudice-free society:

- It is quite possible that a prejudice or tendency to stereotype serves a psychological function. If we are able to remove prejudice within an individual, do we need to replace it with something else to serve the function? If so, with what?
- Is there an age at which prejudice stabilizes? Is there an age beyond which it is virtually impossible to change a person's attitudes? There is current speculation that early adolescence is a crucial period.
- Most of the studies that demonstrate effective prejudice reducing techniques have been conducted in controlled, experimental settings. Are these findings maintained under "real world" conditions? Can we effectively manipulate the "real world" environment?
- Virtually no studies attempt to measure effects of prejudice reduction on a long-range basis. What are the long-term effects? If long-range effects are weak, what is the value of short-term effects?

Despite the relative lack of attention to the reduction of prejudice, there is enough knowledge available. If we are serious about developing the type of society we claim we want, we must begin to apply what we know.

REFERENCES

Allport, Gordon. *The Nature of Prejudice*. Reading, Mass.: Doubleday, 1954.

Amir, Yehuda. "Contact Hypothesis in Ethnic Relations." In *Racial Attitudes in America: Analysis and Findings of Social Psychology*, pp. 319–342. Edited by John Brigham and Theodore Weissbach. New York: Harper and Row, 1972.

Bennett, Christine. "Interracial Acceptance in Desegregated Schools." *Phi Delta Kappan* 60 (1979): 683–684.

Brophy, Ira N. "The Luxury of Anti-Negro Prejudice." *Public Opinion Quarterly* 9 (1946): 456–466.

Carithers, M. W. "School Desegregation and Racial Cleavage 1954–1970: A Review of the Literature." *Journal of Social Issues* 26 (1970): 25–48.

Clore, Gerald L.; Bray, Robert M.; Itkin, Stuart M.; and Murphy, Pamela. "Interracial Attitudes and Behaviors at a Summer Camp." *Journal of Personality and Social Psychology* 36 (1978): 107–116.

Cohen, Elizabeth G. "Modifying the Effects of Social Structure." *American Behavioral Scientist* 16 (1973): 861–879.

Cook, Stuart W. "Motives in a Conceptual Analysis of Attitude-Related Behavior." In *Racial Attitudes in America: Analysis and Findings of Social Psychology*, pp. 250–261. Edited by John Brigham and Theodore Weissbach. New York: Harper & Row, 1972.

Deutsch, Morton, and Collins, Mary A. *Interracial Housing: A Psychological Evaluation of a Social Experiment*. Minneapolis: University of Minnesota Press, 1951.

Fairchild, Halford H., and Gurin, Patricia. "Traditions in the Social Psychological Analysis of Race Relations." *American Behavioral Scientist* 21 (1978): 757–778.

Fishman, Howard, and Fishman, Walda Katz. "A Case Study in Black-Jewish Relations or 'The Only Thing Wrong with Jews is that They Ain't Jewish Enough.'" Paper presented at the Southern Sociological Society Meeting, March 1977. ERIC Reproduction Service, ED 146 285.

Glicksberg, Charles I. "Intercultural Education: Utopia or Reality." *Common Ground* 6 (1946): 64.

Glock, Charles Y.; Wuthnow, Robert; Piliavin, Jane Allyn; and Spencer, Metta. *Adolescent Prejudice.* New York: Harper & Row, 1975.

Harding, John, and Hogrefe, Russell. "Attitudes of White Department Store Employees Toward Negro Co-Workers." *Journal of Social Issues* 8 (1952): 18–28.

Houser, Betsy Bosak. "An Examination of the Use of Audiovisual Media in Reducing Prejudice." *Psychology in the Schools* 15 (January 1978): 116–121.

Kramer, B. M. "Residential Contact as a Determinant of Attitude Toward Negroes." Doctoral dissertation, Harvard University, 1950.

Kraus, Sidney. "Modifying Prejudice: Attitude Change as a Function of the Race of the Communicator." In *Prejudice in Children.* Edited by A. Brown. Springfield, Ill.: Charles C. Thomas, 1972.

Mack, Raymond W. *Prejudice and Race Relations.* Chicago: Quadrangle Books, 1970.

Mack, Raymond W., and Duster, Troy S. *Patterns of Minority Relations.* New York: Anti-Defamation League of B'nai B'rith, 1964.

Mann, John H. "The Differential Nature of Prejudice Reduction." In *Prejudice in Children.* Edited by A. Brown. Springfield, Ill.: Charles C. Thomas, 1972.

Merz, Louise E., and Pearlin, Leonard I. "The Influence of Information on Three Dimensions of Prejudice Toward Negroes." In *Prejudice in Children.* Edited by A. Brown. Springfield, Ill.: Charles C. Thomas, 1972.

Morland, J. Kenneth. "The Development of Racial Bias in Young Children." *Theory Into Practice* 2 (1963): 120–127.

Rose, Peter I. *They and We.* New York: Random House, 1974.

Rubin, I. M. "Increased Self-Acceptance: A Means of Reducing Prejudice." *Journal of Personality and Social Psychology* 5 (1967) 233–238.

Selltiz, Claire, and Cook, Stuart W. "The Effects of Personal Contact in Intergroup Relations." *Theory Into Practice* 2 (1963): 158–165.

Slavin, Robert E. "Effects of Biracial Learning Teams on Cross-Racial Friendships." *Journal of Educational Psychology* 70 (1979): 381–387.

Stouffer, Samuel; Lumsdaine, A. A.; Lumsdaine, M. H.; Williams, R. M., Jr.; Smith, M. B.; Janis, I. L.; Star, S. A.; and Cottrell, L. S., Jr. *The American Soldier.* Vol. 2. Princeton: Princeton University Press, 1949.

Tansik, David A., and Driskill, John D. "Temporal Persistence of Attitudes Induced Through Required Training." *Group and Organization Studies* 2 (1977): 310–321.

Trager, Helen C., and Yarrow, Marian Radke. *They Learn What They Live.* New York: Harper & Row, 1952.

Weigel, R. H.; Wiser, P. L.; and Cook, S. W. "The Impact of Cooperative Learning Experiences on Cross-Ethnic Relations and Attitudes." *Journal of Social Issues* 31 (1975): 219–244.

CHAPTER 8 Racism

8.1 CORNEL WEST

Race Matters

Cornel West is a professor of Afro-American studies and philosophy of religion at Harvard University. His work focuses on black critical thought, cultural criticism, social theory, and the future of American youth. He is known both within academia and in the general public for his ideas on how to overcome crises within black communities. In addition to his writings, West is a respected speaker. He is the author of 13 books, including *Race Matters* (Beacon Press, 1993), from which the following selection has been taken, and *Restoring Hope: Conversations on the Future of Black America* (Beacon Press, 1997).

In this introduction from *Race Matters,* West explores how to set up a discussion of race in America today. He first asserts that race is not a single, separate factor in American society. Rather, it is tied in to economic and political issues and lethargy as part of the complex mix in U.S. life. He then says that before we can have open discussions of race, we must move away from labelling blacks as "them" and basing discussions on how they can fit in. West believes that we must move away from seeing blacks as "problems" in society. Using the Rodney King trial and ensuing riots as an initiating point for discussion, he discusses how current feelings about race in America have been heightened by the effects of media, materialism, and violence. He worries about "the collapse of meaning in life" and states that we must learn compassion and understanding of the history that has led us here.

Key Concept: preparing for discussions of race

What happened in Los Angeles in April of 1992 was neither a race riot nor a class rebellion. Rather, this monumental upheaval was a multiracial, trans-class, and largely male display of justified social rage. For all its ugly, xenophobic resentment, its air of adolescent carnival, and its downright barbaric behavior, it signified the sense of powerlessness in American society. Glib attempts to reduce its meaning to the pathologies of the black underclass, the criminal actions of hoodlums, or the political revolt of the oppressed urban masses miss the mark. Of those arrested, only 36 percent were black, more than a third had full-time jobs, and most claimed to shun political affiliation. What we witnessed in Los Angeles was the consequence of a lethal linkage of economic decline, cultural decay, and political lethargy in American life. Race was the visible catalyst, not the underlying cause.

INTRODUCTION

The meaning of the earthshaking events in Los Angeles is difficult to grasp because most of us remain trapped in the narrow framework of the dominant liberal and conservative views of race in America, which with its worn-out vocabulary leaves us intellectually debilitated, morally disempowered, and personally depressed. The astonishing disappearance of the event from public dialogue is testimony to just how painful and distressing a serious engagement with race is. Our truncated public discussions of race suppress the best of who and what we are as a people because they fail to confront the complexity of the issue in a candid and critical manner. The predictable pitting of liberals against conservatives, Great Society Democrats against self-help Republicans, reinforces intellectual parochialism and political paralysis.

The liberal notion that more government programs can solve racial problems is simplistic—precisely because it focuses *solely* on the economic dimension. And the conservative idea that what is needed is a change in the moral behavior of poor black urban dwellers (especially poor black men, who, they say, should stay married, support their children, and stop committing so much crime) highlights immoral actions while ignoring public responsibility for the immoral circumstances that haunt our fellow citizens.

The common denominator of these views of race is that each still sees black people as a "problem people," in the words of Dorothy I. Height, president of the National Council of Negro Women, rather than as fellow American citizens with problems. Her words echo the poignant "unasked question" of W. E. B. Du Bois, who, in *The Souls of Black Folk* (1903), wrote:

> They approach me in a half-hesitant sort of way, eye me curiously or compassionately, and then instead of saying directly, How does it feel to be a problem? they say, I know an excellent colored man in my town. . . . Do not these Southern outrages make your blood boil? At these I smile, or am interested, or reduce the boiling to a simmer, as the occasion may require. To the real question, How does it feel to be a problem? I answer seldom a word.

Nearly a century later, we confine discussions about race in America to the "problems" black people pose for whites rather than consider what this way of viewing black people reveals about us as a nation.

This paralyzing framework encourages liberals to relieve their guilty consciences by supporting public funds directed at "the problems"; but at the same time, reluctant to exercise principled criticism of black people, liberals deny them the freedom to err. Similarly, conservatives blame the "problems" on black people themselves—and thereby render black social misery invisible or unworthy of public attention.

Hence, for liberals, black people are to be "included" and "integrated" into "our" society and culture, while for conservatives they are to be "well behaved" and "worthy of acceptance" by "our" way of life. Both fail to see that the presence and predicaments of black people are neither additions to nor defections from American life, but rather *constitutive elements of that life.*

To engage in a serious discussion of race in America, we must begin not with the problems of black people but with the flaws of American society—flaws rooted in historic inequalities and longstanding cultural stereotypes. How we set up the terms for discussing racial issues shapes our perception and response to these issues. As long as black people are viewed as a "them," the burden falls on blacks to do all the "cultural" and "moral" work necessary for healthy race relations. The implication is that only certain Americans can define what it means to be American—and the rest must simply "fit in."

The emergence of strong black-nationalist sentiments among blacks, especially among young people, is a revolt against this sense of having to "fit in." The variety of black-nationalist ideologies, from the moderate views of Supreme Court Justice Clarence Thomas in his youth to those of Louis Farrakhan today, rest upon a fundamental truth: white America has been historically weak-willed in ensuring racial justice and has continued to resist fully accepting the humanity of blacks. As long as double standards and differential treatment abound—as long as the rap performer Ice-T is harshly condemned while former Los Angeles Police Chief Daryl F. Gates's antiblack comments are received in polite silence, as long as Dr. Leonard Jeffries's anti-Semitic statements are met with vitriolic outrage while presidential candidate Patrick J. Buchanan's anti-Semitism receives a genteel response—black nationalisms will thrive.

Afrocentrism, a contemporary species of black nationalism, is a gallant yet misguided attempt to define an African identity in a white society perceived to be hostile. It is gallant because it puts black doings and sufferings, not white anxieties and fears, at the center of discussion. It is misguided because—out of fear of cultural hybridization and through silence on the issue of class, retrograde views on black women, gay men, and lesbians, and a reluctance to link race to the common good—it reinforces the narrow discussions about race.

To establish a new framework, we need to begin with a frank acknowledgment of the basic humanness and Americanness of each of us. And we must acknowledge that as a people—*E Pluribus Unum*—we are on a slippery slope toward economic strife, social turmoil, and cultural chaos. If we go down, we go down together. The Los Angeles upheaval forced us to see not only that we are not connected in ways we would like to be but also, in a more profound sense, that this failure to connect binds us even more tightly together. The paradox of race in America is that our common destiny is more pronounced and imperiled precisely when our divisions are deeper. The Civil War and its legacy speak loudly here. And our divisions are growing deeper. Today, eighty-six percent of white suburban Americans live in neighborhoods that are less than 1 percent black, meaning that the prospects for the country depend largely on how its cities fare in the hands of a suburban electorate. There is no escape from our interracial interdependence, yet enforced racial hierarchy dooms us as a nation to collective paranoia and hysteria—the unmaking of any democratic order.

The verdict in the Rodney King case which sparked the incidents in Los Angeles was perceived to be wrong by the vast majority of Americans. But whites have often failed to acknowledge the widespread mistreatment of black people, especially black men, by law enforcement agencies, which helped ignite the spark. The verdict was merely the occasion for deep-seated rage to come to the surface. This rage is fed by the "silent" depression ravaging the country—in which real weekly wages of all American workers since 1973 have declined nearly 20 percent, while at the same time wealth has been upwardly distributed.

The exodus of stable industrial jobs from urban centers to cheaper labor markets here and abroad, housing policies that have created "chocolate cities and vanilla suburbs" (to use the popular musical artist George Clinton's memorable phrase), white fear of black crime, and the urban influx of poor Spanish-speaking and Asian immigrants—all have helped erode the tax base of American cities just as the federal government has cut its supports and programs. The result is unemployment, hunger, homelessness, and sickness for millions.

And a pervasive spiritual impoverishment grows. The collapse of meaning in life—the eclipse of hope and absence of love of self and others, the breakdown of family and neighborhood bonds—leads to the social deracination and cultural denudement of urban dwellers, especially children. We have created rootless, dangling people with little link to the supportive networks—family, friends, school—that sustain some sense of purpose in life. We have witnessed the collapse of the spiritual communities that in the past helped Americans face despair, disease, and death and that transmit through the generations dignity and decency, excellence and elegance.

The result is lives of what we might call "random nows," of fortuitous and fleeting moments preoccupied with "getting over"—with acquiring pleasure, property, and power by any means necessary. (This is not what Malcolm X meant by this famous phrase.) Post-modern culture is more and more a market culture dominated by gangster mentalities and self-destructive wantonness. This culture engulfs all of us—yet its impact on the disadvantaged is devastating, resulting in extreme violence in everyday life. Sexual violence against women and homicidal assaults by young black men on one another are only the most obvious signs of this empty quest for pleasure, property, and power.

Last, this rage is fueled by a political atmosphere in which images, not ideas, dominate, where politicians spend more time raising money than debating issues. The functions of parties have been displaced by public polls, and politicians behave less as thermostats that determine the climate of opinion than as thermometers registering the public mood. American politics has been rocked by an unleashing of greed among opportunistic public officials—who have followed the lead of their counterparts in the private sphere, where, as of 1989, 1 percent of the population owned 37 percent of the wealth and 10 percent of the population owned 86 percent of the wealth—leading to a profound cynicism and pessimism among the citizenry.

And given the way in which the Republican Party since 1968 has appealed to popular xenophobic images—playing the black, female, and homophobic cards to realign the electorate along race, sex, and sexual-orientation lines—it is no surprise that the notion that we are all part of one garment of destiny is discredited. Appeals to special interests rather than to public interests reinforce this polarization. The Los Angeles upheaval was an expression of utter fragmentation by a powerless citizenry that includes not just the poor but all of us.

What is to be done? How do we capture a new spirit and vision to meet the challenges of the post-industrial city, post-modern culture, and post-party politics?

First, we must admit that the most valuable sources for help, hope, and power consist of ourselves and our common history. As in the ages of Lincoln, Roosevelt, and King, we must look to new frameworks and languages to understand our multilayered crisis and overcome our deep malaise.

Second, we must focus our attention on the public square—the common good that undergirds our national and global destinies. The vitality of any public square ultimately depends on how much we *care* about the quality of our lives together. The neglect of our public infrastructure, for example—our water and sewage systems, bridges, tunnels, highways, subways, and streets—reflects not only our myopic economic policies, which impede productivity, but also the low priority we place on our common life.

The tragic plight of our children clearly reveals our deep disregard for public well-being. About one out of every five children in this country lives in poverty, including one out of every two black children and two out of every five Hispanic children. Most of our children—neglected by overburdened parents and bombarded by the market values of profit-hungry corporations—are ill-equipped to live lives of spiritual and cultural quality. Faced with these facts, how do we expect ever to constitute a vibrant society?

One essential step is some form of large-scale public intervention to ensure access to basic social goods—housing, food, health care, education, child care, and jobs. We must invigorate the common good with a mixture of government, business, and labor that does not follow any existing blueprint. After a period in which the private sphere has been sacralized and the public square gutted, the temptation is to make a fetish of the public square. We need to resist such dogmatic swings.

Last, the major challenge is to meet the need to generate new leadership. The paucity of courageous leaders—so apparent in the response to the events in Los Angeles—requires that we look beyond the same elites and voices that recycle the older frameworks. We need leaders—neither saints nor sparkling television personalities—who can situate themselves within a larger historical narrative of this country and our world, who can grasp the complex dynamics of our peoplehood and imagine a future grounded in the best of our past, yet who are attuned to the frightening obstacles that now perplex us. Our ideals of freedom, democracy, and equality must be invoked to invigorate all of us, especially the landless, propertyless, and luckless. Only a visionary leadership that can motivate "the better angels of our nature," as Lincoln said, and activate possibilities for a freer, more efficient, and stable America—only that leadership deserves cultivation and support.

This new leadership must be grounded in grass-roots organizing that highlights democratic accountability. Whoever *our* leaders will be as we approach the twenty-first century, their challenge will be to help Americans determine whether a genuine multiracial democracy can be created and sustained in an era of global economy and a moment of xenophobic frenzy.

Let us hope and pray that the vast intelligence, imagination, humor, and courage of Americans will not fail us. Either we learn a new language of empathy and compassion, or the fire this time will consume us all.

8.2 PEGGY McINTOSH

White Privilege: Unpacking the Invisible Knapsack

Peggy McIntosh is associate director of the Wellesley College Center for Research on Women and cofounder of the Rocky Mountain Women's Institute. Additionally, she is founder and codirector of the national S.E.E.D. (Seeking Educational Equity and Diversity) Project on Inclusive Curriculum. In these projects, she works internationally with college and school faculty in creating gender-fair and multicultural curricula.

Perhaps McIntosh's most influential work is her paper "White Privilege and Male Privilege: A Personal Account of Coming to See Correspondences Through Work in Women's Studies." Her most well-known contributions have come in the pointing-out of the idea of *privilege*, or that set of "taken-for-granted" practices that members of the dominant gender, race, and sexual orientation within the United States seem to have in their lives. The following selection is from an excerpt of "White Privilege and Male Privilege" that was published in the July/August issue of *Peace and Freedom*. In it, McIntosh straightforwardly lists what she calls privileges of being white and heterosexual in the United States. She asserts that these are privileges that are not earned but merely exist by virtue of one's being born white into U.S. society. Although her list is straightforward, McIntosh argues that it is difficult for white heterosexuals to recognize these as unearned privileges that only they are able to receive. She explains that whites are not taught to recognize their own privileges, and they thus deny the resulting advantages that they receive in society. This set of privileges is institutionalized and embedded within society, concludes McIntosh.

Key Concept: whites' privileges in U.S. society

*T*hrough work to bring materials from Women's Studies into the rest of the curriculum, I have often noticed men's unwillingness to grant that they are over-privileged, even though they may grant that women are disadvantaged. They may say they will work to improve women's status, in the society, the university, or the curriculum, but they can't or won't support the idea of lessening men's. Denials which amount to taboos surround the subject of advantages which men gain from women's disadvantages. These denials protect male privilege from being fully acknowledged, lessened or ended.

Thinking through unacknowledged male privilege as a phenomenon, I realized that since hierarchies in our society are interlocking, there was most likely a phenomenon of white privilege which was similarly denied and protected. As a white person, I realized I had been taught about racism as something which puts others at a disadvantage, but had been taught not to see one of its corollary aspects, white privilege, which puts me at an advantage.

I think whites are carefully taught not to recognize white privilege, as males are taught not to recognize male privilege. So I have begun in an untutored way to ask what it is like to have white privilege. I have come to see white privilege as an invisible package of unearned assets which I can count on cashing in each day, but about which I was 'meant' to remain oblivious. White privilege is like an invisible weightless knapsack of special provisions, maps, passports, codebooks, visas, clothes, tools and blank checks.

Describing white privilege makes one newly accountable. As we in Women's Studies work to reveal male privilege and ask men to give up some of their power, so one who writes about having white privilege must ask, "Having described it, what will I do to lessen or end it?"

After I realized the extent to which men work from a base of unacknowledged privilege, I understood that much of their oppressiveness was unconscious. Then I remembered the frequent charges from women of color that white women whom they encounter are oppressive. I began to understand why we are justly seen as oppressive, even when we don't see ourselves that way. I began to count the ways in which I enjoy unearned skin privilege and have been conditioned into oblivion about its existence.

My schooling gave me no training in seeing myself as an oppressor, as an unfairly advantaged person, or as a participant in a damaged culture. I was taught to see myself as an individual whose moral state depended on her individual moral will. My schooling followed the pattern my colleague Elizabeth Minnich has pointed out: whites are taught to think of their lives as morally neutral, normative, and average, and also ideal, so that when we work to benefit others, this is seen as work which will allow "them" to be more like "us."

I decided to try to work on myself at least by identifying some of the daily effects of white privilege in my life. I have chosen those conditions which I think in my case *attach somewhat more to skin-color privilege* than to class, religion, ethnic status, or geographical location, though of course all these other factors are intricately intertwined. As far as I can see, my African American co-workers, friends and acquaintances with whom I come into daily or frequent contact in this particular time, place, and line of work cannot count on most of these conditions.

1. I can if I wish arrange to be in the company of people of my race most of the time.
2. If I should need to move, I can be pretty sure of renting or purchasing housing in an area which I can afford and in which I would want to live.

3. I can be pretty sure that my neighbors in such a location will be neutral or pleasant to me.
4. I can go shopping alone most of the time, pretty well assured that I will not be followed or harassed.
5. I can turn on the television or open to the front page of the paper and see people of my race widely represented.
6. When I am told about our national heritage or about "civilization," I am shown that people of my color made it what it is.
7. I can be sure that my children will be given curricular materials that testify to the existence of their race.
8. If I want to, I can be pretty sure of finding a publisher for this piece on white privilege.
9. I can go into a music shop and count on finding the music of my race represented, into a supermarket and find the staple foods which fit with my cultural traditions, into a hairdresser's shop and find someone who can cut my hair.
10. Whether I use checks, credit cards, or cash, I can count on my skin color not to work against the appearance of financial reliability.
11. I can arrange to protect my children most of the time from people who might not like them.
12. I can swear, or dress in second hand clothes, or not answer letters, without having people attribute these choices to the bad morals, the poverty, or the illiteracy of my race.
13. I can speak in public to a powerful male group without putting my race on trial.
14. I can do well in a challenging situation without being called a credit to my race.
15. I am never asked to speak for all the people of my racial group.
16. I can remain oblivious of the language and customs of persons of color who constitute the world's majority without feeling in my culture any penalty for such oblivion.
17. I can criticize our government and talk about how much I fear its policies and behavior without being seen as a cultural outsider.
18. I can be pretty sure that if I ask to talk to "the person in charge," I will be facing a person of my race.
19. If a traffic cop pulls me over or if the IRS audits my tax return, I can be sure I haven't been singled out because of my race.
20. I can easily buy posters, postcards, picture books, greeting cards, dolls, toys, and children's magazines featuring people of my race.
21. I can go home from most meetings of organizations I belong to feeling somewhat tied in, rather than isolated, out-of-place, outnumbered, unheard, held at a distance, or feared.
22. I can take a job with an affirmative action employer without having co-workers on the job suspect that I got it because of race.
23. I can choose public accommodation without fearing that people of my race cannot get in or will be mistreated in the places I have chosen.
24. I can be sure that if I need legal or medical help, my race will not work against me.

25. If my day, week, or year is going badly, I need not ask of each negative episode or situation whether it has racial overtones.
26. I can choose blemish cover or bandages in "flesh" color and have them more or less match my skin.

I repeatedly forgot each of the realizations on this list until I wrote it down. For me white privilege has turned out to be an elusive and fugitive subject. The pressure to avoid it is great, for in facing it I must give up the myth of meritocracy. If these things are true, this is not such a free country; one's life is not what one makes it; many doors open for certain people through no virtues of their own.

In unpacking this invisible knapsack of white privilege, I have listed conditions of daily experience which I once took for granted. Nor did I think of any of these perquisites as bad for the holder. I now think that we need a more finely differentiated taxonomy of privilege, for some of these varieties are only what one would want for everyone in a just society, and others give licence to be ignorant, oblivious, arrogant and destructive.

I see a pattern running through the matrix of white privilege, a pattern of assumptions which were passed on to me as a white person. There was one main piece of cultural turf; it was my own turf, and I was among those who could control the turf. *My skin color was an asset for any move I was educated to want to make.* I could think of myself as belonging in major ways, and making social systems work for me. I could freely disparage, fear, neglect, or be oblivious to anything outside of the dominant cultural forms. Being of the main culture, I could also criticize it fairly freely.

In proportion as my racial group was being made confident, comfortable, and oblivious, other groups were likely being made inconfident, uncomfortable, and alienated. Whiteness protected me from many kinds of hostility, distress, and violence, which I was being subtly trained to visit in turn upon people of color.

For this reason, the word "privilege" now seems to me misleading. We usually think of privilege as being a favored state, whether earned or conferred by birth or luck. Yet some of the conditions I have described here work to systematically overempower certain groups. Such privilege simply *confers dominance* because of one's race or sex.

I want, then, to distinguish between earned strength and unearned power conferred systemically. Power from unearned privilege can look like strength when it is in fact permission to escape or to dominate. But not all of the privileges on my list are inevitably damaging. Some, like the expectation that neighbors will be decent to you, or that your race will not count against you in court, should be the norm in a just society. Others, like the privilege to ignore less powerful people, distort the humanity of the holders as well as the ignored groups.

We might at least start by distinguishing between positive advantages which we can work to spread, and negative types of advantages which unless rejected will always reinforce our present hierarchies. For example, the feeling that one belongs within the human circle, as Native Americans say, should not be seen as privilege for a few. Ideally it is an *unearned entitlement*. At present, since only a few have it, it is an *unearned advantage* for them. This paper results from a process of coming to see that some of the power which I originally saw as attendant on being a human being in the U.S. consisted in *unearned advantage* and *conferred dominance*.

I have met very few men who are truly distressed about systemic, unearned male advantage and conferred dominance. And so one question for me and others like me is whether we will be like them, or whether we will get truly distressed, even outraged, about unearned race advantage and conferred dominance and if so, what we will do to lessen them. In any case, we need to do more work in identifying how they actually affect our daily lives. Many, perhaps most, of our white students in the U.S. think that racism doesn't affect them because they are not people of color; they do not see "whiteness" as a racial identity. In addition, since race and sex are not the only advantaging systems at work, we need similarly to examine the daily experience of having age advantage, or ethnic advantage, or physical ability, or advantage related to nationality, religion, or sexual orientation.

Difficulties and dangers surrounding the task of finding parallels are many. Since racism, sexism, and heterosexism are not the same, the advantaging associated with them should not be seen as the same. In addition, it is hard to disentangle aspects of unearned advantage which rest more on social class, economic class, race, religion, sex and ethnic identity than on other factors. Still, all of the oppressions are interlocking, as the Combahee River Collective Statement of 1977 continues to remind us eloquently.

One factor seems clear about all of the interlocking oppressions. They take both active forms which we can see and embedded forms which as a member of the dominant group one is taught not to see. In my class and place, I did not see myself as a racist because I was taught to recognize racism only in individual acts of meanness by members of my group, never in invisible systems conferring unsought racial dominance on my group from birth.

Disapproving of the systems won't be enough to change them. I was taught to think that racism could end if white individuals changed their attitudes. [But] a "white" skin in the United States opens many doors for whites whether or not we approve of the way dominance has been conferred on us. Individual acts can palliate, but cannot end, these problems.

To redesign social systems we need first to acknowledge their colossal unseen dimensions. The silences and denials surrounding privilege are the key political tool here. They keep the thinking about equality or equity incomplete, protecting unearned advantage and conferred dominance by making these taboo subjects. Most talk by whites about equal opportunity seems to me now to be about equal opportunity to try to get into a position of dominance while denying that *systems* of dominance exist.

It seems to me that obliviousness about white advantage, like obliviousness about male advantage, is kept strongly inculturated in the United States so as to maintain the myth of meritocracy, the myth that democratic choice is equally available to all. Keeping most people unaware that freedom of confident action is there for just a small number of people props up those in power, and serves to keep power in the hands of the same groups that have most of it already.

Though systemic change takes many decades, there are pressing questions for me and I imagine for some others like me if we raise our daily consciousness on the perquisites of being light-skinned. What will we do with such knowledge? As we know from watching men, it is an open question whether we will choose to use unearned advantage to weaken hidden systems of advantage, and whether we will use any of our arbitrarily-awarded power to try to reconstruct power systems on a broader base.

8.3 CHRISTINE SLEETER

White Racism

Christine Sleeter clearly states that whites approach the idea of racism differently than do people of color. Specifically, whites are silent about racism; they don't talk about racism, and they try to deflect attention away from racism or any discussion of it. White racism is white supremacy, according to Sleeter. She defines it as the institutionalized set of rules and policies, as well as individual sets of beliefs that have given white people control over the power and wealth of America. She believes that this helps to explain why whites do not want to acknowledge the prevalence and power of racism or its impact on society and individuals. Sleeter goes on to say that for whites, multicultural education is about developing positive feelings toward others, with no mention of how racism can be reduced by dismantling the white individual and institutional racism that exists in the United States.

Sleeter is coordinator of the Masters of Arts in Education program at California State University, Monterey Bay. She has written numerous books and articles on multicultural education, with a special emphasis on multicultural education as it relates to teacher education, the social context of multicultural education, white racism, and critical pedagogy. The following selection is from her article "White Racism," *Multicultural Education* (Spring 1994). Sleeter has also edited books for the SUNY Press series The Social Context of Education.

Key Concept: whites' silence about racism

NAMING OUR SILENCE ABOUT WHITE RACISM

With precious few exceptions, White people do not talk about White racism. Instead, we talk about group differences, very often in ways that simplify and devalue others while rendering Whiteness itself as invisible, or "normal." I first noticed White silence about racism about 15 years ago, although I was not able at the time to name it as such. I recall realizing, after having shared many meals with African American friends while teaching in Seattle, that racism and race-related issues were fairly common topics of dinner-table conversation, which African Americans talked about quite openly. It struck me that I could not think of a single instance in which racism had been a topic of dinner-table conversation in White contexts. Race-related issues sometimes came up, but not *racism.* For example, I could remember short discussions about what one would do if a Black family moved next door, or about a very bigotted relative, or about policies such as desegregation or immigration. In these discussions, what was viewed as problematic was people of color themselves, changes in policies that relate to race, or outspoken bigots.

Recently, I was giving a talk about multicultural education to a group of predominantly White teachers at an inservice session. My talk centered around persistent racial, class, and gender disparities in access to various resources such as jobs and housing. My main recommendation to the teachers was that we engage directly in reciprocal dialog with people of color and poor people in our own communities, in order to decide what kind of social system and what kind of schools we actually want, then begin to work collaboratively. I argued that White professionals cannot shape the vision of a multicultural society by ourselves, although we tend to use our status as professionals to assume exactly that role; shaping a vision of multicultural education in our own communities has to be done collaboratively, and must address social inequalities. Afterward, a White teacher approached me with a very puzzled expression on her face, and commented in a rather perplexed tone of voice that she had never heard multicultural education discussed that way. At least she reacted verbally to it; most of the audience simply applauded politely, then went on to the next session. This incident struck me because, although my discussion of racism was not as direct as it might have been, I was still framing multicultural education in a way the White teachers had not even thought about and had difficulty comprehending.

At a recent women's studies conference, participants were asked to divide into racially homogeneous groups to compile a list of the main concerns facing their group. I was in the European-American group, and it floundered. Participants discussed mainly family history and ethnic immigrant background. I suggested that we might address our White racism, but that theme was not taken up. The group tried to place itself on a parallel status with the other racial groups, defining our problems as comparable to theirs. Our Whiteness seemed to be invisible to us—we could discuss our religious, ethnic, and social class differences, but not our common Whiteness or the privileges we gain from White racism (see R. Dyer, "White," *Screen*, 1988).

I suspect that our privileges and silences are invisible to us partly because numerically we constitute the majority of this nation and collectively control a large portion of the nation's resources and media, which enable us to surround ourselves with our own varied experiences and to buffer ourselves from the experiences, and the pain and rage of people of color. But even still, White people do not live in a vacuum; Toni Morrison *(Playing in the dark: Whiteness and the literary imagination,* Harvard University Press, 1992) asks how Whites have managed *not* to see the "thunderous, theatrical presence" of African people in the United States (p. 13). I believe that we cling to filters that screen out what people of color try to tell us because we fear losing material and psychological advantages that we enjoy. Further, we have not yet collectively created a compelling self-identity and sense of meaning that does not entail ravenous materialism and acquisition of power over others.

By White racism (or White supremacy), I am referring to the system of rules, procedures, and tacit beliefs that result in Whites collectively maintaining control over the wealth and power of the nation and the world. For at least 500 years, Europeans and their descendants have taken huge amounts of land, wealth, labor, and other resources from peoples of color around the world. With the exceptions of small, sporadic attempts at restitution, such as that offered belatedly to Japanese American concentration camp survivors, White Americans have never returned or repaid what we have taken. We seem to have agreed tacitly to continue to reap the benefits of the past, and not to talk about it, except largely in ways that render present race relations as legitimate. Current data illustrate the continued advantages Whites enjoy. For example, a recent United Nations report ranks White Americans as having the highest standard of living in the world; Black Americans' living standard ranks 31st and Hispanic Americans' ranks 35th. Of the six nations with the highest living standard, five are predominantly White (R. Wright, "Living standard in U. S. diverse: U. N.," *Kenosha News*, 1993).

As we grow up, Whites become aware that we tend to have more than people of color, and we learn to accept and justify our own position. Until about 40 years ago, it was acceptable in White society to talk openly about presumed shortcomings of groups of color, and the presumed superior intelligence, culture, and morality of Whites. Not all Whites accepted racist beliefs, of course, but they were widely enough held to be openly verbalized.

With the Civil Rights movement, people of color challenged the morality of racism successfully enough that most Whites no longer found it acceptable to voice racist beliefs. So, we simply stopped talking openly about race relations. In general, Whites seem to believe that racism was gone once we eliminated Jim Crow laws, created an ostensibly colorblind legal system (Williams, 1991), and stopped openly saying negative things about groups of color. We maintain a worldview, however, that continues to uphold our racial privileges. We are willing to critique the psychological impact of slavery on Blacks, but not its impact on ourselves. In addition, we continue to obliterate from our historic consciousness information about racism; for example, I have learned to expect only about half of my White teacher education students to have ever heard of Jim Crow laws. ("What, then, was the Civil Rights movement about?" "Well—I'm not sure, I guess.") Groups of color have hoped that we would genuinely accept them as equals if we appreciated the intellectual sophistication of their cultural creations. Too often, however, our response is to experience "other" cultures as a tourist or colonialist would, and tacitly accept White supremacy....

A common White understanding of ethnicity, in fact, "emerged into prominence during a period when the civil rights movement was most active and racial minorities were challenging in basic respects the fairness of the American system" (R. D. Alba, *Ethnic identity: The transformation of White America*, Yale University Press, 1990, p. 317). White society felt threatened, and attempted to reframe ethnicity and race within our own worldview and experience. "The thrust of European-American identity is to defend the individualistic view of the American system, because it portrays the system as open to those who are willing to work hard and pull themselves over barriers of poverty and discrimination" (Alba, p. 317).

We evade discussion of racism because we do not want to give up the lifestyle, privileges, and resources that we control, and that are built on those our ancestors took from others. The very locations on which our homes rest should rightfully belong to Indian nations. Some of us are from families whose wealth was generated partly by slave labor; even if our own familial ancestors did not own slaves or exploit Mexican or Asian laborers, they still did have access to jobs, education, and other opportunities from which Whites barred people of color. To open up a discussion of White racism challenges the legitimacy of White peoples' very lives. Once we are able to say that aloud, we may be able to create a new White discourse that can contribute to a vision of a just future that actually includes all of us, and an agenda for action. But I do not believe we can do that without fully confronting the related layers and processes of White racism.

White people know a great deal about how racism works because we have observed White people intimately all our lives. By examining our own experiences critically, we are uniquely positioned to contribute insights into racism. There are many dimensions of White racism that we need to examine, such as the use of language to frame racial issues in ways that obscure racism (see T. van Dijk, *Elite discourse and racism*, Sage Publications, 1993), connections between White racism and capitalism, roots of White fears and psychological insecurities, the impact of colonialism and slavery on the White psyche, shifts over time in the forms racism takes and the way it is discussed, and factors that differentiate anti-racist Whites from the rest of us. Below I give one example of the kind of analysis in which I believe we should engage.

WHITE RACIAL BONDING

In general, Whites stick together on common definitions of issues that involve race relations, and behave accordingly. We live largely with other Whites, socialize mainly with Whites, consume White media, vote for Whites, and so forth. Although today most Whites profess colorblindness and support for equal opportunity, in fact we behave in a very race-conscious manner. What are some of the processes we use to build and maintain racial solidarity? ...

We are all familiar with some of the more overt ways Whites socialize Whites to accept racism (such as TV stereotypes and expressions of prejudice). But following this experience, I began to pay attention to what I will call "White racial bonding" processes White people engage in everyday. By "racial bonding," I mean simply interactions that have the purpose of affirming a common stance on race-related issues, legitimatizing particular interpretations of groups of color, and drawing conspiratorial we-they boundaries. These communication patterns take forms such as inserts into conversations, race-related "asides" in conversations, strategic eye-contact, and jokes. Often they are so short and sub-tle that they may seem relatively harmless. I used to regard such utterances as annoying expressions of prejudice or ignorance, but that seems to underesti-mate their power to demarcate racial lines and communicate solidarity.

Inserts into conversations may go like this. Two White people are talking ca-sually about various things. One comments, "This community is starting to change. A lot of Mexicans have been moving in." This comment serves as an invitation to White bonding, in which the other person is being asked to agree with the implication that Mexicans create problems and do not belong here, although this has not been said directly. The other person could respond very simply, "Yeah, that's a bummer," affirming the first person's viewpoint; this could be the end of a successful exchange. Or, the other person could com-plain about Mexicans, the ensuing conversation taking the form of Mexican-bashing. In either case, both parties will have communicated agreement that there is a linkage between "Mexicans" and "problems," and will have defined themselves as "insiders" in a network of people who view it as acceptable to articulate a negative valuation of Mexicans. Further, they will have commu-nicated the acceptability of supporting policies limiting Mexican access to the community. Even silence can serve as tacit acquiescence for the purpose of win-ning approval. P. Williams (*The alchemy of race and rights*, Harvard University Press, 1991, p. 126–8) describes in exquisite detail such an exchange in which she participated passively.

How do I know this kind of exchange serves the purpose of racial bond-ing? I know because if I do not give the desired response, the other person very often presses the issue much more explicitly; I also may never hear from the other person again (including relatives). For example, if I change the subject, it usually reappears but more forcefully ("Mexicans bring gang problems, you know; I'm really concerned about the future of this community."). Sometimes I give a response I know the other person is not seeking such as, "Yes, I'm really pleased to see this community becoming more multicultural, I've been working on my Spanish." More often than not, the other person responds with a lecture on problems associated with Mexican American people, and the misguidedness of my judgment. I am usually uncomfortable when people who do not know me well ask what I teach; quite often responses such as "multicultural education" or "urban education" provoke uninvited lectures on race relations, or on their own beliefs as a White liberal (hoping for validation that we share a common viewpoint).

These kinds of interactions seem to serve the purpose of defining racial lines, and inviting individuals to either declare their solidarity or mark them-selves as deviant. Depending on degree of deviance, one runs the risk of losing the other individual's approval, friendship, and company. (This usually occurs in the form of feeling "uncomfortable" around the deviant White person.) Many Whites who do not support racist beliefs, actions, or policies, but who also do not want to risk breaking bonds with other Whites, simply remain silent.

Consideration of White racial bonding has several implications. No White person is exempt from pressures from other White people to "fit in," with the price of conformity to a racial norm very often being approval and friendship. While active anti-racist Whites may not be affected by such processes, I would hypothesize that it does affect Whites who are uncertain about their own racial beliefs and loyalties. J. E. Helms (editor of *Black and white racial identity: Theory, research, and practice,* Greenwood Press, 1990), for example, posits a stage of "reintegration" in White racial identity development in which the White person, after experiencing challenges to her or his previous beliefs about race, returns to those prior, more comfortable and socially acceptable (in White circles) beliefs (see also B. D. Tatum, "Talking about race, learning about racism: The application of racial identity development theory in the classroom," *Harvard Educational Review,* 1992). We all need affective bonds with people. Given the segregation of our society, the strongest bonds are usually with members of our own race. In order to mitigate effects of White racial bonding, potential multicultural education advocates need to develop deep personal bonds with White anti-racists and people of color.

CHAPTER 9 Identity Development

9.1 JEAN S. PHINNEY

Ethnic Identity in Adolescents and Adults: Review of Research

The study of ethnic identity development seeks to answer the question, "How do we come to know who we are ethnically?" In this selection, Jean S. Phinney provides a review of over 70 articles on the topic of ethnic identity development, in particular on the ethnic identity of minority adolescents and adults. Phinney points out that the development of one's identity is not a static process, but rather is constantly undergoing change throughout one's lifetime. According to a stage model presented in the following selection, individuals may go through a stage in which they have not thought much about or examined their ethnic identity. Some individuals may also go through a time when they explore their identity and may finally come to a deeper understanding of what their ethnicity means to their identity.

Phinney is a professor of psychology at California State University, Los Angeles. She has focused much of her research on the development of ethnic and bicultural identity among adolescents. Her interests lie in identifying the factors that influence the development of psychological well-being among minority youth. She is a recipient of a research grant from the National

Institutes of Health, with which she has developed a measure of identity development that is currently being used with adolescents around the world.

Key Concept: review of ethnic identity development

*T*he growing proportion of minority group members in the United States and other Western countries has resulted in an increasing concern with issues of pluralism, discrimination, and racism in the media. However, psychological research on the impact of these issues on the individual is uneven. Most of the research dealing with psychological aspects of contact between racial or ethnic groups has focused on attitudes toward racial or ethnic groups other than one's own and particularly on stereotyping, prejudice, and discrimination. The emphasis has been on attitudes of members of the majority or dominant group toward minority group members; this is a research area of great importance in face of the daily evidence of ethnic tensions and racial violence.

A far less studied aspect of diversity has been the psychological relationship of ethnic and racial minority group members with their own group, a topic dealt with under the broad term *ethnic identity*. The study of attitudes about one's own ethnicity has been of little interest to members of the dominant group, and little attention has been paid by mainstream, generally White researchers to the psychological aspects of being a minority group member in a diverse society

Recent concern with ethnic identity has derived in part from the ethnic revitalization movements in the 1960s. Growing awareness in society of differences associated with ethnic group membership (e.g, lower educational and occupational attainment) has been accompanied by social movements leading to increased ethnic consciousness and pride (Laosa, 1984). Attitudes toward one's ethnicity are central to the psychological functioning of those who live in societies where their group and its culture are at best poorly represented (politically, economically, and in the media) and are at worst discriminated against or even attacked verbally and physically; the concept of ethnic identity provides a way of understanding the need to assert oneself in the face of threats to one's identity (Weinreich, 1983). The psychological importance of ethnic identity is attested to by numerous literary writings of ethnic group members about the struggle to understand their ethnicity (e.g, Du Bois, 1983; Kingston, 1976; Malcolm X, 1970; Rodriguez, 1982).

The issue of ethnic identity has also been brought to the fore by changing demographics, including differential birthrates and increasing numbers of immigrants and refugees throughout the world. Projections suggest that by the mid-1990s, minority youth will constitute more than 30% of the 15- to 25-year-olds in the United States (Wetzel, 1987). The topic not only has important implications within psychology (e.g., Ekstrand, 1986) but also has broad political significance. In response, Canada has developed an explicit policy of multiculturalism and supports continuing study of the issue (Berry, Kalin, & Taylor, 1977). Many European countries will be dealing for years to come with struggles of ethnic minorities to maintain or assert their identities (Kaplan, 1989).

Within the social sciences, many writers have asserted that ethnic identity is crucial to the self-concept and psychological functioning of ethnic group members (e.g., Gurin & Epps, 1975; Maldonado, 1975). Critical issues include the degree and quality of involvement that is maintained with one's own culture and heritage; ways of responding to and dealing with the dominant group's often disparaging views of their group; and the impact of these factors on psychological well-being. These issues have been addressed conceptually from a variety of perspectives (e.g., Alba, 1985; Arce, 1981; Atkinson, Morten, & Sue, 1983; Dashefsky, 1976; DeVos & Romanucci-Ross, 1982; Frideres & Goldenberg, 1982; Mendelberg, 1986; Ostrow, 1977; Parham, 1989; Staiano, 1980; Tajfel, 1978, 1981; Weinreich, 1988; Yancey, Ericksen, & Juliani, 1976; Zinn, 1980).

However, the theoretical writing far outweighs empirical research. Most of the empirical work on ethnic identity has concentrated on young children, with a focus on minority children's racial misidentification or preference for White stimulus figures. This work has been widely discussed and reviewed (e.g., Aboud, 1987; Banks, 1976; Brand, Ruiz, & Padilla, 1974) and is not addressed here. Far less work has been done on ethnic identity beyond childhood and particularly the transition from childhood to adulthood; this gap has been recently noted (Kagitcibasi & Berry, 1989). In published studies on ethnic identity in adolescents and adults, researchers have generally focused on single groups and have used widely discrepant definitions and measures of ethnic identity, which makes generalizations and comparisons across studies difficult and ambiguous. The findings are often inconclusive or contradictory

The topic is of sufficient importance to warrant serious research attention, but in order for the research to yield useful and meaningful results, greater conceptual and methodological clarity is needed. The primary goal of this article is to provide such clarity through a review of the empirical literature on ethnic identity in adolescents and adults. I describe the definitions and conceptual frameworks that have guided empirical research, the way in which the construct has been defined and measured, and the empirical findings. The article concludes with recommendations for future research....

DEFINITIONS OF ETHNIC IDENTITY

Ethnic identity was defined in many ways in the research reviewed. The fact that there is no widely agreed-on definition of ethnic identity is indicative of confusion about the topic. A surprisingly number of the articles reviewed (about two thirds) provided no explicit definition of the construct. The definitions that were given reflected quite different understandings or emphases regarding what is meant by *ethnic identity*.

In a number of articles, ethnic identity was defined as the ethnic component of social identity, as defined by Tajfel (1981): "that part of an individual's self-concept which derives from his knowledge of his membership of a social group (or groups) together with the value and emotional significance attached to that membership" (p.255). Some writers considered self-identification the key aspect; others emphasized feelings of belonging and commitment (Singh, 1977; Ting-Toomey, 1981; Tzuriel & Klein, 1977), the sense of shared values and attitudes (White & Burke, 1987, p. 311), or attitudes toward one's group (e.g., Parham & Helms, 1981; Teske & Nelson, 1973). In contrast to the focus by these writers on attitudes and feelings, some definitions emphasized the cultural aspects of ethnic identity: for example, language, behavior, values, and knowledge of ethnic group history (e.g., Rogler, Cooney, & Ortiz, 1980). The active role of the individual in developing an ethnic identity was suggested by several writers who saw it as a dynamic product that is achieved rather than simply given (Caltabiano, 1984; Hogg, Abrams, & Patel, 1987; Simic, 1987).

In summary researchers appeared to share a broad general understanding of ethnic identity, but the specific aspects that they emphasized differed widely These differences are related to the diversity in how researchers have conceptualized ethnic identity and in the questions they have sought to answer; these issues are reviewed in the next section.

CONCEPTUAL FRAMEWORKS FOR THE STUDY OF ETHNIC IDENTITY

About a quarter of the studies suggested no theoretical framework, but most of the studies were based on one of three broad perspectives: social identity theory, as presented by social psychologists; acculturation and culture conflict, as studied by social psychologists, sociologists, or anthropologists; and identity formation, drawn from psychoanalytic views and from developmental and counseling psychology. There is considerable overlap among the frameworks on which the studies were based, as well as great variation in the extent to which the relevant framework or theory was discussed and applied to the research. However, these three approaches provide a background for understanding the empirical research.

Ethnic Identity and Social Identity Theory

Much of the research on ethnic identity has been conducted within the framework of social identity as conceptualized by social psychologists. One of the earliest statements of the importance of social identity was made by Lewin (1948), who asserted that individuals need a firm sense of group identification in order to maintain a sense of well-being. This idea was developed in considerable detail in the social identity theory of Tajfel and Turner (1979). According [to] the theory, simply being a member of a group provides individuals with a sense of belonging that contributes to a positive self-concept.

However, ethnic groups present a special case of group identity (Tajfel, 1978). If the dominant group in a society holds the traits or characteristics of an ethnic group in low esteem, then ethnic group members are potentially faced with a negative social identity. Identifying with a low-status group may result in low self-regard (Hogg, Abrams, & Patel, 1987; Ullah, 1985). An extensive literature deals explicitly with the notion of "self-hatred" among disparaged ethnic groups, generally with reference to Black Americans (Banks, 1976; V. Gordon, 1980). Much of the research reviewed was concerned with this issue: that is, whether or to what extent membership in, or identification with, an ethnic group with lower status in society is related to a poorer self-concept. A number of studies addressed these issues (Grossman, Wirt, & David, 1985; Houston, 1984; Paul & Fischer, 1980; Tzuriel & Klein, 1977; White & Burke, 1987); the specific findings are discussed later in the article.

Tajfel (1978) asserted that members of low-status groups seek to improve their status in various ways. Individuals may seek to leave the group by "passing" as members of the dominant group, but this solution may have negative psychological consequences. Furthermore, this solution is not available to individuals who are racially distinct and are categorized by others as ethnic group members. Alternative solutions are to develop pride in one's group (Cross, 1978), to reinterpret characteristics deemed "inferior" so that they do not appear inferior (Bourhis, Giles, & Tajfel, 1973), and to stress the distinctiveness of one's own group (Christian, Gadfield, Giles, & Taylor, 1976: Hutnik, 1985).

Social identity theory also addresses the issue of potential problems resulting from participation in two cultures. Both Lewin (1948) and Tajfel (1978) discussed the likelihood that identification with two different groups can be problematic for identity formation in ethnic group members because of the conflicts in attitudes, values, and behaviors between their own and the majority group (Der-Karabetian, 1980; Rosenthal & Cichello, 1986; Salgado de Snyder, Lopez, & Padilla, 1982; Zak, 1973). The issue in this case is whether individuals must choose between two conflicting identities or can establish a bicultural ethnic identity and, if so, whether that is adaptive.

A distinct but related approach to ethnic identity is based on symbolic interactionism and identity theory (Stryker, 1980). Research in this framework emphasizes the importance of shared understandings about the meaning of one's ethnic identity, which derive both from one's own group and from a "countergroup" (White & Burke, 1987).

Acculturation as a Framework for Studying Ethnic Identity

Ethnic identity is meaningful only in situations in which two or more ethnic groups are in contact over a period of time. In an ethnically or racially homogeneous society, ethnic identity is a virtually meaningless concept. The broad area of research that has dealt with groups in contact is the acculturation literature.

The term *ethnic identity* has sometimes been used virtually synonymously with *acculturation*, but the two terms should be distinguished. The concept of acculturation deals broadly with changes in cultural attitudes, values, and behaviors that result from contact between two distinct cultures (Berry, Trimble, & Olmedo, 1986). The level of concern is generally the group rather than the individual, and the focus is on how minority or immigrant groups relate to the dominant or host society. Ethnic identity may be thought of as an aspect of acculturation, in which the concern is with individuals and the focus is on how they relate to their own group as a subgroup of the larger society.

Two distinct models have guided thinking about these questions: a linear, bipolar model and a two-dimensional model. In the linear model, ethnic identity is conceptualized along a continuum from strong ethnic ties at one extreme to strong mainstream ties at the other (Andujo, 1988; Makabe, 1979; Simic, 1987; Ullah, 1985). The assumption underlying this model is that a strengthening of one requires a weakening of the other; that is, a strong ethnic identity is not possible among those who become involved in the mainstream society, and acculturation is inevitably accompanied by a weakening of ethnic identity

In contrast to the linear model, an alternative model emphasizes that acculturation is a two-dimensional process, in which both the relationship with the traditional or ethnic culture and the relationship with the new or dominant culture must be considered, and these two relationships may be independent. According to this view, minority group members can have either strong or weak identifications with both their own and the mainstream cultures, and a strong ethnic identity does not necessarily imply a weak relationship or low involvement with the dominant culture.

This model suggests that there are not only the two acculturative extremes of assimilation or pluralism but at least four possible ways of dealing with ethnic group membership in a diverse society (Berry et al., 1986). Strong identification with both groups is indicative of integration or biculturalism; identification with neither group suggests marginality. An exclusive identification with the majority culture indicates assimilation, whereas identification with only the ethnic group indicates separation. Table I is an illustration of this model and some of the terms that have been used for each of the four possibilities in empirical research. A number of the studies reviewed were based on this model (e.g., M. Clark, Kaufman, & Pierce, 1976; Hutnik, 1986; Ting-Toomey, 1981; Zak, 1973), and in some the authors explored empirical evidence for the bipolar versus the two-dimensional models (e.g., Elias & Blanton, 1987; Zak, 1976). Research on this issue is summarized later.

An important empirical issue in this area has been the question of the extent to which ethnic identity is maintained over time when a minority ethnic group comes in contact with a dominant majority group (DeVos & Romanucci-Ross, 1982; Glazer & Moynihan, 1970; M. Gordon, 1964) and the impact of the process on psychological adjustment (e.g., Berry, Kim, Minde, & Mok, 1987). Underlying both these issues is the theme of culture conflict between two distinct groups and the psychological consequences of such conflicts for individuals. How such conflicts are dealt with at the individual level is part of the process of ethnic identity formation.

Ethnic Identity Formation

Both the social identity and the acculturation frameworks acknowledge that ethnic identity is dynamic, changing over time and context. In a similar vein, several of the definitions cited earlier include the idea that ethnic

TABLE 1

Terms Used for Four Orientations, Based on Degree of Identification With Both One's Own Ethnic Group and the Majority Group

Jean S. Phinney

Identification with majority group	Identification with ethnic group	
	Strong	Weak
Strong	Acculturated Integrated Bicultural	Assimilated
Weak	Ethnically identified Ethnically embedded Separated Dissociated	Marginal

identity is achieved through an active process of decision making and self-evaluation(Caltabiano, 1984; Hogg et al., 1987; Simic, 1987). In a conceptual chapter, Weinreich (1988) asserted that ethnic identity is not an entity but a complex of processes by which people construct their ethnicity. However, in research based on the social identity or acculturation frameworks, investigators in general have not examined ethnic identity at the level of individual change —that is, developmentally

A developmental framework was provided by Erikson's (1968) theory of ego identity formation. According to Erikson, an achieved identity is the result of a period of exploration and experimentation that typically takes place during adolescence and that leads to a decision or a commitment in various areas, such as occupation, religion, and political orientation. The ego identity model, as operationalized by Marcia (1966, 1980), suggests four ego identity statuses based on whether people have explored identity options and whether they have made a decision. A person who has neither engaged in exploration nor made a commitment is said to be *diffuse;* a commitment made without exploration, usually on the basis of parental values, represents a *foreclosed* status. A person in the process of exploration without having made a commitment is in *moratorium;* a firm commitment following a period of exploration is indicative of an *achieved identity* (see Table 2). Although Erikson alluded to the importance of culture in identity formation, this model has not been widely applied to the study of ethnic identity.

The formation of ethnic identity may be thought of as a process similar to ego identity formation that takes place over time, as people explore and make decisions about the role of ethnicity in their lives. A number of conceptual models have described ethnic identity development in minority adolescents or adults. Cross (1978) described a model of the development of Black consciousness in college students during the Civil Rights era. In a dissertation, Kim

TABLE 2

Marcia's Ego Identity Statuses (Top) and
Proposed Stages of Ethnic Identity (Bottom)

Marcia (1966, 1980)	Identity diffusion	Identity foreclosure	Identity crisis[a]	Moratorium	Identity achievement
Cross (1978)		Pre-encounter	Encounter	Immersion/emersion	Internalization
Kim (1981)		White identified	Awakening to social political awareness	Redirection to Asian American consciousness	Incorporation
Atkinson et al. (1983)		Conformity: Preference for values of dominant culture	Dissonance: Questioning and challenging old attitudes	Resistance and immersion: Rejection of dominant culture	Synergetic articulation and awareness
Phinney (1989)	Unexamined ethnic identity:		Ethnic identity search (Moratorium):		Achieved ethnic identity
	Lack of exploration of ethnicity. Possible subtypes:		Involvement in exploring and seeking to understand meaning of ethnicity for oneself		Clear, confident sense of own ethnicity
	Diffusion: Lack of interest in or concern with ethnicity	Foreclosure: Views of ethnicity based on opinions of others			

[a] Identity crisis is not one of Marcia's original four statuses.

(1981) described Asian-American identity development in a group of young adult Asian-American women. A model of ethnic identity formation based on clinical experience was proposed by Atkinson et al. (1983), and Arce (1981) conceptualized the issues with regard to Chicanos.

In a recent article, Phinney (1989) examined commonalities across various models and proposed a three-stage progression from an unexamined ethnic identity through a period of exploration to an achieved or committed ethnic identity (see Table 2). According to this model, early adolescents and perhaps adults who have not been exposed to ethnic identity issues are in the first stage, an unexamined ethnic identity. According to Cross (1978) and others (e.g., Atkinson et al., 1983: Kim, 1981), this early stage is characterized for minorities by a preference for the dominant culture. However, such a preference is not a necessary characteristic of this stage. Young people may simply not be interested in ethnicity and may have given it little thought (their ethnic identity is diffuse). Alternatively, they may have absorbed positive ethnic attitudes from parents or other adults and therefore may not show a preference for the majority group, although they have not thought through the issues for themselves—that is, are foreclosed (Phinney, 1989).

A second stage is characterized by an exploration of one's own ethnicity, which is similar to the moratorium status described by Marcia (1980). This may take place as the result of a significant experience that forces awareness of one's ethnicity ("encounter' according to Cross, 1978, or "awakening," according to Kim, 1981). It involves an often intense process of immersion in one's own culture through activities such as reading, talking to people, going to ethnic museums, and participating actively in cultural events. For some people it may involve rejecting the values of the dominant culture.

The stage model suggests that as a result of this process, people come to a deeper understanding and appreciation of their ethnicity—that is, ethnic identity achievement or internalization. This culmination may require resolution or coming to terms with two fundamental problems for ethnic minorities: (a) cultural differences between their own group and the dominant group and (b) the lower or disparaged status of their group in society (Phinney, Lochner, & Murphy, 1990). The meaning of ethnic identity achievement is undoubtedly different for different individuals and groups because of their different historical and personal experiences. However, achievement does not necessarily imply a high degree of ethnic involvement; one could presumably be clear about and confident of one's ethnicity without wanting to maintain one's ethnic language or customs. A recent conceptual article suggested that the process does not necessarily end with ethnic identity achievement but may continue in cycles that involve further exploration or rethinking of the role or meaning of one's ethnicity (Parham, 1989). A similar idea has been suggested with regard to ego identity (Grotevant, 1987).

Empirical research based on these models has involved describing changes over time in a person's attitudes and understanding about his or her ethnicity. In addition, researchers have looked at factors related to ethnic identity formation, such as parental attitudes and social class, and at correlates, including self-esteem or adjustment and attitudes toward counselors....

EMPIRICAL FINDINGS

Because of the different conceptualizations, definitions, and measures that have been used in the study of ethnic identity, empirical findings are difficult or impossible to compare across studies. Not surprisingly, the findings are often inconsistent.

Self-Esteem, Self-Concept, and Psychological Adjustment

A key issue in conceptual writing about ethnic identity has been the role of group identity in the self-concept: Specifically, does a strong identification with one's ethnic group promote a positive self-concept or self-esteem? Or, conversely, is identification with an ethnic group that is held in low regard by the dominant group likely to lower one's self-esteem? Furthermore, is it possible to hold negative views about one's own group and yet feel good about oneself?

Early interest in these questions stemmed from the work of K. Clark and Clark (1947), which showed that young Black children tended to prefer White dolls to Black dolls. The meaning of such findings continues to be debated, and a number of reviewers have discussed the findings (Aboud, 1987; Banks, 1976; Brand et al., 1974; V. Gordon, 1980). However, this controversy has been dealt with almost entirely in studies with children, and there has been little extension of the work into adolescence and adulthood, the topic of the current review. Given the theoretical importance of this issue, it is surprising that in only 11 of the studies reviewed, the researchers assessed self-esteem or a related construct and examined its relationship to some measure of ethnic identity. The researchers who did address this question presented conflicting results.

Three of the studies suggested positive effects of ethnic identity, although the measures used were different in each case. Among Black early adolescents (ages 13–14) of low socioeconomic status (SES), "acceptance of racial identity," as measured by six items (no reliability given), was found to be significantly related to self-concept as measured by the Tennessee Self Concept Scale (Paul & Fischer, 1980). A study with Anglo-American and Mexican-American junior high school students revealed a positive relationship between self-esteem, assessed by Rosenberg's (1979) Self-Esteem Scale, and ethnic esteem, as measured by adjective ratings of one's own group (Grossman et al, 1985). Among Israeli high school students, ego identity, which is suggestive of good adjustment, was higher among those with high ethnic group identification than among those with low identification (on a scale with reliability of alpha equal to .60), especially among the Oriental Jews, a minority group in Israel (Tzuriel & Klein, 1977).

Four studies revealed no relationship between ethnic identity and various measures of adjustment. A study of Black and White college students revealed no relationship between self-esteem (Rosenberg scale) and ethnic identity, measured in terms of similarity-to-group scores on semantic differential ratings of Blacks and Whites—that is, similarity to a stereotype of one's own group (White & Burke, 1987). Also, for Black college students, "Black consciousness," measured by attitudes toward Blacks and Whites, was unrelated to two measures of self-esteem (Houston, 1984). Among Arab-Israeli college students, self-esteem (Rosenberg scale) was not related to measures of Arab identity (scale reliability = .81) or Israeli identity (scale reliability = .83; Zak, 1976). Finally a study of Italian Australians revealed "Italian identity" (scale reliability = .89) to be unrelated to psychosocial adjustment, according to the Offer Self-Image Questionnaire and the Erikson Psychosocial Stage Inventory (Rosenthal & Cichello, 1986). In summary, these studies of ethnic identity, in which a variety of measures of ethnic identity as a state were used, permit no definitive conclusion about its role in self-esteem.

In contrast to the preceding studies, researchers in four studies examined self-esteem in relation to the stage model of ethnic identity. By analogy with the ego-identity literature, in which positive psychological outcomes have been associated with an achieved identity (Marcia, 1980), the developmental model predicts higher self-esteem in subjects with an achieved ethnic identity. This prediction was supported in a study with 10th-grade Black, Asian-American, and Mexican-American adolescents, in which subjects at higher stages of ethnic identity, as assessed by interviews, were found to have significantly higher scores on all four subscales of a measure of psychological adjustment (self-evaluation, sense of mastery, family relations, and social relations), as well as on an independent measure of ego development (Phinney, 1989). A similar relationship between ethnic identity search and commitment (scale reliabilities = .69 and .59, respectively) and self-esteem was found among college students from four ethnic groups (Asian American, Black, Mexican American, and White); the relationship was stronger among minority group students than among their White peers (Phinney & Alipuria, 1990). A study with Black college students, which was based on Cross's (1978) process model, revealed that low self-esteem was related to the earliest (pre-encounter) stage and to the immersion (moratorium) stage, whereas high self-esteem was associated with the encounter stage, which involves events that precipitate a search or immersion (Parham & Helms, 1985a). In a related study, the pre-encounter and immersion stages were found to be related to feelings of inferiority and anxiety (Parham & Helms, 1985b). These studies suggest that a positive self-concept may be related to the process of identity formation—that is, to the extent to which people have come to an understanding and acceptance of their ethnicity

Ethnic Identity in Relation to the Majority Culture

The acculturation framework for studying ethnic identity suggests that for understanding ethnic identity, it is necessary to consider also the individual's relationship to the dominant or majority group. Whereas a number of the studies reviewed focused on a single ethnic group, without reference to the dominant group (e.g., Asbury, Adderly-Kelly, & Knuckle, 1987; Constantinou & Harvey, 1985; Garcia & Lega, 1979; Keefe, 1986; Masuda, Hasegawa, & Matsumoto, 1973), many researchers took into consideration the relationship to the dominant group.

A central question, as discussed earlier, is whether ethnic identity is directly related to degree of acculturation or whether, conversely, it is independent, so that, for example, one could have a strong ethnic identification and also have strong ties to the dominant culture (see Table 1). Several studies suggest that the two are independent. In a study with adolescent girls of East Indian extraction who were living in England, Hutnik (1986) assessed separately self-identification (as Indian or British) and Indian and British cultural behaviors; the results showed the two dimensions to be unrelated. A similar picture emerged from a study of seven White ethnic groups in Canada (Driedger, 1976). Group scores demonstrated varying degrees of ethnic affirmation and denial for each group, which resulted in three types of ethnic identity, depending on degree of ethnic identification or denial: majority assimilator, ethnic identifiers, and ethnic marginals. Similarly, studies of Armenian Americans (Der-Karabetian, 1980), Jewish Americans (Zak, 1973), and Chinese Americans (Ting-Toomey, 1981) revealed ethnic identity and American identity to be independent dimensions.

However, other studies gave different results. A comparison of bipolar and orthogonal models of ethnic identity among Israelis living in the United States suggested that attitudes and behaviors relative to being Israeli, Jewish, or American were not independent (Elias & Blanton, 1987). Affective measures of the three aspects of identity were positively intercorrelated, whereas behavioral measures were negatively related; subjects who engaged in many typical American behaviors showed fewer Israeli behaviors. In another study of Israelis residing in the United States (Elizur, 1984), Jewish and American identity tended to be negatively related.

More complex results emerged from two studies in which qualitative data were used. An extensive study of Mexican-American and Asian-American adults (M. Clark et al., 1976) revealed six profiles representing different combinations of attitudes, behaviors, and knowledge relative to one's own culture and American culture. A qualitative study of Mexican-American high school students (Matute-Bianchi, 1986) demonstrated five types of ethnic identity, depending on the students' degree of involvement in their own ethnic culture and in the mainstream culture of the high school. Moreover, the types of identity were related to school achievement. Those students who were more embedded in the barrio culture were the least successful academically

The value of studies such as these, in which mainstream as well as ethnic orientation is assessed, has been in emphasizing that ethnic identity is not necessarily a linear construct; it can be conceptualized in terms of qualitatively different ways of relating to one's own and other groups. A problem in using this more complex conceptualization is in assessing the attributes of the contrast group. The characteristics of mainstream culture are far more difficult to define than those of a particular subculture. The issue of measurement of mainstream attitudes belongs properly to the topic of acculturation; these measurement issues were thoroughly discussed by Berry et al. (1986).

The two-dimensional model provides some clarification of the importance of ethnic identity to the self-concept. Some of the contradictions and inconsistencies noted in this review may be a function of differences in the degree to which researchers have considered identification with both the ethnic group and the mainstream culture. For example, although ethnic identity, in the sense of identification with one's ethnic group, can range from strong to weak, an understanding of how ethnic identity is related to self-concept may require also determining an individual's relationship to the majority group. There is some evidence that the acculturated or integrated option may be the most satisfactory and the marginal, the least (Berry et al., 1987). However, the other two possibilities, assimilation and separation, may also provide the basis for a good self-concept, if the person is comfortable with these alternatives and is in an environment that supports them (Phinney et al., 1990).

Changes in Ethnic Identity Related to Generation of Immigration

A second focus of research within the acculturation framework is the way in which ethnic identity changes with contact with another group. Writers generally have agreed that ethnic identity is a dynamic concept, but relatively few have studied it over time. However, a number of researchers have examined changes related to generational status among immigrant groups.

Studies of generational differences in ethnic identity have shown a fairly consistent decline in ethnic group identification in later generations descended from immigrants (Constantinou & Harvey, 1985; Fathi, 1972). Ethnic identity was found to be similarly weaker among those who arrived at a younger age and had lived longer in the new country (Garcia & Lega, 1979; Rogler et al., 1980) and among those with more education (Rogler et al., 1980). However, a study of third- and fourth-generation Japanese-American youth revealed virtually no generational difference (Wooden, Leon, & Toshima, 1988), and a study of Chinese Americans suggests a cyclical process whereby ethnic identity became more important in third- and fourth-generation descendents of immigrants (Ting-Toomey, 1981). A recent study (Rosenthal & Feldman, in press) found that among adolescent Chinese immigrants, ethnic knowledge and be-havior decreased between the first and second generations, but that there was no change in the importance or positive valuation of ethnicity. The authors sug-gest that although some behavioral and cognitive elements of ethnic identity decline, immigrants retain a commitment to their culture. Furthermore, specific programs can foster ethnic identity (Zisenwine & Walters, 1982).

A study of three age groups in Japan (Masuda et al., 1973) illustrates the possible confounding of generation with age and cultural change. Older Japanese scored higher than did younger people in a measure of Japanese identification, in results similar to the generational differences among Japanese immigrants. Comparisons between younger (second-generation) and older (first-generation) subjects may thus tap age as well as cohort differences. In a retrospective interview study with elderly Croatians, Simic (1987) noted an intensification of ethnic sentiments during later life.

Ethnic Identity and Gender

Gender may be a variable in acculturation in those cultures in which men are more likely to get jobs in the mainstream culture while the women re-main at home. There may also be different cultural expectations for men and women, such as the assumption that women are the carriers of ethnic traditions. The very little research that addresses this issue suggests a greater involve-ment in ethnicity by women than by men. Research with Chinese-American college students revealed women to be more oriented to their ancestral culture than were men (Ting-Toomey, 1981), and a drawing study showed higher Black identification in women (Bolling, 1974). Among Irish adolescents in England, girls were significantly more likely than boys to adopt an Irish identity (Ullah, 1985). Japanese girls and women tended to score higher than boys and men on Japanese ethnic identity (Masuda et al., 1973).

In contrast, Jewish boys in Canada were found to show greater preference for Jewish norms than did girls (Fathi, 1972), a fact that the author suggested may be related to the Jewish emphasis on male dominance. Among East Indian and Anglo-Saxon adolescents in England, girls were more inclined than boys to mix with their own group, but they were also more willing to invite home someone from a different group (Hogg et al., 1987). Gender was found to inter-act with ethnic identity on attitudes toward counseling (Ponterotto, Anderson, & Grieger, 1986) and on a measure of visual retention (Knuckle & Asbury, 1986).

In the sparse literature on identity formation, Parham and Helms (1985b) found that Black men were more likely than Black women to endorse attitudes from the earliest stages and less likely to show evidence of the highest stage. A similar trend among Black adolescents was noted by Phinney (1989). These fragmentary results clearly allow no conclusions about sex differences in ethnic identity

Contextual Factors in Ethnic Identity

Ethnic identity is to a large extent defined by context; it is not an issue except in terms of a contrast group, usually the majority culture. The particular context seems to be an essential factor to consider, yet relatively few researchers have examined it in any detail. There is some evidence that ethnic identity varies according to the context (e.g., Vermeulen & Pels, 1984) and the characteristics of the group (Rosenthal & Hrynevich, 1985). Adolescents report that their feelings of being ethnic vary according to the situation they are in and the people they are with (Rosenthal & Hrynevich, 1985). Ethnic identity is positively related to the ethnic density of the neighborhood (Garcia & Lega, 1979) and negatively to the occupational and residential mobility of subjects (Makabe, 1979); it varies among communities within the same state (Teske & Nelson, 1973).

Some writers have suggested that ethnic identity is less likely to be maintained among middle-SES than among lower-SES ethnic group members. Among second-generation Irish adolescents in England, those from lower socioeconomic backgrounds were significantly more likely to identify themselves as Irish than were middle-SES youth, perhaps because they lived in areas with a higher concentration of Irish immigrants. However, research based on the developmental model has revealed no relationship between stages of ethnic identity and social class among high school students (Phinney, 1989) or college students (Phinney & Alipuria, 1990), and racial identity attitudes were not predictive of socioeconomic status among Black college students (Carter & Helms, 1988).

The impact of the context on Black identity has been investigated through studies of transracial adoption. Racial identity was more of a problem for Black children and adolescents adopted into White homes than for those adopted by Black parents, although the self-esteem of the two groups did not differ (McRoy, Zurcher, Lauderdale, & Anderson, 1982). Transracially adopted Hispanic adolescents were similarly likely to identify themselves as Americans, whereas those adopted by Mexican-American couples overwhelmingly called themselves Mexican American (Andujo, 1988). Furthermore, the parental attitudes and perceptions had an important impact on the racial identity of transracial adoptees (McRoy, Zurcher, & Lauderdale, 1984).

There has been little research on such presumably important factors as the relative size of the ethnic group (at the local or the national level) or its status in the community

Ethnic Identity Formation

The developmental model assumes that with increasing age, subjects are more likely to have an achieved ethnic identity Although there is little empirical support for this assumption, some results suggest that there is a developmental progression. In an interview study with Black and White 8th graders, about a third of the subjects showed evidence of ethnic identity search (Phinney & Tarver, 1988); among 10th graders in a related study, the comparable figure was about half (Phinney, 1989). Thus it appeared that the older students had done more searching. In a study based on Cross's (1978) model, Black college students reported their perceptions of themselves over the past, present, and future as shifting from lower to higher levels of Black identity (Krate et al., 1974). Both longitudinal and cross-sectional studies are needed to examine changes toward higher levels of ethnic identity formation.

Although the process model of ethnic identity has not been validated, it provides an alternative way of thinking about ethnic identity. Both attitudes and behaviors with respect to one's own and other groups are conceptualized as changing as one develops and resolves issues and feelings about one's own and other groups. Differing ethnic attitudes and behaviors may therefore reflect different stages of development, rather than permanent characteristics of the group or the individuals studied. Some discrepancies in the findings regarding relationships among components of ethnic identity, reported earlier in this review, may result from studying subjects at different stages of development.

Another topic of interest in this area has been the impact of ethnic identity stages on attitudes regarding the ethnicity of counselors. Black college students in the early stages preferred White counselors (Parham & Helms, 1981), whereas those in the intermediate stages showed a preference for Black counselors (Morten & Atkinson, 1983; Parham & Helms, 1981). Results for subjects at the highest stage are mixed; they may show Black preference (Parham & Helms, 1981) or no preference (Morten & Atkinson, 1983). Stages of ethnic identity development in Blacks are also related to perceptions of White counselors (Pomales, Claiborn, & LaFromboise, 1986).

In examining the relationship of stages of Black identity to Black value orientations, Carter and Helms (1987) found that certain values could be predicted from the stages; for example, the highest stage, internalization, was associated with a belief in harmony with nature.

The study of stages of ethnic identity is at present rudimentary; however, a developmental perspective may be able eventually to provide a more complete understanding of this phenomenon across age. . . .

SUMMARY

In a world where the populations of most countries are increasingly diverse, both ethnically and racially, it is essential to understand the psychological impact of such diversity (Albert, 1988). Although attitudes of the majority toward minority ethnic groups have received most attention, it is equally important to understand how ethnic group members deal with being part of a group that may be disparaged or discriminated against, that must struggle to maintain its own customs and traditions, and that is not well represented in the media, among other problems, The task of understanding ethnic identity is complicated by the fact that the uniqueness that distinguishes each group and setting makes it difficult to draw general conclusions across groups.

There are important research questions to be addressed, such as the role of ethnic identity in self-esteem, its relationship to acculturation, and its place in the development of personal identity. Currently, researchers can offer few answers to these questions because of widely differing approaches to the study of ethnic identity, including lack of agreement on what constitutes its essential components, varying theoretical orientations that have guided the research, and measures that are unique to each group. It is hoped that this article brings some conceptual clarity to this important area and stimulates further research on ethnic identity.

REFERENCES

Aboud, F. (1987). The development of ethnic self-identification and attitudes. In J. Phinney & M. Rotheram (Eds.), *Children's ethnic socialization: Pluralism and development* (pp. 32–55). Newbury Park, CA: Sage.

Alba, R. (1985). *Ethnicity and race in the U.S.A.* London: Routledge & Kegan Paul.

Albert, R. (1988). The place of culture in modern psychology. In P. Bronstein & K. Quina (Eds.), *Teaching a psychology of people: Resources for gender and sociocultural awareness* (pp. 12–18). Washington, DC: American Psychological Association.

Andujo, E. (1988). Ethnic identity of transethnically adopted Hispanic adolescents. *Social Work, 33,* 531–535.

Arce, C. (1981). A reconsideration of Chicano culture and identity. *Daedalus, 110*(2), 177–192.

Asbury, C., Adderly-Kelly, B., & Knuckle, E. (1987). Relationship among WISC-R performance categories and measured ethnic identity in Black adolescents. *Journal of Negro Education, 56,* 172–183.

Atkinson, D., Morten, G., & Sue, D. (1983). *Counseling American minorities.* Dubuque, IA: Wm. C. Brown.

Banks, W. (1976). White preference in Blacks: A paradigm in search of a phenomenon. *Psychological Bulletin, 83,* 1179–1186.

Berry, J., Kalin, R., & Taylor, D. (1977). *Multiculturalism and ethnic attitudes in Canada.* Ottawa, Canada: Minister of Supply and Services.

Berry, J., Kim, U., Minde, T., & Mok, D. (1987). Comparative studies of acculturative stress. *International Migration Review, 21.* 492–511.

Berry, J., Trimble, J., & Olmedo, E. (1986). Assessment of acculturation. In W. Lonner & J. Berry (Eds.), *Field methods in cross-cultural research* (pp. 291–324). Newbury Park, CA: Sage.

Bolling, J. (1974). The changing self-concept of Black children. *Journal of the National Medical Association, 66,* 28–31, 34.

Bourhis, R., Giles, H., & Tajfel, H. (1973). Language as a determinant of Welsh identity. *European Journal of Social Psychology, 3,* 447–460.

Brand, E., Ruiz, R., & Padilla, A. (1974). Ethnic identification and preference: A review. *Psychological Bulletin, 86,* 860–890.

Caltabiano, N. (1984). Perceived differences in ethnic behavior: A pilot study of Italo-Australian Canberra residents. *Psychological Reports, 55,* 867–873.

Carter, R., & Helms, J. (1987). The relationship of Black value-orientations to racial identity attitudes. *Measurement and Evaluation in Counseling and Development, 19,* 185–195.

Carter, R., & Helms, J. (1988). The relationship between racial identity attitudes and social class. *Journal of Negro Education, 57,* 22–30.

Christian, J., Gadfield, N., Giles, H., & Taylor, D. (1976). The multidimensional and dynamic nature of ethnic identity. *International Journal of Psychology, 11,* 281–291.

Clark, K., & Clark, M. (1947). Racial identification and preference in Negro children. In T. Newcomb and E. Hartley (Eds.), *Readings in social psychology* (pp. 551–560). New York: Holt.

Clark, M., Kaufman, S., & Pierce, R. (1976). Explorations of acculturation: Toward a model of ethnic identity. *Human Organization, 35,* 231–238.

Constantinou, S., & Harvey, M. (1985). Dimensional structure and intergenerational differences in ethnicity: The Greek Americans. *Sociology and Social Research, 69,* 234–254.

Cross, W. (1978). The Thomas and Cross models of psychological nigrescence: A literature review. *Journal of Black Psychology, 4,* 13–31.

Dasheksky, A. (Ed.) (1976). *Ethnic identity in society.* Chicago: Rand McNally.

Der-Karabetian, A. (1980). Relation of two cultural identities of Armenian-Americans. *Psychological Reports, 47,* 123–128.

DeVos, G., & Romanucci-Ross, L. (1982). *Ethnic identity: Cultural continuities and change.* Chicago: University of Chicago Press.

Driedger, L. (1976). Ethnic self-identity: A comparison of in-group evaluations. *Sociometry, 39,* 131–141.

Du Bois, W. E. B. (1983). *Autobiography of W. E. B. Du Bois.* New York: International Publishing.

Ekstrand, L. (1986). *Ethnic minorities and immigrants in a cross-cultural perspective.* Lisse, Netherlands: Swets & Zeitlinger.

Elias, N., & Blanton, J. (1987). Dimensions of ethnic identity in Israeli Jewish families living in the United States. *Psychological Reports, 60,* 367–375.

Elizur, D. (1984). Facet analysis of ethnic identity: The case of Israelis residing in the United States. *Journal of General Psychology, 111,* 259–269.

Erikson, E. (1968). *Identity: Youth and crisis.* New York: Norton.

Fathi, A. (1972). Some aspects of changing ethnic identity of Canadian Jewish youth. *Jewish Social Studies, 34,* 23–30.

Frideres, J., & Goldenberg, S. (1982). Myth and reality in Western Canada. *International Journal of Intercultural Relations, 6,* 137–151.

Garcia, M., & Lega, L. (1979). Development of a Cuban ethnic identity questionnaire. *Hispanic Journal of Behavioral Sciences, 1,* 247–261.

Glazer, N., & Moynihan, D. (1970). *Beyond the melting pot.* Cambridge, MA: Harvard University Press.

Gordon, M. (1964). *Assimilation in American life.* London: Oxford University Press.

Gordon, V. (1980). *The self-concept of Black Americans.* Lanham, MD: University Press America.

Grossman, B., Wirt, R., & Davids, A. (1985). Self-esteem, ethnic identity, and behavioral adjustment among Anglo and Chicano adolescents in West Texas. *Journal of Adolescence,8,* 57–68.

Grotevant, H. (1987). Toward a process model of identity formation. *Journal of Adolescent Research, 2,* 203–222.

Gurin, P., & Epps, E. (1975). *Black consciousness, identity, and achievement,* New York: Wiley.

Hogg, M., Abrams, D., & Patel, Y. (1987). Ethnic identity, self-esteem, and occupational aspirations of Indian and Anglo-Saxon British adolescents. *Genetic, Social, and General Psychology Monographs, 113,* 487–508.

Houston, L. (1984). Black consciousness and self-esteem. *Journal of Black Psychology, 11,* 1–7.

Hutnik, N. (1985). Aspects of identity in a multi-ethnic society. *New Community, 12,* 298–309.

Hutnik, N. (1986). Patterns of ethnic minority identification and modes of social adaptation. *Ethnic and Racial Studies, 9,* 150–167.

Kagitcibasi, C., & Berry, J. (1989). Cross-cultural psychology: Current research and trends. In M. Rosenzweig & L. Porter (Eds.), *Annual review of psychology* (Vol. 40, pp. 493–531). Palo Alto, CA: Annual Reviews.

Kaplan, R. (1989, July). The Balkans: Europe's third world. *The Atlantic, 263,* 16–22.

Keefe, S. (1986). Southern Appalachia: Analytical models, social services, and native support systems. *American Journal of Community Psychology, 14,* 479–498.

Kim, J. (1981). *The process of Asian-American identity development: A study of Japanese American women's perceptions of their struggle to achieve Positive identities.* Unpublished doctoral dissertation, University of Massachusetts.

Kingston, M. (1976). *The woman warrior.* South Yarmouth, MA: J. Curley.

Knuckle, E., & Asbury, C. (1986). Benton revised visual retention test: Performance of Black adolescents according to age, sex, and ethnic identity. *Perceptual and Motor Skills, 63,* 319–327.

Krate, R., Leventhal, G., & Silverstein, B. (1974). Self-perceived transformation of Negro-to-Black identity. *Psychological Reports, 34,* 1071–1075.

Laosa, L. (1984). Social policies toward children of diverse ethnic, racial and language groups in the United States. In H. Stevenson & A. Siegel (Eds.), *Child development research and social policy* (pp. 1–109). Chicago: University of Chicago Press.

Lewin, K. (1948). *Resolving social conflicts.* New York: Harper.

Makabe, T. (1979). Ethnic identity scale and social mobility: The case of Nisei in Toronto. *The Canadian Review of Sociology and Anthropology, 16,* 136–145.

Malcolm X. (1965). *Autobiography of Malcolm X.* New York: Golden Press.

Maldonado, D., Jr. (1975). Ethnic self-identity and self-understanding. *Social Casework, 56,* 618–622.

Marcia, J. (1966). Development and validation of ego-identity status. *Journal of Personality and Social Psychology, 3,* 551–558.

Marcia, J. (1980). Identity in adolescence. In J. Adelson (Ed.), *Handbook of adolescent psychology* (pp. 159–187). New York: Wiley.

Masuda, M., Hasegawa, R., & Matsumoto, G. (1973). The ethnic identity questionnaire: A comparison of three Japanese age groups in Tachikawa, Japan, Honolulu, and Seattle. *Journal of Cross-Cultural Psychology, 4,* 229–244.

Matute-Bianchi, M. (1986). Ethnic identities and pattern of school success and failure among Mexican-descent and Japanese-American students in a California high school: An ethnographic analysis. *American Journal of Education, 95,* 233–255.

McRoy, R., Zurcher, L., & Lauderdale, M. (1984). The identity of transracial adoptees. *Social Casework, 65,* 34–39.

McRoy, R., Zurcher, L., Lauderdale, M., & Anderson, R. (1982). Self-esteem and racial identity in transracial and inracial adoptees. *Social Work, 27,* 522–526.

Mendelberg, H. (1986). Identity conflict in Mexican-American adolescents. *Adolescence, 21,* 215–222.

Morten, G., & Atkinson, D. (1983). Minority identity development and preference for counselor race. *Journal of Negro Education, 52,* 156–161.

Ostrow, M. (1977). The psychological determinants of Jewish identity. *Israel Annals of Pyschiatry and Related Disciplines, 15,* 313–335.

Parham, T. (1989). Cycles of psychological nigrescence. *The Counseling Psychologist, 17,* 187–226.

Parham, T., & Helms, J. (1981). The influence of Black student's racial identity attitudes on preferences for counselor's race. *Journal of Counseling Psychology, 28,* 250–257.

Parham, T., & Helms, J. (1985a). Attitudes of racial identity and self-esteem of Black students: An exploratory investigation. *Journal of College Student Personnel, 26,* 143–147.

Parham, T., & Helms, J. (1985b). Relation of racial identity attitudes to self-actualization and affective states of Black students. *Journal of Counseling Psychology, 32,* 431–440.

Paul, M., & Fischer, J. (1980). Correlates of self-concept among Black early adolescents. *Journal of Youth and Adolescence, 9,* 163–173.

Phinney, J. (1989). Stages of ethnic identity in minority group adolescents. *Journal of Early Adolescence, 9,* 34–49.

Phinney, J., & Alipuria, L. (1990). Ethnic identity in older adolescents from four ethnic groups. *Journal of Adolescence, 13.*

Phinney, J., Lochner, B., & Murphy, R. (1990). Ethnic identity development and psychological adjustment in adolescence. In A. Stiffman & L. Davis (Eds.), *Ethnic issues in adolescent mental health.* Newbury Park, CA: Sage.

Phinney, J., & Tarver, S. (1988). Ethnic identity search and commitment in Black and White eighth graders. *Journal of Early Adolescence, 8,* 265–277.

Pomales, J., Claiborn, C., & LaFromboise, T. (1986). Effect of Black students' racial identity on perceptions of White counselors varying in cultural sensitivity. *Journal of Counseling Psychology, 33,* 57–61.

Ponterotto, J., Anderson, W., & Grieger, I. (1986). Black students' attitudes toward counseling as a function of racial identity. *Journal of Multicultural Counseling and Development, 14,* 50–59.

Rodriguez, R. (1982). *Hunger of memory.* Boston: Godine.

Rogler, L., Cooney, R., & Ortiz, V. (1980). Intergenerational change in ethnic identity in the Puerto Rican family. *International Migration Review, 14,* 193–214.

Rosenberg, M. (1979). *Conceiving the self.* New York: Basic Books.

Rosenthal, D., & Cichello, A. (1986). The meeting of two cultures: Ethnic identity and psychosocial adjustment of Italian-Australian adolescents. *International Journal of Psychology, 21,* 487–501.

Rosenthal, D., & Feldman, S. (in press). The nature and stability of ethnic identity in Chinese youth: Effects of length of residence in two cultural contexts. *Journal of Cross-Cultural Psychology.*

Rosenthal, D., & Hrynevich, C. (1985). Ethnicity and ethnic identity: A comparative study of Greek-, Italian-, and Anglo-Australian adolescents. *International Journal of Psychology, 20,* 723–742.

Salgado de Snyder, N., Lopez, C. M., & Padilla, A. M. (1982). Ethnic identity and cultural awareness among the offspring of Mexican interethnic marriages. *Journal of Early Adolescence, 2,* 277–282.

Simic, A. (1987). Ethnicity as a career for the elderly: The Serbian-American case. *Journal of Applied Gerontology, 6,* 113–126.

Singh, V. (1977). Some theoretical and methodological problems in the study of ethnic identity: A cross-cultural perspective. *New York Academy of Sciences: Annals, 285,* 32–42.

Staiano, K. (1980). Ethnicity as process: The creation of an Afro-American identity. *Ethnicity, 7,* 27–33.

Stryker, S. (1980). *Symbolic interactionism: A social structural version.* Menlo Park, CA: Benjamin Cummings.

Tajfel, H. (1978). *The social psychology of minorities.* New York: Minority Rights Group.

Tajfel, H. (1981). *Human groups and social categories.* Cambridge, England: Cambridge University Press.

Tajfel, H., & Turner, J. (1979). An intergrative theory of intergroup conflict. In W. Austin & S. Worchel (Eds.), *The social psychology of intergroup relations* (pp. 34–47). Monterey, CA: Brooks/Cole.

Teske, R., & Nelson, B. (1973). Two scales for the measurement of Mexican-American identity. *International Review of Modern Sociology, 3,* 192–203.

Ting-Toomey, S. (1981). Ethnic identity and close friendship in Chinese-American college students. *International Journal of Intercultural Relations, 5,* 383–406.

Tzuriel, D., & Klein, M. M. (1977). Ego identity: Effects of ethnocentrism, ethnic identification, and cognitive complexity in Israeli, Oriental, and Western ethnic groups. *Psychological Reports, 40,* 1099–1110.

Ullah, P. (1985). Second generation Irish youth: Identity and ethnicity. *New Community, 12,* 310–320.

Vermeulen, H., & Pels, T. (1984). Ethnic identity and young migrants in The Netherlands. *Prospects, 14,* 277–282.

Weinreich, P. (1983). Emerging from threatened identities. In G. Breakwell (Ed.), *Threatened identities* (pp. 149–185). New York: Wiley.

Weinreich, P. (1988). The operationalization of ethnic identity. In J. Berry & R. Annis (Eds.), *Ethnic psychology: Research and practice with immigrants, refugees, native peoples, ethnic groups and sojourners* (pp. 149–168). Amsterdam: Swets & Zeitlinger.

Wetzel, J. (1987). *American youth: A statistical snapshot.* Washington, DC: William T. Grant Foundation.

White, C., & Burke, P. (1987). Ethnic role identity among Black and White college students: An interactionist approach. *Sociological Perspectives, 30,* 310–331.

Wooden, W., Leon, J., & Toshima, M. (1988). Ethnic identity among Sansei and Yonsei church-affiliated youth in Los Angeles and Honolulu. *Psychological Reports, 62,* 268–270.

Yancey, W., Ericksen, E., & Juliani, R. (1976). Emergent ethnicity: A review and reformulation. *American Sociological Review, 41,* 391–403.

Zak, I. (1973). Dimensions of Jewish-American identity. *Psychological Reports, 33,* 891–900.

Zak, I. (1976). Structure of ethnic identity of Arab-Israeli students. *Psychology Reports, 38,* 239–246.

Zinn, M. (1980) Gender and ethnic identity among Chicanos. *Frontiers, 5,* 18–24.

Zisenwine, D., & Walters, J. (1982). Jewish identity: Israel and the American adolescent. *Forum on the Jewish People, Zionism, and Israel, 45,* 79–84.

Teaching White Students About Racism

Beverly Daniel Tatum predicts that the development of ethnic identity for whites in the United States will take a different path than for minorities. Because of a political and social system that places whites in positions of power, she says, their struggles with coming to understand who they are ethnically deal with different issues and points. For instance, one struggle is when individuals move beyond the point of thinking that they are "normal," that everyone is just like them, to the recognition that they live in a society that validates their ethnicity while devaluing other ethnicities. In laying out the six-stage model developed by Janet Helms, Tatum asserts that for whites there are two major developmental tasks in the process of identity development. First, whites must recognize and then work to abandon individual racism. Later, though, there is a difficult effort to develop a positive white identity. Tatum includes the words of her teacher education students as examples of the various stages of the development of white identity. The words give rich details of the emotional struggles in developing white identity.

Tatum is a professor of psychology and education at Mount Holyoke College in South Hadley, Massachusetts. Her work focuses on racial identity development and its impact on the classroom. She has widespread recognition in both the academic and popular arenas for her writings and presentations, and she was one of three authors to appear with President Bill Clinton at a 1997 national town meeting on race. The following selection is from her article "Teaching White Students About Racism: The Search for White Allies and the Restoration of Hope," *Teachers College Record* (summer 1994). Tatum has also published a popular book titled *Why Are All the Black Kids Sitting Together in the Cafeteria?* (Basic Books, 1997).

Key Concept: white identity development

UNDERSTANDING WHITE IDENTITY DEVELOPMENT

As Janet Helms explains in her model of white racial identity development, "racial identity development theory concerns the psychological implications of racial group membership, that is belief systems that evolve in reaction to perceived differential racial-group membership."[1] In U.S. society, where racial-group membership is emphasized, it is assumed that the development of a racial identity will occur in some form in everyone. However, the process will unfold in different ways for whites and people of color because of the different social positions they occupy in this society. For whites, there are two major developmental tasks in this process, the abandonment of individual racism and the recognition of and opposition to institutional and cultural racism. Helms writes: "Concurrently, the person must become aware of her or his Whiteness, learn to accept Whiteness as an important part of herself or himself, and to internalize a realistically positive view of what it means to be White."[2] Helms's six-stage model can then be divided into two major phases, the first being the abandonment of racism (a process that begins with the Contact stage and ends with the Reintegration stage). The second phase, defining a positive white identity, begins with the Pseudo-Independent stage and reaches fruition at the Autonomy stage.

Contact Stage

The first stage of racial identity for whites (the Contact stage) is a stage at which there is little attention paid to the significance of one's racial group membership. Individuals at this stage of development rarely describe themselves as white. If they have lived, worked, or gone to school in predominantly white settings, they may simply think of themselves as like the majority of those around them. This view is exemplified by the comment one of my white students made when asked to describe herself in terms of her class and ethnic background. She summed up her middle-class, white European background by saying, "I'm just normal." This sense of being part of the racial norm is taken for granted without conscious consideration of the systematically conferred advantages given to whites simply because of their racial group membership.[3]

While they have been influenced by the prevailing societal stereotypes of people of color, there is typically limited awareness of this socialization process. Often individuals at the Contact stage perceive themselves as completely free of prejudice, unaware of their own assumptions about other racial groups. I would describe the majority of the white men and women I have had in my course over the last twelve years as being in this stage of development at the start of the semester.

Disintegration Stage

However, participating in a classroom where the social consequences of racial group membership are explicitly discussed as part of the course content typically propels white students from the first stage to the next, referred to by Helms as the Disintegration Stage.[4] At this stage, white students begin to see how much their lives and the lives of people of color have been affected by racism in our society. The societal inequities they now notice are in direct contradiction to the idea of an American meritocracy, a concept that has typically been an integral part of their earlier socialization. The cognitive dissonance that results is part of the discomfort experienced at this stage. One response to this discomfort is to deny the validity of the information that is being presented to them, or to withdraw from the class psychologically, if not physically.[5] However, if they remain engaged, white students at the disintegration stage typically want to deal with the guilt and other uncomfortable feelings by doing something, by taking action of some sort to interrupt the racism they now see around them. If students have learned (as I hope they have) that racism can take both active forms (e.g., verbal harassment, physical violence, intentional acts of discrimination) and passive forms (e.g., silence in the presence of another's racist remarks, unexamined policies and practices that disproportionately impact people of color, the failure to acknowledge the contributions of people of color), then they recognize that an active response to racism is required to interrupt its perpetuation in our society.

"But what action can I take?" is a common question at this point in their development. Jerri, a white woman from an upper-middle-class family, expressed this sentiment clearly in her journal.

> Another thing I realized when I got to college was the privileges attached to being white. My family had brought me up trying to make me aware of other people and their differences—but they never explained the power I had. I do not take advantage of my power—at least I try not to, but it seems inevitable. I feel helpless. There is so much I want to do—to help. What can I do? I do not want to help perpetuate racism, sexism and stereotypes.

Helping students think this question through for themselves is part of our responsibility as educators who have accepted the challenge of teaching about racism. Heightening student awareness about racism without also providing some hope for social change is a prescription for despair. We all have a sphere of influence, some domain in which we exercise some level of power and control. For students, the task may be to identify what their own sphere of influence is (however large or small) and to consider how it might be used to interrupt the cycle of racism.[6]

However, once again, students find that they can think of many more examples of racist behavior than they can think of examples of antiracist behavior. Many white students have experienced their most influential adult role models, their parents, as having been the source of overtly expressed racial prejudices. The following excerpts from the journals of two students illustrate this point:

> Today was the first class on racism. . . . Before today I didn't think I was exposed to any form of racism. Well, except for my father. He is about as prejudiced as they come. [Sally, a white female]

> It really bothers me that stereotypes exist because it is from them that I originally became uninformed. My grandmother makes all kinds of decisions based on stereotypes—who to hire, who to help out. When I was growing up, the only black people that I knew were adults [household help], but I admired them just as much as any other adult. When I expressed these feelings to my parents, I was always told that the black people that I knew were the exceptions and that the rest of the race were different. I, too, was taught to be afraid. [Barbara, a white woman]

Others experienced their parents as passively silent on the subject of racism, simply accepting the status quo. As one young man from a very privileged background wrote:

> It is easy to simply fade into the woodwork, run with the rest of society, and never have to deal directly with these problems. So many people I know from home... have simply accepted what society has taught them with little if any question. My father is a prime example of this. His overriding preaching throughout my childhood dealt with simply accepting reality. [Carl, a white male]

Those white students whose parents actively espoused antiracist values still felt unprepared for addressing racism outside of the family circle, a point highlighted by the following journal entry, written by Annette, a white female college senior;

> Talking with other class members, I realized how exceptional my parents were. Not only were they not overtly racist but they also tried to keep society's subtle racism from reaching me. Basically I grew up believing that racism was no longer an issue and all people should be treated as equals. Unfortunately, my parents were not being very realistic as society's racism did begin to reach me. They did not teach me how to support and defend their views once I was interacting in a society without them as a buffer.

How do they learn how to interrupt someone else's racist (or sexist/anti-Semitic/homophobic) joke or challenge someone's stereotype if they have never seen anyone else do it? Despite the lack of examples, many students will begin to speak up about racism to their friends and family members. They often find that their efforts to share their new knowledge and heightened awareness with others are perceived negatively. Alice, a white woman, wrote:

> I never realized how much sexism and racism there still is on TV. I don't know if I'll ever be able to watch TV in the same way again. I used to just watch TV shows, laugh at the funny jokes, and not think about sexism or racism.... I know my friends and family probably don't think I'm as much fun as I used to be because I can't watch TV without making an issue of how racist and sexist most shows are.

The fear of being alienated from these friends and family members is real, and is part of the social pressure experienced by those at the Disintegration stage of development to back away from this new awareness of racism. The dilemma of noticing racism and yet feeling the societal pressure not to notice, or at least not to speak up, is resolved for some at the Reintegration stage.

Reintegration Stage

At the Reintegration stage, whites may turn to explanations for racism that put the burden of change on those who are the targets of racism.

Race-related negative conditions are assumed to result from Black people's inferior social, moral, and intellectual qualities, and thus it is not unusual to find persons in the Reintegration stage selectively attending to and/or reinterpreting information to conform to societal stereotypes of black people.[7]

As Wellman clearly illustrates, such thinking allows the white individual to relieve himself or herself of guilt as well as responsibility for working toward social change.[8]

Because the pressure to ignore racism and to accept the socially sanctioned stereotypes is so great, unless we talk about the interpersonal challenges that often confront students at this point in their understanding, we place them at risk of getting stuck in the Reintegration stage. Identifying these challenges for students does not solve the problem for them, but it does help them to recognize the source of some of the discomfort they may experience. It is hoped that this recognition allows them to respond in ways that will allow for continued growth in their own racial identity development.

Pseudo-Independent Stage

Continued, ongoing dialogue about race-related issues is one way to promote such growth. As the students' understanding of the complexity of institutional racism in our society deepens, the likelihood of resorting to "blame-the-victim" explanations lessens. Such deepening awareness is associated with the commitment to unlearn one's own racism, and marks the movement into the next stage of development in Helms's model, the Pseudo-independent stage. This stage marks the beginning of the second phase of this developmental process, creating a positive definition of whiteness.

At the Pseudo-independent stage, the individual may try to deal with some of the social pressures experienced at earlier stages by actively seeking friendships with those who share an antiracist perspective. In particular, some white students may want to distance themselves psychologically from their own racial group by seeking out relationships with people of color. An example of this can be seen in the following journal entry:

> One of the major and probably most difficult steps in identity development is obtaining or finding the consciousness of what it means to be white. I definitely remember many a time that I wished I was not white, ashamed of what I and others have done to the other racial groups in the world.... I wanted to pretend I was black, live with them, celebrate their culture, and deny my whiteness completely. Basically, I wanted to escape the responsibility that came with identifying myself as "white." [Lisa, a white female]

How successful these efforts to escape whiteness via people of color are will depend in part on the racial-identity development of the people of color involved.[9] However, even if these efforts to build interracial relationships are successful, the individual must eventually confront the reality of his or her own whiteness.

We all must be able to embrace who we are in terms of our racial cultural heritage, not in terms of assumed superiority or inferiority, but as an integral part of our daily experience in which we can take pride. But for many white students who have come to understand the reality of racism in all of our lives, whiteness is still at this stage experienced as a source of shame rather than a source of pride. Efforts to define a positive white identity are still tentative. The confusion experienced at this stage is clearly expressed by Bob, a white male struggling with these issues. Five weeks into the semester, he wrote:

> There have been many talk shows on in the past week that have focused on race. Along with the readings I'm finding that I'm looking at the people and topics in very different ways than I had in the past. I'm finding that this idea of white identity is more important than I thought. Yet white identity seems very hard to pin hole. I seem to have an idea and feel myself understanding what I need to do and why and then something presents itself that throws me into mass confusion. I feel that I need some resource that will help me through the process of finding white identity.

Immersion/Emersion

The next stage of white racial identity development, Immersion/Emersion, is a stage at which individuals intensify their efforts to create a positive self-definition as a white person. Helms writes, "The person in this stage is searching for the answers to the questions: 'Who am I racially?' and 'Who do I want to be?' and 'Who are you really?'"[10] Students at this stage actively seek white role models who might provide examples for nonoppressive ways of being white. Such examples might be found in the form of biographies or autobiographies of white individuals who have been engaged in a similar process. Unfortunately, these materials are not easily found because the lives of white antiracists or "allies" have not generally been subjects of study....

Participation in white consciousness-raising groups organized specifically for the purpose of examining one's own racism is often helpful in this process. At Mount Holyoke College, where I currently teach, such a group was formed (White Women Against Racism) following the 1992 acquittal of the Los Angeles police officers involved in the beating of Rodney King. Support groups of this nature help to combat the social isolation antiracist whites often experience, and provide encouragement for continued development of a self-definition as a white ally.

It is at this stage that the feelings of guilt and shame are replaced with feelings of pride and excitement. Helms writes,

> The person may begin to feel a euphoria perhaps akin to a religious rebirth. These positive feelings not only help to buttress the newly developing White identity, but provide the fuel by which the person can truly begin to tackle racism and oppression in its various forms.[11]

Mary, a senior writing her last journal entry of the semester, reflected this excitement at the changes she was observing in herself:

> This past weekend I went to New York. . . . As always we drove through Harlem on our way downtown. For the first time in four years I didn't automatically feel nervous when we turned that corner. For the first time I took an active interest in what was going on in the neighborhood and in the neighborhood itself. When the bus driver pointed out some points of interest like the Apollo, I actually recognized the names and was truly appreciative that the driver had pointed them out. I know this doesn't sound like much to get excited about, and in all honesty it doesn't really excite me either. In a way though, I guess this serves as an object lesson of sorts for me; I CAN unlearn the racism that I've been taught. It required some thought beforehand, but it certainly wasn't difficult by any means. Clearly, the next step is to identify something new to focus on and unlearn THAT as well. I can't help feeling like this is how a toddler must feel—each step is a challenge and although sometimes you fall, you don't usually hurt yourself. But overwhelmingly, each step is exciting and an accomplishment.

NOTES

1. Janet E. Helms, *Black and White Racial Identity: Theory, Research and Practice* (Westport, Conn.: Greenwood Press, 1990).
2. Ibid., p. 55.
3. For further discussion of the concept of white privilege and the advantages systematically conferred on whites, see Peggy McIntosh's working paper, *White Privilege and Male Privilege: A Personal Account of Coming to see Correspondences through Work in Women's Studies* (Wellesley, Mass.: Wellesley College Center for Research on Women).
4. Helms, *Black and White Racial Identity*, chap. 4, p. 58.
5. Tatum, "Talking about Race, Learning about Racism."
6. For a discussion of the use of action-planning projects in a course on racism, see ibid.
7. Helms, *Black and White Racial Identity*, p. 60.
8. David Wellman, *Portraits of White Racism* (New York: Cambridge University Press, 1977).
9. For further discussion of the interaction effect of stages of racial-identity development for people of color and for whites, see Tatum, "Talking about Race, Learning about Racism."
10. Helms, *Black and White Racial Identity*, p. 62.
11. Ibid.

PART THREE

Studying the Field of Multicultural Education

On the Internet . . .

Sites appropriate to Part Three

The Educational Resources Information Center (ERIC) is an online searchable index to virtually all articles published in educational journals. The index can be searched to find articles on many subjects within the field of education.

```
http://www.accesseric.org:81/
```

This Web site examines the concept of cultural literacy through the use of E. D. Hirsch's ideas. It answers the questions of what is the cultural literacy movement, what is good about it, and what are its flaws.

```
http://www.ils.nwu.edu/~e_for_e/nodes/
   NODE-94-pg.html
```

This Web site provides links to authors, journals, and books that are within the field of critical pedagogy. It includes discussions of contemporary philosophy, media criticism, and cultural studies.

```
http://www.cudenver.edu/~mryder/itc_data/
   postmodern.html
```

CHAPTER 10

The

Conservative Tradition

10.1 ARTHUR M. SCHLESINGER, JR.

The Disuniting of America

Arthur M. Schlesinger, Jr., is a well-known historian and author. He combines his scholarly work with political work, gaining the description "scholar-activist." He has been a professor at Harvard University, and he has also worked for presidents of the United States, including as adviser to John F. Kennedy. He has also written a number of presidential speeches over the years, and he worked for the Office of War Information during World War II. He is perhaps best known for his presidential histories, most famously his biographies of the Kennedys. Schlesinger also wrote books on the Andrew Jackson and Franklin D. Roosevelt presidencies. He has twice won the Pulitzer Prize for his writings on history. The following selection is from an article in the Winter 1991 issue of *American Educator*, titled "The Disuniting of America."

One of Schlesinger's key concerns in his writings is the "cult of ethnicity" and his fear that the focus on ethnicity has fragmented society and is threatening to destroy America's common core and America itself. Schlesinger begins his selection by laying out some of the inconsistencies in the beliefs throughout U.S. history. For example, one creed says that all men are created equal, yet America allowed slavery. With an Anglo-Saxon domination throughout history, ethnic groups started standing up for civil rights. This created what Schlesinger calls an "ethnic upsurge," and he gives this movement credit for correcting a lot of inequities. But his main point in this selection is that too much of a focus on ethnicity emphasizes difference, puts walls between peoples, and tries to revise history in incorrect ways.

Schlesinger also describes the role of historians in defining and shaping a national identity.

Key Concept: concerns about the "cult of ethnicity"

What then, is the American, this new man?" This was the question famously asked two centuries ago by French immigrant J. Hector St. John de Crevecoeur in his book *Letters from an American Farmer.*

Crevecoeur ruminated over the astonishing diversity of the settlers— "a mixture of English, Scotch, Irish, French, Dutch, Germans, and Swedes," a "strange mixture of blood" that you could find in no other country. "From this promiscuous breed," he wrote, "that race now called Americans has arisen."

What, Crevecoeur mused, were the characteristics of this suddenly emergent American race? He provided a classic answer to his own question: "He is an American, who leaving behind him all his ancient prejudices and manners, receives new ones from the new mode of life he has embraced, the new government he obeys, and the new rank he holds. The American is a new man, who acts upon new principles.... *Here individuals of all nations are melted into a new race of men.*"

Crevecoeur's conception was of a brand-new nationality created by individuals who, in repudiating their homelands and joining to make new lives, melted away ancient ethnic differences. Most of those intrepid Europeans who had torn up their roots to brave the wild Atlantic saw America as a transforming nation, banishing old loyalties and forging a new national identity based on common political ideals.

This conception prevailed through most of the two centuries of the history of the United States. But lately a new conception has arisen. The escape from origins has given way to the search for roots. The "ancient prejudices and manners" disclaimed by Crevecoeur have made a surprising comeback.

The new gospel condemns Crevecoeur's vision of individuals of all nations melted into a new race in favor of an opposite vision: a nation of groups, differentiated in their ancestries, inviolable in their diverse identities. The contemporary ideal is shifting from assimilation to ethnicity, from integration to separatism.

The ethnic upsurge has had some healthy consequences. The republic has at last begun to give long-overdue recognition to the role and achievements of groups subordinated and ignored during the high noon of male Anglo-Saxon dominance—women, Americans of South and East European ancestry, black Americans, Indians, Hispanics, Asians. There is far better understanding today of the indispensable contributions minorities have made to American civilization.

But the cult of ethnicity, pressed too far, exacts costs. Instead of a transformative nation with an identity all its own, America increasingly sees itself as preservative of old identities. Instead of a nation composed of individuals making their own free choices, America increasingly sees itself as composed of groups more or less indelible in their ethnic character. The national ideal had once been *e pluribus unum.* Are we now to belittle *unum* and glorify *pluribus?* Will the center hold? Or will the melting pot yield to the Tower of Babel?

A struggle to redefine the national identity is taking place in many arenas —in our politics, our voluntary organizations, our churches, our language— and in no arena more crucial than our system of education. The schools and colleges of the republic train the citizens of the future. They have always been battlegrounds for debates over beliefs, philosophies, values.

What students learn in schools vitally affects other arenas of American life —the way we see and treat other Americans, the way we conceive the purpose of the republic. The debate about the curriculum is a debate about what it means to be an American. What is ultimately at stake is the shape of the American future.

I.

How could Crevecoeur's "promiscuous breed" be transformed into a "new race"? This question preoccupied another young Frenchman who arrived in America three quarters of a century after Crevecoeur. "Imagine, my dear friend, if you can," Alexis de Tocqueville wrote back to France, "a society formed of all the nations of the world... people having different languages, beliefs, opinions: in a word, a society without roots, without memories, without prejudices, without routines, without common ideas, without a national character, yet a hundred times happier than our own." What alchemy could make this miscellany into a single society?

The answer, Tocqueville concluded, lay in the commitment of Americans to democracy and self-government. Civic participation, Tocqueville argued in *Democracy in America,* was the great educator and the great unifier. Immigrants, Tocqueville said, become Americans through the exercise of the political rights and civic responsibilities bestowed on them by the Declaration of Independence and the Constitution.

Half a century later, when the next great foreign commentator on American democracy James Bryce wrote *The American Commonwealth,* immigration had vastly increased and diversified. What struck Bryce was what had struck Tocqueville: "the amazing solvent power which American institutions, habits, and ideas exercise upon newcomers of all races... quickly dissolving and assimilating the foreign bodies that are poured into her mass."

A century after Tocqueville, another foreign visitor, Gunnar Myrdal of Sweden, called the cluster of ideas, institutions, and habits "the American Creed." Americans "of all national origins, regions, creeds, and colors," Myrdal wrote in 1944, hold in common "the *most explicitly expressed* system of general ideals" of any country in the West: the ideals of the essential dignity and equality of all human beings, of inalienable rights to freedom, justice, and opportunity.

The schools teach the principles of the Creed, Myrdal said; the churches preach them; the courts hand down judgments in their terms. Myrdal saw the Creed as the bond that links all Americans, including nonwhite minorities, and as the spur forever goading Americans to live up to their principles. "America," Myrdal said, "is continuously struggling for its soul."

The new race received its most celebrated metaphor in 1908 in a play by Israel Zangwill, an English writer of Russian Jewish origin. *The Melting-Pot* tells the story of a young Russian Jewish composer in New York. David Quixano's artistic ambition is to write a symphony expressing the vast, harmonious interweaving of races in America, and his personal hope is to overcome racial barriers and marry Vera, a beautiful Christian girl. "America," David cries, "is God's crucible, the great Melting-Pot where all the races of Europe are melting and re-forming! . . . God is making the American."

Yet even as audiences cheered *The Melting-Pot*, Zangwill's metaphor raised doubts. One had only to stroll around the great cities to see that the melting process was incomplete. Ethnic minorities were forming their own *quartiers* in which they lived in their own way—not quite that of the lands they had left but not that of Anglocentric America either: Little Italy, Chinatown, Yorkville, Harlem, and so on.

In having his drama turn on marriage between people of different races and religions, Zangwill, who had himself married a Christian, emphasized where the melting pot must inexorably lead: to the submergence of separate ethnic identities in the new American race. Soon ethnic spokesmen began to appear, moved by real concern for distinctive ethnic values and also by real if unconscious vested interest in the preservation of ethnic constituencies. Even some Americans of Anglo-Saxon descent deplored the obliteration of picturesque foreign strains for the sake of insipid Anglocentric conformity. The impression grew that the melting pot was a device to impose Anglocentric images and values upon hapless immigrants—an impression reinforced by the rise of the "Americanization" movement in response to the new polyglot immigration.

Gunnar Myrdal in 1944 showed no hesitation in declaring the American Creed the common possession of all Americans, even as his great book, *An American Dilemma,* provided a magistral analysis of America's most conspicuous failure to live up to the Creed: the treatment by white Americans of black Americans.

Noble ideals had been pronounced as if for all Americans, yet in practice they applied only to white people. White settlers had systematically pushed the American Indians back, killed their braves, seized their lands, and sequestered their tribes. They had brought Africans to America to work their plantations and Chinese to build their railroads. They had enunciated glittering generalities of freedom and withheld them from people of color. Their Constitution protected slavery, and their laws made distinctions on the basis of race. Though they eventually emancipated the slaves, they conspired in the reduction of the freedmen to third-class citizenship. Their Chinese Exclusion acts culminated in the total prohibition of Asian immigration in the Immigration Act of 1924. It occurred to damned few white Americans in these years that Americans of color were also entitled to the rights and liberties promised by the Constitution.

Yet what Bryce had called "the amazing solvent power" of American institutions and ideas retained its force, even among those most cruelly oppressed and excluded. Myrdal's polls of Afro-America showed the "determination" of blacks "to hold to the American Creed." Ralph Bunche, one of Myrdal's collaborators, observed that every man in the street—black, red, and yellow as well as white—regarded America as the "land of the free" and the "cradle of liberty." The American Creed, Myrdal surmised, meant even more to blacks than to whites, since it was the great means of pleading their unfulfilled rights.

The second world war gave the Creed new bite. Hitler's racism forced Americans to look hard at their own racial assumptions. Emboldened by the Creed, blacks organized for equal opportunities in employment, opposed segregation in the armed forces, and fought in their own units on many fronts. After the war, the civil rights revolution, so long deferred, accelerated black self-reliance. So did the collapse of white colonialism around the world and the appearance of independent black states.

Across America minorities proclaimed their pride and demanded their rights. Women, the one "minority" that in America constituted a numerical majority, sought political and economic equality. Jews gained new solidarity from the Holocaust and then from the establishment of a Jewish state in Israel. Changes in the immigration law dramatically increased the number arriving from Hispanic and Asian lands, and, following the general example, they asserted their own prerogatives. American Indians mobilized to reclaim their rights and lands long since appropriated by the white man; their spokesmen even rejected the historic designation in which Indians have taken deserved pride and named themselves Native Americans. The civil rights revolution provoked new expressions of ethnic identity by the now long-resident "new migration" from southern and eastern Europe—Italians, Greeks, Poles, Czechs, Slovaks, Hungarians.

The pressure for the new cult of ethnicity came less from the minorities en masse than from their often self-appointed spokesmen. Most ethnics, white and nonwhite, saw themselves primarily as Americans. Still, ideologues, with sufficient publicity and time, could create audiences. Spokesmen with a vested interest in ethnic identification turned against the ideal of assimilation. The melting pot, it was said, injured people by undermining their self-esteem. It denied them heroes—"role models," in the jargon—from their own ethnic ancestries. Praise now went to the "unmeltable ethnics."

In 1974, after testimony from ethnic spokesmen denouncing the melting pot as a conspiracy to homogenize America, Congress passed the Ethnic Heritage Studies Program Act—a statute that, by applying the ethnic ideology to all Americans, compromised the historic right of Americans to decide their ethnic identities for themselves. The act ignored those millions of Americans —surely a majority—who refused identification with any particular ethnic group.

The ethnic upsurge (it can hardly be called a revival because it was unprecedented) began as a gesture of protest against the Anglocentric culture. It became a cult, and today it threatens to become a counter-revolution against the original theory of America as "one people," a common culture, a single nation.

... The great American asylum, as Crevecoeur called it, open, as George Washington said, to the oppressed and persecuted of all nations, has been from the start an experiment in a multi-ethnic society. This is a bolder experiment than we sometimes remember. History is littered with the wreck of states that tried to combine diverse ethnic or linguistic or religious groups within a single sovereignty. Today's headlines tell of imminent crisis or impending dissolution in one or another multi-ethnic polity—the Soviet Union, India, Yugoslavia, Czechoslovakia, Ireland, Belgium, Canada, Lebanon, Cyprus, Israel, Ceylon, Spain, Nigeria, Kenya, Angola, Trinidad, Guyana. ... The list is almost endless.

The ethnic revolt against the melting pot has reached the point, in rhetoric at least, though not I think in reality, of a denial of the idea of a common culture and a single society. If large numbers of people really accept this, the republic would be in serious trouble. The question poses itself: how to restore the balance between *unum* and *pluribus?*

The old American homogeneity disappeared well over a century ago, never to return. Ever since, we have been preoccupied in one way or another with the problem, as Herbert Croly phrased it eighty years back in *The Promise of American Life*, "of keeping a highly differentiated society fundamentally sound and whole."

The genius of America lies in its capacity to forge a single nation from peoples of remarkably diverse racial, religious, and ethnic origins. It has done so because democratic principles provide both the philosophical bond of union and practical experience in civic participation. The American Creed envisages a nation composed of individuals making their own choices and accountable to themselves, not a nation based on inviolable ethnic communities. The Constitution turns on individual rights, not on group rights. Law, in order to rectify past wrongs, has from time to time (and in my view often properly so) acknowledged the claims of groups; but this is the exception, not the rule.

Our democratic principles contemplate an open society founded on tolerance of differences and on mutual respect. In practice, America has been more open to some than to others. But it is more open to all today than it was yesterday and is likely to be even more open tomorrow than today. The steady movement of American life has been from exclusion to inclusion.

Historically and culturally this republic has an Anglo-Saxon base; but from the start the base has been modified, enriched, and reconstituted by transfusions from other continents and civilizations. The movement from exclusion to inclusion causes a constant revision in the texture of our culture. The ethnic transfusions affect all aspects of American life—our politics, our literature, our music, our painting, our movies, our cuisine, our customs, our dreams.

Black Americans in particular have influenced the ever-changing national culture in many ways. They have lived here for centuries, and, unless one believes in racist mysticism, they belong far more to American culture than to the culture of Africa. Their history is part of the Western democratic tradition, not an alternative to it. No one does black Americans more disservice than those Afrocentric ideologues who would define them out of the West.

The interplay of diverse traditions produces the America we know. "Paradoxical though it may seem," Diane Ravitch has well said, "the United States has a common culture that is multicultural." That is why unifying political ideals coexist so easily and cheerfully with diversity in social and cultural values. Within the overarching political commitment, people are free to live as they choose, ethnically and otherwise. Differences will remain; some are reinvented; some are used to drive us apart. But as we renew our allegiance to the unifying ideals, we provide the solvents that will prevent differences from escalating into antagonism and hatred.

One powerful reason for the continuing movement in America from exclusion to inclusion is that the American Creed facilitates the appeal from the actual to the ideal. When we talk of the American democratic faith, we must understand it in its true dimensions. It is not an impervious, final, and complacent orthodoxy, intolerant of deviation and dissent, fulfilled in flag salutes, oaths of allegiance, and hands over the heart. It is an ever-evolving philosophy, fulfilling its ideals through debate, self-criticism, protest, disrespect, and irreverence; a tradition in which all have rights of heterodoxy and opportunities for self-assertion. The Creed has been the means by which Americans have haltingly but persistently narrowed the gap between performance and principle. It is what all Americans should learn, because it is what binds all Americans together.

Americans of whatever origin should take pride in the distinctive inheritance to which they have all contributed, as other nations take pride in their distinctive inheritances.

Our schools and colleges have a responsibility to teach history for its own sake—as part of the intellectual equipment of civilized persons—and not to degrade history by allowing its contents to be dictated by pressure groups, whether political, economic, religious, or ethnic. The past may sometimes give offense to one or another minority; that is no reason for rewriting history. Properly taught, history will convey a sense of the variety, continuity, and adaptability of culture, of the need for understanding other cultures, of the ability of individuals and peoples to overcome obstacles, of the importance of critical analysis and dispassionate judgment in every area of life.

It has taken time to make our values real for all our citizens, and we still have a good distance to go, but we have made progress. If we now repudiate the quite marvelous inheritance that history bestows on us, we invite the fragmentation of the national community into a quarrelsome spatter of enclaves, ghettos, tribes. The bonds of cohesion in our society are sufficiently fragile, or so it seems to me, that it makes no sense to strain them by encouraging and exalting cultural and linguistic apartheid.

The question America confronts as a pluralistic society is how to vindicate cherished cultures and traditions without breaking the bonds of cohesion —common ideals, common political institutions, common language, common culture, common fate—that hold the republic together. Our task is to combine due appreciation of the splendid diversity of the nation with due emphasis on the great unifying Western ideas of individual freedom, political democracy, and human rights. These are the ideas that define the American nationality and that today empower people of all continents, races, and creeds.

10.2   E. D. HIRSCH, JR.

American Diversity and Public Discourse

E. D. Hirsch, Jr., is a professor of English at the University of Virginia in Charlottesville, Virginia, and president of the Core Knowledge Foundation. He emphasizes the idea that a core set of knowledge and literacy should form the foundation of American society. In his writings he lays out the cultural literacy that he and other conservative scholars believe form the core of what makes American strong and coherent and, therefore, that all people should know. At the end of the book from which the following selection is taken, *Cultural Literacy: What Every American Needs to Know* (Houghton Mifflin, 1987), he has included a checklist of over 1,000 discrete items that he feels every literate American ought to know, including dates, names, pieces of literature, and political concepts.

In the following selection, Hirsch states that diversity is fine but that America must have a core of common culture. He notes that America has a set of traditions, myths, ceremonies, and values that are durable. The English language, for instance, has survived throughout U.S. history and has held the country together. The core of a national vocabulary has served generation after generation, and Hirsch believes that it is this core that maintains the coherence of the country. He worries that this common cultural literacy has been lost and that youngsters may actually need to be reintroduced to this cultural vocabulary.

Key Concept: a common cultural core that keeps America coherent

OUR TRADITIONS OF DIVERSITY AND UNITY

... To acknowledge the importance of minority and local cultures of all sorts, to insist on their protection and nurture, to give them demonstrations of respect in the public sphere are traditional aims that should be stressed even when one is concerned, as I am, with national culture and literacy. But this [selection] is not ... an inquiry into the multifarious local and ethnic traditions that are found in the United States. It is for the Amish to decide what Amish traditions are, but it is for all of us to decide collectively what our American traditions are, to decide what "American" means on the other side of the hyphen in

165

Italo-American or Asian-American. What national values and traditions really belong to national cultural literacy?

The larger national culture must be extremely capacious and somewhat vague. That is the case in a large monocultural country like France, and it is even more emphatically so in a deliberately diversified one like our own. What is common to our broad culture? Besides the English language and the national legal codes, American culture possesses first of all a civil religion that underlies our civil ethos. Our civil ethos treasures patriotism and loyalty as high, though perhaps not ultimate, ideals and fosters the belief that the conduct of the nation is guided by a vaguely defined God. Our tradition places importance on carrying out the rites and ceremonies of our civil ethos and religion through the national flag, the national holidays, and the national anthem (which means "national hymn"), and supports the morality of tolerance and benevolence, of the Golden Rule, and communal cooperation. We believe in altruism and self-help, in equality, freedom, truth telling, and respect for the national law.

Besides these vague principles, American culture fosters such myths about itself as its practicality, ingenuity, inventiveness, and independent-mindedness, its connection with the frontier, and its beneficence in the world (even when its leaders do not always follow beneficent policies). It acknowledges that Americans have the right to disagree with the traditional values but nonetheless acquiesce in the dominant civil ethos to the point of accepting imprisonment as the ultimate means of expressing dissent.

Although these principles have not been immune to internal attack in American history, they have nonetheless proved durable. Our national culture was created at the start of the modern age, when dogmatic, sectarian religion had already come under the devastating criticism of the Enlightenment, and when American civil religion, in the vague form in which our founders created it, began to accommodate itself to the secularism of the modern age. This civil religion, "big-tented and tolerant," as [*Washington Post* commentator] Charles Krauthammer calls it, lends coherence to the larger American public culture and is the basic source of American values.

Although some modern secularists do not accept public religious expressions of any sort, and do not regard them as the necessary source of social bonding and civic virtue, their position has not been sustained by history. The American civil religion, as expressed in our national rites and symbols, is in fact a central source of coherence in American public culture, holding together various and even contradictory elements of its tradition. Secularists who deplore any public references to God, and regard benevolent social ideas as ultimate civic principles, are, in the end, just another species of hyphenated Americans —secularist-Americans—who form a large class but acquiesce in the second side of the American hyphen like most of us who sing the national hymn, pledge allegiance ("under God") to the flag, know that all are "endowed by their Creator" with inalienable rights.

When George Washington in his Farewell Address said that "religion and morality are indispensable supports" of the American commonwealth, these sentiments were by no means peculiar to him. Those who collaborated in writing his address included Alexander Hamilton, James Madison, and John Jay, and their sentiments represented ideas expressed elsewhere by other founders, including Jefferson. The American founders were well aware of the paradox that precisely because established sectarian religion must be forbidden, a non-sectarian civil "religion" must be put in its stead to secure a good and harmonious democracy. Since the people are to govern themselves, they must govern on high, broadly religious principle for the larger public good as well as for their own private good.

Such religious sentiments must have expression in rituals and sacred texts. The civil religion honors the values of tolerance, equality, freedom, patriotism, duty, and cooperation; it has symbols and rites like the flag, public oaths, and the holidays. It also has its own bible, a knowledge of which is at the heart of cultural literacy. That bible was not decided upon by a synod once and for all. No doubt some of its "books"—the Declaration of Independence, the Gettysburg Address, some parts of the Bible itself—will always belong in it, but our consensual form of civil religion is much like our legal system in that it allows for change and amendment.

I am not the first to make this observation about our civil bible. Horace Kallen, that enthusiast for cultural pluralism, proposes that the following make up its canon:

> Its book of Genesis would of course be the Declaration of Independence, which is also the simplest, clearest, most comprehensive yet briefest telling of the American Idea. It sets the theme and whatever follows is a variation upon it.

Kallen lists his preferences for additional sacred texts.

> George Washington's letter to the Jewish Congregation at Newport; Jefferson's First and Second Inaugurals; his Virginia Bill of Religious Liberty; his letters to John Adams on Natural Aristocracy; certain articles from the *Federalist;* the Constitution; certain decisions and statements of John Marshall's. The Bible might include James Madison's "Memorial and Remonstrance"; James Monroe's promulgation of the Monroe Doctrine; the Constitution of the American Anti-Slavery Society; Horace Mann's Twelfth Report to the Massachusetts Board of Education; the Seneca Falls Declaration on Women's Rights; Abraham Lincoln's "House Divided" speech; John Brown's speech to the Court that sentenced him . . .

And so on for a couple of paragraphs, through the Truman Doctrine and the reports of Truman's Commission on Higher Education and on Civil Rights.

Kallen's list is dated, too long, and too narrowly based in his own values. It takes too little account of the distinction between what is broadly and consensually established among Americans over the generations and what he thinks it would be good to throw in. But Kallen rightly includes contemporary documents because the American bible is constantly being brought up to date through new additions, as is the American Constitution through new interpretations. Cultural revision is one of our best traditions.

There is, of course, a very good reason why the principle of cultural revision should parallel our principle of legal change and constitutional reinterpretation. They are fundamentally similar. The Constitution has biblical status for the nation, but it is understood to be amendable because it serves a principle more ultimate than itself—that of the sovereignty of the people. The bible of the American civil religion is based on fundamental principles of justice, freedom, and equality that permit progress and change.

One recent addition to the current American bible is the "I Have a Dream" speech by Martin Luther King, Jr., which self-consciously draws on earlier texts of the American bible to make its new contribution, just as the writers of the New Testament deliberately reappropriated the words of the Old. I have placed in italics King's quotations from and allusions to documents that belong to the cultural literacy of every American.

> I have a dream that one day this nation will rise up and live out the true meaning of its creed: *We hold these truths to be self-evident; that all men are created equal....* I have a dream that one day *every valley shall be exalted, every hill and mountain shall be made low, the rough places will be made plains, and the crooked places will be made straight, and the glory of the Lord shall be revealed, and all flesh shall see it together....* This will be the day when *all of God's children* will be able to sing with new meaning, *My country 'tis of thee, sweet land of liberty, of thee I sing. Land where my fathers died, land of the pilgrims' pride, from every mountainside, let freedom ring....* When we let freedom ring, when we let it ring from every village and every hamlet, from every state and every city, we will be able to speed up that day when all of God's children, black men and white men, Jews and Gentiles, Protestants and Catholics, will be able to join hands and sing in the words of that old Negro spiritual, *Free at last! Free at last! Thank God Almighty, we are free at last!*

THE VOCABULARY OF A PLURALISTIC NATION

... By accident of history, American cultural literacy has a bias toward English literate traditions. Short of revolutionary political upheaval, there is absolutely nothing that can be done about this. It is not a weakness of our literate culture that it has its origins in English traditions, for, like all other literate traditions connected with great national languages, the English tradition is broad and heterogeneous and grows ever more so. For many centuries it has embraced a wide range of materials, as evidenced in Hugh Blair's *Rhetoric*, which contains elements from many lands and cultures. Yet Blair's book did not contain any items from his native land. Many national cultures are neglected in our national vocabulary—not just Scottish, Welsh, and Irish, but also German, French, Spanish, and Italian. Dozens of other cultures could consider themselves disenfranchised by the continued dominance in our nation of English literate culture. What have Americans to do, in any ethnic or national sense, with 1066 or Chaucer or Milton? Nonetheless, we have kept and still need to keep English culture as the dominant part of our national vocabulary for purely functional reasons.

After more than two hundred years of national life, the main elements of our vocabulary have transcended the sphere of contention and dispute. We do not argue whether Abraham Lincoln in his log cabin belongs in the vocabulary of literate Americans, any more than we argue about spelling. No matter how value-laden or partisan some of these common elements were in their origins long ago, they now exist as common materials of communication. History has decided what those elements are. They are the medium of public discourse, the instruments through which we are able to communicate our views to one another and make decisions in a democratic way.

It is cultural chauvinism and provincialism to believe that the content of our vocabulary is something either to recommend or deplore by virtue of its inherent merit. Think how well the French or Chinese have done without Shakespeare or George Washington, and how well we have done without Racine or Lao-tse. No doubt it benefits the French and Chinese to learn about Shakespeare and Washington, just as it benefits us to learn about Racine and Lao-tse. But the benefit we derive is to come to the tolerant understanding that no single national vocabulary is inherently superior or privileged above all others.

That is the virtue of broadening our horizons by encountering cultures other than our own. We discover not only that other cultures have produced other successful vocabularies for dealing with life, but also that all of the great national vocabularies, including our own, have a relativity about them. Each vocabulary would be different if history had been different—if Shakespeare had never been born, for instance, or if he had chosen not to write about Hamlet. The specific contents of the different national vocabularies are far less important than the fact of their being shared.

Any true democrat who understands this, whether liberal or conservative, will accept the necessary conservatism that exists at the core of the national vocabulary, which must serve all sorts and conditions of people from all generations. Changes at its core must occur with glacial slowness if it is to accommodate all the people and serve as our universal medium of communication.

Many Americans who have graduated from high school in the recent past have been deprived of the cultural vocabulary that was commonly possessed by educated persons in past generations. Some repair work is necessary for them and for the members of the current school generation. They must be reintroduced to the cultural vocabulary that continues to be the foundation for literate national communication. The new illiteracy is sometimes excused by the argument that our schools are now educating larger portions of our population. The point is that we are *not* educating them. We undertook the great task of universal education precisely in order to produce a truly literate population, but we have not succeeded in that task in recent years. We must assure that new generations will continue to be enfranchised in our medium of national communication as securely as they are enfranchised at the polls.

There is a second respect in which the national vocabulary must be enhanced for the current school generation. As national and international life has come to contain an increasingly technical element, the idea of literacy has gradually come to include a larger vocabulary of shared scientific and technical knowledge. Especially today, when political decisions in our democracy have an increasingly technical element, our schools should enhance scientific and technical vocabularies. We require not only that ordinary citizens be scientifically literate but that technicians and scientists master the nonscientific literate culture. To explain the implications of their work to others, experts must be aware of the shared associations in our literate vocabulary and be able to build analogies on those associations.

Both of these proposals—bridging the generation gap in cultural literacy and enhancing its scientific component—are closely tied to basic principles of the American republic. I have in mind the Founding Fathers' idea of a literate and informed citizenry. Essential to this concept is the principle that, when desirable, the main features and implications of the most arcane specialty can be explained to literate and educated citizens. Economic issues can be discussed in public. The moral dilemmas of new medical knowledge can be weighed. The implications of technological change can become subjects of informed public discourse—not about technical details, but about the broad issues of the debate. Otherwise we are in danger of falling victims to technological intimidation.

The founders of our republic had in mind a Ciceronian ideal of education and discourse in a republic. Cicero claimed that he could explain Greek science and philosophy or anything else to his fellow Romans in ordinary Latin terms, and he did. Our founders greatly admired Cicero's aims. Thomas Jefferson used the concepts in the Declaration of Independence and constantly referred to Cicero's writings in the notebook he kept. John Adams quoted Cicero at length in his *Preface on Government* and said of him that "all the ages of the world have not produced a greater statesman and philosopher combined."

The Ciceronian ideal of universal public discourse was strong in this country into the early twentieth century. In the Roman republic of Cicero's time, such discourse was chiefly oral, and the education Cicero sought was in "rhetoric" rather than "literacy." But the terms are equivalent. Literacy—reading and writing taken in a serious sense—is the rhetoric of our day, the basis of public discourse in a modern republic. The teaching of Ciceronian literacy as our founders conceived it is a primary but currently neglected responsibility of our schools.

CHAPTER 11 Critical Pedagogy

11.1 PAULO FREIRE

Pedagogy of the Oppressed

The writings of Paulo Freire (1921–1997) are a direct result of his life and circumstances in Brazil. His family lost their middle-class status during the depression of the 1930s, and he experienced poverty, hunger, malnourishment, and the accompanying falling behind in school. This life experience led him to work among the poor during his adolescent years to try to help peasants and workers in a project of liberation, a project he worked on for the rest of his life. In trying to help the poor to understand their legal rights, he turned his efforts to adult literacy programs and to methods of educating the poor and illiterate. In 1964, as a result of his work with the poor in Brazil, he was arrested, imprisoned, and then forced into exile. He returned 16 years later to become the appointed minister of education in Rio de Janeiro. He also served as a professor at Harvard University, and in 1986 he received the United Nations Educational, Scientific and Cultural Organization (UNESCO) Prize for Education. His books include *Pedagogy of the Oppressed* (Continuum, 1970), from which the following selection has been taken; *Education for Critical Consciousness* (Seabury Press, 1973); and *Pedagogy of Hope: Reliving Pedagogy of the Oppressed* (Continuum, 1994).

In the following selection, Freire describes what he means by his concept of a pedagogy of the oppressed. He begins by explaining that both the oppressed and those who cause others to be oppressed are being dehumanized. People who want to overcome oppression, whether part of the oppressed or the oppressors, must unveil that oppression and commit themselves to its transformation. And to do this, Freire says, humanists must "authentically commit themselves to the people [and] must re-examine themselves constantly." They must be virtually converted to the life of the people. The key, Freire says, is "critical and liberating dialogue," which engages the people who are oppressed, rather than serving as an imposition by the oppressors.

Key Concept: recognizing and ending dehumanization

While the problem of humanization has always, from an axiological point of view, been man's central problem, it now takes on the character of an inescapable concern. Concern for humanization leads at once to the recognition of dehumanization, not only as an ontological possibility but as an historical reality. And as man perceives the extent of dehumanization, he asks himself if humanization is a viable possibility. Within history, in concrete, objective contexts, both humanization and dehumanization are possibilities for man as an uncompleted being conscious of his incompletion.

But while both humanization and dehumanization are real alternatives, only the first is man's vocation. This vocation is constantly negated, yet it is affirmed by that very negation. It is thwarted by injustice, exploitation, oppression, and the violence of the oppressors; it is affirmed by the yearning of the oppressed for freedom and justice, and by their struggle to recover their lost humanity.

Dehumanization, which marks not only those whose humanity has been stolen, but also (though in a different way) those who have stolen it, is a *distortion* of the vocation of becoming more fully human. This distortion occurs within history; but it is not an historical vocation. Indeed, to admit of dehumanization as an historical vocation would lead either to cynicism or total despair. The struggle for humanization, for the emancipation of labor, for the overcoming of alienation, for the affirmation of men as persons would be meaningless. This struggle is possible only because dehumanization, although a concrete historical fact, is *not* a given destiny but the result of an unjust order that engenders violence in the oppressors, which in turn dehumanizes the oppressed.

Because it is a distortion of being more fully human, sooner or later being less human leads the oppressed to struggle against those who made them so. In order for this struggle to have meaning, the oppressed must not, in seeking to regain their humanity (which is a way to create it), become in turn oppressors of the oppressors, but rather restorers of the humanity of both.

This, then, is the great humanistic and historical task of the oppressed: to liberate themselves and their oppressors as well. The oppressors, who oppress, exploit, and rape by virtue of their power, cannot find in this power the strength to liberate either the oppressed or themselves. Only power that springs from the weakness of the oppressed will be sufficiently strong to free both. Any attempt to "soften" the power of the oppressor in deference to the weakness of the oppressed almost always manifests itself in the form of false generosity; indeed, the attempt never goes beyond this. In order to have the continued opportunity to express their "generosity," the oppressors must perpetuate injustice as well. An unjust social order is the permanent fount of this "generosity," which is nourished by death, despair, and poverty. That is why the dispensers of false generosity become desperate at the slightest threat to its source.

True generosity consists precisely in fighting to destroy the causes which nourish false charity. False charity constrains the fearful and subdued, the "rejects of life," to extend their trembling hands. True generosity lies in striving so that these hands—whether of individuals or entire peoples—need be extended less and less in supplication, so that more and more they become human hands which work and, working, transform the world.

This lesson and this apprenticeship must come, however, from the oppressed themselves and from those who are truly solidary with them. As individuals or as peoples, by fighting for the restoration of their humanity they will be attempting the restoration of true generosity. Who are better prepared than the oppressed to understand the terrible significance of an oppressive society? Who suffer the effects of oppression more than the oppressed? Who can better understand the necessity of liberation? They will not gain this liberation by chance but through the praxis of their quest for it, through their recognition of the necessity to fight for it. And this fight, because of the purpose given it by the oppressed, will actually constitute an act of love opposing the lovelessness which lies at the heart of the oppressors' violence, lovelessness even when clothed in false generosity....

The pedagogy of the oppressed, as a humanist and libertarian pedagogy, has two distinct stages. In the first, the oppressed unveil the world of oppression and through the praxis commit themselves to its transformation. In the second stage, in which the reality of oppression has already been transformed, this pedagogy ceases to belong to the oppressed and becomes a pedagogy of all men in the process of permanent liberation. In both stages, it is always through action in depth that the culture of domination is culturally confronted.[1] In the first stage this confrontation occurs through the change in the way the oppressed perceive the world of oppression; in the second stage, through the expulsion of the myths created and developed in the old order, which like specters haunt the new structure emerging from the revolutionary transformation.

The pedagogy of the first stage must deal with the problem of the oppressed consciousness and the oppressor consciousness, the problem of men who oppress and men who suffer oppression. It must take into account their behavior, their view of the world, and their ethics. A particular problem is the duality of the oppressed: they are contradictory, divided beings, shaped by and existing in a concrete situation of oppression and violence.

Any situation in which "A" objectively exploits "B" or hinders his pursuit of self-affirmation as a responsible person is one of oppression. Such a situation in itself constitutes violence, even when sweetened by false generosity, because it interferes with man's ontological and historical vocation to be more fully human. With the establishment of a relationship of oppression, violence has *already* begun. Never in history has violence been initiated by the oppressed. How could they be the initiators, if they themselves are the result of violence? How could they be the sponsors of something whose objective inauguration called forth their existence as oppressed? There would be no oppressed had there been no prior situation of violence to establish their subjugation.

Violence is initiated by those who oppress, who exploit, who fail to recognize others as persons—not by those who are oppressed, exploited, and unrecognized. It is not the unloved who initiate disaffection, but those who cannot love because they love only themselves. It is not the helpless, subject to terror, who initiate terror, but the violent, who with their power create the concrete situation which begets the "rejects of life." It is not the tyrannized who initiate despotism, but the tyrants. It is not the despised who initiate hatred, but those who despise. It is not those whose humanity is denied them who negate man, but those who denied that humanity (thus negating their own as well). Force is used not by those who have become weak under the preponderance of the strong, but by the strong who have emasculated them.

For the oppressors, however, it is always the oppressed (whom they obviously never call "the oppressed" but—depending on whether they are fellow countrymen or not—"those people" or "the blind and envious masses" or "savages" or "natives" or "subversives") who are disaffected, who are "violent," "barbaric," "wicked," or "ferocious" when they react to the violence of the oppressors.

Yet it is—paradoxical though it may seem—precisely in the response of the oppressed to the violence of their oppressors that a gesture of love may be found. Consciously or unconsciously, the act of rebellion by the oppressed (an act which is always, or nearly always, as violent as the initial violence of the oppressors) can initiate love. Whereas the violence of the oppressors prevents the oppressed from being fully human, the response of the latter to this violence is grounded in the desire to pursue the right to be human. As the oppressors dehumanize others and violate their rights, they themselves also become dehumanized. As the oppressed, fighting to be human, take away the oppressors' power to dominate and suppress, they restore to the oppressors the humanity they had lost in the exercise of oppression.

It is only the oppressed who, by freeing themselves, can free their oppressors. The latter, as an oppressive class, can free neither others nor themselves. It is therefore essential that the oppressed wage the struggle to resolve the contradiction in which they are caught; and the contradiction will be resolved by the appearance of the new man: neither oppressor nor oppressed, but man in the process of liberation. If the goal of the oppressed is to become fully human, they will not achieve their goal by merely reversing the terms of the contradiction, by simply changing poles.

... [A]nother issue of indubitable importance arises: the fact that certain members of the oppressor class join the oppressed in their struggle for liberation, thus moving from one pole of the contradiction to the other. Theirs is a fundamental role, and has been so throughout the history of this struggle. It happens, however, that as they cease to be exploiters or indifferent spectators or simply the heirs of exploitation and move to the side of the exploited, they almost always bring with them the marks of their origin: their prejudices and their deformations, which include a lack of confidence in the people's ability to think, to want, and to know. Accordingly, these adherents to the people's cause constantly run the risk of falling into a type of generosity as malefic as that of the oppressors. The generosity of the oppressors is nourished by an unjust order, which must be maintained in order to justify that generosity. Our converts, on the other hand, truly desire to transform the unjust order; but because of their background they believe that they must be the executors of the transformation. They talk about the people, but they do not trust them; and trusting the people is the indispensable precondition for revolutionary change. A real humanist can be identified more by his trust in the people, which engages him in their struggle, than by a thousand actions in their favor without that trust.

Those who authentically commit themselves to the people must reexamine themselves constantly. This conversion is so radical as not to allow of ambiguous behavior. To affirm this commitment but to consider oneself the proprietor of revolutionary wisdom—which must then be given to (or imposed on) the people—is to retain the old ways. The man who proclaims devotion to the cause of liberation yet is unable to enter into *communion* with the people, whom he continues to regard as totally ignorant, is grievously self-deceived. The convert who approaches the people but feels alarm at each step they take, each doubt they express, and each suggestion they offer, and attempts to impose his "status," remains nostalgic towards his origins. . . .

Critical and liberating dialogue, which presupposes action, must be carried on with the oppressed at whatever the stage of their struggle for liberation. The content of that dialogue can and should vary in accordance with historical conditions and the level at which the oppressed perceive reality. But to substitute monologue, slogans, and communiqués for dialogue is to attempt to liberate the oppressed with the instruments of domestication. Attempting to liberate the oppressed without their reflective participation in the act of liberation is to treat them as objects which must be saved from a burning building; it is to lead them into the populist pitfall and transform them into masses which can be manipulated.

At all stages of their liberation, the oppressed must see themselves as men engaged in the ontological and historical vocation of becoming more fully human. Reflection and action become imperative when one does not erroneously attempt to dichotomize the content of humanity from its historical forms.

The insistence that the oppressed engage in reflection on their concrete situation is not a call to armchair revolution. On the contrary, reflection—true reflection—leads to action.

NOTES

1. This appears to be the fundamental aspect of Mao's Cultural Revolution.

Insurgent Multiculturalism and the Promise of Pedagogy

Henry A. Giroux is a prolific writer who has published over 200 articles, chapters, and books in the past 20 years. He is currently director of the Waterbury Forum in Education and Cultural Studies at Pennsylvania State University, and he previously taught at Miami University in Florida, Tufts University in Medford, Massachusetts, and Boston University in Massachusetts. His main areas of focus are critical pedagogy, the politics of curriculum and education, popular culture, and issues of power in general. Some of his books are *Living Dangerously: Multiculturalism and the Politics of Difference* (Peter Lang, 1993) and *Border Crossings: Cultural Workers and the Politics of Education* (Routledge, 1992). He has received much recognition for his books, some of which have been named the most significant books in education by the American Educational Studies Association for several years. *Living Dangerously* was named "Outstanding Book on the Subject of Human Rights in North America" by the Gustavus Myers Center for the Study of Human Rights. Important to Giroux has been his work with the respected educator Paulo Freire, and he serves on the International Advisory Board of the Paulo Freire Institute in Brazil.

The following selection has been taken from chapter 15, "Insurgent Multiculturalism and the Promise of Pedagogy," of *Multiculturalism: A Critical Reader,* edited by David Theo Goldberg (Blackwell, 1994). In it, Giroux takes an activist stance toward what multiculturalism means. As he describes, conservatives want to shut out all talk of white power and racism. Giroux wants to make multicultural education more political and to make these issues central rather than ignore them. With regard to what he calls "insurgent multiculturalism," Giroux wants to "strip white supremacy of its legitimacy and authority." Giroux believes that multiculturalism must be ethically and politically based to allow students and teachers to understand how power works and how power relations can be transformed. He

considers his suggestions practical, and he describes how pedagogy and
curriculum can develop such practices within multicultural education.

Key Concept: making multiculturalism ethically and politically active

*Henry A.
Giroux*

INTRODUCTION

Multiculturalism has become a central discourse in the struggle over issues regarding national identity, the construction of historical memory, the purpose
of schooling, and the meaning of democracy. While most of these battles have
been waged in the university around curriculum changes and in polemic exchanges in the public media, today's crucial culture wars increasingly are being
fought on two fronts. First, multiculturalism has become a "tug of war over who
gets to create public culture,"[1] Second, the contested terrain of multiculturalism
is heating up between educational institutions that do not meet the needs of a
massively shifting student population and students and their families for whom
schools increasingly are perceived as merely one more instrument of repression.

In the first instance, the struggle over public culture is deeply tied to
a historical legacy that affirms American character and national identity in
terms that are deeply exclusionary, nativist, and racist. Echoes of this racism
can be heard in the voices of public intellectuals such as George Will, Arthur
Schlesinger Jr, and George Gilder. Institutional support for such racism can be
found in neoconservative establishments such as the Olin Foundation and the
National Association of Scholars.

In the second instance, academic culture has become a contested space
primarily because groups that have been traditionally excluded from the public
school curriculum and from the ranks of higher education are now becoming
more politicized and are attending higher education institutions in increasing
numbers. One consequence of this developing politics of difference has been a
series of struggles by subordinate groups over access to educational resources,
gender and racial equity, curriculum content, and the disciplinary-based organization of academic departments.

While it has become commonplace to acknowledge the conflicting meanings of multiculturalism, it is important to acknowledge that in its conservative
and liberal forms multiculturalism has placed the related problems of white
racism, social justice, and power off limits, especially as these might be addressed as part of a broader set of political and pedagogical concerns. In what
follows, I want to reassert the importance of making the pedagogical more political. That is, I want to analyze how a broader definition of pedagogy can be
used to address how the production of knowledge, social identities, and social
relations might challenge the racist assumptions and practices that inform a variety of cultural sites, including but not limited to the public and private spheres
of schooling. Central to this approach is an attempt to define the pedagogical
meaning of what I will call an insurgent multiculturalism. This is not a multiculturalism that is limited to a fascination with the construction of identities,
communicative competence, and the celebration of tolerance. Instead, I want to

shift the discussion of multiculturalism to a pedagogical terrain in which relations of power and racialized identities become paramount as part of a language of critique and possibility.

In part, this suggests constructing "an educational politics that would reveal the structures of power relations at work in the racialization of our social order" while simultaneously encouraging students to "think about the invention of the category of whiteness as well as that of blackness and, consequently, to make visible what is rendered invisible when viewed as the normative state of existence: the (white) point in space from which we tend to identify difference."[2] As part of a language of critique, a central concern of an insurgent multiculturalism is to strip white supremacy of its legitimacy and authority. As part of a project of possibility, and insurgent multiculturalism is about developing a notion of radical democracy around differences that are not exclusionary and fixed, but that designate sites of struggle that are open, fluid, and that will provide the conditions for expanding the heterogeneity of public spaces and the possibility for "critical dialogues across different political communities and constituencies."[3] ...

TOWARD AN INSURGENT MULTICULTURALISM

> To make a claim for multiculturalism is not ... to suggest a juxtaposition of several cultures whose frontiers remain intact, nor is it to subscribe to a bland "melting-pot" type of attitude that would level all differences. It lies instead, in the intercultural acceptance of risks, unexpected detours, and complexities of relation between break and closure.[4]

Multiculturalism like another broadly signifying term is multiaccentual and must be adamantly challenged when defined as part of the discourse of domination or essentialism. The challenge the term presents is daunting given the way in which it has been appropriated by various mainstream and orthodox positions. For example, when defined in corporate terms it generally is reduced to a message without critical content. Liberals have used multiculturalism to denote a pluralism devoid of historical contextualization and the specificities of relations of power or they have depicted a view of cultural struggle in which the most fundamental contradictions "implicating race, class, and gender can be harmonized within the prevailing structure of power relation."[5] For many conservatives, multiculturalism has come to signify a disruptive, unsettling, and dangerous force in American society. For some critics, it has been taken up as a slogan for promoting an essentializing identity politics and various forms of nationalism. In short, multiculturalism can be defined through a variety of ideological constructs, and signifies a terrain of struggle around the reformation of historical memory, national identity, self- and social representation, and the politics of difference.

Multiculturalism is too important as a political discourse to be exclusively appropriated by liberals and conservatives. This suggests that if the concept of multiculturalism is to become useful as a pedagogical concept, educators need to appropriate it as more than a tool for critical understanding and the pluralizing of differences; it must also be used as an ethical and political referent which allows teachers and students to understand how power works in the interest of dominant social relations, and how such relations can be challenged and transformed. In other words, an insurgent multiculturalism should promote pedagogical practices that offer the possibility for schools to become places where students and teachers can become border crossers engaged in critical ethical reflection about what it means to bring a wider variety of cultures into dialogue with each other, to theorize about cultures in the plural, within rather than outside "antagonistic relations of domination and subordination."[6]

In opposition to the liberal emphasis on individual diversity, an insurgent multiculturalism also must address issues regarding group differences and how power relations function to structure racial and ethnic identities. Furthermore, cultural differences cannot be merely affirmed to be assimilated into a common culture or policed through economic, political, and social spheres that restrict full citizenship to dominant groups. If multiculturalism is to be linked to renewed interests in expanding the principles of democracy to wider spheres of application, it must be defined in pedagogical and political terms that embrace it as a referent and practice for civic courage, critical citizenship, and democratic struggle. Bhikhu Parekh provides a definition that appears to avoid a superficial pluralism and a notion of multiculturalism that is structured in dominance. He writes:

> Multiculturalism doesn't simply mean numerical plurality of different cultures, but rather a community which is creating, guaranteeing, encouraging spaces within which different communities are able to grow at their own pace. At the same time it means creating a public space in which these communities are able to interact, enrich the existing culture and create a new consensual culture in which they recognize reflections of their own identity.[7]

In this view, multiculturalism becomes more than a critical referent for interrogating the racist representations and practices of the dominant culture, it also provides a space in which the criticism of cultural practices is inextricably linked to the production of cultural spaces marked by the formation of new identities and pedagogical practices that offers a powerful challenge to the racist, patriarchal, and sexist principles embedded in American society and schooling. Within this discourse, curriculum is viewed as a hierarchical and representational system that selectively produces knowledge, identities, desires, and values. The notion that curriculum represents knowledge that is objective, value free, and beneficial to all students is challenged forcefully as it becomes clear that those who benefit from public schooling and higher education are generally white, middle-class students whose histories, experiences, language, and knowledge largely conform to dominant cultural codes and practices. Moreover, an insurgent multiculturalism performs a theoretical service by addressing curriculum as a form of cultural politics which demands linking the production and legitimation of classroom knowledge, social identities, and values to the institutional environments in which they are produced.

As part of a project of possibility, I want to suggest some general elements that might inform an insurgent multicultural curriculum. First, a multicultural curriculum must be informed by a new language in which cultural differences are taken up not as something to be tolerated by as essential to expanding the discourse and practice of democratic life. It is important to note that multiculturalism is not merely an ideological construct, it also refers to the fact that by the year 2010, people of color will be the numerical majority in the United States. This suggests that educators need to develop a language, vision, and curriculum in which multiculturalism and democracy become mutually reinforcing categories. At issue here is the task of reworking democracy as a pedagogical and cultural practice that contributes to what John Dewey once called the creation of an articulate public. [Historian and intellectual] Manning Marable defines some of the essential parameters of this task.

> Multicultural political democracy means that this country was not built by and for only one group—Western Europeans; that our country does not have only one language—English; or only one religion—Christianity; or only one economic philosophy—corporate capitalism. Multicultural democracy means that the leadership within our society should reflect the richness, colors and diversity expressed in the lives of all of our people. Multicultural democracy demands new types of power sharing and the reallocation of resources necessary to great economic and social development for those who have been systematically excluded and denied.[8]

Imperative to such a task is a reworking of the relationship between culture and power to avoid what Homi Bhabha has called "the subsumption or sublation of social antagonism . . . the repression of social divisions . . . and a representation of the social that naturalizes cultural difference and turns it into a 'second'-nature argument."[9]

Second, as part of an attempt to develop a multicultural and multiracial society consistent with the principles of a democratic society, educators must account for the fact that men and women of color are disproportionately underrepresented in the cultural and public institutions of this country. Pedagogically this suggests that a multicultural curriculum must provide students with the skills to analyze how various audio, visual, and print texts fashion social identities over time, and how these representations serve to reinforce, challenge, or rewrite dominant moral and political vocabularies that promote stereotypes that degrade people by depriving them of their history, culture, and identity.

This should not suggest that such a pedagogy should solely concentrate on how meanings produce particular stereotypes and the uses to which they are put. Nor should a multicultural politics of representation focus exclusively on producing positive images of subordinated groups by recovering and reconstituting elements of their suppressed histories. While such approaches can be pedagogically useful, it is crucial for critical educators to reject any approach to multiculturalism that affirms cultural differences in the name of an essentialized and separatist identity politics. Rather than recovering differences that sustain their self-representation through exclusions, educators need to demonstrate how differences collide, cross over, mutate, and transgress in their negotiations and struggles. Differences in this sense must be understood not through the fixity of place or the romanticization of an essentialized notion of history and experience but through the tropes of indeterminacy, flows, and translations.

In this instance, multiculturalism can begin to formulate a politics of representation in which questions of access and cultural production are linked to what people do with the signifying regimes they use within historically-specific public spaces.

While such approaches are essential to giving up the quest for a pure historical tradition, it is imperative that a multicultural curriculum also focus on dominant, white institutions and histories to interrogate them in terms of their injustices and their contributions for "humanity." This means, as [author and Harvard professor] Cornel West points out that

> to engage in a serious discussion of race in America, we must begin not with the problems of black people but with the flaws of American society—flaws rooted in historical inequalities and longstanding cultural stereotypes.... How we set up the terms for discussing racial issues shapes our perception and response to these issues. As long as black people are viewed as "them," the burden falls on blacks to do all the "cultural" and "moral" work necessary for healthy race relations. The implication is that only certain Americans can define what it means to be American —and the rest must simply "fit in."[10]

In this sense, multiculturalism is about making whiteness visible as a racial category; that is, it points to the necessity of providing white students with the cultural memories that enable them to recognize the historically- and socially constructed nature of their own identities. Multiculturalism as a radical, cultural politics should attempt to provide white students (and others) with the self-definitions upon which they can recognize their own complicity with or resistance to how power works within and across differences to legitimate some voices and dismantle others. Of course, more is at stake here than having whites reflect critically on the construction of their own racial formation and their complicity in promoting racism. Equally important is the issue of making all students responsible for their practices, particularly as these serve either to undermine or expand the possibility for democratic public life.

Third, a multicultural curriculum must address how to articulate a relationship between unity and difference that moves beyond simplistic binarisms. This is, rather than defining multiculturalism against unity or simply for difference, it is crucial for educators to develop a unity-in-difference position in which new, hybrid forms of democratic representation, participation, and citizenship provide a forum for creating unity without denying the particular, multiple, and the specific. In this instance, the interrelationship of different cultures and identities become borderlands, sites of crossing, negotiation, translation, and dialogue. At issue is the production of a border pedagogy in which the intersection of culture and identity produces self-definitions that enables teachers and students to authorize a sense of critical agency. Border pedagogy points to a self/other relationship in which identity is fixed as neither Other nor the same; instead, it is both and, hence, defined within multiple literacies that become a referent, critique, and practice of cultural translation, a recognition of no possibility of fixed, final, or monologically authoritative meaning that exists outside of history, power, and ideology.

Within such a pedagogical cartography, teachers must be given the opportunity to cross ideological and political borders as a way of clarifying their own moral vision, as a way of enabling counterdiscourses, and, as Roger Simon points out, as a way of getting students "beyond the world they already know in order to challenge and provoke their inquiry and challenge of their existing views of the way things are and should be."[11]

Underlying this notion of border pedagogy is neither the logic of assimilation (the melting pot) nor the imperative to create cultural hierarchies, but the attempt to expand the possibilities for different groups to enter into dialogue to understand further the richness of their differences and the value of what they share in common.

Fourth, an insurgent multiculturalism must challenge the task of merely re-presenting cultural differences in the curriculum; it must also educate students of the necessity for linking a justice of multiplicity to struggles over real material conditions that structure everyday life. In part, this means understanding how structural imbalances in power produce real limits on the capacity of subordinate groups to exercise a sense of agency and struggle. It also means analyzing specific class, race, gender, and other issues as social problems rooted in real material and institutional factors that produce specific forms of inequality and oppression. This would necessitate a multicultural curriculum that produces a language that deals with social problems in historical and relational terms, and uncovers how the dynamics of power work to promote domination within the school and the wider society. In part, this means multiculturalism as a curricula discourse and pedagogical practice must function in its dual capacity as collective memory and alternative reconstruction. History, in this sense, is not merely resurrected but interrogated and tempered by "a sense of its liability, its contingency, its constructedness."[12] Memory does not become the repository of registering suppressed histories, albeit critically, but of reconstructing the moral frameworks of historical discourse to interrogate the present as living history.

Finally, a multicultural curriculum must develop, in public schools and institutions of higher education, contexts that serve to refigure relations between the school, teachers, students, and the wide community. For instance, public schools must be willing to develop a critical dialogue between the school and those public cultures within the community dedicated to producing students who address the discourse and obligations of power as part of a larger attempt at civic renewal and the reconstruction of democratic life. At best, parents, social activists, and other socially-concerned community members should be allowed to play a formative role in crucial decisions about what is taught, who is hired, and how the school can become a laboratory for learning that nurtures critical citizenship and civic courage. Of course, the relationship between the school and the larger community should be made in the interest of expanding "the social and political task of transformation, resistance, and radical democratization.[13] In both spheres of education, the curriculum needs to be decentralized to allow students to have some input into what is taught and under what conditions. Moreover, teachers need to be educated to be border crossers, to explore zones of cultural difference by moving in and out of the resources, histories, and narratives that provide different students with a sense of identity, place, and possibility. This does not suggest that educators become tourists traveling to exotic lands; on the contrary, it points to the need for them to enter into negotiation and dialogue around issues of nationality, difference, and identity so as to be able to fashion a more ethical and democratic set of pedagogical relations between themselves and their students while simultaneously allowing students to speak, listen, and learn differently within pedagogical spaces that are safe, affirming, questioning, and enabling.

In this instance, a curriculum for a multicultural and multiracial society provides the conditions for students to imagine beyond the given and to embrace their identities critically as a source of agency and possibility. In addition, an insurgent multiculturalism should serve to redefine existing debates about national identity while simultaneously expanding its theoretical concerns to more global and international matters. Developing a respect for cultures in the plural demands a reformulation of what it means to be educated in the United States and what such an education implies for the creation of new cultural spaces that deepen and extend the possibility of democratic public life. Multiculturalism insists upon challenging old orthodoxies and reformulating new projects of possibility. It is a challenge that all critical educators need to address.

NOTES

1. Alice Kessler-Harris, "Cultural Locations: Positioning American Studies in the Great Debate," *American Quarterly*, 44, 3 (1992), p. 310.

2. Hazel Carby, "The Multicultural Wars," in *Black Popular Culture*, ed. Gina Dent (Seattle: Bay Press, 1992), pp. 193–4.

3. Kobena Mercer, "Back to my Routes: A Postscript on the 80s," *Ten. 8*, 2, 3 (1992), p. 33.

4. Trinh T. Minh-Ha, *Woman, Native, Other: Writing Postcoloniality and Feminism* (Bloomington: Indiana University Press, 1989), p. 232.

5. E. San Juan Jr, *Racial Formations/Critical Transformations: Articulations of Power in Ethnic and Racial Studies in the United States* (Atlantic Highlands, NJ: Humanities Press, 1992), p. 101.

6. Hazel Carby, "Multi-Culture," *Screen Education*, 34 (Spring 1980), p. 65.

7. Bhabha and Parekh, "Identities on Parade: A Conversation," p. 4.

8. Manning Marable, *Black America: Multicultural Democracy* (Westfield, NJ: Open Media, 1992), p. 13.

9. Homi K. Bhabha, "A Good Judge of Character: Men, Metaphors, and the Common Culture: in *Race-ing Justice, Engendering Power: Essays on Anita Hill, Clarence Thomas, and the Construction of Social Reality*, ed. Toni Morrison (New York: Pantheon, 1992), p. 242.

10. Cornel West, "Learning to Talk of Race," p. 24.

11. Roger I. Simon, *Teaching Against the Grain* (New York: Bergin and Garvey Press, 1992), p. 17.

12. Henry Louis Gates Jr, "The Black Man's Burden," *Black Popular Culture*, ed. Gina Dent (Seattle: Bay Press, 1992), p. 76.

13. Judith Butler, "Contingent Foundations: Feminism and the Question of 'Postmodernism'," in *Feminists Theorize the Political*, eds Judith Butler and Joan Scott (New York: Routledge, 1991), p. 13.

PART FOUR

Multicultural Education for All Students

On the Internet . . .

Sites appropriate to Part Four

The American Association of University Women (AAUW) is a national organization that promotes education and equity for all women and girls. It sponsors research, community action projects, fellowships and grants, and funds for legal efforts.

    http://www.aauw.org

The National Clearinghouse for Bilingual Education (NCBE) works to collect, analyze, and disseminate information relating to the effective education of linguistically and culturally diverse learners in the United States. It works with local districts and states to develop educational programs.

    http://www.ncbe.gwu.edu

The National MultiCultural Institute (NMCI) provides workshops and conferences on working within a multicultural society. It provides training materials that help educators to learn how to work with diverse learners and others within schools and society.

    http://www.nmci.org

CHAPTER 12 Gender

12.1 AMERICAN ASSOCIATION OF UNIVERSITY WOMEN

How Schools Shortchange Girls

The American Association of University Women (AAUW) is an organization of college and university graduates that was founded in 1881 to work for the advancement of women. In 1990 the AAUW commissioned the Wellesley College Center for Research on Women to do an in-depth study and to report on the treatment of girls from early childhood through grade 12. The purpose of the report is to help advise educators and government policymakers on educational policy issues relating to equality of educational opportunities for girls and young women in school. The selection that follows is from the AAUW's executive summary of their findings, *How Schools Shortchange Girls: A Study of Major Findings on Girls and Education* (1992).

   Some of the main findings from the AAUW study are that girls receive significantly less academic encouragement in classrooms than boys, that the curriculum often leaves out the contributions and experiences of girls and women, that race and class interact to lead to even further differential treatment, and that girls are less likely to pursue math or science courses and careers than boys are. The study encourages educators to take seriously the provision of equal educational opportunities for girls and young women.

Key Concept: gender equity in schools

*F*or those who believe that equitable education for all young Americans is the greatest source of a nation's strength, *The AAUW Report: How Schools*

Shortchange Girls, will not be reassuring. Commissioned by the AAUW Educational Foundation and developed by the Wellesley College Center for Research on Women, the study challenges the common assumption that girls and boys are treated equally in our public schools.

Ironically, AAUW's first national study—undertaken in 1885—was initiated to dispel the commonly accepted myth that higher education was harmful to women's health. This latest report presents the truth behind another myth—that girls and boys receive equal education.

While most of us are painfully aware of the crisis in American education, few understand or acknowledge the inequities that occur daily in classrooms across the country. Didn't we address that problem in Title IX of the 1972 Education Amendments, which prohibits discrimination in educational institutions receiving federal funds? Many of us worked hard to ensure that this legislation would be passed. Its passage, however, did not solve the problem.

This report is a synthesis of all the available research on the subject of girls in school. It presents compelling evidence that girls are not receiving the same quality, or even quantity, of education as their brothers.

The implications of the report's findings are enormous. Women and children are swelling the ranks of the poor, at great cost to society. Yet our education policymakers are failing to address the relationship between education and the cycle of poverty. The shortchanging of girls is not even mentioned in the current educational restructuring debate.

A well-educated work force is essential to the country's economic development, yet girls are systematically discouraged from courses of study essential to their future employability and economic well-being. Girls are being steered away from the very courses required for their productive participation in the future of America, and we as a nation are losing more than one-half of our human potential. By the turn of the century, two out of three new entrants into the work force will be women and minorities. This work force will have fewer and fewer decently paid openings for the unskilled. It will require strength in science, mathematics, and technology—subjects girls are still being told are not suitable for them.

The AAUW Report presents a base for a new and enlightened education policy—a policy that will ensure that this nation will provide the best possible education for all its children. It provides policymakers with impartial data on the ways in which our school system is failing to meet the needs of girls and with specific strategies that can be used to effect change. The wealth of statistical evidence must convince even the most skeptical that gender bias in our schools is shortchanging girls—and compromising our country.

The AAUW Educational Foundation is proud to present *The AAUW Report: How Schools Shortchange Girls,* made possible through the generosity of the many supporters of the Eleanor Roosevelt Fund. This report is destined to add

a new dimension to the education debate. The evidence is in, and the picture is clear: shortchanging girls—the women of tomorrow—shortchanges America.
— *Alice McKee, President AAUW Educational Foundation*

American Association of University Women

WHY A REPORT ON GIRLS?

The invisibility of girls in the current education debate suggests that girls and boys have identical educational experiences in school. Nothing could be further from the truth. Whether one looks at achievement scores, curriculum design, or teacher-student interaction, it is clear that sex and gender make a difference in the nation's public elementary and secondary schools.

The educational system is not meeting girls' needs. Girls and boys enter school roughly equal in measured ability. Twelve years later, girls have fallen behind their male classmates in key areas such as higher-level mathematics and measures of self-esteem. Yet gender equity is still not a part of the national debate on educational reform.

Neither the *National Education Goals* issued by the National Governors Association in 1990 nor *America 2000*, the 1991 plan of the President and the U.S. Department of Education to "move every community in America toward these goals," makes any mention of providing girls equitable opportunities in the nation's public schools. Girls continue to be left out of the debate—despite the fact that for more than two decades researchers have identified gender bias as a major problem at all levels of schooling.

Schools must prepare both girls and boys for full and active roles in the family, the community, and the work force. Whether we look at the issues from an economic, political, or social perspective, girls are one-half of our future. We must move them from the sidelines to the center of the education-reform debate.

A critical step in correcting educational inequities is identifying them publicly. *The AAUW Report: How Schools Shortchange Girls* provides a comprehensive assessment of the status of girls in public education today. It exposes myths about girls and learning, and it supports the work of the many teachers who have struggled to define and combat gender bias in their schools. The report challenges us all—policymakers, educators, administrators, parents, and citizens—to rethink old assumptions and act now to stop schools from shortchanging girls.

Our public education system is plagued by numerous failings that affect boys as negatively as girls. But in many respects girls are put at a disadvantage simply because they are girls. *The AAUW Report* documents this in hundreds of cited studies.

When our schools become more gender-fair, education will improve for all our students—boys as well as girls—because excellence in education cannot be achieved without equity in education. By studying what happens to girls in school, we can gain valuable insights about what has to change in order for each student, every girl and every boy, to do as well as she or he can.

WHAT THE RESEARCH REVEALS

What Happens in the Classroom?

- Girls receive significantly less attention from classroom teachers than do boys.
- African American girls have fewer interactions with teachers than do white girls, despite evidence that they attempt to initiate interactions more frequently.
- Sexual harassment of girls by boys—from innuendo to actual assault—in our nation's schools is increasing.

A large body of research indicates that teachers give more classroom attention and more esteem-building encouragement to boys. In a study conducted by Myra and David Sadker, boys in elementary and middle school called out answers eight times more often than girls. When boys called out, teachers listened. But when girls called out, they were told to "raise your hand if you want to speak." Even when boys do not volunteer, teachers are more likely to encourage them to give an answer or an opinion than they are to encourage girls.

Research reveals a tendency, beginning at the preschool level, for educators to choose classroom activities that appeal to boys' interests and to select presentation formats in which boys excel. The teacher-student interaction patterns in science classes are often particularly biased. Even in math classes, where less-biased patterns are found, psychologist Jacquelynne Eccles reports that select boys in each math class she studied received particular attention to the exclusion of all other students, female and male.

Teaching methods that foster competition are still standard, although a considerable body of research has demonstrated that girls—and many boys as well—learn better when they undertake projects and activities cooperatively rather than competitively.

Researchers, including Sandra Damico, Elois Scott, and Linda Grant, report that African American girls have fewer interactions with teachers than do white girls, even though they attempt to initiate interactions more often. Furthermore, when African American girls do as well as white boys in school, teachers often attribute their success to hard work while assuming that the white boys are not working up to their potential.

Girls do not emerge from our schools with the same degree of confidence and self-esteem as boys. The 1990 AAUW poll, *Shortchanging Girls, Shortchanging America,* documents a loss of self-confidence in girls that is twice that for boys as they move from childhood to adolescence. Schools play a crucial role in challenging and changing gender-role expectations that undermine the self-confidence and achievement of girls.

Reports of boys sexually harassing girls in schools are increasing at an alarming rate. When sexual harassment is treated casually, as in "boys will be boys," both girls and boys get a dangerous, damaging message: "girls are not worthy of respect; appropriate behavior for boys includes exerting power over girls."

American Association of University Women

- The contributions and experiences of girls and women are still marginalized or ignored in many of the textbooks used in our nation's schools.
- Schools, for the most part, provide inadequate education on sexuality and healthy development despite national concern about teen pregnancy, the AIDS crisis, and the increase of sexually transmitted diseases among adolescents.
- Incest, rape, and other physical violence severely compromise the lives of girls and women all across the country. These realities are rarely, if ever, discussed in schools.

Curriculum delivers the central message of education. It can strengthen or decrease student motivation for engagement, effort, growth, and development through the images it gives to students about themselves and the world. When the curriculum does not reflect the diversity of students' lives and cultures, it delivers an incomplete message.

Studies have shown that multicultural readings produced markedly more favorable attitudes toward nondominant groups than did the traditional reading lists, that academic achievement for all students was linked to use of nonsexist and multicultural materials, and that sex-role stereotyping was reduced in students whose curriculum portrayed males and females in nonstereotypical roles. Yet during the 1980s, federal support for reform regarding sex and race equity dropped, and a 1989 study showed that of the ten books most frequently assigned in public high school English courses only one was written by a woman and none by members of minority groups.

The "evaded" curriculum is a term coined in this report to refer to matters central to the lives of students that are touched on only briefly, if at all, in most schools. The United States has the highest rate of teenage childbearing in the Western industrialized world. Syphilis rates are now equal for girls and boys, and more teenage girls than boys contract gonorrhea. Although in the adult population AIDS is nine times more prevalent in men than in women, the same is not true for young people. In a District of Columbia study, the rate of HIV infection for girls was almost three times that for boys. Despite all of this, adequate sex and health education is the exception rather than the rule.

Adolescence is a difficult period for all young people, but it is particularly difficult for girls, who are far more likely to develop eating disorders and experience depression. Adolescent girls attempt suicide four to five times as often as boys (although boys, who choose more lethal methods, are more likely to be successful in their attempts).

Perhaps the most evaded of all topics in schools is the issue of gender and power. As girls mature they confront a culture that both idealizes and exploits the sexuality of young women while assigning them roles that are clearly less valued than male roles. If we do not begin to discuss more openly the ways in which ascribed power—whether on the basis of race, sex, class, sexual orientation, or religion—affects individual lives, we cannot truly prepare our students for responsible citizenship.

How Do Race/Ethnicity and Socioeconomic Status Affect Achievement in School?

- Girls from low-income families face particularly severe obstacles. Socioeconomic status, more than any other variable, affects access to school resources and educational outcomes.
- Test scores of low-socioeconomic-status girls are somewhat better than for boys from the same background in the lower grades, but by high school these differences disappear. Among high-socioeconomic-status students, boys generally outperform girls regardless of race/ethnicity.
- Too little information is available on differences among various groups of girls. While African Americans are compared to whites, or boys to girls, relatively few studies or published data examine differences by sex *and* race/ethnicity.

All girls confront barriers to equal participation in school and society. But minority girls, who must confront racism as well as sexism, and girls from low-income families face particular severe obstacles. These obstacles can include poor schools in dangerous neighborhoods, low teacher expectations, and inadequate nutrition and health care.

Few studies focus on issues affecting low-income girls and girls from minority groups—unless they are pregnant or drop out of school. In order to develop effective policies and programs, a wide range of issues—from course-taking patterns to academic self-esteem—require further examination by sex, race/ethnicity, and socioeconomic status.

How Are Girls Doing in Math and Science?

- Differences between girls and boys in math achievement are small and declining. Yet in high school, girls are still less likely than boys to take the most advanced courses and be in the top-scoring math groups.
- The gender gap in science, however, is *not* decreasing and may, in fact, be increasing.
- Even girls who are highly competent in math and science are much less likely to pursue scientific or technological careers than are their male classmates.

Girls who see math as "something men do" do less well in math than girls who do not hold this view. In their classic study, Elizabeth Fennema and Julia Sherman reported a drop in both girls' math confidence and their achievement in the middle school years. The drop in confidence *preceded* the decline in achievement.

Researcher Jane Kahle found that boys come to science classes with more out-of-school familiarity and experience with the subject matter. This advantage is furthered in the classroom. One study of science classrooms found that 79 percent of all student-assisted science demonstrations were carried out by boys.

We can no longer afford to disregard half our potential scientists and science-literate citizens of the next generation. Even when girls take math and science courses and do well in them, they do not receive the encouragement they need to pursue scientific careers. A study of high school seniors found that 64 percent of the boys who had taken physics and calculus were planning to major in science and engineering in college, compared to only 18.6 percent of the girls who had taken the same subjects. Support from teachers can make a big difference. Studies report that girls rate teacher support as an important factor in decisions to pursue scientific and technological careers.

Tests: Stepping Stones or Stop Signs?

- Test scores can provide an inaccurate picture of girls' and boys' abilities. Other factors such as grades, portfolios of student work, and out-of-school achievements must be considered in addition to test scores when making judgments about girls' and boys' skills and abilities.
- When scholarships are given based on the Scholastic Aptitude Test (SAT) scores, boys are more apt to receive scholarships than are girls who get equal or slightly better high school grades.
- Girls and boys with the same Math SAT scores do not do equally well in college—girls do better.

In most cases tests reflect rather than cause inequities in American education. The fact that groups score differently on a test does not necessarily mean that the test is biased. If, however, the score differences are related to the validity of the test—for example, if girls and boys know about the same amount of math but boys' test scores are consistently and significantly higher—then the test is biased.

A number of aspects of a test—beyond that which is being tested—can affect the score. For example, girls tend to score better than boys on essay tests, boys better than girls on multiple-choice items. Even today many girls and boys come to a testing situation with different interests and experiences. Thus a reading-comprehension passage that focuses on baseball scores will tend to favor boys, while a question testing the same skills that focuses on child care will tend to favor girls.

Why Do Girls Drop Out and What Are the Consequences?

- Pregnancy is not the only reason girls drop out of school. In fact, less than half the girls who leave school give pregnancy as the reason.
- Dropout rates for Hispanic girls vary considerably by national origin: Puerto Rican and Cuban American girls are more likely to drop out than are boys from the same cultures or other Hispanic girls.
- Childhood poverty is almost inescapable in single-parent families headed by women without a high school diploma: 77 percent for whites and 87 percent for African Americans.

In a recent study, 37 percent of the female dropouts compared to only 5 percent of the male dropouts cited "family-related problems" as the reason they left high school. Traditional gender roles place greater family responsibilities on adolescent girls than on their brothers. Girls are often expected to "help out" with caretaking responsibilities; boys rarely encounter this expectation.

However, girls as well as boys also drop out of school simply because they do not consider school pleasant or worthwhile. Asked what a worthwhile school experience would be, a group of teenage girls responded, "School would be fun. Our teachers would be excited and lively, not bored. They would act caring and take time to understand how students feel.... Boys would treat us with respect. If they run by and grab your tits, they would get into trouble."

Women and children are the most impoverished members of our society. Inadequate education not only limits opportunities for women but jeopardizes their children's—and the nation's—future.

12.2 CAROL GILLIGAN AND JANE ATTANUCCI

Two Moral Orientations: Gender Differences and Similarities

Carol Gilligan is a professor of gender studies at Harvard University. Her groundbreaking book *In a Different Voice: Psychological Theory and Women's Development* (Harvard University Press, 1982) was a component in her being selected by *Ms.* magazine as 1984 Woman of the Year. Her research led to the founding of the Harvard Project on Women's Psychology and Girls' Development.

Jane Attanucci is an associate professor of human development and family studies at Wheelock College in Boston, Massachusetts. Attanucci is a 1990 recipient of the National Academy of Education Spencer Fellowship, and she was a National Institute of Mental Health (NIMH) postdoctoral fellow at Massachusetts Mental Health Center. One focus of her work is the area of moral development

In the following selection from "Two Moral Orientations: Gender Differences and Similarities," *Merrill-Palmer Quarterly* (vol. 34, no. 3, 1988), Gilligan and Attanucci compare the moral development theory of psychologist Lawrence Kohlberg with the moral development of women. They use Kohlberg as a contrast because Kohlberg did not look at the experiences and life expectations of girls and women in forming his conception of moral development. In Kohlberg's highest stages, those that describe the most morally developed people, a person makes judgments based on the rights involved, independent of the needs and values of those around him. Gilligan and Attanucci present the voices of women as they make life decisions, and they present an alternative suggestion of moral orientation that takes into account aspects of women's development. In this conception, moral development is seen in terms of conflicting responsibilities to self and others. What is seen in these women's voices is a moral imperative to care and to nonviolence.

Key Concept: women's moral development

*P*revious interpretations of individual, cultural, and sex differences in moral reasoning have been constrained by the assumption that there is a single moral perspective, that of justice. The analysis of women's moral judgments clarified an alternative approach to moral decision making which was designated the *care perspective* (Gilligan, 1982)....

The distinction made here between a justice orientation and a care orientation pertains to the ways in which moral problems are conceived and reflects different dimensions of human relationships that give rise to moral concern. A justice perspective draws attention to problems of inequality and oppression and holds up an ideal of reciprocal rights and equal respect for individuals. A care perspective draws attention to problems of detachment or abandonment and holds up an ideal of attention and response to need.

Two moral injunctions, not to treat others unfairly and not to turn away from someone in need, capture these different concerns. From a developmental standpoint, both inequality and attachment are universal human experiences: All children are born into a situation of inequality and no child survives in the absence of some kind of adult attachment. These two intersecting dimensions of equality and attachment characterize all forms of human relationship. All relationships can be described in both sets of terms: as unequal or equal and as attached or detached. Because everyone has been vulnerable both to oppression and to abandonment, two moral visions—one of justice and one of care—recur in human experience.

Psychologists studying moral development have equated morality with justice, characterized the parent-child relationships as a relationship of inequality, and contrasted it with the equality of peer relations. Previous discussions of "two moralities" (Haan, 1978; Youniss, 1980) have been cast in terms of inequality and equality, following the Piaget (1932/1965) equation of moral development with the development of the idea of justice and his distinction between relationships of constraint and relationships of cooperation.

Although the dimensions of constraint and cooperation represent the opposite poles of inequality and equality in relationships, neither addresses the dimension of attachment and detachment, responsiveness and failures to respond, in those relationships. The present discussion of two moral orientations refers instead to the dimensions of attachment and equality in all relationships and considers moral development in terms of both changes in the understanding of what fairness means and in terms of changes in the understanding of what constitutes care. Because problems of inequality and problems of detachment arise throughout human life and in both public and private realms, it would be expected that equality and attachment would persist as moral concerns.

The present paper is a report of the results of three studies undertaken to investigate the two moral orientations and to determine to what extent men and women differentially raise concerns about justice and care in discussing moral conflicts in their lives. The examples presented in Table 1, drawn from discussions of real-life dilemmas, illustrate the concept of moral orientation. Each pair of dilemmas reveals how a problem is seen from a justice perspective and from a care perspective. In each pair of examples, the justice construction is the more familiar one, capturing the way such problems are usually defined from a moral standpoint.

TABLE 1

Examples of Justice Care Perspectives in Real-Life Moral Domain Data

Justice	Care
1J [If people were taking drugs and I was the only one who wasn't I would feel it was stupid, I know for me what is right is right and what's wrong is wrong... it's like a set of standards I have.] *(High School Student)*	1C [If there was one person it would be a lot easier to say no, I could talk to her, because there wouldn't be seven others to think about. I do think about them, you know, and wonder what they say about me and what it will mean... I made the right decision not to because my real friends accepted my decision.] *(High School Student)*
2J [The conflict was that by all rights she should have been turned into the honor board for violation of the alcohol policy.] [I liked her very much.] [She is extremely embarrassed and upset. She was contrite, she wished she had never done it. She had all the proper levels of contriteness and guilt and] [I was supposed to turn her in and didn't.] *(Medical Student)*	2C [It might just be his business if he wants to get drunk every week or it might be something that is really a problem and that should be dealt with professionally; and to be concerned about someone without antagonizing them or making their life more difficult than it had to be; maybe there was just no problem there.] [I guess in something like a personal relationship with a proctor you don't want to just go right out there and antagonize people, because that person will go away and if you destroy any relationship you have, I think you have lost any chance of doing anything for a person.] *(Medical Student)*
3J [I have moral dilemmas all the time, but I have no problem solving them usually. I usually resolve them according to my internal morality... the more important publicly your office is, to me the more important it is that you *play by the rules* because society hangs together by these rules and in my view, if you cheat on them, even for a laudatory purpose, eventually you break the rules down, because it is impossible to draw any fine lines.] *(Lawyer)*	3C [I have to preside over these decisions and try to make them as nondisastrous as possible for the people who are most vulnerable. The fewer games you play the better, because you are really dealing with issues that are the very basis to people's day-to-day well-being, and it is people's feelings, people's potential for growth, and you should do everything in your power to smooth it.] *(Lawyer)*

In 1J, a peer pressure dilemma is presented in terms of how to uphold one's moral standards and how to withstand the pressure from one's friends to deviate from what one knows for oneself to be right. In 1C, a similar decision (not to smoke) is cast in terms of how to respond both to one's friends and to oneself. The rightness of the decision not to smoke is established in terms of the fact that it did not break relationships: "My real friends accepted my decision." Attention to one's friends, to what they say and how choices affect the friendship, is presented as a moral concern.

In the second pair of examples, the dilemma of whether to report someone who has violated the medical school's alcohol policy is posed differently from the justice and care perspectives. The decision not to tell is reasoned in different ways. A clear example of justice tempered by mercy is presented in 2J. The student believes that the violator should be turned in ("I was supposed to turn her in") and justifies not doing so on the grounds that she deserved mercy because "She had all the proper level of contriteness" that was appropriate for the situation.

In 2C, a student decides not to turn a proctor in for drinking because it would "destroy any relationship you have" and therefore would "hurt any chance of doing anything for that person." In this construction, turning in the person is seen as impeding efforts to help. The concern about maintaining the relationship in order to be able to help is not mentioned in 2J. Similarly, the concern about maintaining the honor board policy is not mentioned in 2C.

A further illustration of how justice and care perspectives restructure moral understanding can be seen by observing that in 2J the student justifies not turning in the violator because of questions about the rightness of the alcohol policy itself. But in 2C the student considers whether what was deemed a problem was really a problem for the other person. The case of 2C illustrates what is meant by striving to see the other person in his or her own particular terms. It also exemplifies the contrast between this endeavor and the effort to establish, independently of persons, the legitimacy of existing rules and standards.

The third pair of examples further illustrates the distinction between establishing and maintaining existing rules and universal impartial standards (3J) and attending to people in their particular circumstances and minimizing the damaging effects of legal decisions (3C). In 3J, the lawyer affirms the value of the American legal system, dismissing the "impossible . . . fine lines." In 3C, the lawyer struggles with those same fine lines in order to protect those personally vulnerable to society's "game." These interpretations of the same legal system differ; neither is entirely wrong or naive. In 3J, the lawyer asserts the necessity of our legal system to hold society together. But in 3C, the lawyer appeals to the injunction not to abandon those in need.

It is important to emphasize that these examples were selected to highlight the contrast between a justice perspective and a care perspective. It must be stressed, however, that most people who participated in this research used considerations of both justice and care in discussing a moral conflict they faced.

In the present study two questions were posed: (a) In the evidence of justice and care orientations in people's discussion of real-life moral conflict, do people represent both orientations equally or do they tend to focus on one and minimally represent the other? And (b) Is there a relationship between moral orientation and gender?

TABLE 2

Gender and Age of Subjects by Study

	15–22 Years	*23–34 Years*	*35–77 Years*	*n*
Study 1				
Women	4	2	5	11
Men	4	1	5	10
Study 2				
Women	9	4	0	13
Men	12	14	0	26
Study 3				
Women	10	0	0	10
Men	10	0	0	10

METHOD

Subjects were drawn from three research studies. In each study, the subjects were asked to describe a real-life moral dilemma. All three samples consisted of men and women who were matched for levels of education; the adults were matched for professional occupations. See Table 2 for the distribution of subjects, by sample, in age and gender categories.

Study 1. The design matched participants for high levels of education and professional occupations to examine the variables of age, gender, and type of dilemma. The adolescents and adults included were 11 women and 10 men. The racial composition (19 white and 2 minority) was not statistically random, as race was not a focal variable of the study.

Study 2. First-year students were randomly selected from two prestigious northeastern medical schools to be interviewed as part of a longitudinal study of stress and adaptation in physicians.[1] The 26 men and 13 women students represented the proportions of each gender in the class at large. The 19 white and 20 minority students (Black, Hispanic and Asian Americans) were selected to balance the sample's racial composition (the only sample in the present study with such a design). The students ranged in age from 21 to 27 years.

Study 3. The 10 female and 10 male participants were randomly selected from a coeducational private school in a midwestern city. The 19 white and 1 minority student ranged in age from 14 to 18 years.

All participants were asked the following series of questions about their personal experience of moral conflict and choice:

1. Have you ever been in a situation of moral conflict where you had to make a decision but weren't sure what was the right thing to do?
2. Could you describe the situation?
3. What were the conflicts for you in that situation?
4. What did you do?
5. Do you think it was the right thing to do?
6. How do you know?

The interviewer asked questions to encourage the participants to clarify and elaborate their responses. For example, participants were asked what they meant by words like *responsibility, obligation, moral, fair, selfish,* and *caring.* The interviewers followed the participants' logic in presenting the moral problem, most commonly querying, "Anything else?"

The interviews were conducted individually, tape recorded, and later transcribed. The moral conflict questions were one segment of an interview which included questions about morality and identity (Gilligan et al., 1982). The interviews lasted about 2 hours.

Data Analysis

The real-life moral dilemmas were analyzed by using methods described in Lyons's *Manual for Coding Real-Life Dilemmas* (1982). The Lyons procedure[2] is a content analysis which identifies moral considerations. The unit of analysis is the *consideration,* defined as each idea the participant presents in discussing a moral problem. The units are designated in Table 1 with brackets.

To reach an acceptable level of reliability in identifying considerations required extensive training. The three coders trained by Lyons were blind to the gender, age, and race of the participants and achieved high levels of intercoder reliability (a range of 67% to 95%, and a mean of 80% agreement, across samples of randomly selected cases). Typically, a real-life moral dilemma consisted of 7 considerations, with a range of 4 to 17. A minimum of four considerations was required for the present analysis. When only four considerations were present, in all but one case, the four considerations were in one orientation. The coder classified these considerations as either justice or care.

The Lyons score was simply the predominant, most frequent, mode of moral reasoning (justice or care). For the present study, *predominance* was redefined so that a real-life moral dilemma consisting of only care or justice considerations was labeled *Care Only* or *Justice Only.* A dilemma consisting of 75% or more care or justice considerations was labeled *Care Focus* or *Justice Focus,* respectively. A dilemma in which less than 75% of the total number of considerations were care or justice was placed in the *Care Justice* category.

TABLE 3

Number of Participants by Moral Orientation Category

	Care Only	Care Focus	Care Justice	Justice Focus	Justice Only
Observed	5	8	27	20	20
Expected	.64	4	70	4	.64

RESULTS

The real-life dilemma data are summarized from three studies with comparable designs. That is, samples with male and female subjects are matched for high socioeconomic status. Frequencies and statistical tests are presented across samples. The statistical comparison of samples on moral orientation is not significant ($\chi^2(4, N = 80) = 9.21$ n.s.). Parallel tests have been performed for each sample and discrepancies from the overall pattern are reported and discussed.

Two observations can be made from the data in Table 3: First, the majority of people represent both moral orientations; 69% compared to the 31% who use Care or Justice Only. Second, two thirds of the dilemmas are in the Focus categories (Care Only, Care Focus, Justice Only, Justice Focus), and only one third are in the Care Justice category. The question addressed by Table 3 is, Do people tend to focus their discussion of a moral problem in one or the other orientation?

For the typical case, the ratio of care to justice considerations is Care Only 7:0; Care Focus 6:1; Care Justice 5:2, 4:3, 3:4, 2:5; Justice Focus 1:6; and Justice Only 0:7. Using a binomial model, if an equal probability of care and justice considerations in an account of a real-life moral dilemma ($p = .5$) is assumed, then a random sampling of moral considerations (typically $N = 7$) over 80 trials (80 participants' single dilemmas) would result in an expected binomial distribution. To test whether the distribution of scores fit the expected distribution, the χ^2 goodness of fit test is applied. The observed distribution differs significantly from the expected, $\chi^2(4, N = 80)$ 133.8, $p < .001$, and provides supporting evidence for the contention that an individual's moral considerations are not random but tend to be focused in either the care or justice orientation.

In Table 4 the distribution of moral orientations for each gender is presented. The statistical test of gender differences is based on a combination of Care Only and Care Focus, as well as a combination of Justice Only and Justice Focus in order to have expected values greater than 5: $\chi^2(2, N = 80) = 18.33$, $p < .001$. This test demonstrates the relationship between moral orientation and gender in which both men and women present dilemmas in the Care Justice category, but Care Focus is much more likely in the moral dilemma of a woman and Justice Focus more likely in the dilemma of a man. In fact, if women were excluded from a study of moral reasoning, Care Focus could easily be overlooked.

201

TABLE 4

Frequency of Moral Orientation Categories by Gender of Participants

	Care Only	Care Focus	Care Justice	Justice Focus	Justice Only
Women	5	7	12	6	4
Men	0	1	15	14	16

The relationship between moral orientation and age was not tested because the majority of participants were adolescents and young adults, providing little age range. Furthermore, in the present study, age was confounded with sample (i.e., the young adults were the medical students), making interpretation difficult.

The medical student data (Study 2) raised further questions of Interpretation which bear on the issues addressed in this analysis. First, the dilemmas from the medical students, when tested separately, do not show the same relationship between gender and moral orientation, $\chi^2(2, n = 39) = 4.36$, n.s. However, consistent with the overall findings, the two Care Focus dilemmas were presented by women.

As for the pattern of difference in this racially diverse sample, the Care Focus dilemmas were presented by one white woman and one minority woman. The relationship between moral orientation and race for both men and women was that the dilemmas presented by white students were more likely to fall in the Care Justice category and dilemmas of minority students in the Justice Focus category (Fisher's Exact $p = .045$ for women, and $p = .0082$ for men).

DISCUSSION

The present exploration of moral orientation has demonstrated that: (a) Concerns about justice and care are both represented in people's thinking about real-life moral dilemmas, but people tend to focus on one set of concerns and minimally represent the other. And (b) there is an association between moral orientation and gender such that both men and women use both orientations, but Care Focus dilemmas are more likely to be presented by women and Justice Focus dilemmas by men.

Analysis of care and justice as distinct moral orientations that address different moral concerns leads to a consideration of both perspectives as constitutive of mature moral thinking. The tension between these perspectives is suggested by the fact that detachment, which is the mark of mature moral judgment in the justice perspective, becomes the moral problem in the care perspective, that is, the failure to attend to need. Conversely, attention to the particular needs and circumstances of individuals, the mark of mature moral judgment in the care perspective, becomes the moral problem in the justice perspective, that is, failure to treat others fairly, as equals. Care Focus and Justice Focus reasoning suggest a tendency to lose sight of one perspective in arriving at moral decision. That the focus phenomenon was demonstrated by two thirds of both men and women in the present study suggests that this liability is shared by both sexes.

This finding provides an empirical explanation for the equation of morality with justice in the theories of moral development that are derived from all-male research samples (Kohlberg, 1969, 1984; Piaget, 1932/1965). If women were eliminated from the present study, the focus on care would virtually disappear. Given the presence of justice concerns, most of the dilemmas described by women could be analyzed for justice considerations without reference to care considerations.

In addition, the Care Focus dilemmas presented by women offer an explanation for the fact that within a justice conception of morality, moral judgments of girls and women have appeared anomalous and difficult to interpret; Piaget (1932/1965) cites this explanation as the reason for studying boys. Furthermore, finding Care Focus mainly among women indicates why the analysis of women's moral thinking elucidated the care perspective as a distinct moral orientation and why the considerations of care that has been noted in dilemmas presented by men did not seem fully elaborated (Gilligan & Murphy, 1979).

The evidence of orientation focus as an observable characteristic of moral judgment does not justify the conclusion that focus is a desirable attribute of moral decision. However, careful attention to women's articulation of the care perspective has led to a different conception of the moral domain and to a different way of analyzing the moral judgment of both men and women.

The category Care Justice in our findings raises important questions that merit investigation in future research. Dilemmas in this "bifocal" category were equally likely among men and women in our study. It is possible that interviews involving more dilemmas and further questioning might reveal the focus phenomenon to be more common. But it is also possible that such studies might find and elucidate further an ability to sustain two moral perspectives, an ability, which according to the present data, seems equally characteristic of men and women.

The findings presented here suggest that people know and use both moral orientations. Although Care Focus dilemmas are raised by women, it is important to emphasize that the focus phenomenon in two moral orientations is replicated in an all-female sample of students in a private girls' high school. The moral dilemmas of these 48 adolescent girls are distributed as follows: Care Focus, 22; Care Justice, 17; and Justice Focus, 9. This distribution offers significantly from the expected binomial distribution, as well. The statistical test is based on a combination of Care Only and Care Focus, as well as a combination of Justice Only and Justice Focus in order to have expected values greater than 5: $\chi^2(2, N = 48) = 154.4, p < .001)\ldots$

The promise of approaching moral development in terms of moral orientation lies in its potential to transform debates over sex differences in moral reasoning into serious questions about moral perspectives that are open to empirical study. If moral maturity consists in the ability to sustain concerns about justice and care and if the focus phenomenon indicates a tendency to lose sight of one set of concerns, then the encounter with orientation difference can tend to offset errors in moral perception. Like the moment when the ambiguous figure shifts from a vase to two faces, the recognition that there is another way to look at a problem may expand moral understanding.

NOTES

1. Nineteen other medical students who could not (two would not) describe a situation of moral conflict are not in the present study. We acknowledge the bias created by such attrition. Their response may reflect the pressures on first-year medical students in a context which discourages the uncertainty about knowing what is the right thing to do. Generalizations about physicians from this specific study would be unwarranted, however, as several physicians who participated in Study 1 provided both care and justice perspectives on their experiences of conflict and choice.

2. Lyon's coding sheet (Lyons, 1983) specifies five categories that establish whether the consideration is assigned to justice or care. Intercoder reliability is computed across categories. In the present study, most of the considerations coded fit Categories 2 and 3 under justice and care. When we ran our analysis using only these categories, some subjects were lost due to an insufficient number of considerations, but the direction of the findings as reported in the results section (with all categories included) remained. This fact is significant because Categories 2 and 3 under justice and care best capture our distinction between justice and care: concern with fulfilling obligations, duty or commitments, or maintaining standards or principles of fairness (justice), and concern with maintaining or restoring relationships, or with responding to the weal and woe of others (care). Lyons's Categories 1, 4, and 5 under justice and care are consistent with her focus on the perspective taken toward others. Yet Categories 1, 4, and 5 can readily be confused with a conception of justice and care as bi-polar opposites of a single dimension of moral reasoning or as mirror image conceptions where justice is egoistic and uncaring and caring is altruistic and unjust. Because these categories were rarely evident in the current data, these questions, although important for other researchers to consider, are only marginally relevant to the present discussion.

REFERENCES

GILLIGAN, C. (1982). *In a different voice: Psychological theory and women's development*. Cambridge, MA: Harvard University Press.

GILLIGAN, C., & MURPHY, J. (1979). Development from adolescence to adulthood: The philosopher and the dilemma of the fact. In D. Kuhn (Ed.), *Intellectual development beyond childhood* (pp. 85–99). San Francisco: Jossey-Bass.

HAAN, N. (1978). Two moralities in action contexts: Relationships to thought, ego regulation and development. *Journal of Personality and Social Psychology, 36,* 286–305.

KOHLBERG, L. (1969). Stage and sequence: The cognitive-developmental approach to socialization. In D. A. Goslin (Ed.), *Handbook of socialization theory and research* (pp. 347–480). Chicago: Rand McNally.

KOHLBERG, L. (1984). *The psychology of moral development, Vol.* 2. San Francisco: Harper & Row.

LYONS, N. (1982). *Conceptions of self and morality and modes of moral choice: Identifying justice and care in judgments of actual moral dilemmas.* Unpublished doctoral dissertation, Harvard University, Cambridge, MA.

LYONS, N. (1983). Two perspectives: On self, relationships, and morality. *Harvard Educational Review, 53,* 125–145.

PIAGET, J. (1965). *The moral judgment of the child.* New York: Free Press. (Original work published 1932)

YOUNISS, J. (1980). *Parents and peers in social development.* Chicago: University of Chicago Press.

CHAPTER 13 Race

13.1 GLORIA LADSON-BILLINGS

But That's Just Good Teaching!

Gloria Ladson-Billings gives a clear definition of culturally relevant pedagogy: a teacher utilizes a student's own culture as a vehicle for learning. In
this pedagogy, students need to be able to maintain their cultural integrity.
In more fully describing culturally relevant pedagogy, Ladson-Billings states
that students must experience academic success, students must develop and
maintain cultural competence, and "students must develop a critical consciousness through which they challenge the status quo of the current social
order." Although Ladson-Billings is writing about good education for African
American students specifically, she emphasizes that these practices would
be good for all students. She gives examples of teachers' words and teaching activities that exemplify the kind of culturally relevant teaching that is
good for all students.

    Ladson-Billings is a professor of curriculum and instruction at the Uni-
versity of Wisconsin. She writes on multicultural education in general and
on race-related issues in particular. Her special focus is on African American education. The following selection is from the article "But That's Just
Good Teaching! The Case for Culturally Relevant Pedagogy," *Theory Into
Practice* (Summer 1995). Ladson-Billings has also published in a number
of educational journals and is coeditor, with Carl Grant, of *Dictionary of
Multicultural Education* (Oryx Press, 1997).

Key Concept: culturally relevant pedagogy

*F*or the past 6 years I have been engaged in research with excellent
teachers of African American students (see, for example, Ladson-Billings, 1990,

1992b, 1992c, 1994). Given the dismal academic performance of many African American students (The College Board, 1985), I am not surprised that various administrators, teachers, and teacher educators have asked me to share and discuss my findings so that they might incorporate them in their work. One usual response to what I share is the comment around which I have based this article. "But, that's just good teaching!" Instead of some "magic bullet" or intricate formula and steps for instruction, some members of my audience are shocked to hear what seems to them like some rather routine teaching strategies that are a part of good teaching. My response is to affirm that, indeed, I am describing good teaching, and to question why so little of it seems to be occurring in the classrooms populated by African American students.

The pedagogical excellence I have studied is good teaching, but it is much more than that. This article is an attempt to describe a pedagogy I have come to identify as "culturally relevant" (Ladson-Billings, 1992a) and to argue for its centrality in the academic success of African American and other children who have not been well served by our nation's public schools. First, I provide some background information about other attempts to look at linkages between school and culture. Next, I discuss the theoretical grounding of culturally relevant teaching in the context of a 3-year study of successful teachers of African American students. I conclude this discussion with further examples of this pedagogy in action.

LINKING SCHOOLING AND CULTURE

Native American educator Cornel Pewewardy (1993) asserts that one of the reasons Indian children experience difficulty in schools is that educators traditionally have attempted to insert culture into the education, instead of inserting education into the culture. This notion is, in all probability, true for many students who are not a part of the White, middle-class mainstream. For almost 15 years, anthropologists have looked at ways to develop a closer fit between students' home culture and the school. This work has had a variety of labels including "culturally appropriate" (Au & Jordan, 1981), "culturally congruent" (Mohatt & Erickson, 1981) "culturally responsive" (Cazden & Leggett, 1981; Erickson & Mohatt, 1982), and "culturally compatible" (Jordan, 1985; Vogt, Jordan, & Tharp, 1987). It has attempted to locate the problem of discontinuity between what students experience at home and what they experience at school in the speech and language interactions of teachers and students. These sociolinguists have suggested that if students' home language is incorporated into the classroom, students are more likely to experience academic success.

Villegas (1988), however, has argued that these micro-ethnographic studies fail to deal adequately with the macro social context in which student failure takes place. A concern I have voiced about studies situated in speech and language interactions is that, in general, few have considered the needs of African American students.[1]

Irvine (1990) dealt with the lack of what she termed "cultural synchronization" between teachers and African American students. Her analysis included the micro-level classroom interactions, the "mid-level" institutional context (i.e., school practices and policies such as tracking and disciplinary practices), and the macro-level societal context. More recently Perry's (1993) analysis has included the historical context of the African American's educational struggle. All of this work—micro through macro level—has contributed to my conception of culturally relevant pedagogy.

WHAT IS CULTURALLY RELEVANT PEDAGOGY?

In the current attempts to improve pedagogy, several scholars have advanced well-conceived conceptions of pedagogy. Notable among these scholars are Shulman (1987), whose work conceptualizes pedagogy as consisting of subject matter knowledge, pedagogical knowledge, and pedagogical content knowledge, and Berliner (1988), who doubts the ability of expert pedagogues to relate their expertise to novice practitioners. More recently, Bartolome (1994) has decried the search for the "right" teaching strategies and argued for a "humanizing pedagogy that respects and uses the reality, history, and perspectives of students as an integral part of educational practice" (p. 173).

I have defined culturally relevant teaching as a pedagogy of opposition (1992c) not unlike critical pedagogy but specifically committed to collective, not merely individual, empowerment. Culturally relevant pedagogy rests on three criteria or propositions: (a) Students must experience academic success; (b) students must develop and/or maintain cultural competence; and (c) students must develop a critical consciousness through which they challenge the status quo of the current social order.

Academic Success

Despite the current social inequities and hostile classroom environments, students must develop their academic skills. The way those skills are developed may vary, but all students need literacy, numeracy, technological, social, and political skills in order to be active participants in a democracy. During the 1960s when African Americans were fighting for civil rights, one of the primary battlefronts was the classroom (Morris, 1984). Despite the federal government's failed attempts at adult literacy in the South, civil rights workers such as Septima Clark and Esau Jenkins (Brown, 1990) were able to teach successfully those same adults by ensuring that the students learned that which was most meaningful to them. This approach is similar to that advocated by noted critical pedagogue Paulo Freire (1970).

While much has been written about the need to improve the self-esteem of African American students (see for example, Banks & Grambs, 1972; Branch & Newcombe, 1986; Crooks, 1970), at base students must demonstrate academic competence. This was a clear message given by the eight teachers who participated in my study.[2] All of the teachers demanded, reinforced, and produced academic excellence in their students. Thus, culturally relevant teaching requires that teachers attend to students' academic needs, not merely make them "feel good." The trick of culturally relevant teaching is to get students to "choose" academic excellence.

In one of the classrooms I studied, the teacher, Ann Lewis,[3] focused a great deal of positive attention on the African American boys (who were the numerical majority in her class). Lewis, a White woman, recognized that the African American boys possessed social power. Rather than allow that power to influence their peers in negative ways, Lewis challenged the boys to demonstrate academic power by drawing on issues and ideas they found meaningful. As the boys began to take on academic leadership, other students saw this as a positive trait and developed similar behaviors. Instead of entering into an antagonistic relationship with the boys, Lewis found ways to value their skills and abilities and channel them in academically important ways.

Cultural Competence

Culturally relevant teaching requires that students maintain some cultural integrity as well as academic excellence. In their widely cited article, Fordham and Ogbu (1986) point to a phenomenon called "acting White," where African American students fear being ostracized by their peers for demonstrating interest in and succeeding in academic and other school related tasks. Other scholars (Hollins, 1994; King, 1994) have provided alternate explanations of this behavior.[4] They suggest that for too many African American students, the school remains an alien and hostile place. This hostility is manifest in the "styling" and "posturing" (Majors & Billson, 1992) that the school rejects. Thus, the African American student wearing a hat in class or baggy pants may be sanctioned for clothing choices rather than specific behaviors. School is perceived as a place where African American students cannot "be themselves."

Culturally relevant teachers utilize students' culture as a vehicle for learning. Patricia Hilliard's love of poetry was shared with her students through their own love of rap music. Hilliard is an African American woman who had taught in a variety of schools, both public and private for about 12 years. She came into teaching after having stayed at home for many years to care for her family. The mother of a teenaged son, Hilliard was familiar with the music that permeates African American youth culture. Instead of railing against the supposed evils of rap music, Hilliard allowed her second grade students to bring in samples of lyrics from what both she and the students determined to be non-offensive rap songs.[5] Students were encouraged to perform the songs and the teacher reproduced them on an overhead so that they could discuss literal and figurative meanings as well as technical aspects of poetry such as rhyme scheme, alliteration, and onomatopoeia.

Thus, while the students were comfortable using their music, the teacher used it as a bridge to school learning. Their understanding of poetry far exceeded what either the state department of education or the local school district required. Hilliard's work is an example of how academic achievement and cultural competence can be merged.

Another way teachers can support cultural competence was demonstrated by Gertrude Winston, a White woman who has taught school for 40 years.[6] Winston worked hard to involve parents in her classroom. She created an "artist or craftsperson-in-resident" program so that the students could both learn from each other's parents and affirm cultural knowledge. Winston developed a rapport with parents and invited them to come into the classroom for 1 or 2 hours at a time for a period of 2–4 days. The parents, in consultation with Winston, demonstrated skills upon which Winston later built.

For example, a parent who was known in the community for her delicious sweet potato pies did a 2-day residency in Winston's fifth grade classroom. On the first day, she taught a group of students[7] how to make the pie crust. Winston provided supplies for the pie baking and the students tried their hands at making the crusts. They placed them in the refrigerator overnight and made the filling the following day. The finished pies were served to the entire class.

The students who participated in the "seminar" were required to conduct additional research on various aspects of what they learned. Students from the pie baking seminar did reports on George Washington Carver and his sweet potato research, conducted taste tests, devised a marketing plan for selling pies, and researched the culinary arts to find out what kind of preparation they needed to become cooks and chefs. Everyone in Winston's class was required to write a detailed thank you note to the artist/craftsperson.

Other residencies were done by a carpenter, a former professional basketball player, a licensed practical nurse, and a church musician. All of Winston's guests were parents or relatives of her students. She did not "import" role models with whom the students did not have firsthand experience. She was deliberate in reinforcing that the parents were a knowledgeable and capable resource. Her students came to understand the constructed nature of things such as "art," "excellence," and "knowledge." They also learned that what they had and where they came from was of value.

A third example of maintaining cultural competence was demonstrated by Ann Lewis, a White woman whom I have described as "culturally Black" (Ladson-Billings, 1992b; 1992c). In her sixth grade classroom, Lewis encouraged the students to use their home language while they acquired the secondary discourse (Gee, 1989) of "standard" English. Thus, her students were permitted to express themselves in language (in speaking and writing) with which they were knowledgeable and comfortable. They were then required to "translate" to the standard form. By the end of the year, the students were not only facile at this "code-switching" (Smitherman, 1981) but could better use both languages.

Critical Consciousness

Culturally relevant teaching does not imply that it is enough for students to chose academic excellence and remain culturally grounded if those skills and abilities represent only an individual achievement. Beyond those individual characteristics of academic achievement and cultural competence, students must develop a broader sociopolitical consciousness that allows them to critique the cultural norms, values, mores, and institutions that produce and maintain social inequities. If school is about preparing students for active citizenship, what better citizenship tool than the ability to critically analyze the society?

Freire brought forth the notion of "conscientization," which is "a process that invites learners to engage the world and others critically" (McLaren, 1989, p. 195). However, Freire's work in Brazil was not radically different from work that was being done in the southern United States (Chilcoat & Ligon, 1994) to educate and empower African Americans who were disenfranchised.

In the classrooms of culturally relevant teachers, students are expected to "engage the world and others critically." Rather than merely bemoan the fact that their textbooks were out of date, several of the teachers in the study, in conjunction with their students, critiqued the knowledge represented in the textbooks, and the system of inequitable funding that allowed middle-class students to have newer texts. They wrote letters to the editor of the local newspaper to inform the community of the situation. The teachers also brought in articles and papers that represented counter knowledge to help the students develop multiple perspectives on a variety of social and historical phenomena.

Another example of this kind of teaching was reported in a Dallas newspaper (Robinson, 1993). A group of African American middle school students were involved in what they termed "community problem solving" (Tate, 1995). The kind of social action curriculum in which the students participated is similar to that advocated by scholars who argue that students need to be "centered" (Asante, 1991; Tate, 1994) or the *subjects* rather than the objects of study.

CULTURALLY RELEVANT TEACHING IN ACTION

As previously mentioned, this article and its theoretical undergirding come from a 3-year study of successful teachers of African American students. The teachers who participated in the study were initially selected by African American parents who believed them to be exceptional. Some of the parents' reasons for selecting the teachers were the enthusiasm their children showed in school and learning while in their classrooms, the consistent level of respect they received from the teachers, and their perception that the teachers understood the need for the students to operate in the dual worlds of their home community and the White community.

In addition to the parents' recommendations, I solicited principals' recommendations. Principals' reasons for recommending teachers were the low number of discipline referrals, the high attendance rates, and standardized test scores.[8] Teachers whose names appeared as both parents' and principals' recommendations were asked to participate in the study. Of the nine teachers' names who appeared on both lists, eight were willing to participate. Their participation required an in-depth ethnographic interview (Spradley, 1979), unannounced classroom visitations, videotaping of their teaching, and participation in a research collective with the other teachers in the study. This study was funded for 2 years. In a third year I did a follow-up study of two of the teachers to investigate their literacy teaching (Ladson-Billings, 1992b; 1992c).

Initially, as I observed the teachers I could not see patterns or similarities in their teaching. Some seemed very structured and regimented, using daily routines and activities. Others seemed more open or unstructured. Learning seemed to emerge from student initiation and suggestions. Still others seemed eclectic—very structured for certain activities and unstructured for others. It seemed to be a researcher's nightmare—no common threads to pull their practice together in order to relate it to others. The thought of their pedagogy as merely idiosyncratic, a product of their personalities and individual perspectives, left me both frustrated and dismayed. However, when I was able to go back over their interviews and later when we met together as a group to discuss their practice, I could see that in order to understand their practice it was necessary to go beyond the surface features of teaching "strategies" (Bartolome, 1994). The philosophical and ideological underpinnings of their practice, i.e. how they thought about themselves as teachers and how they thought about others (their students, the students' parents, and other community members), how they structured social relations within and outside of the classroom, and how they conceived of knowledge, revealed their similarities and points of congruence.[9]

All of the teachers identified strongly with teaching. They were not ashamed or embarrassed about their professions. Each had chosen to teach and, more importantly, had chosen to teach in this low-income, largely African American school district. The teachers saw themselves as a part of the community and teaching as a way to give back to the community. They encouraged their students to do the same. They believed their work was artistry, not a technical task that could be accomplished in a recipe-like fashion. Fundamental to their beliefs about teaching was that all of the students could and must succeed. Consequently, they saw their responsibility as working to guarantee the success of each student. The students who seemed furthest behind received plenty of individual attention and encouragement.

The teachers kept the relations between themselves and their students fluid and equitable. They encouraged the students to act as teachers, and they, themselves, often functioned as learners in the classroom. These fluid relationships extended beyond the classroom and into the community. Thus, it was common for the teachers to be seen attending community functions (e.g., churches, students' sports events) and using community services (e.g., beauty parlors, stores). The teachers attempted to create a bond with all of the students, rather than an idiosyncratic, individualistic connection that might foster an unhealthy competitiveness. This bond was nurtured by the teachers' insistence on creating a community of learners as a priority. They encouraged the students to learn collaboratively, teach each other, and be responsible for each other's learning.

As teachers in the same district, the teachers in this study were responsible for meeting the same state and local curriculum guidelines.[10] However, the way they met and challenged those guidelines helped to define them as culturally relevant teachers. For these teachers, knowledge is continuously recreated, recycled, and shared by the teachers and the students. Thus, they were not dependent on state curriculum frameworks or textbooks to decide what and how to teach.

For example, if the state curriculum framework called for teaching about the "age of exploration," they used this as an opportunity to examine conventional interpretations and introduce alternate ones. The content of the curriculum was always open to critical analysis.

The teachers exhibited a passion about what they were teaching—showing enthusiasm and vitality about what was being taught and learned. When students came to them with skill deficiencies, the teachers worked to help the students build bridges or scaffolding so that they could be proficient in the more challenging work they experienced in these classrooms.

For example, in Margaret Rossi's sixth grade class, all of the students were expected to learn algebra. For those who did not know basic number facts, Rossi provided calculators. She believed that by using particular skills in context (e.g., multiplication and division in the context of solving equations), the students would become more proficient at those skills while acquiring new learning.

IMPLICATIONS FOR FURTHER STUDY

I believe this work has implications for both the research and practice communities. For researchers, I suggest that this kind of study must be replicated again and again. We need to know much more about the practice of successful teachers for African American and other students who have been poorly served by our schools. We need to have an opportunity to explore alternate research paradigms that include the voices of parents and communities in non-exploitative ways.[11]

For practitioners, this research reinforces the fact that the place to find out about classroom practices is the naturalistic setting of the classroom and from the lived experiences of teachers. Teachers need not shy away from conducting their own research about their practice (Zeichner & Tabachnick, 1991). Their unique perspectives and personal investment in good practice must not be overlooked. For both groups—researchers and practitioners alike—this work is designed to challenge us to reconsider what we mean by "good" teaching, to look for it in some unlikely places, and to challenge those who suggest it cannot be made available to all children.

NOTES

1. Some notable exceptions to this failure to consider achievement strategies for African American students are *Ways With Words* (Heath, 1983); "Fostering Early Literacy Through Parent Coaching" (Edwards, 1991); and "Achieving Equal Educational Outcomes for Black Children" (Hale-Benson, 1990).

2. I have written extensively about this study, its methodology, findings, and results elsewhere. For a full discussion of the study, see Ladson-Billings (1994).

3. All study participants' names are pseudonyms.

4. At the 1994 annual meeting of the American Educational Research Association, King and Hollins presented a symposium entitled, "The Burden of Acting White Revisited."

5. The teacher acknowledged the racism, misogyny, and explicit sexuality that is a part of the lyrics of some rap songs. Thus, the students were directed to use only those songs they felt they could "sing to their parents."

6. Winston retired after the first year of the study but continued to participate in the research collaborative throughout the study.

7. Because the residency is more than a demonstration and requires students to work intensely with the artist or craftsperson, students must sign up for a particular artist. The typical group size was 5–6 students.

8. Standardized test scores throughout this district were very low. However, the teachers in the study distinguished themselves because students in their classrooms consistently produced higher test scores than their grade level colleagues.

9. As I describe the teachers I do not mean to suggest that they had no individual personalities or practices. However, what I was looking for in this study were ways to describe the commonalties of their practice. Thus, while this discussion of culturally relevant teaching may appear to infer an essentialized notion of teaching practice, none is intended. Speaking in this categorical manner is a heuristic for research purposes.

10. The eight teachers were spread across four schools in the district and were subjected to the specific administrative styles of four different principals.

11. Two sessions at the 1994 annual meeting of the American Educational Research Association in New Orleans entitled, "Private Lives in Public Conversations: Ethics of Research Across Communities of Color," dealt with concerns for the ethical standards of research in non-White communities.

REFERENCES

Asante, M. K. (1991). The Afrocentric idea in education. *Journal of Negro Education, 60,* 170–180.

Au, K., & Jordan, C. (1981). Teaching reading to Hawaiian children: Finding a culturally appropriate solution. In H. Trueba, G. Guthrie, & K. Au (Eds.), *Culture and the bilingual classroom: Studies in classroom ethnography* (pp. 69–86). Rowley, MA: Newbury House.

Banks, J., & Grambs, J. (Eds), (1972). *Black self-concept: Implications for educational and social sciences.* New York: McGraw-Hill.

Bartolome, L. (1994). Beyond the methods fetish: Toward a humanizing pedagogy. *Harvard Educational Reviews, 64,* 173–194.

Berliner, D. (1988, October). Implications of studies of expertise in pedagogy for teacher education and evaluation. In *New directions for teacher assessment* (Invitational conference proceedings). New York: Educational Testing Service.

Branch, C., & Newcombe, N. (1986). Racial attitudes among young Black children as a function of parental attitudes: A longitudinal and cross-sectional study. *Child Development, 57,* 712–721.

Brown, C. S. (Ed.), (1990). *Ready from within: A first person narrative.* Trenton, NJ: Africa World Press.

Cazden, C., & Leggett, E. (1981). Culturally responsive education: Recommendations for achieving Lau remedies II. In H. Trueba, G. Guthrie, & K. Au (Eds.), *Culture and the bilingual classroom: Studies in classroom ethnography* (pp. 69–86). Rowley, MA: Newbury House.

Chilcoat, G. W., & Ligon, J. A. (1994). Developing democratic citizens: The Mississippi Freedom Schools as a model for social studies instruction. *Theory and Research in Social Education, 22,* 128–175.

The College Board. (1985). *Equality and excellence: The educational status of Black Americans.* New York: Author.

Crooks, R. (1970). The effects of an interracial preschool program upon racial preference, knowledge of racial differences, and racial identification. *Journal of Social Issues, 26,* 137–148.

Edwards, P. A. (1991). Fostering early literacy through parent coaching. In E. Hiebert (Ed.), *Literacy for a diverse society: Perspectives, programs, and policies* (pp. 199–123). New York: Teachers College Press.

Erickson, F., & Mohatt, C. (1982). Cultural organization and participation structures in two classrooms of Indian students. In G. Spindler (Ed.), *Doing the ethnography of schooling* (pp. 131–174). New York: Holt, Rinehart & Winston.

Fordham, S., & Ogbu, J. (1986). Black students' success: Coping with the burden of "acting White." *Urban Review, 18,* 1–31.

Freire, P. (1970). *Pedagogy of the oppressed.* New York: Herder & Herder.

Gee, J. P. (1989). Literacy, discourse, and linguistics: Introduction. *Journal of Education, 171,* 5–17.

Hale-Benson, J. (1990). Achieving equal educational outcomes for Black children. In A. Baron & E. E. Garcia (Eds.), *Children at risk: Poverty, minority status, and other issues in educational equity* (pp. 201–215). Washington, DC: National Association of School Psychologists.

Heath, S. B. (1983). *Ways with words.* Cambridge, U.K.: Cambridge University Press.

Hollins, E. R. (1994, April). *The burden of acting White revisited: Planning school success rather than explaining school failure.* Paper presented at the annual meeting of the American Educational Research Association, New Orleans.

Irvine, J. J. (1990). *Black students and school failure.* Westport, CT: Greenwood Press.

Jordan, C. (1985). Translating culture: From ethnographic information to educational program. *Anthropology and Education Quarterly, 16,* 105–123.

King, J. (1994). *The burden of acting White re-examined: Towards a critical genealogy of acting Black.* Paper presented at the annual meeting of the American Educational Research Association, New Orleans.

Ladson-Billings, G. (1990). Like lightning in a bottle: Attempting to capture the pedagogical excellence of successful teachers of Black students. *International Journal of Qualitative Studies in Education, 3,* 335–344.

Ladson-Billings, G. (1992a). Culturally relevant teaching: The key to making multicultural education work. In C. A. Grant (Ed.), *Research and multicultural education* (pp. 106–121). London: Falmer Press.

Ladson-Billings, G. (1992b). Liberatory consequences of literacy: A case of culturally relevant instruction for African-American students. *Journal of Negro Education, 61,* 378–391.

Ladson-Billings, G. (1992c). Reading between the lines and beyond the pages: A culturally relevant approach to literacy teaching. *Theory Into Practice, 31,* 312–320.

Ladson-Billings, G. (1994). *The dreamkeepers: Successful teaching for African-American students.* San Francisco: Jossey-Bass.

McLaren, P. (1989). *Life in schools.* White Plains, NY: Longman.

Majors, R., & Billson, J. (1992). *Cool pose: The dilemmas of Black manhood in America.* New York: Lexington Books.

Mohatt, G., & Erickson, F. (1981). Cultural differences in teaching styles in an Odawa school: A sociolinguistic approach. In H. Trueba, G. Guthrie, & K. Au (Eds.), *Culture and the bilingual classroom: Studies in classroom ethnography* (pp. 105–119). Rowley, MA: Newbury House.

Morris, A. (1984). *The origins of the civil rights movement: Black communities organizing for change.* New York: The Free Press.

Perry, T. (1993). *Toward a theory of African-American student achievement.* Report No. 16. Boston, MA: Center on Families, Communities, Schools and Children's Learning, Wheelock College.

Pewewardy, C. (1993). Culturally responsible pedagogy in action: An American Indian magnet school. In E. Hollins, J. King, & W. Hayman (Eds.), *Teaching diverse populations: Formulating a knowledge base* (pp. 77–92). Albany: State University of New York Press.

Robinson, R. (1993, Feb. 25). P. C. Anderson students try hand at problem-solving. *The Dallas Examiner,* pp. 1, 8.

Shulman, L. (1987). Knowledge and teaching: Foundations of the new reform. *Harvard Educational Review, 57,* 1–22.

Smitherman, G. (1981). *Black English and the education of Black children and youth.* Detroit: Center for Black Studies, Wayne State University.

Spradley, J. (1979). *The ethnographic interview.* New York: Holt, Rinehart & Winston.

Tate, W. F. (1994). Race, retrenchment, and reform of school mathematics. *Phi Delta Kappan, 75,* 477–484.

Tate, W. F. (1995). "Returning to the Root: A Culturally Relevant Approach to Mathematics Pedagogy. *Theory into Practice, 34.*

Villegas, A. (1988). School failure and cultural mismatch: Another view. *The Urban Review, 20,* 253–265.

Vogt, L., Jordan, C., & Tharp, R. (1987). Explaining school failure, producing school success: Two cases. *Anthropology and Education Quarterly, 18,* 276–286.

Zeichner, K. M., & Tabachnick, B. R. (1991). Reflections on reflective teaching. In B. R. Tabachnick & K. M. Zeichner (Eds.), *Inquiry-oriented practices in teacher education* (pp. 1–21). London: Falmer Press.

13.2 KAREN SWISHER AND DONNA DEYHLE

Adapting Instruction to Culture

"American Indian students come to learn about the world in ways that differ from those of non-Indian students." In this selection, taken from the chapter titled "Adapting Instruction to Culture" of the book *Teaching American Indian Students* edited by John Reyhner (University of Oklahoma Press, 1994), Karen Swisher and Donna Deyhle summarize research on the learning styles of American Indian students. They also show how learning styles affect learning in a classroom where the teaching is oriented toward different learning styles. According to Swisher and Deyhle, American Indian student learning styles in general tend to include the following: learn privately before performing, volunteering, or speaking publicly; learn by observing and reflecting; and learn through cooperation. Students' learning styles are influenced by home and cultural socialization. By understanding the ways that American Indian students learn, according to Swisher and Deyhle, teachers can avoid creating classroom environments that diminish the traditional culture of American Indians, as well as create environments for more positive learning experiences for students.

Swisher is an associate professor in the College of Education and the Center for Indian Education at Arizona State University. She is also editor of the *Journal of American Indian Education.* Swisher's focus in her research and teaching is on American Indian education and multicultural education, with an emphasis on learning styles and the effects on learning and on issues such as dropouts. Deyhle is an associate professor of cultural foundations and ethnic studies at the University of Utah. Her interests are in the areas of anthropology of education, ethnographies of education, American Indian education, and multicultural education. She received her Ph.D. in educational anthropology from the University of New Mexico. Deyhle has conducted a number of research studies with an ethnographic approach in Brazil, Australia, Peru, Wales, and the Navajo reservation. Both Swisher and Deyhle have received national honors and awards from educational associations.

Key Concept: learning styles of American Indian students

LEARNING TO LEARN

> When I make an assignment my Indian students are reluctant to finish quickly or to correct other peers' papers. My Anglo students are quick to jump into the task. The Indian students seem to need time to think about things before they take action on their assignment. It is almost like they have to make sure they can do it before they try. Or, on the other hand, they seem to just not care about doing their assignments. (teacher, personal communication, 1987)

It is generally accepted in the literature that the ways in which children have learned to learn prior to entering the formal education environment are influenced by early socialization experiences (John 1972; Philips 1972; Cazden 1982). Different sociocultural environments cause behaviors to differ from culture to culture.

Differences between the home learning style and the school learning style are often manifested when an Indian child goes to school. Wax, Wax, and Dumont described one such conflict, in which performance does not precede competence:

> Indians tend to ridicule the person who performs clumsily: an individual should not attempt an action unless he knows how to do it; and if he does not know, then he should watch until he has understood. In European and American culture generally, the opposite attitude is usually the case; we "give a man credit for trying" and we feel that the way to learn is to attempt to do. (1964, 95)

Werner and Begishe (1968) presented evidence from the Navajos to illustrate how home culture affects styles of learning. They reported that Navajos seem to be unprepared or ill at ease if pushed into early performance without sufficient thought or the acquisition of mental competence preceding the actual physical activity. This philosophy suggests, "If at first you don't think, and think again, don't bother trying." In contrast, the white culture's approach, which stresses performance as a prerequisite for the acquisition of competence, is summed up in the philosophy "If at first you don't succeed, try, try, again" (1968, 1–2).

Longstreet (1978) also reported how Navajo children have learned to learn. She observed that Navajo children watch an activity repeatedly before attempting any kind of public performance. They do not have an adult close by helping and correcting them; instead, they observe and review the performance in their heads until they can perform the task well in front of an audience.

Brewer, in describing learning at home and school for Oglala Sioux children, said that observation, self-testing in private, and then demonstration of a task for approval were essential steps in learning. "Learning through public mistakes was not and is not a method of learning which Indians value" (1977, 3).

In pointing out how culturally influenced styles may conflict with one another, Appleton (1983), in a report titled "Culture: A Way of Reading," described differences in Yaqui Indian learning style. In the typical public school classroom, Appleton wrote, Yaqui children avoid unfamiliar ground, where trial and error or an inquiry method of reasoning was required. Instead, they come to school believing that a respectful attitude toward any task includes doing the task well. For Yaquis, doing an activity according to recommended or correct form is as important as the purpose or goal of the activity, and if it cannot be done well, there is little reason to engage in the activity at all.

These Navajo, Oglala Sioux, and Yaqui examples exhibit home socialization practices that influence the way these Indian children learn to learn. These children preferred to learn privately and to gain competence before publicly performing. Although each group was different and distinct from the others in language and other aspects of their particular culture, a similar approach to learning seems to be prevalent.

EXPERIENCING THE WORLD: A VISUAL APPROACH TO LEARNING

I study like this. The teacher lectures and then I take notes. And then I read them over. I study them. And then when I take a test I see the study notes in my mind (her hands quickly outline a rectangular shape). I see the paper and then I know where the answers are when I see the paper in my mind. (Navajo student, personal communication, 1988).

Within the last two decades researchers have investigated the visual approach that many Indian groups use as a method by which they come to know and understand the world. John suggested that there is considerable agreement among social scientists, educators, and others "that the Indian children of the Southwest are visual in their approaches to their world" (1972, 333). Impressions formed by careful observation are lasting impressions. She reported that Navajo children learn by looking: "They scrutinize the face of adults; they recognize at great distances their family's livestock. They are alert to danger signs of changing weather or the approach of predatory animals" (1972, 333). Appleton, in describing Yaqui children, said they are encouraged to learn by watching and modeling; "learning the correct way to do a task by watching it being performed repeatedly by others is highly reinforced" (1983, 173).

Indian children of the Northwest also exhibit the same sort of visual strength in how they view their world. For example, Kwakiutl children apparently have learned to learn by observation (Philion and Galloway 1969; Rohner 1965; Wolcott 1967). Rohner (1965) found that in their homes, Kwakiutl children learned by observation, manipulation, and experimentation, but in school the learning experience was limited to verbal instruction, reading, and writing. Philion and Galloway (1969), in their research with Kwakiutl children and the reading process, stated that the children displayed remarkable ability in visual discrimination. By imitating the behavior of others, very young children (ages four or five) were able to perform complicated sets of actions without verbal directions.

Kleinfeld (1973) described the extraordinary accuracy of Eskimos in memory of visual information. Their figural and spatial abilities enabled them to draw maps of the terrain that were accurate in significant detail and in spatial arrangements.

The visual strength of Indian children in the Southwest has also been the subject of reports by Cazden and John (1971) and John-Steiner and Osterreich (1975). Philips (1972) added to the literature on observations of visual strength from her work with Warm Springs Oregon Indian children. When viewed as cultural strengths and not weaknesses or deficiencies, the natural skills and abilities of Indian children contribute to a total picture of that child's learning style.

FIELD DEPENDENCE AND FIELD INDEPENDENCE: THE INFLUENCE OF CULTURE

> Yeah, when I think about this field dependent/independent stuff, my Indian students seem to be more field sensitive. They do better when they understand the total picture. (teacher, personal communication, 1988)

Although field dependence/independence is the most thoroughly researched dimension of cognitive style (Cazden and Leggett 1981), there are few reports devoted to study of this dimension with American Indian students. The work of Ramirez and Castaneda (1974) with Mexican American children has provided a framework for looking at the impact of culture on learning styles of Indian children. Ramirez and Castaneda examined field dependence/independence in light of cultural differences among Mexican Americans and postulated that Mexican American youth tend to grow up in a culture in which family organization tends to produce primarily field dependent or, as they term it, field sensitive learning styles. Conversely, children reared in formally organized families that promote strong individual identity tend to be more field independent (Cohen 1969). It has been speculated that viewed from this paradigm, Indian children tend to be more field sensitive. However, in one study of field dependence/independence in Navajo children, Dinges and Hollenbeck (1978) found that their Navajo sample scored significantly higher in a field independent direction than did the white sample. Their findings contrast with previous research and hypothesized results, which suggested that there is a direct relationship among family organization, cultural isolation, and field dependence/field independence for cultures of the United States and in other cultures of the world. They attempted to determine that a similar relationship also holds for other American Indian groups but found contrasting data. They suggested a multi-factor explanation comprising genetic, environmental, experiential, and linguistic factors unique to the Navajo to account for the outcomes.

In summary, the body of research, although small, on learning styles of American Indian students presents some converging evidence that suggests common patterns or methods in the way these students come to know or understand the world. They approach tasks visually, seem to prefer to learn by careful observation preceding performance, and seem to learn in their natural settings experientially. Research with other student groups has clearly illustrated that differences in learning style (whether they be described as relational/analytical, field dependent/independent, or global/linear) can result in "academic disorientation." While it is not clear where Indian students fit on this continuum, it is clear from the research summarized in the previous section that American Indian students come to learn about the world in ways that differ from those of non-Indian students.

SHOWING COMPETENCE: PUBLIC AND PRIVATE TALK

I have noticed that when I asked a question, the [Pima] students would not respond; there was dead silence. But when I made a comment without questioning, they were more likely to respond and join in the discussion. (teacher, personal communication, 1988)

The way in which people prefer to demonstrate learning is an important corollary to the way in which they prefer to learn. As Mehan has described,

To be successful in classroom lessons, students must not only know the *content* of academic subjects, they must know the appropriate *form* in which to cast their academic knowledge. Although it is incumbent upon students to display *what* they know during lessons, they must also know *how* to display it. (1981, 51)

There is evidence that the ways in which children acquire and demonstrate knowledge are influenced by accustomed cultural norms and socialization practices (Cohen 1969). A body of recent research on minority children has produced studies that show different reactions to cooperative versus competitive situations, questioning techniques, classroom pace, and classroom organization. Included in this research is considerable ethnographic evidence on children's responses to different interactional situations in school and in their home and community. Classroom studies of Indian children's interactional styles or demonstration of knowledge have come to focus on the continuity/discontinuity spectrum as it relates to a child's home and school environments. The interactional style of the home environment sometimes conflicts or interferes with the interactional style required for successful participation in the classroom (Cazden 1982; Dumont 1972; Erickson and Mohatt 1982; Philips 1972, 1983; Van Ness 1981).

In particular, recent studies point to the different cultural orientation Indian children experience when participating in classroom learning. One of the most extensive studies was done by Philips (1972). Examining participant structures and communicative competence with children from the Warm Springs Indian Reservation in Oregon, Philips observed that Indian children were reluctant to participate in structures that required large and small group recitations. However, they were more talkative than non-Indian children in the last two structures, in which students initiated the interaction with the teacher or worked on student-led group projects. She noted that Warm Springs Indian children failed to participate verbally in their classrooms because the norms for social performance in their community did not support public linguistic performance, although the school environment demanded it. Philips's study revealed that observation, careful listening, supervised participation, and individualized self-correction or testing were modes of learning in the Warm Springs Indian community. She concluded that this process of competence acquisition may help to explain the Warm Springs Indian children's reluctance to speak in front of their classmates. An incongruity exists in that the processes of acquisition of knowledge and demonstration of knowledge in the classroom are "collapsed into the single act of answering questions or reciting when called upon to do so by the teacher, particularly in the lower grades" (1972, 388).

Other ethnographic research suggests that the communication difficulty experienced by the Warm Springs Indian children when participant structures are teacher dominated and require public recitations may be generalized to other groups of American Indian children as well as other minority group children. Dumont (1972) found a similar situation in a study that contrasted two Cherokee classrooms. In one classroom, teacher-dominated recitations were a predominant structure and the children were silent. In the other classroom the children were observed to talk excitedly and productively about all of their learning tasks because they could choose when and how to participate and the teacher encouraged small group student-directed projects. The landmark research conducted by Philips and Dumont presents frameworks for analyzing the interactional structure that exists in schools attended by children from other tribal groups. This research indicates that some Indian children are more apt to participate actively and verbally in group projects and in situations where they volunteer participation. Conversely, these Indian children are less apt to perform on demand when they are individually "put on the spot" by teachers who expect them to answer questions in front of other students.

COOPERATING AND COMPETING:
THE INDIVIDUAL AND THE GROUP

You put them out on the basketball court and they are competitive as can be. But in the classroom they don't want to compete against each other. I can ask a question and when a student responds incorrectly no other student will correct him. They don't want to look better than each other or to put another student down. The Anglo students are eager to show that they know the correct answer. They want to shine, the Indian students want to blend into the total class. (teacher, personal communication, 1988)

There is evidence that Indian children are predisposed to participate more readily in group or team situations. While much of the evidence on cooperation versus competition is anecdotal, Miller and Thomas (1972) and Brown (1977) conducted studies with Blackfeet and Cherokee Indian children, respectively, using the Madsen Cooperation Board to examine cooperative and competitive behaviors. Miller and Thomas found dramatic differences between Canadian Blackfoot children and Canadian white children while playing a game that permitted either competitive or cooperative behavior, but rewarded cooperative behavior. White children behaved competitively even when it was maladaptive to do so, while Blackfoot children cooperated. Brown found Cherokee children to be more cooperative and less competitive than white American children. There was a negative relationship between the cooperative behavior of Cherokee children and their school achievement. In other words, the students' cooperative behavior produced lower achievement. In the Cherokee classroom society, children closely followed traditional Cherokee norms such as maintaining harmonious relations and, more important, held fast to standards of achievement that all children could meet (Brown 1977). High-ability students, who did not want to violate this norm, did not display their competence, and the result was lowered achievement for many Cherokee students.

The implications of this research are that if Indian children have learned to learn in a cooperative way, they may experience conflicts when they enter the competitive world of the classroom. It also confirms the findings of ethnographic studies that suggest that many Indian students avoid competition when they view it as unfair (Dumont 1972; Wax, Wax, and Dumont 1964).

It is apparent that many Indian children tend to avoid individual competition, especially when it makes one individual appear to be better than another. In fact, in many Indian societies an individual's humility is something to be respected and preserved. Havighurst observed that "Indian children may not parade their knowledge before others nor try to appear better than their peers" (1970, 109).

In looking at competition and the peer society of Indian youth, Wax stated that

> It has frequently been observed that Indian pupils hesitate to engage in an individual performance before the public gaze, especially where they sense competitive assessment against their peers. Indian children do not wish to be exposed as inadequate before their peers, and equally do not wish to demonstrate by their individual superiority the inferiority of their peers. On the other hand, where performance is socially defined as benefitting the peer society, Indians become excellent competitors (as witness their success in team athletics). (1971, 85)

What the literature suggests is that for Indian children from certain groups, public display of knowledge that is not in keeping with community or group norms may be an unreasonable expectation. It may be an experience that causes Indian children to withdraw and act out the stereotype of the "silent Indian child."

TEACHING STYLE: ADAPTATION
TO LEARNING STYLE

The teaching style or method one chooses to transmit learning can have a significant effect on whether students learn or fail. As John suggested,

> Styles of teaching are, in part, an expression of the goals of education. When working with Indian children, educators choose methods of instruction that zero in on what they wish to accomplish instead of methods that reflect the developmental stages of children or respond to the specific features of tribal life. (1972, 332)

There are many variables to consider in choosing teaching methods that will lead to optimal learning in a particular situation. Among those variables, the culture of the learner has only recently been considered anything other than a deficiency to be remedied. As Burgess pointed out, "Unfortunately, many instructors ignore culture and its impact on learning both in 'content' and 'style,' rather than devising methods and techniques through which culturally diverse individuals approach problem solving" (1978, 52).

Leacock (1976) provided a strong argument for understanding culture and its influence on instruction. She believed that "true cultural insight" enables one to look beyond differences that are superficial and socially determined to the integrity of the individual; it prevents misinterpretation of behaviors that do not follow an accustomed pattern. Leacock cited as an example teachers' misinterpretation of the pervading "cooperative spirit" in Indian societies and a reluctance of Indian children to compete with peers as a lack of desire and motivation. In essence, she was saying that cultural differences are often misinterpreted and that the lens through which the teacher views behavior is colored by the ways in which atypical behaviors were characterized during the teacher-training process. For example, "timidity" is often interpreted as lack of initiative, motivation, or competitive spirit; but viewed through a more culturally relativistic lens, timid behavior might reveal a reluctance to compete with one's peers or to display learning in a way not congruent with the child's life-style. Wax, Wax, and Dumont reported similar conflicts when teachers misinterpret cultural behavior. They concluded,

> When Indian children err, their elders, "explain," which as we understood it means that they painstakingly and relatively privately illustrate or point out the correct procedure or proper behavior. However ... teachers in school do not understand this. Their irate scolding becomes an assault on the child's status before his peers. (At the same time, the teacher diminishes his own stature, inasmuch as respected elders among Indians control their tempers and instruct in quiet patience.) (1964, 95)

Mohatt and Erickson's (1981) study of cultural differences in teaching styles in an Odawa school supports the differences between participant structures Philips (1972) found in Warm Springs and illustrates that teachers who viewed cultural differences as strengths were able to create the type of atmosphere that motivates learning. In this study an Odawa Indian and a non-Indian teacher were observed to see if there were differences in their teaching styles. Although both teachers were effective and experienced, they varied as to their teaching strategies. The Odawa teacher's strategies reflected Odawa cultural patterns of what is appropriate in ordinary social relations between adults and children, which were then manifested in the pacing of classroom activities and interactions with students.

In most classrooms teachers tend to introduce almost all new concepts and give all instructions verbally (Rohner 1965; Appleton 1983). This teaching style conflicts with the traditional cultural patterns reinforced in many Indian communities, where visual perception is encouraged. As John speculates, "If the description of the ways in which young Navajo children learn is correct, that is, that they tend to approach their world visually and by quiet, persistent exploration, then a style of teaching stressing overt verbal performance is alien to such a child" (1972, 338). This is not to say that Indian children should not be expected to respond to verbal instructions or perform verbally, but, rather, that new concepts might be presented through alternative modes or teaching styles and that Indian children might be invited to display their learning in alternative interactions. For example, Cazden and Leggett (1981) recommended that because children differ in sensory modality strength, their learning may be limited by overly verbal environments, and therefore schools should deliberately plan more multisensory instruction. While Cazden and Leggett were referring to children in bilingual classrooms, they do use the term "bilingual classrooms" to refer to any classroom that includes minority children. Their recommendation makes sense for teachers of Indian children.

IN THE CLASSROOM: TRANSLATING THEORY INTO PRACTICE

The premise of this [selection] is that although Indian students come to school with an approach to learning which is culturally influenced and often different from those of mainstream American students, the styles that teachers use to deliver instruction are essentially the same for everyone. Philips capsulized this attitude when she said,

> Surprisingly little attention has been given to the teaching methods used in teaching ethnic minority students in this country. Particularly when the notion of culturally relevant curriculum materials has been around as long as it has. It is as if we have been able to recognize that there are cultural differences in what people learn, but not in how they learn. (1983, 132–33)

Advocating for Hispanic High School Students

Alicia Paredes Scribner is an associate professor in the area of social and cultural aspects of schooling at Southwest Texas State University. Throughout her work, she combines the study of school culture with the psychological aspects of student development. In articles such as the following, "Advocating for Hispanic High School Students: Research-Based Educational Practices," *The High School Journal* (April/May 1995), she focuses on how school change can reflect race, culture, and ethnicity.

Scribner states as her goal for this selection drawing "attention to research-based educational practices that can ameliorate those conditions of education that prevent Hispanic high school students from reaching their full potential." To this end, she lays out several problematic conditions for Hispanic students, then suggests some effective and promising practices for changing those conditions. In studying how to work toward dropout prevention, she recommends emphasizing conditions that keep students in school. In looking at effective instruction, she contends that the whole school climate needs to be culturally supportive. In examining the psychoeducational assessment of Hispanic students, she recommends using alternative measures that are advocacy-oriented. And to help educators to understand the issues involved in the acculturation of Hispanic students into the American school, Scribner encourages educators to support feelings of acceptance and pride in the students' cultural identities.

Key Concept: effective educational practices for Hispanic students

*M*arshall High School is located in a large metropolis in the Southwest region of the United States. The school population is predominantly minority, the largest subgroup of which is Hispanic. Over the last few years, Marshall High School has posted a dramatic increase in achievement scores. The dropout rate has shown a steady decline over the same period. A close look at student, teacher, and instructional characteristics of this high school indicate that the general approach to teaching is advocacy-oriented. Teachers work collaboratively to consider relevant home, community, school, classroom, and student factors when designing effective instructional practices for their students. Teachers understand second language acquisition and provide effective instruction to *enhance the linguistic competence of their students. Teachers display an unusual commitment to their profession and to their students. They have high expectations for their students and communicate these expectations to them. Students feel appreciated and respected. Referrals for formal psychoeducational assessment are rarely made without a well-planned and organized system of instruction that has carefully considered how the ecology of the learning environment may be contributing to the student's learning difficulty. The school administration and faculty are sensitive to acculturative stress and understand that a new culture and educational system may cause temporary adjustment problems for immigrant students. The overall school environment fosters a receptive context in which students learn and develop skills to assist them in transitioning to higher education or the world of work.*

The school described above is an imaginary one. It represents a model for improved teaching and learning conditions that will lead to academic achievement for Hispanics and other language minority students. If we are going to reverse the tide of underachievement of language minority students and reduce the dramatic rate of Hispanic high school dropouts, we indeed need to improve the way we teach Hispanic secondary students, who represent a large segment of the student population. Marshall High School should be the rule, rather than the exception.

Students from diverse cultural and linguistic backgrounds who attend school throughout the United States face many challenges in the process of acquiring their education. The majority of these students come from homes where English is not the primary language. A large number are limited English proficient (LEP) and hold immigrant status; concentrations of immigrants are usually found in poor neighborhoods. Data indicate that in 1990, about 43 percent of all LEP students were immigrants (U.S. Bureau of the Census, 1992). Both LEP and immigrant students are almost twice as likely to be poor. Many may have significant health and emotional needs as a result of trauma experienced in war-torn countries or refugee camps. They may be highly transient, making instruction difficult; they often arrive at school after the academic year has started, or leave before the academic year is ended (McDonnell and Hill, 1993). In addition, factors such as family dislocations, uncertainty and stress associated with poverty, mobility within school districts, changing school curricula and changing family roles are not always compatible with a stable school experience (Paredes Scribner, 1994).

This article draws attention to research-based educational practices that can ameliorate those conditions of education that prevent Hispanic high school students from reaching their full potential. Specifically, it is argued that there are selected practices that can contribute to dropout prevention, effective instruction, appropriate assessment, and reducing acculturative stress for Hispanic high school students. Recent research arms the committed school staff who advocate for Hispanic high school students with an array of promising practices that can make the imaginary Marshall High School real.

DROPOUT PREVENTION

A combination of poor instruction, repeated academic failure, feelings of alienation, lack of self-esteem, teenage pregnancy, overage for grade level and lack of parent involvement result in conditions that lead to student dropout. Data from the 1990 U.S. Census show that more than 135,000 individuals between the ages of 16 and 19 did not complete high school. The graduation rate in this country is 68.7 percent. However, accurate dropout data are difficult to report because of the different definitions of what constitutes a student dropout. A far greater number of student dropouts are not accounted for due to attrition from public high school enrollment between the ninth grade and the expected graduation in the 12th grade, four years later (Johnson, 1994). National figures indicate that in 1992, nearly half of the Hispanics ages 18–24 had dropped out of high school, a rate that has steadily been rising since the mid-1980s. In Texas, attrition rates indicate that for Hispanics the percentage change from 1985–86 to 1991–92 represents an increase of 9% over the eight-year period (Johnson, 1994).

The reasons for the high dropout rate of Hispanic high school students versus other minority groups are complex. Robledo Montecel explains that " . . . for Hispanics dropping out is part of the experience of being poor and Hispanic" ("High dropout rate," 1994). The problem may have its roots much earlier than high school. The average three to five-year-old Hispanic child has a one in three chance of getting into a preschool program and faces a good chance of being enrolled in a minority elementary school with limited resources and a shortage of facilities. Other reasons focus on the relevance of classroom instruction.

Those students from Hispanic backgrounds that make it as far as high school face the likelihood that the school will not offer the necessary preparatory courses required for college. It is common practice in school districts across the country to assign students to courses on the basis of standardized test scores. Based on these scores, students are tracked into college preparatory, regular or vocational coursework. Due to cultural and linguistic factors, Hispanic and other language minority students seldom get tracked into the college preparatory courses. Data from the High School and Beyond Study (Carroll, 1988) indicate that by their senior year, 73.8% of Hispanic youth have been enrolled in curricular programs that make a college education impossible. In an effort to achieve excellence, many states have instituted even more rigorous graduation standards by developing competency tests tied to educational reforms. The raising of standards without improving classroom instruction further penalizes language minority students, resulting in disproportionately high dropout rates.

Effective Practices

Rather than concentrate on the reasons why students drop out of school, we need to emphasize conditions that keep students in school. Delgado-Gaitan (1988) identified outside support as a major component in the lives of students who stayed in school. Students who stayed in school exhibited a higher degree of conformity to the school's regulations. They received qualitatively different social and emotional familial support from their families to help them deal with school rules and conflicts than did students who dropped out. Family members attended school activities, met regularly with school personnel and involved themselves in every possible way to keep the students in school. Although many of the parents in Delgado-Gaitans's study had themselves dropped out of school, they believed their children should get an education. In the same study, the alternative high school setting provided an environment in which concern for the total individual and the development of his/her abilities were emphasized. In other words, the focus was on the value of the person, rather than the value of the institution. Other studies (Hill, 1979; Mare, 1980; Paredes Scribner, 1989) link level of parental education and reinforcement history with student high school completion.

Students themselves form their own attitudes about the value of education. Low self-esteem, feelings of isolation and alienation and, ultimately, feeling inconsequential to the larger society contribute to school dropout (Reyes & Jason, 1993). The practice most cited for improving student retention is simply to make schooling more engaging, teaching more "active," and learning a more collaborative experience (Bermudez, 1994; Garcia, 1994; Oakes & Lipton, 1994; Sosa, 1993). Students should never experience the "pobrecito (poor student) syndrome." Teachers should be personally committed to the well-being of each child, eliminate ability grouping, establish on-site homework and tutoring by other students, if necessary, and be held accountable for high expectations for all students (Garcia, 1994).

In addition, recommendations for dropout prevention advocate keeping students with the same teachers for the last three years of high school, block scheduling so that there is a small core of teachers knowledgeable about each child and planning instructional strategies accordingly, coordinated coursework and rigorous academic programs, parental support networks and mentor programs, as well as a paid work experience beginning at the middle school level (Duran, 1989; Garcia, 1994; Oakes & Lipton, 1994; Reyes & Jason, 1993). Effective educational programs that have relevance to real life experiences will stimulate students, excite them about learning, and keep them in school.

EFFECTIVE INSTRUCTION

Among the most critical problems school districts face in providing adequate education for Hispanic students is the lack of appropriately trained teaching personnel and limited resources to meet the substantial needs of the LEP population in the nation's schools (McDonnell & Hill, 1993; U.S. General Accounting Office, 1994). Until very recently, language minority students who manifested learning difficulties were considered difficult to teach or linguistically deprived due to limited skills in the English language. Schools were essentially absolved of responsibility for the education of these students (Lucas, Henze, & Donato, 1990). Over the years, changes were made as a result of legal decisions (Diana

v. Board of Education, 1970; Lau v. Nichols, 1973). Nevertheless, the greater emphasis has been on elementary school-age students, paying little attention to the needs of language minority students at the secondary levels.

Trends show significant changes in the profiles of Hispanic high school populations. Secondary Hispanic students may range from those who come with strong educational backgrounds from their home country to those who have never had formal education. Those who have attended "secundaria" in their native countries may have higher levels of literacy skills than their American peers. While those students who have never attended school or whose educational history is characterized by interruptions have limited or no literacy skills in their native language. Variance within the Hispanic student population has made research difficult at this level. Larger urban districts across the United States may serve over 100 language groups, but not all language communities represent the same rate of English language proficiency. The National Advisory and Coordinating Council on Bilingual Education (1988) estimated that among Vietnamese and Hispanic communities, the largest language groups, about three out of four persons are LEP, in contrast to the four or five out of ten that characterize other language communities. If immigration patterns continue at the current rate, by the year 2026 our schools will be attempting to educate approximately 15 million students from culturally and linguistically diverse backgrounds, or 25% of the total elementary and secondary school enrollment (Garcia, 1994).

Even though the numbers of LEP students of high school age keep growing, few secondary bilingual programs exist to provide the needed support to students in their native language. The status of instruction to LEP students indicates that these students receive limited support in understanding academic subjects such as math, social studies and science (U.S. General Accounting Office, 1994). The General Accounting Office (GAO) report, which examined learning conditions for LEP students in five selected school districts in preparation for the reauthorization of federal elementary and secondary education programs, further states that students spend their time with teachers who do not understand their native language and who have little or no training in how to communicate with them.

These students are typically offered low level courses and English as a second language classes that emphasize segmented skills, worksheets and offer little opportunity for oral language development and interactive learning. In middle school and high school, the low level courses may result in passing grades, but the students are not acquiring the necessary learning to succeed in college or to get a decent job. Schools must be more accountable for the quality of instruction students receive.

Effective Practices

Providing adequate education for Hispanic high school students begins with the recruitment of both inservice and preservice teachers, preferably bilingual, who advocate for culturally and linguistically diverse language learners

(Bermudez, 1994; Garcia, 1994; Sosa, 1993). In a report published by the National Clearinghouse of Bilingual Education (Minicucci & Olsen, 1992, p. 15), the authors summarize effective practices in high schools that appear to be meeting the challenges of educating language minority students:

- there is a school-wide vision which includes English learners;
- there is a culturally supportive climate;
- there is ongoing training and staff support involving all teachers in the preparation and planning of programs for students learning English; and
- there is coordination and articulation between the ESL/Bilingual department and other departments, and between different grade levels.

Moreover, Lucas, et al. (1990) summarized features of effective instructional programs for Hispanic high school students. Effective programs placed value on the students' language and culture. The faculty and administration had high student expectations and made the education of language minority students a priority. Teacher staff development addressed not only effective instructional practices, learning styles and literacy skills in the content areas, but also training in crosscultural counseling. Small class size, particularly in ESL and primary language instruction, was the norm. Tracking language minority students in low level courses was avoided. Instead, there was an established system of academic support which closely monitored student progress. Parental involvement was fostered by the availability of Spanish-speaking staff, English instruction for parents, and their involvement in planning their child's course schedules. Finally, the faculty and staff shared a strong commitment to empower language minority students.

PSYCHOEDUCATIONAL ASSESSMENT

Hispanic student underachievement often results in referrals for psychoeducational assessment. At a loss to know what to do with language minority students who exhibit learning difficulties, teachers look to special education for solutions. Current methods of assessing cognitive and linguistic needs of Hispanic students fail to measure the depth and range of students' knowledge, problem-solving and critical thinking (Fradd, 1993).

Procedures to assess language proficiency fail to accurately assess the student's linguistic competence in both the native language and English. Language assessments are characterized by looking at criteria such as phonology (sound system/pronunciation), morphology (vocabulary and word usage), syntax (grammar), fluency (smoothness of communication), semantics (meaning), and pragmatics (functional use of language). Phonology, morphology and syntax are emphasized to the exclusion of semantics and pragmatics (Quinn, 1994). Some linguists consider phonology, morphology and syntax to be surface level structures of language; semantics and pragmatics are considered the deeper structures of language (Cummins, 1984). If only standardized, norm-referenced tests are used to assess language and other skills, the examiner does not get a full picture of the student's abilities in either the native language or English. How well a student performs on these measures becomes a function of his/her language ability, not his/her cognitive ability.

Formal, standardized testing typically used in schools was designed to provide feedback on how well specific knowledge and skills are learned. This type of assessment focuses on how students handle tasks on a single occasion under severe time constraints. Decisions determining eligibility for special education services are made, in part, on the basis of evidence from formal aptitude and achievement tests that indicate severe discrepancies between the student's cognitive ability and achievement. Historically, such measures have had detrimental consequences for LEP students because this population of students tends to perform lower than other groups on such tests (Palmer, Olivarez, Willson, & Fordyce, 1989; Valencia & Aburto, 1991). As a result of decisions made on the basis of standardized, norm-referenced tests, a disproportionate number of language minority students are represented in special education programs throughout the United States (Duran, 1989; Figueroa, 1989, 1990; Ortiz, 1986; Rueda, 1989).

Effective Practices

Promising assessment practices for language minority students propose alternative measures that are advocacy-oriented. Alternative assessment trends attempt to link assessment to instruction, making the psychoeducational assessment a fair and diagnostic process by considering the appropriateness of the curriculum and implementing a system of prereferral intervention. Beginning with a valid assessment of ability in the native language as well as English, appropriate interventions are designed to address the student's communicative competence (Duran, 1988).

Alternative assessment techniques include systematic observation of students, mediated learning experiences, and test-teach-test paradigms which focus on the process of learning instead of the products of learning. Using the Learning Potential Assessment Device (LPAD), a diagnostic system proposed by Fouerstein and his associates (1979), the examiner attempts to assess the student's learning capacity and degree of modifiability. This model is also applied to Vygotsky's (1978) theory of zone of proximal development (ZPD) as an index of cognitive modifiability. Zone of proximal development refers to the improvement a child makes on a mental task with mediated training. Here the examiner's goal is to increase the student's repertoire of problem-solving behaviors. The greater the degree of improvement, the higher the student's ability.

Advocacy-oriented assessment practices begin with a review of the student's educational history, informal assessment of skills in the native language and English, effective instruction to meet the student's needs, and appropriate educational interventions to give the student every opportunity to succeed in school. Cummins (1989) recommends that assessment go beyond looking for the learning difficulty as an inherent problem within the child. Instead, he recommends we look at how learning problems may be pedagogically induced or inherent in the instructional experience of the child.

Alicia Paredes
Scribner

ACCULTURATION

Students may also exhibit learning difficulties as a result of adjustment problems. These may range from shyness to acting-out behaviors or even more serious psychological problems. Culture exerts an effect on behavior and it is important for assessment personnel in the schools to understand cultural identity and self concept "within an often hostile environment and the attainment of status within the school's social structure" (Zapata, 1995, p. 90). In the process of acculturation, immigrant students may experience adjustment problems due to several reasons. Relocation to a new country, new school and new culture may result in feelings of isolation and anonymity for students. Friends and relatives are left behind resulting in discontinuity of everything that is familiar to the individual. Some families experience a conflict of values and role reversal when the more acculturated children assume financial and social responsibilities for the non-English speaking parents. In the academic setting the language barrier may result in inappropriate grade placement which further makes adjustment more difficult. The social need to adapt and be accepted by their mainstream peers may create anxiety. How well the students and families will adjust in the adopted country is a function of acculturation.

Acculturation refers to the changes that occur as a result of continuous contact between two distinct cultures (Berry, Trimble, & Olmedo, 1986). A significant deterrent to acculturation may be found in the attitudes of both the immigrant group and the larger society. The literature on acculturation is beginning to address problems of racism and negative attitudes in the United States because of changing demographic trends and the influx of peoples from many different parts of the world. The extent to which new immigrants are acculturated in the larger society depends on (1) the importance new arrivals place on identifying or maintaining cultural characteristics of their ethnic groups, and (2) the importance they attribute to maintaining positive relationships with the larger society and other ethnic groups (Phinney, Chavira, & Williamson, 1992). Majority cultural groups represented in most high schools throughout the United States have the potential of either easing the acculturation process or inducing barriers for new immigrant students.

Effective Practices

Responding to a need for school professionals to understand the acculturation of school children, Berry and his colleagues (Berry, Kim, Power, Young, & Bujaki, 1989) have developed a model of acculturation which sets forth four modes of acculturation. The first is *assimilation,* which occurs when ethnic groups choose to identify solely with the dominant society. *Integration* occurs when ethnic groups successfully involve themselves with the dominant culture and retain their traditional culture. They are equally comfortable in both cultures. *Separation* occurs when the ethnic group has little or no interaction with the dominant culture. The last, *marginality,* occurs when the ethnic group experiences a loss of one's culture or origin and there is also a lack of involvement with the dominant society. Marginality can create anxiety so severe as to produce neurotic or deviate behavior. Students who feel they are in this "no man's land" are at risk for drugs, dropping out of school and suicide ("LEP Students and Acculturation," 1991).

Despite variations in the degree of acculturation, Hispanic students' aspirations tend to be about the same as those of Anglo students (Chahin, 1983; Hispanic Research Center, 1991). However, school experiences tend to limit the opportunities of some students. The quality of school experience, the opportunity to acquire literacy skills in English and the opportunity to maintain identity with the native language and culture will contribute to academic success. Ethnic identity can impact Hispanic children's relationships with peers and teachers, as well as their long-term life and career development (Baron, 1991). Thus, acculturative stress can be reduced by having a culturally responsive curriculum that includes values of culturally and linguistically diverse students (Cummins, 1989).

How Hispanic high school students are perceived is a function of the extent to which schools emphasize multicultural curricula, the recruitment of multicultural staff, and the involvement of parents. Schools that possess these characteristics have a positive impact on both teachers and students (Moore, 1988). Academic achievement of minorities involves crossing cultural boundaries (Ogbu, 1994). High achievers in all cultures share similar qualities. They are more likely to be involved in more school activities than are low achievers, and high achievers view themselves as having high academic abilities and putting forth more effort (Pollard, 1989).

Phiney, el al., (1992) surveyed a group of high school and college students from four different ethnic groups to explore the relationship between acculturation attitudes and self-esteem. They found that youth strongly endorsed integration over the other modes of acculturation. This finding indicates that maintaining a positive identification with one's own and the mainstream culture provides "a more solid basis for self-esteem" (p. 310). As far back as the 1970s, work by Ramirez and his associates (as cited in Padilla, 1995) showed that participation in two cultures was not necessarily problematic.

A positive atmosphere in the school setting will support feelings of acceptance and pride in one's cultural identity. Compatibility between ethnic identity and school culture typically results in academic success (Matute-Bianchi, 1989). Students that successfully achieve the *integration* mode will maintain loyalty to their traditional culture along with responding to the demands of the dominant culture.

SUMMARY

The research-based practices reviewed in this article seem to point in the same direction. The Marshall High Schools of our nation are places where

(1) dropout rates are low;
(2) teachers spend longer periods of time with the same group of students;
(3) students are rarely placed in low level classes;
(4) parents are involved in their children's education in some way; and
(5) cultural identity and ethnic pride are fostered within a positive school climate.

Clearly, the evidence documented in the studies, research reports and recent reviews of culturally diverse student populations have added to our knowledge about the impact an advocacy-oriented school environment can have on Hispanic student academic success. Marshall High School need not be imaginary. By sharing a school-wide commitment to implementing a comprehensive plan that focuses on effective practices for dropout prevention, effective instruction, psychoeducational assessment, and acculturation, the research-based practices presented in this article are attainable.

Asian-American Children: A Diverse Population

The following selection by Valerie Ooka Pang, which is from "Asian-American Children: A Diverse Population," *The Educational Forum* (Fall 1990), lays out the demographics of Asian Americans. Pang's purpose in this selection is to bring attention to the diversity that exists within Asian Americans and to break the stereotype that they are all the same. She describes some of the key issues that affect Asian American students. One is whether students were born in the United States or are immigrants. This will affect how they identify themselves, what activities and groups they join, and their views of language and family. Many Asian American children feel "marginal," or conflicted between becoming assimilated into the dominant culture or retaining their home cultures. Pang talks about the problems of holding the "model minority" myth. This causes heightened anxiety and frustration for students, and their skills in areas other than science and technology are often overlooked. Pang concludes, "Asian-American students cannot have equal educational opportunity when their educational experience is shaped by inaccurate information and naive beliefs."

Pang is a professor at San Diego State University in California, and she is a senior fellow of the Annenberg Institute for School Reform, Brown University, in Providence, Rhode Island. She also serves as adviser for various groups that make media productions dealing with children's issues, especially television shows like *Sesame Street* and *Mister Rogers' Neighborhood*. Her interests are in culturally meaningful teaching, and she has published articles in journals such as *Phi Delta Kappan, Harvard Educational Review,* and *Multicultural Education*.

Key Concept: the diversity within the Asian American population

*T*o many teachers, Asian-American students seem to look and be alike—they are model minority students. Like many other stereotypes, this perception is easier believed than carefully examined. In fact, most Asian-American students are neither "super brains" nor "gang members." They do represent many cognitive strengths and weaknesses, have diverse ethnic roots, live in many parts of the United States, and range from being newly immigrated to having roots over 200 years old.[1] Without basic knowledge of the diversity of the particular population, schools cannot provide an equal chance for all to develop their intellect and skills.[2]

237

*Valerie Ooka
Pang*

Asian-Americans encompass a number of highly diverse groups, including those of the Cambodian, Chinese, East Indian, Filipino, Guamanian, Hawaiian, Hmong, Indonesian, Japanese, Korean, Laotian, Samoan, and Vietnamese heritages. The U.S. Bureau of the Census included smaller Asian-American groups within the category of all other Asians in the 1980 Census. These were Bangladeshi, Bhutanese, Bornean, Burmese, Celbesian, Cernan, Indochinese, Iwo-Jiman, Javenese, Malayan, Maldivian, Nepali, Okinawan, Sikkimese, Singaporean, and Sri Lankan.[3] In toto, they make up the fastest growing minority group in the United States. From 1970 to 1980, the Asian population increased by approximately 143 percent.[4] In 1985, Asian-American population was estimated to be 5.1 million and projected to increase to 10 million by the year 2000, approaching four percent of the national population.[5] The 1984 Elementary and Secondary School Civil Rights Survey reported an Asian-American student population of just about one million.[6] Taking into consideration birthrate and continued immigration, it may be safely surmised that the figure has further increased in more recent years.

Though the number of children who are of mixed parentage is not known, it is important to note that Asian-American youth include a number of Eurasian-Americans, Asian Latino-Americans, Asian Black-Americans, Asian Native-Americans, and others. Interracial marriages have been occurring since the first Filipino immigrants made Louisiana their home in 1763 and wed outside their ethnic community.[7] More recently, of course, there have been many mixed children conceived during the Vietnam war who were rejected both in Vietnam due to their White-American roots, and in the U.S. because of their Vietnamese backgrounds.[8] Many families also include intraracial marriages among different Asian-American groups. Thus, it is not uncommon for children to have both Chinese and Japanese roots or Filipino and Vietnamese heritages.

Before getting into the general discussion of Asian-American population, a word must be said about the label, "Oriental." Though this term is often used in education to identify students with Asian roots, its use in reference to U.S. citizens and residents ignores the negative connotations of an outgroup status, of foreigners, and perhaps even of "yellow peril." Asian-Americans have resided in the United States for over 200 years, some being able to trace their roots back over ten generations. Also, soldiers from the Filipino-American community fought in the War of 1812.[9] It is more appropriate to call these people "Asian-American" or, more inclusively, "Asian- and Pacific Islander-American."

FACTORS CONTRIBUTING TO DIVERSITY

Asian-American students, native or immigrant. An important variable when dealing with Asian-American population is place of birth, American born or immigrant. The experiences of the two groups may differ greatly, and so does the manner in which they identify themselves. Though it is dangerous to overgeneralize across individuals within a group, American-born students are likely to be more highly assimilated into the mainstream,[10] especially those who do not reside in ethnic communities.[11] For example, many Japanese-American students who live in middle-class suburban neighborhoods[12] may not choose to identify themselves along ethnic lines.[13] Matute-Bianchi found such high school students from central California identify themselves through their school activities like student government and social clubs, rather than through ancestry. They did not want to engage in school activities that were ethnically tied. For example, though attempts had been made at one school to establish a club focusing on Japanese history, no students of Japanese descent joined the group.

However, many American-born, limited English proficient students may readily identify themselves through ethnic lines, and even boast, "I can be President of the United States." These children may come to school unable to speak English because they have spoken their ancestral languages all their lives. Kindergarten could be the very first setting requiring them to use English. On the other hand, many American-born students speak only English.[14] They can be categorized as being bicultural, and they may look positively at ethnic membership and life in an environment that mixes both mainstream and traditional Asian values.[15] These children may be family oriented, respect elders, and value education, while at the same time participate in mainstream, after-school activities like football or ballet. They may not choose to take part in Asian-American activities at school, but can be members of, for example, a local Buddhist temple, participating in ethnically specific activities in that context.[16]

Like their American-born counterparts, immigrant students clearly demonstrate a wide range of approaches to their background. There are highly assimilated ones who may feel compelled to blend into American society and so relinquish ancestral cultural values, behaviors, and traditions. They may, for example, refuse to speak their first language, and view their ethnic ties as obstacles to being accepted into the mainstream. In contrast, there are those who are extremely proud of their background. The parents of these children speak their ancestral language at home,[17] and children may attend a special Saturday or after-school language school built to ensure that the values, beliefs, and language of the originating culture remain in the community.[18]

Many from Asian countries have migrated to the United States in search of economic stability. Prior to 1965, Chinese-American, Filipino-American, Japanese-American, and Korean-American communities consisted of families who had long American roots, since immigration had been prohibited for the Chinese after 1882, the Japanese and Koreans after 1924, and the Filipinos after 1934 (the Filipino Exclusion Act).[19] With the Immigration Act of 1965, the numbers of Chinese, Korean, and Filipino immigrants dramatically rose. More recently, after the governments of South Vietnam, Cambodia, and Laos fell in 1975, there were thousands of Vietnamese, Chinese, Cambodians, and other Asian refugees who fled Southeast Asia because of political strife.[20] The largest proportion of the refugee population were Vietnamese with smaller numbers of Laotians, Chinese-Vietnamese, and Hmong refugees. They represented a large diversity in socioeconomic and educational levels.[21] Some were fluent English speakers and others had no English language skills at all. With all this influx, difficulties have sometimes developed between immigrant and American-born Asian students. Differences between the two categories of students, their values and feelings,[22] can affect their interactions at school.

Possible intragroup conflicts. Many Asian-Americans have found themselves with increasing feelings of marginality,[23] as the pressure of cultural assimilation can produce ambivalent feelings about ethnic group membership.[24] Marginality refers to conflicting attitudes that may develop when a member of a minority group finds himself or herself at cultural odds with the dominant society, and the marginal person can develop personality traits of insecurity, hypersensitivity, and excessive self-consciousness. Even within the Asian-American population itself, those students whose families have old roots within the United States may not feel comfortable with new immigrant students. They may fear being identified with the immigrants who, they feel, are old fashioned, "nerds," or "weird" in dress and behavior. When new immigrants are being harassed by other students, the better established ones may feel the pressure to "join in" the mainstream so as not to be perceived as being associated with the newcomers. Or they may ignore the harassment, without trying to discourage the taunting. Educators should be aware of this possible area of conflict and not routinely choose other Asian-Americans as buddies for immigrant students, assuming incorrectly that older ones can be of the most help to the new arrivals. Asking students to volunteer for this responsibility may reduce the potential for such conflict.

The second source of intragroup conflict may lie in the past, "old country" animosities. Many new immigrant students may find themselves placed in classes with others from groups that, historically, have been fierce enemies. Antagonism has cropped up in some school incidents involving Asian-American students battling each other. In one instance, a teacher who had Vietnamese-American and Cambodian-American students learned about these animosities in a peer teaching situation. The Vietnamese-American student had lived in the United States for about seven years and spoke English well. The Cambodian-American student had been in the United States for only three years and was having some difficulties understanding the material. The teacher mistakenly assumed that they would be happy to work with each other, since they had similar refugee experiences. He asked the Vietnamese youth to help the Cambodian. Since such students generally have a high regard for teachers, they were rather reluctant to speak out, but the Vietnamese student explained diplomatically that he did not think the other student would accept his help. This greatly surprised the teacher, but the prediction of the student was confirmed when the Cambodian student said, "I do not want to accept help from a Vietnamese." These feelings were worked through, but even then it was difficult for the students who had been in adversary roles to view situations in a new light. These historical sentiments often come with new immigrants, and teachers need to be aware of such long-standing animosities.

Of course, immigrant and American-born youth may not generally form close friendships with each other. There can exist a mutual feeling of mistrust, reflecting a lack of understanding of each other's values and beliefs. Sometimes language barriers contribute to the distance. Those born in the U.S. who do not speak an ancestral language may feel unable to communicate with immigrants who are speaking a first language other than English. And, on their part, immigrant youngsters may not understand English sufficiently well to feel comfortable participating in peer group conversations. School staff should be sensitive to these possible sources of conflict in encouraging cooperative activities. Students with varied roots can be placed in small mixed groupings where personal experiences can help reduce prejudicial attitudes. Here, again, the danger of overgeneralizing is ever present, as the dynamics between groups are not always apparent. Teachers need to react to their Asian-American students as individuals, and to understand how the differing experiences of these students can influence their behaviors in school. . . .

SOCIOPSYCHOLOGICAL AND ACADEMIC NEEDS

Self concept and psychological needs.   To many school personnel, Asian-American students appear to have fewer and less severe personal problems than other students. Though teachers are often aware of the academic problems of those from Southeast Asia, the needs of other students may not be readily apparent. It is easy for teachers to spot problems of language proficiency, but it is much more difficult to identify internal conflicts in students.

Needless to say, Asian-American students must deal with the stresses of racism and the existence of conflicting cultural messages communicated by frequently portrayed images of Asian-Americans. One of those images is the "model minority" classification, which can be accompanied by the belief that they are the students who raise the grading curve. They are usually not the football stars or cheerleaders, and they may be perceived as "nerds." Students who do well must cope with this social image, and it is not always an asset to stand out academically, to be considered "eggheads." Yet, they oftentimes come from families in which education is highly valued. Parents will sacrifice material comfort in order to provide the best educational experience for their children.[25] Some parents expect not only "good" grades but also "exceptionally high" grades from their offspring. Thus, students who feel pressure from their families must deal with possible rejection from their peers.

On the other hand, there are Asian-American children who are not intellectually gifted and cannot reach the high academic standards which parents or teachers have set for them. These students have a difficult time dealing with negative feelings of being a "loser." One *sansei* (third generation Japanese-American) high school student said about himself, "My folks just gave up on me because I didn't get into college." Unfortunately, this message was also reiterated by his teacher who told the student, "Your sister was an *A* student—how come you only get *C*'s? You're not trying." The model minority image can be a terrible liability for those students who are not academically inclined, especially when teachers assume that children from certain Asian-American groups will be top achievers. These students are trying to deal with the powerful process of assimilation, and mixed messages regarding their acceptance into mainstream society can be a heavy burden for them to carry.

The impact of being a member of a visibly different minority group can also have a forceful effect on the fragile and developing self image of children. The findings of a study examining the self-concept of Asian-American youth show a disturbing pattern of generally lower levels of self-esteem than Caucasian and Black American youngsters.[26] Another study reported Vietnamese-American students to score lowest on overall self concept in comparison to non-Vietnamese Asian, Caucasian, Black-American, and Mexican-American students.[27] Similarly, Korean-American and Chinese-American students may not feel as positive about their physical self image as Black- or White-American students.[28] In yet another study of the general self concept of Japanese-American students in the fourth through sixth grades, lower physical self concept scores were seen offset by high academic self image scores to make the general scores less than revealing.[29] These findings may be surprising to many teachers who believe Asian-American students are well adjusted, competent students. Such studies point to the need for schools to take steps to help Asian-American students develop more positive perceptions of themselves. . . .

The inaccurate "model minority" myth and belief in the homogeneity of the Asian-American student population have limited the development of educational programs that fully address their varied needs. New perspectives on these children should be adopted by school personnel.

One area of concern is self concept of which a global view may not be sufficient to clarify their feelings of specific inadequacies. Asian-American children may also suffer from test anxiety and pressures for high academic achievement. Some appear to be highly influenced by a desire to please their parents, an impetus potentially stronger than direct parental pressure. Additionally, teachers may be unconsciously contributing to the heightened anxiety in students by assuming most Asian-American students to be high achievers. Another important concern is the inability of many school staff to recognize feelings of depression, frustration, and desperation in these students. Schools should consider instituting programs to help students and parents to understand better the pressures for high academic achievement and to assist highly anxious students to develop effective coping skills.

There is also the need for schools to institute educational programs to help Asian-American children become confident in communication skills, both oral and written. Because these students often exhibit competencies in technical and scientific fields, school personnel may overlook their lower grades in English, creative writing, or composition. There are some Asian groups whose children are dropping out of school at a very high rate, and the effects can be devastating on the economic and political survival of their communities. In addition, there are high numbers of "at risk" students in certain groups to call for a balanced view of Asian-American students and their families. Like any other group, they have strengths and needs. We are still saddled with an educational system that has difficulty dealing with children who come to school with varying values, languages, and motivational backgrounds. Understanding the great diversity within the group is crucial, otherwise their needs may continue to be overlooked. Creation of alternatives in curriculum, counseling, and instructional strategies demand a change in our attitudes toward, and knowledge of, these students. Asian-American students cannot have equal educational opportunity when their educational experience is shaped by inaccurate information and naive beliefs.

REFERENCES

1. Fred Cordova, *Filipinos: Forgotten Asian Americans* (Dubuque, Iowa: Kendall/Hunt Publishing Co., 1983).
2. Margie Kitano, "Early Education for Asian-American Children," in *Understanding the Multicultural Experience in Early Childhood Education*, eds. Olivia Saracho and Bernard Spodek (Washington, D.C.: National Association for the Education of Young Children, 1983), pp. 45–66.
3. Robin W. Gardner, Bryant Robey, and Peter C. Smith, *Asian Americans: Growth, Change, and Diversity* (Washington, D.C.: Population Reference Bureau, 1985).
4. Bob Suzuki, "Asian Americans in Higher Education: Impact of Changing Demographics and Other Social Forces." (Paper presented at the National Symposium on the Changing Demographics of Higher Education, the Ford Foundation, New York, April 1988).
5. Jayjia Hsai, *Asian Americans in Higher Education and at Work,* (Hillsdale, N.J.: Lawrence Erlbaum Associates, 1988).
6. DBS Corporation, *Elementary and Secondary Civil Rights Survey 1984* (Washington, D.C.: Office for Civil Rights, U.S. Office of Education, June 1986; ERIC Document Reproduction Service No. ED 271 545).
7. Cordova, *Filipinos.*
8. Jean Carlin and Burton Sokoloff, "Mental Health Treatment Issues for Southeast Asian Refugee Children," in *Southeast Asian Mental Health: Treatment, Prevention, Services, Training and Research,* ed. Tom Owan (Washington, D.C.: U.S. Department of Health and Human Services, 1985; DSHS Publication No. ADM 85–1399), pp. 91–112.
9. Cordova, *Filipinos.*
10. Amado Cabezas, *Early Childhood Development in Asian and Pacific American Families: Families in Transition* (San Francisco: Asian Inc., 1981).
11. David Sue, Derald Sue, and Diane Sue, "Psychological Development of Chinese-American Children," in *The Psychological Development of Minority Group Children,* ed. Gloria Powell (New York: Brunner/Mazel Publishers, 1983), pp. 159–166.
12. Harry Kitano, *Japanese Americans: The Evolution of a Subculture* (New Jersey: Prentice-Hall, 1976).
13. Maria Matute-Bianchi, "Ethnic Identities and Patterns of School Success and Failure among Mexican-Descent and Japanese-American Students in a California High School: An Ethnographic Analysis," *American Journal of Education* 94 (November 1986): 233–255.
14. Cabezas, *Early Childhood Development.*
15. David Sue and Derald Sue, "Chinese American Personality and Mental Health," *Amerasia Journal* 1 (Fall 1971): 95–98.

16. Matute-Bianchi, "Ethnic Identities."

17. Grace Guthrie, *A School Divided* (Hillsdale, N.J.: Lawrence Erlbaum Associates, 1985); Bok-Lim Kim, "The Korean-American Child at School and at Home." (Report of a project funded by the Administration for Children, Youth, and Families, U.S. Department of Health, Education, and Welfare, Washington, D.C., 1980).

18. Guthrie, *A School Divided*.

19. Bok-Lim Kim, *The Asian Americans: Changing Patterns, Changing Needs* (Montclair, N.J.: Association of Korean Christian Scholars in North America, 1978).

20. Shirley Hume, "U.S. Immigration Policy and Asian and Pacific Americans: Aspects and Consequences," in *Civil Rights Issues of Asian and Pacific Americans: Myths and Realities* (Washington, D.C.: U.S. Commission on Civil Rights, May 1979), pp. 283–291.

21. Ruben Rumbaut, "Mental Health and the Refugee Experience: A Comparative Study of Southeast Asian Refugees," in *Southeast Asian Mental Health: Treatment, Prevention, Services, Training and Research*, ed. Tom Owan (Washington, D.C.: U.S. Department of Health and Human Services, 1985; DSHS Publication No. ADM 85–1399), pp. 433–486.

22. Genevieve Lau, "Chinese American Early Childhood Socialization in Communication," Doctoral dissertation, Stanford University, 1988.

23. Sue and Sue, "Chinese American Personality."

24. Milton Gordon, *Assimilation in American Life* (New York: Oxford University Press, 1964).

25. Elliott Mordkowitz and Herbert Ginsburg, "The Academic Socialization of Successful Asian-American College Students." (Paper presented at the Annual Meeting of the American Educational Research Association, San Francisco, April 1986).

26. Romeria Tidwell, "Gifted Students' Self-images as a Function of Identification Process, Race and Sex," *Journal of Pediatric Psychology* 5 (March 1980): 57–69.

27. Nguyen T. Oanh and William B. Michael, "The Predictive Validity of Each of Ten Measures of Self-Concept Relative to Teacher's Ratings of Achievement in Mathematics and Reading of Vietnamese Children and of Those from Five Other Ethnic Groups," *Educational and Psychological Measurement* 37 (Winter 1977): 1005–1016.

28. Theresa Chang, "The Self-Concept of Children in Ethnic Groups: Black American and Korean American," *Elementary School Journal* 76 (October 1975): 52–58; David Fox and Valerie Jordan, "Racial Preference and Identification of American Chinese, Black and White Children," *Genetic Psychology Monographs* 88 (November 1973): 220–286.

29. Valerie Ooka Pang, Donald Mizokawa, James Morishima, and Roger Olstad, "Self Concepts of Japanese-American Children," *Journal of Cross-Cultural Psychology* 16 (March 1985): 99–109.

CHAPTER 14 Language

14.1 JIM CUMMINS

The Two Faces of Language Proficiency

Jim Cummins is a professor in and head of the Modern Language Centre of the Ontario Institute for Studies in Education. His research interests include patterns of language acquisition and academic development among minority students and the effects of teaching practices on the development of language and literacy. Cummins has published a number of articles and books and is considered a leading authority in multicultural education and language development. The following selection is from his book *Empowering Minority Students* (California Association for Bilingual Education, 1989).

After detailing the misconceptions commonly held about bilingual education, Cummins distinguishes between surface, or conversational, skills in the school language (English in the United States) and academic skills in that language. The problem is that if a student speaks English well enough to go about daily life without too many problems, then teachers assume the student can take tests measuring academic performance in English. But, as Cummins points out, conversational skills are quite different than academic skills. Conversational skills are gained in about two years and are gained in context. They can be aided by such cues as body language and gestures. Academic language skills, on the other hand, take at least five years to learn at the level of proficiency on tests. Thus, teachers must take care not to assume academic competence based on perceived conversational competence.

Key Concept: distinguishing between conversational and academic language skills

*T*here are two major misconceptions regarding the nature of language proficiency that have been (and still are) prevalent among educators. These misconceptions have important *practical* implications for the way educators interact with language minority students. Both involve a confusion between the surface or conversational aspects of children's language and deeper aspects of proficiency that are more closely related to children's conceptual and academic development. The first misconception entails identifying children's control over the surface structures of standard English with their ability to think logically. Children who speak a non-standard variety of English (or their L1) are frequently thought to be handicapped educationally and less capable of logical thinking. This assumption derives from the fact that children's language is viewed as inherently deficient as a tool for expressing logical relations.

The second misconception is in many respects the converse of the first. In this case, children's good control over the surface features of English (i.e. their ability to converse adequately in English) is taken as an indication that all aspects of their "English proficiency" have been mastered to the same extent as native speakers of the language. In other words, conversational skills are interpreted as a valid index of overall proficiency in the language. In the case of both of these misconceptions, a close relationship is assumed between the two faces of language proficiency, the conversational and the academic....

HOW LONG DOES IT TAKE MINORITY STUDENTS TO ACQUIRE ENGLISH?

A considerable amount of research from both Europe and North America suggests that minority students frequently develop fluent surface or conversational skills in the school language but their academic skills continue to lag behind grade norms (Cummins, 1984; Skutnabb-Kangas and Toukomaa, 1976). It is important for educators to be aware of this research since failure to take account of the distinction between conversational and academic language skills can result in discriminatory testing of minority students and premature exit from bilingual programs into all-English programs. Specifically, the presence of adequate surface structure leads teachers and psychologists to eliminate "limited English proficiency" as an explanation for children's academic difficulty. The result is that minority children's low academic performance is attributed to deficient cognitive abilities (e.g. "learning disabilities," educable mental retardation) or to lack of motivation to succeed academically.

Some concrete examples will help illustrate how this process operates. These examples are taken from a Canadian study in which the teacher referral forms and psychological assessments of more than 400 language minority students were analyzed (Cummins, 1984). Throughout the teacher's referral forms and psychologists' assessment reports there are references to the fact that children's English communicative skills are considerably better developed than their academic language skills (e.g. reading achievement). For example:

PS (094): referred for reading and arithmetic difficulties in grade 2; teacher commented that "since PS attended grade 1 in Italy, I think his main problem is language, although he understands and speaks English quite well."

DM (105): Arrived from Portugal at age 10 and was placed in a grade 2 class; three years later, in grade 5, her teacher commented that "her oral answering and comprehension is so much better than her written work that we feel a severe learning problem is involved, not just her non-English background."

GG (184): Although he had been in Canada for less than a year, in November of the grade 1 year the teacher commented that "he speaks Italian fluently and English as well." However, she also referred him for psychological assessment "because he is having a great deal of difficulty with the grade 1 program" and she wondered if he had "specific learning disabilities or if he is just a very long way behind children in his age group."

These examples illustrate the influence of the environment in developing English conversational skills. In many instances in this study language minority students were considered to have sufficient English proficiency to take a verbal IQ test within about a year of arrival in Canada. Similarly, in the United States, language minority students are often considered to have developed sufficient English proficiency to cope with the demands of an all-English classroom after a relatively short amount of time in a bilingual program (in some cases as little as six months).

Recent research suggests that very different time periods are required for minority students to achieve peer-appropriate levels in conversational skills in the second language as compared to academic skills. Specifically, conversational skills often approach native-like levels within about two years of exposure to English whereas a period of five years or more may be required for minority students to achieve as well as native speakers in academic aspects of language proficiency (Collier, 1987; Collier & Thomas, 1988; Cummins, 1981c, 1984; Wong Fillmore, 1983). Academic language proficiency refers to both reading and writing abilities and to content areas where students are required to use their language abilities for learning (e.g. science, social studies, etc).

The pattern is well-illustrated in Collier's studies. These involved more than 2,000 limited-English-proficient students and were carried out in an affluent suburban school district where all instruction was through English. She reported that it took a minimum of 4 to 9 years for these students to attain grade norms in different aspects of English academic skills. It is noteworthy that these figures represent the time period required for the *most advantaged* limited-English-proficient students to perform as well as their native English-speaking peers and a longer time period can be expected for less advantaged students.

The relatively long period of time required for language minority students to attain grade norms in academic aspects of English can be attributed to the fact that native English speakers continue to make significant progress in English academic skills (e.g. vocabulary knowledge, reading and writing skills, etc) year after year. They do not stand still waiting for the minority student to catch up. In conversational skills, on the other hand, after the first six years of life, changes tend to be more subtle.

In addition, in face-to-face conversation the meaning is supported by a range of contextual cues (e.g. the concrete situation, gestures, intonation, facial expression, etc) whereas this is seldom the case for academic uses of language (e.g. reading a text). Typical everyday conversational interactions can be characterized as context-embedded and cognitively-undemanding while academic tasks tend to become increasingly context-reduced and cognitively-demanding as students advance through the grades. The approximate time periods involved in developing peer-appropriate conversational and academic communicative proficiency are outlined in Figure 1.

FIGURE 1

Length of Time Required to Achieve Age-Appropriate Levels of Conversational and Academic Language Proficiency

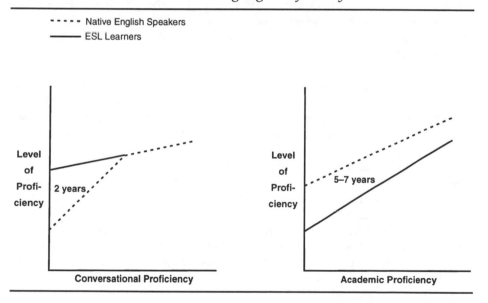

The practical implications of this distinction can be seen in the fact that educators often fail to take account of the difference between these two aspects of proficiency when they teach and assess minority students. For example, in the Cummins (1984) study, it was found that because students often appeared to be fluent in English, psychologists tended to assume that they had overcome all problems in learning English and consequently IQ tests administered in English were valid. The data clearly showed that this assumption was unfounded. Students were frequently labelled as "learning disabled" or "retarded" on the basis of tests administered within one or two years of the students' exposure to

English in school. In fact, the research data show that even students who had been instructed through English for three years in school were performing at the equivalent of 15 IQ points below grade norms as a direct result of insufficient time to catch up with their native English-speaking peers (Cummins, 1981, 1984).

The same logic applies to the exiting of minority students prematurely to all-English programs. Educators frequently assume that students are ready to survive without support in an all-English classroom on the basis of the fact that they appear to be fluent in English. This surface fluency may mask significant gaps in the development of academic aspects of English. The result is that after premature exit from the bilingual program, the student performs considerably below grade level in the regular classroom.

The fact that minority students may require upwards of five years to catch up to native-English-speaking students in English academic skills does not, in itself, necessarily imply that these students should be in withdrawal ESL [English as a second language] or bilingual classes for this period. It does imply, however, that instruction in mainstream classes after students have been exited from ESL or bilingual programs must be tuned to students' level of English in order to provide them with the comprehensible input necessary to sustain academic growth (Krashen, 1981; Wong Fillmore, 1983). In addition, academic growth will be fostered by context-embedded instruction that validates students' background experiences by encouraging them to express, share, and amplify these experiences....

In short, the research evidence suggests that although there are large individual differences between children in the rapidity with which they acquire different aspects of English proficiency (Wong Fillmore, 1983), verbal tests of psychological functioning or achievement tend to underestimate minority students' academic potential until they have been learning the school language for *at least* 4–5 years.

Another implication of these findings is that for students who have been learning the school language for less than this period, it becomes extremely problematic to attempt any diagnosis of categories such as "learning disability" since any genuine learning problems are likely to be masked by as yet inadequately developed proficiency in the school language. The unresolved problems inherent in disentangling the assessment of language and academic skills among minority students can be seen in the fact that, in Texas, Hispanic students are still over-represented by a factor of 300% in the "learning disabilities" category (Ortiz and Yates, 1983).

THE CONVERSATIONAL/ACADEMIC LANGUAGE PROFICIENCY PRINCIPLE

The evidence presented above suggests the importance of distinguishing children's ability to function conversationally in English from their ability to function academically in English. Academic uses of language often require the ability to manipulate language without the support provided in an in-terpersonal communicative context (e.g. negotiation of meaning, immediate feedback, etc).

This distinction is a convenient and, I believe, important one. However, any dichotomy inevitably oversimplifies the reality. Thus, it is appropriate to clarify certain aspects of the distinction. First, it refers not to two totally sep-arate aspects of language functioning but to a continuum of uses of language that children gradually acquire as they develop during the preschool and school years. The conversational/academic continuum is not identical to the distinc-tion between oral and written uses of language. Written uses do tend to require explicit and decontextualized use of language, since the communicative partner is not present and a shared context often cannot be assumed, but many oral lan-guage interactions, both in school and outside school, are also decontextualized to a greater or lesser extent and thus would be characterized as "academic" (see Biber, 1986, for an intriguing investigation of these issues). A central as-pect of what I have termed "academic" language proficiency is the ability to make complex meanings explicit in either oral or written modalities by means of *language itself* rather than by means of paralinguistic cues (e.g. gestures, in-tonation etc). Experience of these uses of language in oral interactions prior to school clearly helps to prepare children to use and understand the increasingly decontextualized language demands of school.

Similar distinctions have been made by a number of other investigators (see Cummins, 1984 for a review). Snow (1983), for example, distinguishes be-tween contextualized and decontextualized language and argues that exposure to decontextualized language use at home is an important predictor of academic success at school. In a study of approximately 150 English-French bilingual children in grades 2–5, Snow, Cancino, Gonzalez and Shriberg (1987) reported a strong relationship between children's ability to give formal definitions of words and their performance on a standardized reading test. Foley (1987) has reported similar results in a case study of successful and unsuccessful Spanish-English bilingual readers.

On the basis of her extensive ethnographic study among middle-class and lower-class families, Heath (1983) argues that the differences between social classes in learning to read derives from more than just differential access to literacy materials at home. What is more significant is the extent to which lit-eracy activities are integrated with children's daily lives. The black and white *Maintown* (middle-class) children in her study experienced activities such as in-venting narratives related to the stories that were read to them and comparing book characters with real people they knew. They learned to view language as an artifact separate from its use in face-to-face communicative contexts.

Heath (1986) enumerates some of the ways in which schools expect chil-dren to be able to use language before they begin formal schooling:

1. Use language to label and describe the objects, events and information that non-intimates present to them;
2. Use language to recount in a predictable order and format past events or information given to them by non-intimates;

3. Follow directions from oral and written sources without needing sustained personal reinforcement from adults or peers;
4. Use language to sustain and maintain the social interactions of the group;
5. Use language to obtain and clarify information from non-intimates;
6. Use language on appropriate occasions to account for one's unique experiences, to link these to generally known ideas or events, and to create new information or to integrate ideas in innovative ways.

Heath points out that those students who achieve academic success either bring to school all of these language uses, and the cultural norms that lie behind them, or they learn quickly to intuit the rules of these language uses for both speaking and writing. Minority children who have these functions of language available in their L1 can transfer them easily to English, given appropriate opportunities in English.... Thus, both in-school and out-of-school occasions (in both L1 and L2) that require explanation of facts and assumptions not shared by others provide practice in the kind of decontextualized and impersonal language that is important for academic success. Heath suggests, for example, that a child who listens to a bank teller explain to her mother the rules for opening a savings account learns something about how to present information to someone who does not already share it, a use of language that will be invoked in much of the child's writing in school.

The relevance for academic success of these competencies in varied uses of language can be seen from the fact that as students progress through the grades, they are increasingly required to manipulate language in cognitively-demanding and decontextualized situations that differ significantly from everyday conversational interactions. In writing, for example, they must learn to continue to produce language without the prompting that comes from a conversational partner and they must plan large units of discourse, and organize them coherently, rather than planning only what will be said next.

It is important for educators to realize that children come to school with different degrees of exposure to decontextualized language. When students have had little exposure to such uses of language prior to school and instruction in school assumes that these uses have been developed already, the resulting "mismatch" can cause considerable initial confusion for children. This mismatch in the pragmatic or functional aspects of language is very different from the "linguistic mismatch."... The latter mismatch entails a switch between the language of the home (e.g. Spanish) and the language of the school (English) and is not *in itself* a major cause of academic problems for minority students. However, "pragmatic mismatches" in the ways of using language (as discussed by Heath [1983] and Snow [1983]) are potentially more serious causes of difficulty for minority students. The potential for such mismatches is minimized when initial instruction in school is highly context-embedded or "interactive/experiential."...[1]

In short, the notion of "academic" aspects of language proficiency involves a complex array of linguistic competencies that are discussed in more detail elsewhere (e.g. Cummins and Swain, 1986; Heath, 1983; Lindfors, 1980; Snow, 1983). For purposes of this monograph, it is sufficient to emphasize that the general distinction between conversational and academic aspects of language proficiency (or contextualized and decontextualized uses of language) carries important implications for the education of language minority students.

251

Jim Cummins

CONCLUSION

... [M]inority students' educational failure cannot be attributed solely to linguistic factors. However, misconceptions about language on the part of educators have clearly contributed to students' difficulties; in fact, it is argued ... that the persistence of these misconceptions about language is a *symptom* of the underlying educational structure that disables minority students. For educators, a first step in becoming conscious of the ways in which this underlying structure operates to promote discriminatory assessment, placement and instruction of minority students is to critically examine the notion of "language proficiency" and how it affects performance on psychometric tests. Specifically, it is necessary to acknowledge that students' surface fluency in English cannot be taken as indicative of their overall proficiency in English. Similarly, ESL teachers and bilingual educators should realize that their task is to develop *academic* skills in English, not just conversational skills. Academic skills in English usually require most of the elementary school years to develop to grade norms, and, as discussed in the following chapter, are more dependent on children's conceptual foundation in L1 than on their English conversational fluency.[2]

It is also crucial for educators and policy-makers to face up to the implications for intervention of the fact that children are not failing in school because of lack of English fluency. Lack of English fluency may be a secondary contributor to children's academic difficulty but the fundamental causal factors of both success and failure lie in what is communicated to children in their interactions with educators. This is clearly expressed by Isidro Lucas (1981) in describing a research study he carried out in the early 1970's with Puerto Rican students in Chicago designed to explore the reasons for student dropout. Although he prepared questionnaires in both Spanish and English, he never had to use the Spanish version. The reason was that

> "All my dropout respondents spoke good understandable English. They hadn't learned math, or social sciences, or natural sciences, unfortunately. But they had learned English.... No dropout mentioned lack of English as the reason for quitting. As it evolved through questionnaires and interviews, theirs was a more subtle story—of alienation, of not belonging, of being 'push-outs'.... To my surprise, dropouts expressed more confidence in their ability to speak English than did the stay-ins (seniors in high school). For their part, stay-ins showed more confidence in their Spanish than did dropouts.... I had to conclude that identity, expressed in one's confidence and acceptance of the native culture, was more a determinant of school stay-in power than the mere acquisition of the coding-decoding skills involved in a different language, English" (p. 19).

In short, understanding why and how minority students are failing academically requires that educators dig a little deeper than superficial linguistic mismatches between home and school or insufficient exposure to English. Underachievement is not caused by lack of fluency in English. Underachievement is the result of particular kinds of interactions in school that lead minority students to mentally withdraw from academic effort.

NOTES

1. Among the communication activities in school that provide students with opportunities to develop decontextualized uses of language in meaningful contexts are many kinds of cooperative learning activities (see Kagan, 1986). The same goal is also achieved by *barrier games*. In this type of activity children work in pairs and each member of a pair is given a picture or object that the other child cannot see because of a barrier (e.g. a low cardboard screen) put up between the two children. The partners then talk to each other to determine differences and similarities between the two pictures. A variation is to have one child draw a picture related to a particular topic and then describe the picture to her partner who attempts to draw the picture as it is described (see New Zealand Department of Education, 1988, for further excellent examples that can be used to promote communication skills among both minority and non-minority students).

2. It is emphasized in subsequent chapters that the distinction between conversational and academic aspects of language proficiency does *not* imply that academic skills should be developed through decontextualized instruction. On the contrary, high levels of literacy and critical thinking can be promoted effectively only by interactive/experiential instruction that encourages students' oral and written expression.

14.2 LILY WONG FILLMORE AND
CONCEPCIÓN VALADEZ
Teaching Bilingual Learners

The following selection is from "Teaching Bilingual Learners," in Merlin C. Wittrock, ed., *Handbook of Research on Teaching,* 3rd ed. (Macmillan, 1986). In it Lily Wong Fillmore and Concepción Valadez give the definition of bilingual education that is still commonly used today, the one that was established with the 1974 Bilingual Act. Briefly, under this definition instruction is given in both English and the student's native language so that the student can learn effectively. *Maintenance* bilingual education programs allow students to continue receiving instruction in both languages even after English is learned. *Transitional* programs try to move students into English-only instruction. In determining effective teaching strategies, it appears that immersion is best, but there are many variables that affect its success. One effective strategy seems to be to put limited English proficiency (LEP) students in regular English-speaking classrooms but to group them with other LEP students for some activities.

Fillmore is a professor of language, literacy, and culture in education. Her background and Ph.D. is in linguistics. Her interest in second language learning and the education of language-minority students was fueled by early volunteer experiences teaching children of migrant farmworkers in California's agricultural areas, where she learned that efforts needed to be undertaken to help teach children English as a second language. Fillmore is project director and principal investigator for The Family, Community and the University Partnership, which prepares professionals to work with American Indian communities. She also serves as adviser to several language-related organizations, including the University of California's Linguistic Minority Research Institute. In 1993 she was chosen Honoree of the Year by the National Association of Bilingual Educators.

Valadez is an associate professor at the University of California, Los Angeles, in the area of urban schooling: curriculum, teaching, leadership and policy studies. She has published articles and books on language education, and her interests are language education, bilingualism, literacy, and testing of linguistic minorities.

Key Concept: strategies for bilingual education

Bilingual education rests on the following assumptions:

1. Students who are less than fully proficient in the school language will have difficulty deriving academic benefit from their educational experience, since the inability to understand the language in which instruction is given precludes comprehension of the content of that instruction.

2. It takes LEP [limited English proficiency] students time to acquire the level of proficiency in English that is needed to participate effectively in all-English classes. During the time it takes to learn English, they will get little out of their school experience if they are instructed exclusively in that language.

3. Instruction in the native language of LEP students allows them to participate in school and to acquire the skills and knowledge covered in the curriculum while they are learning English. It also allows them to make use of skills, knowledge, and experiences they already have, and to build on those prior assets in school.

4. Knowledge and skills are more easily acquired by LEP students in their native language; but computational skills and many literacy skills acquired in the native language can be transferred to the new language once it is mastered. Hence time spent in learning materials in the native language is not time that is lost with respect to the coverage of subject matter in school.

5. Students need adequate exposure to the language of school in order to acquire it as a second language; this exposure to English is best when it takes place in settings in which the learners' special linguistic needs help to shape the way the language gets used. Subject matter instruction given in English can provide the exposure that LEP students need, as long as it is appropriately tailored for them. Subject matter instruction in the school language is an essential component of bilingual education.

6. Formal instruction in English as a second language (ESL) can help students get started learning the language. ESL, whether it is formal or informal, is an integral part of American bilingual education programs.

7. The academic potential of all children, including those served by bilingual programs, has the best chance of being realized when their language skills, their social and cultural experiences, and their knowledge of the world are affirmed in school; these are the foundations of academic development.

The term "bilingual education" is used in reference to a variety of instructional programs, some of which are bilingual, others of which are not. The definition of bilingual education most commonly assumed in the U.S. is the one given in the 1974 version of the Bilingual Education Act [Title VII, Elementary and Secondary Education Act]:

> The term "program of bilingual education" means a program of instruction, designed for children of limited English-speaking ability in elementary or secondary schools, in which, with respect to the years of study to which such program is applicable—"(i) there is instruction given in, and study of, English and, to the extent necessary to allow a child to progress effectively through the educational system, the native language of the children of limited English-speaking ability, and such instruction is given with appreciation of the cultural heritage of such children, and with respect to elementary school instruction, such instruction shall, to the extent necessary, be in all courses or subjects of study which will allow a child to progress effectively through the educational system." (Sec. 703, (a)(4)(A))

Bilingual programs come in many forms, but their defining characteristics are these:

- Instruction is given in two languages: in the U.S., English is one, and the home language of the LEP students served by the program the other;
- Instruction in the language of the school is given in a way that permits students to learn it as a second language.

Programs vary considerably in the extent to which each of the two components is emphasized in their objectives, and in how they are realized. Some of this variation stems from a general confusion over the roles and functions played by language in these two aspects of bilingual programs. In particular, the distinction between *language of instruction*, that is, language used as the vehicle by which instruction and information are communicated to students in textbooks and in classrooms, and *language instruction*, that is, instruction in which language itself is the object being taught, is one that is often confused in discussions pertaining to these components.

A typology of bilingual education based in part on differing degrees of emphasis on objectives was proposed by Fishman and Lovas (1970). A similar but more complex typology was advanced by Mackey (1970), whose typology is based on the distribution of the languages with respect to the entire learning environment including home, school, area, and national goals and patterns of usage. In some cases, the primary objectives of the program are the development of English language skills, and enabling LEP students served by the program to make a shift as expeditiously as possible to an all-English program of studies. Fishman and Lovas characterize such programs as "transitional" in orientation. Transitional bilingual programs offer LEP students dual-language instruction but only until they have acquired enough English to deal with instruction given exclusively in that language. The rationale for using the students' native language in school is that it permits them to deal with school while they are learning English; the goal is reached when they can be placed in all-English classes at their appropriate grade level. Transitional programs differ from English as a second language programs in that the LEP students' native or first language (L1) is used as a language of instruction along with English, the language the students are learning as their second language (L2), whereas in ESL programs, LEP students are taught English through the exclusive use of English. The major aim of both is to help LEP students deal successfully with instruction given in English. However, transitional programs match the defining characteristics of bilingual education programs, while ESL programs do not, despite the similarity in aim. The likely outcome of transitional bilingual education is a limited bilingualism; many students shift away from the use of their L1 altogether when its use is no longer supported outside of the home.

A second major category of bilingual programs according to the Fishman and Lovas typology can be described as "maintenance" in orientation. Under the Fishman and Lovas framework, two other categories of programs can be distinguished: there are, in addition to maintenance programs, those whose aim is "monoliterate bilingualism" and those whose aim is "partial bilingualism," the differences among them having to do with the extent to which they promote literacy in the two languages of instruction. In maintenance programs, the objective is to develop full literacy skills in both languages. In monoliterate programs, the goal is to develop oral language skills in the home language, but not literacy skills, which are developed only in the societal language. In partial bilingualism programs, literacy in the home language is promoted, but not in all subject areas. In this discussion, all three are subsumed under the broadly drawn category of maintenance programs since they are not so different in their basic orientation, and the concern here is in the primary objectives and rationales that determine the nature of any given program.

Maintenance programs differ from transitional ones in that LEP students can remain in them even after they have become fully proficient in English. The students' L1 is seen as more than a temporary medium of instruction, a stopgap measure that allows them to get some benefit from school while they are learning English; it is seen as an alternative medium of instruction which serves as a legitimate means by which these students can continue to gain access to the curriculum even after they have learned English. The rationale for maintenance programs is that the continued use of both languages in school will enable the students served by these programs to develop mature skills in both languages and to achieve full bilingualism eventually. In this type of program, the emphasis is not only on the development of English language proficiency, but on maintaining and developing L1 proficiency as well. In contrast to transitional programs where bilingualism is viewed as a means by which English proficiency can be achieved, in these programs, it is seen as a worthwhile end in itself.

The differences between these two categories of programs add up to a major contrast in orientation: transitional programs are fundamentally compensatory in their orientation, while maintenance programs are augmentary in theirs. The differences between transitional and maintenance programs that have been identified here are reflected in the instructional issues that arise in each. In transitional programs, for example, questions related to establishing the levels of L2 proficiency needed to handle the exclusive use of that language in instructional materials and activities are crucial since they determine eligibility for such programs. Such questions are not as important in maintenance programs since students can remain in them even after they are proficient enough in English to handle all-English instruction. In this review, issues related to both types of programs are discussed, but the reader will find a greater emphasis on issues related to transitional programs than on those associated with maintenance programs. The reason for that is simple: Most bilingual programs are of the first type; the second is an ideal that is seldom realized....

...Let us now consider what have been found to be relatively effective ways of organizing instructional programs and of using language in teaching from the standpoint of enabling LEP students to develop the language skills they need for school. The research that has focused on this issue is not extensive, but it is consistent in showing that methods involving the teaching of subject matter directly in the target language such as that used in the Canadian immersion bilingual education programs produce the best results. While the second-language skills acquired by students have been found to be less than perfect even in the most successful of these programs (cf. Selinker, Swain, & Dumas, 1975; Swain, 1983), the methods followed in these programs have nonetheless worked exceedingly well. The immersion students have acquired L2 skills that enable them to perform as well in school as comparable students who have been taught exclusively in the L1. Studies comparing different methods of language use in bilingual instruction have found the direct method to be more effective for L2 learning than the concurrent method (Wong Fillmore, 1982; Legarreta, 1979) despite the fact that students may hear more English used in classes following the concurrent method (Legarreta, 1977). The critical factor in the relatively successful programs has been that the two languages of instruction have been kept completely separate either by time or by subject matter. When the L2 is used, it is the only language used, and teachers do what they can to convey the information they are trying to impart during the lesson in whatever way they can short of resorting to the students' L1. In fact, in many ways successful bilingual classes are organized in ways that allow them to emulate immersion classes for at least a part of the day. The key characteristics of the immersion technique... are these: (a) The classes are linguistically homogeneous (that is, all of the students are more or less at the same L2 proficiency level); (b) although teachers are bilingual and can understand the students when they use the L1, they themselves use the L2 only when interacting with them; (c) teachers teach subject matter exclusively in the L2, making sure that students understand what is being taught by whatever means they have available to them, through games, songs, and activities that involve the student in understanding and learning by doing rather than just by listening; and (d) the new language serves a real communicative function from the very beginning, and is to be learned in the context of use. The linguistic homogeneity of these classes is critical to the success of the method. Teachers find it easiest and most natural to make the linguistic adjustments needed by learners when it is clear that everyone needs them. As we have tried to show, speech (including that used by teachers in lessons) works as input for language learning only when it has been custom-tailored to fit the linguistic needs of the learners in question. It is far more difficult to deal with the needs of heterogeneous groups because what is fitting for some students is not for others. This difficulty, it appears, accounts for why teachers sometimes resort to using translations in linguistically heterogeneous classes, as noted earlier.

The problem for bilingual teachers is that most classes are heterogeneous in L2 proficiency, even when the students are all from the same L1 background. How can instruction be organized so that language can use used in ways that promote L2 development? The solution that has been adopted in many programs has been to group the students by L2 proficiency for instruction given in that language. This allows teachers to attend to the special needs of each group of students separately, and for everyone to be on an equal linguistic footing during group instruction. In this way, teachers create periods in which immersion teaching techniques can be used effectively. This being the case, would LEP students be better served in segregated classes? We believe not. The research evidence suggests that students need the immersion type of activity that can be provided most easily in segregated groups, but they also need to have contact with classmates who are fluent speakers of the L2 in order to develop a native-like control of that language. They would profit from being in integrated classes for some part of each day. The ideal situation for language learning, according to educators who specialize in the development of language skills during the elementary school years (cf. Lindfors, 1983 and Urzua, 1981) consists of instructional activities that allow children to interact freely in the course of working on mutually involving tasks that invite discussion, questioning, responding, and so forth. A certain amount of social engineering and structuring is needed to make such activities really work for language learning, however. Left on their own, students may not be inclined to interact in ways that are helpful from the standpoint of language learning. Children may find it just as hard as teachers do to consider the linguistic needs of learners in linguistically mixed groups, or they may engage in the use of "foreigner talk," which gives the learners an erroneous idea of what the L2 is really like. It takes planning to create instructional activities that minimize such problems, and constant monitoring to make sure that such activities work as they should. Among the most promising efforts in this regard have been programs that make use of peer tutoring as a method of getting English-speaking students to interact with LEP students in bilingual programs in ways that enhance language learning (cf. Johnson and August, 1981)....

CONCLUSION

In view of the controversy surrounding bilingual education, it is easy to see how its true objectives and potential benefits have become secondary to all else. It offers children a chance to survive in school without giving up their cultural identities. It allows them to become bilingual and to enjoy the social and cognitive benefits that bilingualism offers individuals. All of them will learn English eventually. However, it takes more than learning a second language to be bilingual and to get the full benefits of bilingualism. Social factors can exert a considerable influence on the outcome of the second-language learning process. In order to become true bilinguals these children must hang onto and develop their knowledge of the native language as they acquire English. In this society, however, the learning of English all too often means the loss of the L1. Countless groups have lost their languages in the process of learning English, despite their best efforts to preserve them (Fishman, 1980a, 1980b). In the research that has been discussed in this [selection], we have seen that much of the emphasis in bilingual education has been to help students learn English. However, it can be argued that with or without such help, there is little danger that LEP students who have gone through the American school system can avoid learning English. The social forces that impel them to learn English are sufficiently great that they will learn it sooner or later. English is the predominant language of the society they live in, and these students know they have to learn it. They are surrounded by it wherever they go, including the bilingual classroom, as we have seen. Any English instruction they are given there facilitates the process, but it is not, in most cases, a necessity. The real problem for these students is that they are likely to acquire English but end up nevertheless without the resources that allow them to take part in the society they are growing up in. For many of them, the price paid for learning English is the mother tongue and their cultural identity. All too often, this leads to the loss of many of the cultural resources to which that language gives them access. What is lost in surrendering the native language may be the connectedness with primary group and community that gives an individual the personal stability needed for coping with adult responsibilities and opportunities. In the long run, however, the greatest loss may be to the society. The immigrant groups whose children are the LEP students in our schools today have enormous cultural resources and talent to contribute to their adopted society. These contributions can help to invigorate and enrich the society as they have in the past. The learning of English will give LEP students access to the opportunities offered by the society, but if the unique resources that their cultures have given them are lost in the process they will have less to give back to the society as adults.

REFERENCES

Bilingual Education Act (Title VII, ESEA), Public Law 93–380, 20 U.S.C., 800b, (1974, August 21).

Fishman, J. A. (1980a). Bilingualism and biculturalism as individual and as societal phenomena. *Journal of Multilingual and Multicultural Development, 1,* 3–16.

Fishman, J. A. (1980b). Bilingual education in the United States under ethnic community auspices. In J. E. Alatis (Ed.), *Georgetown University Roundtable on Languages and Linguistics 1980.* Washington, DC: Georgetown University Press.

Fishman, J. A., & Lovas, J. (1970). Bilingual education in a sociolinguistic perspective. *TESOL Quarterly, 4*(3), 215–222.

Johnson, D. M., & August, D. (1981). Social factors in second language acquisition: Peer tutoring intervention. In P. Gonzales (Ed.). *Proceedings of the Eighth Annual International Bilingual Bicultural Education Conference.* Rosslyn, VA: National Clearinghouse for Bilingual Education.

Legarreta, D. (1977). Language choice in bilingual classrooms. *TESOL Quarterly, 11*(1), 9–16.

Lindfors, J. (1983). Exploring in and through language. In M. A. Clarke and J. Handscombe (Eds.), *On Tesol '82: Pacific perspectives on language learning and teaching.* Washington, DC: Teachers of English to Speakers of Other Languages.

Mackey, W. F. (1970). A typology of bilingual education. *Foreign Language Annals, 3,* 596–608.

Selinker, L., Swain, M., & Dumas, G. (1975). The interlanguage hypotheses extended to children. *Language Learning, 25*(1), 139–152.

Swain, M. (1983, October). *Communicative competence: Some roles of comprehensible input and comprehensible output in its development.* Paper presented at the 10th University of Michigan Conference on Applied Linguistics, Ann Arbor, MI. [To appear in S. Gass and C. Madden (Eds.), *Input in Second Language Acquisition.* Rowley, MA: Newbury House].

Urzua, C. (1981). *Talking purposefully.* Silver Springs, MD: Institute of Modern Language.

Wong Fillmore, L. (1982). Instructional language as linguistic input: Second language learning in classrooms. In L. C. Wilkinson (Ed.) *Communicating in the classroom.* New York: Academic Press.

CHAPTER 15 Social Class

15.1 JEAN ANYON

Social Class and School Knowledge

Jean Anyon is a professor at Rutgers University in Newark, New Jersey. She has published extensively on how social class affects schooling, especially in inner-city settings. Her recent book *Ghetto Schooling: A Political Economy of Urban Educational Reform* (Teachers College Press, 1997) is a study of reform efforts in an inner-city school, placed within the sociohistorical context of a lower-income community.

Anyon presents a study of four types of schools in the following selection from "Social Class and School Knowledge," *Curriculum Inquiry* (vol. 11, no. 1, 1981). She found that social stratification of knowledge is clear, with sharp differences between the different schools. As Anyon defines the four types of schools studied, she explains that the differences lie not only along economic levels but also along the types of work the parents do. The types of schools were "working-class," "middle-class," "affluent professional," and "executive elite" schools. Anyon was especially interested in the reproductive aspects of knowledge, or those that contribute directly to the legitimation and perpetuation of existing ideologies and practices, and the nonreproductive aspects, or those that facilitate transformation of ideologies and practices. Her findings show that the schools differ with regard to whose history is taught, what the main goal of life is taught to be, the acceptability of the expression of creative ideas, and access to how to control ideas that dominate society. Anyon also found that within all schools there are possibilities for students to become transformative.

Key Concept: social stratification of knowledge

When Max Weber and Karl Marx suggested that there were identifiable and socially meaningful differences in the educational knowledge made available to literati and peasant, aristocrat and laborer, they were of course discussiing earlier societies. Recent scholarship in political economy and sociology of knowledge has also argued, however, that in advanced industrial societies such as Canada and the U.S., where the class structure is relatively fluid, students of different social class backgrounds are still likely to be exposed to qualitatively different types of educational knowledge. Students from higher social class backgrounds may be exposed to legal, medical, or managerial knowledge, for example, while those of the working classes may be offered a more "practical" curriculum (e.g., clerical knowledge, vocational training) (Rosenbaum 1976; Karabel 1972; Bowles and Gintis 1976). It is said that such social class differences in secondary and postsecondary education are a conserving force in modern societies, an important aspect of the reproduction of unequal class structures (Karabel and Halsey 1977; Apple 1979; Young and Whitty 1977).

The present article examines data on school knowledge collected in a case study of five elementary schools in contrasting social class settings in two school districts in New Jersey. The data suggest, and the article will argue, that while there were similarities in curriculum topics and materials, there were also subtle as well as dramatic differences in the curriculum and the curriculum-in-use among the schools. The study reveals that even in an elementary school context, where there is a fairly "standardized" curriculum, social stratification of knowledge is possible. The differences that were identified among the schools suggest as well that rather than being simply conserving or "reproductive," school knowledge embodies contradictions that have profound implications for social change. The reproductive and nonreproductive possibilities of school knowledge involve theoretical implications of the data and will be delineated after the data have been presented....

The terminology defining social classes and differentiating the schools in this study is to be understood in a technical sense, as reflected in the process by which the sample of schools was selected. Thus, the schools in this study were differentiated not only by income level as an indicator of parent access to capital, but also by the kind of *work* that characterized the majority of parents in each school.

The first three schools were in a medium-size city district in northern New Jersey, and the final two were in a nearby New Jersey suburban district. In each of the three city schools, approximately 85% of the students were white. In the fourth school, 90% were white, and in the last school, all were white.

The first two schools are designated *working-class schools*, because the majority of the students' fathers (and approximately one-third of their mothers) were in unskilled or semiskilled occupations, with somewhat less than one-third of the fathers being skilled workers. Most family money incomes were at or below $12,000 during the period of the study, as were 38.6% of all U.S. families (U.S. Bureau of the Census 1979, p. 2, Table A). The third school is designated the *middle-class school*, although because of residence patterns the parents were a mixture of highly skilled, well-paid blue collar and white collar workers, as well as those with traditional middle-class occupations such as public school teachers, social workers, accountants, and middle-managers. There were also several local doctors and town merchants among the parents. Most family money incomes were between $13,000 and $25,000 during the period of the study, as were 38.9% of all U.S. families (U.S. Bureau of the Census 1979, p. 2, Table A).

The fourth school is designated the *affluent professional school*, because the bulk of the students' fathers were highly-paid doctors such as cardiologists; television or advertising executives; interior designers; or other affluent professionals. While there were a few families less affluent than the majority (e.g., the families of the superintendent of schools and of several professors at nearby universities, as well as several working-class families), there were also a few families who were more affluent. The majority of family money incomes were between $40,000 and $80,000 during the period of the study, as were approximately 7% of all U.S. families.[1]

The final school is called the *executive elite school*. The majority of pupils' fathers in this school were vice presidents or more advanced corporate executives in U.S.-based multinational corporations or financial firms on Wall Street. Most family money incomes were over $100,000 during the period of the study, as were less than 1% of U.S. families (see Smith and Franklin 1974)....

CONCLUSION AND IMPLICATIONS

I would conclude that despite similarities in some curriculum topics and materials, there are profound differences in the curriculum and the curriculum-in-use in the sample of schools in this study. What counts as knowledge in the schools differs along dimensions of structure and content. The differences... will be assessed for social and theoretical implications. The assessment will focus on reproductive and nonreproductive aspects of knowledge in each social-class setting. "Reproductive" will refer to aspects of school knowledge that contribute directly to the legitimation and perpetuation of ideologies, practices, and privileges constitutive of present economic and political structures. "Non-reproductive" knowledge is that which facilitates fundamental transformation of ideologies and practices on the basis of which objects, services, and ideas (and other cultural products) are produced, owned, distributed, and publicly evaluated. The present definition of social change as fundamental transformation transcends the goals of, but does not deny the importance of, humanitarian efforts and practices in institutions such as the school. As we shall see, however, the genesis of truly transformative activity is in the contradictions within and between social settings.

In the working class schools there are two aspects of school knowledge that are reproductive. First, and quite simply, students in these schools were not taught their own history—the history of the American working class and its situation of conflict with powerful business and political groups, e.g., its long history of dissent and struggle for economic dignity. Nor were these students taught to value the interests which they share with others who will be workers. What little social information they were exposed to appears to provide little or no conceptual or critical understanding of the world or their situation in the world. Indeed, not knowing the history of their own group—its dissent and conflict—may produce a social amnesia or "forgetting" (Jacoby, 1975). Such "forgetting" by the working class has quietistic implications in the social arena and potentially reproductive consequences.

A second reproductive aspect of school knowledge in these working-class schools was the emphasis in curriculum and in classrooms on mechanical behaviors, as opposed to sustained conception. This is important to a reproduction of the division of labor at work and in society between those who plan and manage (e.g., technical professionals, executives) and the increasing percentage of the work force whose jobs entail primarily carrying out the policies, plans, and regulations of others. These working-class children were not offered what for them would be *cultural capital*—knowledge and skill at manipulating ideas and symbols in their own interest, e.g., historical knowledge and analysis that legitimates their dissent and furthers their own class in society and in social transformation.

These aspects of school knowledge in the working-class schools contribute to the reproduction of a group in society who may be without marketable knowledge; a reserve group of workers whose very existence, whose availability for hire, for example, when employed workers strike, serves to keep wages down and the work force disciplined. A reserve group is, of course, essential to capitalism because lower wages permit profit accumulation, which is necessary to the viability of firms, banks, state budgets and other bank-financed budgets of, one could argue, the entire system.

On the other hand, however, there is a major contradiction in school knowledge in these working-class schools, and from this may emerge a situation that is potentially socially transformative. Teacher control of students is a high priority in these schools, as in other schools. What the teachers attempted, in these two working-class schools, however, was *physical* control. There was little attempt to win the hearts and minds of these students. Now, our own era in history is one in which social control is achieved primarily through the dominant ideology and the perceived lack of ideological alternatives. But the working-class children in the schools studied here were taught very little of the ideology that is central to stable reproduction of the U.S. system, e.g., traditional bodies of knowledge that include the ideologies of an alleged lack of social alternatives to capitalist organization, patriotism and nationalism, faith in one's own chance of "making it big," and belief that the economy and polity are indeed designed in the interests of the average man and woman. In some cases, children in this study gave evidence that they had already rejected the ideologies of patriotism and of equal chances for themselves.

The absence of traditional bodies of knowledge and ideology may make these children vulnerable to alternative ideas; the children may be more open to ideas that support fundamental social change. Indeed, some of the children were already engaged in struggle against what was to them an exploitative group—the school teachers and administrators. They were struggling against the imposition of a foreign curriculum. They had "seen through" that system. The children's struggle, however, was destructive to themselves. Really *useful* knowledge for these students, e.g., honest "citizenship" education, would authenticate students' own meanings and give them skills to identify and analyze their own social class and to transform a situation that some already perceive is not in their own interest.

A social and theoretical implication of the education of the working-class students in this study, then, is that while a reserve pool of marginally employed workers is perhaps assured by modern schooling, ideological hegemony is not. Ideological hegemony is, rather, extremely tenuous, and the working class may be less ideologically secured than some other social groups. What is important is to make available to working-class students the cultural and ideological tools to begin to transform perspicacity into power.[2]

In the middle-class school, the children I observed were not taught the history of workers or of dissent, nor were they instructed to unify around common interests they will have as wage earners in a system in which many middle-class jobs are becoming increasingly like industrial and clerical jobs—mechanical and rote (for example, computer, technical, and social work; other service jobs; perhaps teaching; nursing and other formerly professional jobs). There were, however, distinguishing characteristics of knowledge in this middle-class school that are important primarily because of the social-class location of the families. For example, the notion of knowledge as originating in external and externally approved sources, as generated and validated by experts, may yield a passive stance before ideas and ideology and before the creation or legitimation of new ideas. This, of course, has implications of intellectual passivity, and ideological quietude. Moreover, school knowledge in the middle-class school was highly commodified. The reification of ideas and knowledge into given facts and "generalizations" that exist separately from one's biography or discovery contributes to the commodification of knowledge. It is true that knowledge in the working-class schools was reified as well. However, in order to be a commodity, a product must have some value in the marketplace and must be perceived as having some value, or no one would "buy" it. That is, it must have an exchange value. Traditional conceptual or academic knowledge in the working-class schools is not perceived by many teachers or students as having exchange value in the marketplace, or workplace, of working-class jobs. Therefore, it does not have commodity status. In the social class position of the present middle-class school, however, the teachers and students perceive the knowledge to have market value: there is a perceived chance that if one can accumulate facts, information and "generalizations," one can exchange them for college entrance or for a white-collar (perhaps even professional) job. But as is true of all commodities, when one exchanges an object, one gives up its use for oneself. Furthermore, a commodity is useful only in an exchangeable, objectified form. Forms in which knowledge is useful for reflection, critical thought, or making sense do not generate as much value in the competition for college entrance and the majority of U.S. jobs.

Commodification of knowledge in the middle-class school is reproductive in part because it helps to legitimate and reproduce the ideology of production for consumption, for example, production of knowledge and other cultural products for the market rather than for personal use or for social transformation. (An actively consuming public is, of course, a material necessity in a capitalist system, and thus legitimation of the ideology of consumption—of production *for* consumption—has direct economic reproductive consequences as well.)

There is a second aspect of knowledge in the middle-class school that is reproductive. This is also a part of the apparent acceptance or belief in the possibility of success for oneself. It is a social fact of major importance that the U.S. middle class is a group whose recent history has shown rapidly decreasing economic stability for individual families. There is, thus, material reason for the reification of knowledge into accumulatable form and for the anxiety which the children manifest concerning tests, college, and jobs. For example, the amount of attention one must pay to "getting ahead" not only leaves little interest or time for critical attention, but it also actively fosters and strengthens belief in the ideologies of upward mobility and success. For example, "If I do not believe that there is a chance for me, and that I can succeed, why should I try so hard? Why go along?" I must *believe* in order to work hard; and to work hard increases the personal (psychological) necessity of my belief. So, the perception of social possibilities for the middle class hinted at in this study and the ideologized and reified school knowledge found in their schooling contribute not only to some of them "getting ahead," but to the production of a class with perhaps the highest degree of mystification and ideological internalization. This, of course, is reproductive.

There is, however, a potentially nonreproductive contradiction to be foreseen regarding school knowledge and the lives of these children. Many of those whose schooling and families have promised them a high reward for working hard and doing well will actually *not* succeed in the job market. This situation, after years of schooling in ideology and promises, may serve to generate cynicism or, more constructively, a critical view of the system. Also, the fact that many of these students will go to college may expose them to alternative ideas. They may be exposed to authors and professors who present alternative views and critical assessments of the social order. From this new knowledge and social perspective, they may, perhaps, be moved to utilize their own curiosity, to begin to use knowledge to question what is. Such questioning is a beginning of any socially transformative activity.

In the affluent professional school there are several aspects of school knowledge that are reproductive. First, the children are taught what is, for most of them, their own history—the history of the wealthy classes. They are taught that the power of their own group is legitimate. They are, as well, taught ways of expressing and using such ideas—that ideology—in their own interests. They are being provided with cultural capital. Indeed, the fact that the knowledge of their own group is socially prestigious knowledge enhances the exchange value of their knowledge as capital. Moreover, because many affluent professional jobs (doctor, lawyer, professor, scientist) still require conception and creativity and independent thought, many of the children in this school will be in the privileged position of having the *use* value of their knowledge (for personal creativity, for example) be at the same time its *exchange* value (for example, they will get paid for doing creative, conceptual work).

A second aspect of school knowledge that is reproductive here is its nascent empiricism (by empiricism I refer to the emphasis in adult science on basing knowledge on experience and on appearances, on observable data this experience produces.) As the basis for knowledge or explanations, empiricism is socially reproductive when it provides a framework for allegedly independent thought. Empiricism uses characteristics of observable data and characteristics of the observed relationships between data for its explanations; empiricism eschews explanations and analyses which are based on transcendent and nonempirical knowledge (see Bernstein 1978). This mode of inquiry thus uses categories and explanations that are confined to what already exists, to what can be observed. This mitigates against challenges to the necessity or naturalness of these categories and of what exists. School science programs and math manipulables make a small contribution, then, to the legitimation of empiricism as a way of seeking and testing knowledge, and to the acceptance of what is, as opposed to what could be. The programs are, in this case, a potential invisible boundary of the social thought of these children.

Accompanying the nascent empiricism in this affluent professional school is the emphasis on individual development as a primary goal of education (as opposed, for example, to the development of the priority of collective goals). A priority on personal expression, personal "meaning making" and the "construction of reality" mitigates against collectivistic values and meanings and solutions; it is thereby reproductive of values important to an individualistic, privately owned, and competitive economy.

Finally, the emphasis in the curriculum and classrooms on active use of concepts and ideas by students, as opposed to a stress on mechanics or rote behaviors, facilitates the perpetuation of an unequal division of labor in U.S. society, where some (these children?) will plan and others (working-class and middle-class children?) will have jobs that entail carrying out the plans.

There are, however, basic contradictions apparent in the school knowledge of these affluent professional children. In these conflicts one can see powerful implications for social transformation. For example, the contradiction between attempting as a student, and making sense as an adult, presumably later in one's professional creative labors, in a society where many things do *not* make sense and are irrational is a conflict which may generate political radicalism. Such a conflict may lead to intellectuals who are highly critical of the system and who attempt to persuade others by disseminating their own views. Or, it may lead to political activism, to overt attempts to take physical action against perceived political and economic irrationalities, as, for example, the students in Students for a Democratic Society (SDS)—a radical, anti-Vietnam War group—a majority of whom were from affluent professional families. Indeed, as Alvin Gouldner points out (1979), almost all leaders of social revolutions in the modern era have come from families of comparatively high standing in their society who were exposed to large amounts of cultural capital (e.g., Marx, Engels, the majority of the early Bolsheviks, Mao Tse-tung, Chou En-Lai, Ho Chi Minh, and Fidel Castro).

It is probably true that the conflict inherent in attempting to make sense in a world that is in many ways irrational is present for all children in all schools and social classes. What makes the conflict a potentially powerful force in the affluent professional school, however, is first the social-class position of these children, their cultural capital, and future access to information, power, and further cultural capital afforded to them by their social position. A second factor important here is the nature of their schooling. These children were told, and encouraged, more than the children in any other school to be creative, to think for themselves, and to make sense. It is indeed because of such encouragement to the young that the increasingly ideological notions of freedom and democracy can be turned back upon the economically and politically powerful and made into truly transformative demands.

Another contradiction to the school knowledge of these children that is nonreproductive is the contradiction between the value placed on creativity and personal decision making, and the systematic, increasingly rationalized nature of school and professional work in U.S. society. This conflict, already apparent in the use of science and reading programs in this school, is a contradiction that suggests possible later conflicts between the use and exchange values of knowledge in adult work, for example, between one's own creativity and the increasing rationalization and control of professional work by technology, bureaucratic trends, and centralization. It also suggests class conflict between affluent professionals, with their own interests and skills and relative power in the bureaucracy on one hand, and the capitalists, who are their "bosses" and who hold the purse strings, on the other. Conflict between the educated classes and the ruling class has long been a source of movement for social transformation. Indeed, as Gouldner (1979) reminds us, it has been this class—the educated, the intellectuals—who have, to date, taken control in periods of revolutionary upheaval, e.g., in the early Soviet Union and China. It is, then, important to provide the children of the affluent professional class with school knowledge that is not just conceptual, analytical, and expressive, but that is also critical and collective. Such knowledge would foster responsiveness not only to the needs of individual "meaning making" and development, but to the development of a wider social collectivity that, not coincidentally, would affirm the needs of the working and middle classes as well.

The executive elite school offers cultural capital to its children, whose families as a class have the major portion of available physical capital in society. These children are taught the history of "ruling" groups, and that rule by the wealthy and aristocratic is rational and natural, going back, for example, to the Ancient Greeks. Such knowledge is, for them, symbolic capital. They are provided with other kinds of symbolic capital as well—practice in manipulating socially prestigious language and concepts in systematic ways. They are told the importance of controlling ideas and given some insight into controlling ideas in their own (Western) culture. The fact that the culture of their social class is the dominant and most prestigious one enhances the exchange value or "worth" of their knowledge in the marketplace.

Some of these children had a fair amount of class consciousness, if this is defined as knowledge of themselves as part of a group in society and in history, and an appreciation of their own group's interests as opposing the interests of other groups in society (e.g., plebs, strikers). While class consciousness among the working classes is likely to be nonreproductive, such a consciousness among the capitalist class is, of course, likely to increase their efforts to win conflicts, to conserve culture, and to maintain their social position, e.g., to prevent what

[English historian Arnold] Toynbee said was the "decay of civilization from within."

School knowledge in the executive elite school was the most "honest" about society, U.S. social problems, and social irrationalities. It was sometimes expressive of liberal concerns, as well. Indeed, it came the closest to being socially critical. The children were given analytical and unsentimental insight into the system. Whereas, for example, middle-class children might see a pluralism of equal or competing ethnic cultures, the children of the executive elite might perceive social class and economic conflict. Thus, these children may be less ideologically mystified than, for example, the middle-class students. The executive elite students—in different and more socially profitable ways than the working-class students—may see more clearly through the rhetoric of nationalism and equal opportunity to the raw facts of class and class conflict.

There is a potential contradiction here in the "clarity" of understanding the system that may, in the particular context of the social-class position of these children, have transformative possibilities. This is the contradiction for them between the use and exchange values in their knowledge: the contradiction between using knowledge for pleasure and enjoying one's class privilege, for example, and the exchange value of knowledge when it must be used to maintain that privilege. Two particular characteristics the empower this contradiction for these children (because the contradiction does appear in weaker forms in other schools) are, first, that extreme pressure is necessary, and excruciating struggle is demanded in a capitalist political democracy to actually maintain one's position of economic power and privilege. To grow up in the modern capitalist class is not only to enjoy travel, luxury, good schools, and financial wealth; it is also to have to maintain power in the face of others competing with you, within an irrational economic system that is increasingly difficult to predict, manage, and control—not only in the U.S. but in a rebellious Third World, as well. To be the "best," one must continually "beat the best." This is severe pressure. Second, to be a powerful capitalist, one must cause suffering and actually exploit others. Indeed, one's wealth and power are possible only because there are others (e.g., a reserve "pool" of workers) who do not have power and resource. These two "facts of life" of "being a capitalist" mean that if one is not ideologically secured, one may reject these demands. In contrapuntal fashion, the pressures, the irrationalities, and the exploitative characteristics of one's role in the system may one day cause the system to be perceived as the enemy—to be destroyed, rather than exploited. One thinks, as examples, of ruling class "children" who have rejected their privileges for radical politics and who have attempted to destroy members of their own class (the Baader-Meinhoff Group in Germany, the Red Brigades in Italy, or, indeed, the Weathermen in the U.S.). While such efforts at social transformation are violent and irrational and are not condoned, they must be acknowledged as nonreproductive in intent.

By situating school knowledge in its particular social location, we can see how it may contribute to contradictory social processes of conservation and transformation. We see the schools reproducing the tensions and conflicts of the larger society. It becomes apparent as well that an examination of only one social site may blur the distinctions and subtleties that a comparative study illuminates. That is, a social phenomenon may differ by social class; and indeed similar (or the same) phenomena may have different meanings in different social contexts.

This study has suggested, as well, that there are class conflicts in educational knowledge and its distribution. We can see class conflict in the struggle to impose the knowledge of powerful groups on the working class and in student resistance to this class-based curriculum. We can see class conflict in the contradictions within and between school knowledge and its economic and personal values, and in attempts to impose liberal public attitudes on children of the rich.

Class conflict in education is thus not dormant, nor a relic of an earlier ear; nor is the outcome yet determined. No class is certain of victory, and ideological hegemony is not secure. Those who would struggle against ideological hegemony must not confuse working-class powerlessness with apathy, middle-class ideology with its inevitability, or ruling-class power and cultural capital with superior strength or intelligence. Just as blacks were not the happy-go-lucky fellows of former stereotypes, so the working class is not dull or acquiescent, and the rich are not complacent or secure. Indeed, perhaps the most important implication of the present study is that for those of us who are working to transform society, there is much to do, at all levels, in education.

NOTES

1. This figure is an estimate. According to the Bureau of the Census, only 2.6% of families in the United States had money incomes of $50,000 or over in 1977 (U.S. Bureau of the Census 1979, Table A p. 2). For figures on income at these higher levels, see Smith and Franklin (1974).

2. It is interesting to note (as information that supports my interpretation of a "perspicacious" working class) that several academic surveys in the 1960s (reported the Vietnam War) and throughout the war, Americans with only a grade-school education were much stronger for withdrawal from the war than Americans with a college education. Zinn argues that "the regular polls, based on samplings, underestimated the opposition to the war among lower-class people" (p. 482). Just as the earliest anti-Vietnam protests came out of the Civil Rights movement as blacks began being drafted, so opposition was stronger earlier in working-class communities as young men from these communities were drafted.

REFERENCES

APPLE, MICHAEL. *Ideology and curriculum*. Boston: Routledge and Kegan Paul, 1979.
BERNSTEIN, RICHARD. *The restructuring of social and political theory*. Philadelphia: University of Pennsylvania Press, 1978.

BOWLES, SAMUEL, and GINTIS, HERBERT. *Schooling in capitalist America: Educational reform and the contradictions of economic life.* New York: Basic Books, 1976.

GOULDNER, ALVIN. *The future of intellectuals and the rise of the new class.* New York: Seabury Press, 1979.

JACOBY, RUSSELL. *Social amnesia.* Boston: Beacon Press. 1975.

KARABEL, JEROME. "Community colleges and social stratification." *Harvard Educational Review* 42, no. 4 (November 1972): 521–562.

___, and HALSEY, A.H. *Power and ideology in education.* New York: Oxford University Press, 1977.

ROSENBAUM, JAMES. *Making inequality: The hidden curriculum of high school tracking.* New York: Wiley, 1976.

SMITH, JAMES, and FRANKLIN, STEPHAN. "The concentration of personal wealth, 1922–1969." *American Economic Review* 64, no. 4 (May 1974): 162–167.

UNITED STATES BUREAU OF THE CENSUS. "Money income in 1977 of families and persons in the United States." In *Current population reports,* Series P–60, no. 118. Washington, D.C.: United States Government Printing Office, 1979.

YOUNG, MICHAEL, and WHITTY, GEOFF. *Society, state and schooling.* Sussex, England: Falmer Press, 1977.

ZINN, HOWARD. A people's history of the United States. New York: Harper and Row, 1980.

The Importance of Class in Multiculturalism

In the following selection, Joe L. Kincheloe and Shirley R. Steinberg argue that class differences are increasing and that any efforts to disregard discussions of class in society are attempts to perpetuate the status quo. They propose what they call "a critical multicultural pedagogy of empowerment for the poor." Such an education would need to include several features. There must be a recognition of class bias within education, with an understanding of the nature and effects of the polarization of wealth. There must be a political vision and an ability to organize the poor into resistance. And there must be the development of the knowledge and skills required to escape poverty.

Kincheloe and Steinberg have written or edited a number of books together. Kincheloe is a professor of cultural studies and pedagogy at Pennsylvania State University in University Park, Pennsylvania, while Steinberg teaches at Adelphi University in New York City. Together, they have edited the books *Thirteen Questions: Reframing Education's Conversation* (Peter Lang, 1992), *Kinderculture: The Corporate Construction of Childhood* (Westview, 1997), and the book from which the following selection is drawn, *Changing Multiculturalism* (Open University Press, 1997). Kincheloe focuses his research on pedagogy, popular culture, and issues of race, class, and gender. Steinberg focuses on the construction of childhood consciousness and the corporate curriculum.

Key Concept: education for empowering the poor

The study of class as an important social force in Western society has never been more important than it is at the end of the twentieth century, with the massive redistribution of wealth from the poor to the wealthy. In 1980, for example, the average corporate chief executive officer (CEO) in the USA earned 38 times the salary of the average factory worker. By 1990 the average CEO earned 72 times as much as a teacher and 93 times as much as a factory worker (Coontz 1992; West 1993; Sleeter and Grant 1994).

THE INTENSIFICATION OF CLASS INEQUALITY

When such unequal realities exist and continue to grow, the importance of the study of class and the need for class analysis in a critical multiculturalism expands. When the specific dynamics of the polarization of wealth in the USA are analysed in further detail, new insights into mobility are uncovered. Americans have always placed great value on hard work. People who work hard should be rewarded for their effort—indeed, Americans believe that the backbone of society rests upon hard work. Most Americans would be surprised to find out, therefore, that the redistribution of wealth of the past fifteen years has been accomplished inversely in relation to hard work. Much of the new wealth created in the 1980s and 1990s did not come from inventing a better mousetrap or long hours of study or working overtime. Most new wealth befell those with enormous assets who were able to reap 'instant wealth' from rapidly fluctuating return rates on their speculative investments. Dividends, tax shelters, interest and capital gains were at the centre of the action—not hard work (Coontz 1992). The connection between class position and one's willingness to work hard may be less direct than many Americans have assumed. The attempt to dismiss class as an American issue must be exposed for what it is—an instrumental fiction designed to facilitate the perpetuation of the status quo by pointing to the poor's laziness and incompetence as the causes of their poverty....

A CRITICAL MULTICULTURAL PEDAGOGY OF EMPOWERMENT FOR THE POOR

... [C]ritical multiculturalists advocate a politically informed, socially contextualized, ethically grounded, power sensitive pedagogy for students from poor backgrounds. Such a cultural and institutional education would possess several features.

(1) The recognition of class bias within education.   Teachers, students, cultural critics and political leaders must understand the subtle and hidden ways in which class bias filters into educational policy, schooling and the cultural curriculum. Schools, media, religious groups and politicians often maintain that Western capitalist societies are lands of wealth and opportunity open to all who are willing to work. Lessons are taught daily that former communist nations in Eastern Europe and Third World societies in Africa, Asia and Latin America are stricken by poverty and its concurrent social problems, but that Western societies are above such pathology. Indeed, countries like the USA, Britain, Canada, Australia and New Zealand constantly use their expertise to repair the problems of other, less developed nations. Implicitly embedded in such a curriculum is the notion that Western societies are at their essence white and middle class nations. They are populated by upwardly mobile white men who are the smartest, most industrious people in the world. Their main concern is to make a prosperous life for themselves and their families—an objective that operates in the best interests of everyone on the planet.

273

In the school curriculum the poor are rarely studied. In elementary and secondary social studies curricula the contributions of workers are erased, as textbooks and curriculum guides depict a world where factory and business owners and politicians do all the work. At an implicit, subtextual level such teaching inscribes irrelevancy on the lives of the working classes. The study of the past is an examination of 'the lives of the rich and famous'. One can almost hear Robin Leach's grating voice uncritically enshrining and ennobling the behaviours of the privileged, especially when they are engaged in morally reprehensible practices such as slavery, conquest of indigenous peoples, political and economic colonization and urbanization. Such activities are often presented unambiguously as heroic acts of 'progress' that brought honour and wealth to the motherland. The brutal, often genocidal, features of these practices are too often ignored. Students and citizens involved in a pedagogy of empowerment gain the ability to expose features of the class-biased curriculum that operate daily in their lives (Swartz 1993; Sleeter and Grant 1994).

(2) The appreciation of the nature and effects of the polarization of wealth. Again, everyone benefits, the poor in particular, from an understanding of the way power works and poverty develops. Such knowledge empowers the poor not only to escape such forces themselves but to initiate public, institutional and private conversations about the relationship between poverty and wealth. Such knowledge empowers the poor to 'call' media commentators and political leaders on the superficial and misleading pronouncements that pass for an analysis of the causes of poverty (Jones 1992). Western peoples—Americans in particular—have yet to discuss the social, political and economic aspects of privilege *vis-à-vis* deprivation. In this context students and citizens will learn that the polarization of wealth and the economic perspectives that allowed it to happen have created a situation where our society's economic machine no longer needs young inexperienced people. Adolescence as a preparatory stage for adulthood is obsolete. In the 1990s it has become a corral for unneeded young people drifting in a socio-economic purgatory (for more information on these changing conditions of youth in the late twentieth century see Steinberg and Kincheloe 1997). Demographers report that elderly men have the highest suicide rate. Perceived by society and themselves as socially superfluous, old men are removed from the workforce, stripped of a future and left to wait for death. Over the past quarter century the group that witnessed the fastest growing suicide rate was males aged fifteen to nineteen (Gaines 1990). Stripped of their hopes for socio-economic mobility and burdened with the masculine expectation for self-sufficiency, these young men reflect the Western social dilemma in the 1990s. Critical multiculturalism must provide a voice of hope, an avenue of participation for students and citizens victimized by contemporary economic strategies and youth policies.

(3) The articulation of a political vision. Any pedagogy of empowerment that fails to produce a political vision that grounds the political organization of theeconomically marginalized will fail. The poor must gain the political savvy

to uncover hegemonic ideological attempts to disempower them. In this context they will turn such political knowledge into the political clout to resist those who attempt to undermine their solidarity by appealing to their racial, gender, ethnic or religious prejudices (Jennings 1992). A critical multicultural political vision understands that the traditional route to socio-economic mobility has, contrary to the prevailing wisdom, involved first achieving income stability and then investing in education (Coontz 1992). In the light of this understanding the basis of an economic empowerment policy should revolve around job creation/full employment policies that provide child care for workers and reward and punish businesses on the basis of their contributions to the creation of good jobs and democratic workplaces in poor areas. The critical multicultural political vision calls for an increase in wages and a commitment to end welfare by providing jobs to welfare recipients. In two-parent families where one or two of the parents is a full-time worker or in single-parent families where the parent works either full-time or part-time, work should be rewarded. Health care for such workers should be guaranteed and tax burdens should be reduced (Ellwood 1988; West 1992; Nightingale 1993). Obviously, such a political vision is not popular in Western societies at the end of the century. Thus, it will take a monumental effort on the part of the poor and their allies to generate support for the policies demanded by the vision.

(4) The development of the knowledge and skills required to escape poverty. The core of the critical multicultural pedagogy of empowerment revolves around an understanding of the impediments to social and economic mobility and the specifics of how one gets around such social, cultural and educational roadblocks. As a rigorous multidimensional course of study, the empowerment curriculum views men and women in more than simply egoistic, self-centred and rationalist terms. Individuals, especially poor ones, need help making meaning in their lives, developing sense of purpose, constructing a positive identity and cultivating self-worth. Unlike previous forms of conservative and liberal education, the pedagogy of empowerment would address these issues, using the categories covered in this [selection] as the programme's theoretical basis. Understanding socio-economic class in the larger context of historical power relations, students would understand that poverty is not simply a reflection of bad character or incompetence. In this context students would appreciate the organizational dynamics necessary to the effort to 'pull oneself up by one's bootstraps'—an undertaking often referenced but infrequently explained. The empowerment curriculum would help poor individuals to develop strategies to take control of schools, social agencies, health organizations and economic organizations. Understanding how these organizations work to undermine the interests of the poor, with their narrow and often scientifically produced definitions of normality, intelligence, family stability etc., the curriculum helps students to devise strategies to resist the imposition of policies grounded on such definitions (Ellwood 1988; Jennings 1992; West 1992).

The curriculum begins with the personal experiences of working class students but moves to understandings far beyond them; teachers constantly relate what is being learned back to student experience. Concepts and information about the world are integrated into what students already know. Such data are then analysed in the light of questions of economic justice, environmental/ecological connections to class bias, an understanding of Western modernist ways of seeing the world and the needs of democracy. Such understandings help to create a critical consciousness grounded on an appreciation of both the way ideology works to convince the marginalized of their own inferiority and how empowered people are capable of generating democratic change. Students with a critical consciousness are able to point out the ways the power bloc enforces its dominance and how in the electronic world of postmodernity the process takes on new degrees of impact and complexity. Empowered students who possess a critical multicultural consciousness draw upon the reality of everyday conflict in their lives, their recognition of the gap between the promise of democracy and the despair they have experienced as members of the low socio-economic class to illustrate to all the reality of injustice. In this emotional connection of lived experience to larger conceptual understanding, students and teachers begin to get in touch with their passion, the lived impact of their encounter with critical multiculturalism (Sleeter and Grant 1994; Britzman and Pitt 1996; Giroux 1997a).

In the light of the engagement with this passionate new consciousness, all forms of knowledge are opened to question. Here, an important skill for poor students involves the ability to reveal the power interests hidden within allegedly neutral knowledge forms. Thus, a central feature of any critical multicultural curriculum involves an analysis of existing literary works, important philosophical, political and religious texts and particular accounts of history that shape a curriculum—the Eurocentric canon, for example. In this analysis students explore where such knowledge comes from, why particular knowledge forms have not been included and the strengths and limitations of the ways of knowing that accompany the canonical discourse. What we are describing here is rigorous scholarly activity that refuses to dispense information to students dispassionately, but insists on engaging students in the discovery of personal meanings within knowledge and in the production of knowledge. As subjugated groups begin to make sense of their histories and their personal worlds, critical multiculturalists display their respect for the intellect of members of such groups by not simply accepting any meaning they make or knowledge they produce as authentic. Critical multicultural teachers and cultural workers engage the knowledge production of particular individuals, inducing them to become more and more aware of the socio-political, cultural and moral dynamics embedded within their constructions. It is not uncommon to find racist and sexist undercurrents that undermine the dignity of non-whites and women. In this context critical multiculturalists have no problem challenging the assumptions behind such knowledge. Such engagements with canon, meaning making and critiques provide not only empowerment and cognitive development, but also a form of cultural capital that emerges from an understanding of the discourse of education. Education can be thought of as a discourse community with its own rules of knowledge, decorum and success. In the process of engaging students with the issues discussed here, critical multicultural teachers from elementary school to college are consciously involved in introducing students to this educational discourse community. Students from subjugated groups typically feel that they are not a part of the school community, that they don't possess the secret knowledge that will let them into the club. The type of critical education discussed here provides students from lower socio-economic class backgrounds with a sense of belonging that holds implications not only for their lives in school but for vocational, spiritual and interpersonal domains as well (Darder 1991; Harred 1991; Hauser 1991).

(5) Awareness of the liabilities and possibilities of resistance. When marginalized students come to the conclusion—and most of them eventually do—that education is set up to reward the values of the already successful, those whose culture most accurately reflects the mainstream, they have to negotiate how they react to this realization. Most lower socio-economic class students are, understandably, confused and dislocated because of this reality. Critical multiculturalism is devoted to helping marginalized students make sense of this reality and facilitating the formulation of the resistance to it. A central lesson for angry marginalized students involves developing an awareness of the costs of various forms of resistance. Rejection of middle class propriety often expresses itself as an abrasive classroom behaviour antithetical to mutual respect and focused analysis. Critical multiculturalists believe that the outcome of marginalized student resistance does not have to be disempowerment. To formulate an emancipatory form of resistance we draw upon the world of cultural analyst John Fiske (1993). Fiske argues that marginalized peoples comprise localized power groups who typically produce popular forms of knowledge. Such knowledge forms are powerful and can be drawn upon for psychic protection from the ideological teachings of the power bloc. Marginalized knowledge forms or, as we described them earlier, subjugated knowledge allow the oppressed to make sense of their social and educational experiences from a unique vantage point and in the process to reconstruct their identities. Critical multiculturalists both study these knowledge forms and encourage their students to explore their origins and effects. Without such understanding and encouragement, we fear that lower socio-economic class anger over the unfairness and oppression they encounter will turn violent.

Obviously, it already has in many places, but what we have observed so far may simply represent the tip of the iceberg. Marginalized peoples become violent when they are not heard. Obviously racial and class violence has a plethora of causes, but one of the most important involves the fact that the power bloc often does not listen to non-white or poor people. In this context studies indicate that while violence can be observed at all socio-economic levels, it is concentrated among males from poor backgrounds. As the disparity of wealth increases, the impulse for violence also grows. We can see such an impulse quite clearly in a variety of popular cultural forms consumed by working class men and women, young males in particular, including heavy metal music, violent movies and professional wrestling (Gaines 1990; Fiske 1993). To avoid the escalation of violence among the oppressed, issues of social and economic justice will have to be taken seriously by individuals from various social sectors. Without dramatic action, Western societies face a violent opening of the new millennium. Constructive, non-violent strategies of resistance must be carefully studied in the coming years.

(6) Emphasis on the ability to organize the poor.   Many observers consistently underestimate the localizing power of the poor to assert themselves. The localizing power of the poor is a social resource typically misunderstood by the power bloc that helps to define the parameters of what the power bloc can or cannot do. When thoughtfully organized, the poor can extend the influence of such power and move it in an emancipatory direction. Such organization increases the odds that the poor will be able to draw upon the subversive power of their localized or subjugated knowledge. An empowering aspect of such knowledge involves the insight it can provide into the connections between the actions of various power blocs—consistencies in the ways such power wielders attempt to maintain the status quo. One of the roles of critical multiculturalists... involves pointing out and conceptually extending such subjugated understandings. For example, an organized group of poor people would understand the class elitism at work both in a school curriculum that focused on the 'great contributions' of business, industrial and political leaders and in newspapers and TV reports that provide business news and not labour news. Though they occur in different social venues, these realities work to undermine the power and importance of the poor and working class. Such an understanding leads to the possibility of an informed resistance.

Any organizational efforts for the empowerment of the marginalized must understand that power does not flow in some unidirectional hierarchy from the powerful to the oppressed. Though their power is weak in relation to the power bloc, the oppressed possess a variety of means of eluding the control of oppressors—in many historical cases this bottom-up power has led to the overthrow of the power bloc. Organizational efforts to mobilize the disempowered must always be mindful of this potential and appreciate the marginalized individual's capacity to use his or her creativity and localized knowledge to question dominant ideologies and the hegemonic purposes of its institutions. The very lower socio-economic class students who are saddled with the disempowering burden of a low IQ, for example, are the students who because of their social location are empowered to recognize the foibles and naiveté of privileged individuals with high IQs. On many occasions we have heard the oppressed laugh at the incompetence of high-status individuals whom they had encountered at some point during their lives. Such a subjugated knowledge can serve as a conceptual basis for rejecting the cognitive essentialism of intelligence tests and the psychic scars and socio-economic disempowerment that accompany them. Such understandings can be used as a foundation for the development of a counter-hegemonic and empowered consciousness. They can experientially ground the development of counter-organizations that produce counter-histories and counter-knowledges of the relationships between the marginalized and the privileged. New forms of political organizations and pedagogical interventions must be formulated that draw upon both subjugated understandings of the privileged and critical multicultural understandings of how power works (Wartenberg 1992; Fiske 1993; West 1993; Britzman and Pitt 1996; Carspecken 1996).

Joe L. Kincheloe
and Shirley R.
Steinberg

REFERENCES

Britzman, D. and Pitt, A. (1996) On refusing one's place: the ditchdigger's dream, in J. Kincheloe, S. Steinberg and A. Gresson (eds) *Measured Lies: The Bell Curve Examined*. New York: St Martin's Press.

Carspecken, P. (1996) The set-up: crocodile tears for the poor, in J. Kincheloe, S. Steinberg and A. Gresson (eds) *Measured Lies: The Bell Curve Examined*. New York: St Martin's Press.

Coontz, S. (1992) *The Way We Never Were: American Families and the Nostalgia Trap*. New York: Basic Books.

Darder, A. (1991) *Culture and Power in the Classroom: a Critical Foundation for Bicultural Education*. Westport, CT: Bergin and Garvey.

Ellwood, D. (1988) *Poor Support: Poverty in the American Family*. New York: Basic Books.

Fiske, J. (1993) *Power Plays, Power Works*. New York: Verso.

Gaines, D. (1990) *Teenage Wasteland: Suburbia's Dead End Kids*. New York: Harper Perennial.

Giroux, H. (1997a) *Pedagogy and the Politics of Hope: Theory, Culture, and Schooling*. Boulder, CO: Westview Press.

Harred, J. (1991) Collaborative learning in the literature classroom: old problems revisited, paper presented at the Conference on College Composition and Communication, Boston.

Hauser, J. (1991) Critical inquiries, uncertainties and not faking it with students, paper presented at the Annual Conference of the Center for Critical Thinking and Moral Critique, Rohnert Park, CA.

Jennings, J. (1992) Blacks, politics, and the human service crisis, in J. Jennings (ed.) *Race, Politics, and Economic Development: Community Perspectives*. New York: Verso.

Jones, M. (1992) The black underclass as systematic phenomenon, in J. Jennings (ed.) *Race, Politics, and Economic Development: Community Perspectives*. New York: Verso.

Nightingale, C. (1993) *On the Edge: a History of Poor Black Children and Their American Dreams*. New York: Basic Books.

Sleeter, C. and Grant, C. (1994) *Making Choices from Multicultural Education: Five Approaches to Race, Class, and Gender*. New York: Merrill.

Steinberg, S. and Kincheloe, J. (1997) *Kinderculture: Corporate Constructions of Childhood*. Boulder, CO: Westview Press.

Swartz, E. (1993) Multicultural education: disrupting patterns of supremacy in school curricula, practices, and pedagogy, *Journal of Negro Education*, 62(4): 493–506.

Wartenberg, T. (1992b) Situated social power, in T. Wartenberg (ed.) *Rethinking Power*. Albany, NY: SUNY Press.

West, C. (1992) Nihilism in black America, in G. Dent (ed.) *Black Popular Culture*. Seattle: Bay Press.

West, C. (1993) *Race Matters*. Boston: Beacon Press.

PART FIVE

Multicultural Practices in the Schools

On the Internet . . .

Sites appropriate to Part Five

The National Association for Multicultural Education (NAME) brings together educators from K–12, college, university, and adult education to learn about and discuss the field of multicultural education. Educators in NAME create both research and teaching strategies for multicultural education.

```
http://www.inform.umd.edu/NAME/index.html
```

Teaching Tolerance is a free magazine that provides educators with ideas, information, and resources for promoting multicultural understanding in schools and communities.

```
http://www.splcenter.org/
    teachingtolerance//tt-1.html
```

The Educational Resources Information Center (ERIC) periodically produces documents containing materials and information gathered about a particular topic. This Web site is titled "A Community Guide to Multicultural Education Programs," and it was published by the ERIC Clearinghouse on Urban Education.

```
http://eric-web.tc.columbia.edu/guides/
    pg6.html
```

CHAPTER 16 Multicultural Classrooms

16.1 LOUISE DERMAN-SPARKS

Empowering Children to Create a Caring Culture in a World of Differences

Louise Derman-Sparks is director of the Anti-Bias Leadership Project in Pasadena, California. She has focused on antibias and antiracist education, especially for early childhood. She has written articles and books on the topics, including a teacher's guide for implementing an antibias curriculum into an early childhood classroom called *Anti-Bias Curriculum: Tools for Empowering Young Children*. Her works give recommendations to teachers for implementing the ideas. The following selection is from an article titled "Empowering Children to Create a Caring Culture in a World of Differences," *Childhood Education* (Winter 1993/1994).

In the following selection, Derman-Sparks focuses on working with young children to create a climate of antibias. She begins by describing how early—between two and four years old—that children pick up on gender and racial bias. Using the words of young children, she describes how schools and teachers can unintentionally create and reinforce racial, gender, and cultural biases. She then lays out how teachers can create a curriculum and an environment that is purposefully antibiased and antiracist. To be effective, says Derman-Sparks, there must be "a caring culture in which children can be empowered." And she emphasizes that teachers need to actively engage themselves in this effort in their own lives as well. Teachers' attempting to become antiracist is where the efforts need to begin, according to Derman-Sparks. In this effort, teachers need to engage in reflective thinking, planning, and locating resources, and then they must create the same experiences for children by using the students' own experiences and interests.

Key Concept: creating an antiracist climate for young children

*R*acism, sexism, classism, heterosexism and ableism are still deeply entrenched and pervasive in society, making it very difficult for millions of children to be "Freedom's Child." What must we do as educators to ensure that all children can develop to their fullest potential—can truly become "Freedom's Child"?

CHILDREN'S DEVELOPMENT OF IDENTITY AND ATTITUDES

Take a moment to listen to the voices of children. Members of the Anti-Bias Curriculum Task Force developed the anti-bias approach after a year spent collecting and analyzing children's thinking and trying out activities. They collected the following anecdotes:

- Steven is busy being a whale on the climbing structure in the 2-year-old yard. Susie tries to join him. "Girls can't do that!" he shouts.
- Robby, 3 years old, refuses to hold the hand of a dark-skinned classmate. At home, he insists, after bathing, that his black hair is now "white because it is clean."
- "You aren't really an Indian," 4-year-old Rebecca tells one of her child care teachers. "Where are your feathers?"
- "Malcolm can't play with us. He's a baby," Linda tells their teacher. Malcolm, another 4-year-old, uses a wheelchair.

Those voices reflect the impact of societal bias on children. Now, listen to voices of children in programs that practice anti-bias curriculum:

- Maria, 4 years old, sees a stereotypical "Indian warrior" figure in the toy store. "That toy hurts Indian people's feelings," she tells her grandmother.
- Rebecca's kindergarten teacher asks the children to draw a picture of what they would like to be when they grow up. Rebecca draws herself as a surgeon—in a pink ball gown and tiara.

- After hearing the story of Rosa Parks and the Montgomery bus boy-cott, 5-year-old Tiffany, whose skin is light brown, ponders whether she would have had to sit in the back of the bus. Finally, she firmly asserts, "I'm Black and, anyway, all this is stupid. I would just get off and tell them to keep their old bus."
- In the school playground, 5-year-old Casey and another white friend, Tommy, are playing. Casey calls two other boys to join them. "You can't play with them. They're Chinese eyes," Tommy says to him. Casey replies, "That's not right. All kinds of kids play together. I know. My teacher tells me civil rights stories."

Children do not come to preschool, child care centers or elementary school as "blank slates" on the topic of diversity. Facing and understanding what underlies their thoughts and feelings are key to empowering children to resist bias. . . .

WHAT EMPOWERING CHILDREN TO CREATE A CARING CULTURE REQUIRES OF US

CLARITY ABOUT GOALS   The following goals are for *all* children. The specific issues and tasks necessary for working toward these goals will vary for children, depending on their backgrounds, ages and life experiences.

Nurture each child's construction of a knowledgeable, confident self-concept and group identity.   To achieve this goal, we must create education conditions in which all children are able to like who they are without needing to feel superior to anyone else. Children must also be able to develop biculturally where that is appropriate.

Promote each child's comfortable, empathic interaction with people from diverse backgrounds.   This goal requires educators to guide children's development of the cognitive awareness, emotional disposition and behavioral skills needed to respectfully and effectively learn about differences, comfortably negotiate and adapt to differences, and cognitively understand and emotionally accept the common humanity that all people share.

Foster each child's critical thinking about bias.   Children need to develop the cognitive skills to identify "unfair" and "untrue" images (stereotypes), comments (teasing, name-calling) and behaviors (discrimination) directed at one's own or others' identities. They also need the emotional empathy to know that bias hurts.

Cultivate each child's ability to stand up for her/himself and for others in the face of bias. This "activism" goal requires educators to help every child learn and practice a variety of ways to act: a) when another child acts in a biased manner toward her/him, b) when a child acts in a biased manner toward another child, c) when an adult acts in a biased manner. Goal 4 builds on goal 3 as critical thinking and empathy are necessary components of acting for oneself or others in the face of bias.

These four goals interact with and build on each other. We cannot accomplish any one goal without the other three. *Their combined intent is to empower children to resist the negative impact of racism and other "isms" on their development and to grow into adults who will want and be able to work with others to eliminate all forms of oppression.* In other words, the underlying intent is not to end racism (and other "isms") in one generation by changing children's attitudes and behaviors, but rather to promote critical thinkers and activists who can work for social change and participate in creating a caring culture in a world of differences.

PREPARING OURSELVES   Effective anti-bias education requires every teacher to look inward and commit to a lifelong journey of understanding her/his own cultural beliefs, while changing the prejudices and behaviors that interfere with the nurturing of all children. Teachers need to know:

- how to see their own culture in relationship to society's history and current power realities
- how to effectively adapt their teaching style and curriculum content to their children's needs
- how to engage in cultural conflict resolution with people from cultural backgrounds other than their own
- how to be critical thinkers about bias in their practice
- how to be activists—engaging people in dialogue about bias, intervening, working with others to create change.

Achieving these goals takes commitment and time, and is a developmental process for adults as well as for children. One must be emotionally as well as cognitively involved and ready to face periods of disequilibrium and then reconstruction and transformation.

IMPLEMENTATION PRINCIPLES AND STRATEGIES

To create a caring culture in which children can be empowered, teachers must be "reflective practitioners" who can think critically about their own teaching practice and adapt curriculum goals and general strategies to the needs of their children.

CRITICAL THINKING   Be aware of "tourist multicultural curriculum" and find ways to eliminate tourism from your program. Tourist multicultural curriculum is the most commonly practiced approach in early childhood education and elementary school today. The majority of commercial curriculum materials currently available on the market and many published curriculum guides reflect a tourist version of multicultural education. Unfortunately, tourist multicultural curriculum is a simplistic, inadequate version of multicultural education.

In a classroom practicing a tourist approach, the daily "regular" curriculum reflects mainstream European American perspectives, rules of behavior, images, learning and teaching styles. Activities about "other" cultures often exhibit the following problems:

Disconnection: Activities are added on to the curriculum as special times, rather than integrated into all aspects of the daily environment and curriculum.

Patronization: "Other" cultures are treated as "quaint" or "exotic." This form of tourism does not teach children to appreciate what all humans share in common.

Trivialization: Cultural activities that are disconnected from the daily life of the people trivialize the culture. A typical example is multicultural curriculum that focuses on holidays—days that are different from "normal" days. Children do not learn about how people live their lives, how they work, who does what in the family—all of which is the essence of a culture. Other forms of trivialization include: turning cultural practices that have deep, ritual meaning into "arts and crafts" or dance activities, or asking parents to cook special foods without any further lessons about the parents' cultures.

Misrepresentation: Too few images of a group oversimplifies the variety within the group. Use of images and activities based on traditional, past practices of an ethnic group rather than images of contemporary life confuse children. Misusing activities and images that reflect the culture-of-origin of a group to teach about *the life of cultures in the U.S.* conveys misconceptions about people with whom children have little or no face-to-face experience.

In sum, tourist multicultural curriculum does not give children the tools they need to comfortably, empathetically and fairly interact with diversity. Instead, it teaches simplistic generalizations about other people that lead to stereotyping, rather than to understanding of differences. Moreover, tourist curriculum, because it focuses on the unusual and special times of a culture and neglects how people live their daily lives, does not foster children's understanding and empathy for our common humanity. Moving beyond tourist multicultural curriculum is key to our profession's more effective nurturing of diversity.

INCORPORATE MULTICULTURAL AND ANTI-BIAS ACTIVITIES INTO DAILY CURRICULUM PLANNING   Diversity and anti-bias topics are integral to the entire curriculum at any education level. One practical brainstorming technique for identifying the numerous topic possibilities is "webbing."

Step one is determining the center of the "web." This can be: 1) an issue raised by the children (e.g., a person who is visually impaired cannot work);

2) any number of traditional preschool "units" (e.g., my body, families, work); 3) High/Scope's (Weikart, 1975) "key experiences" (e.g., classification or seriation); 4) any of the traditional content areas of the primary curriculum (science, math, language arts, physical and health curriculum).

Step two involves brainstorming the many possible anti-bias, multicultural issues that stem from the subject at the web's center. *Step three* involves identifying specific content for a particular classroom based on contextual/developmental analysis. *Step four* involves listing possible activities that are developmentally and culturally appropriate for your particular class.

CULTURAL APPROPRIATENESS: ADULT/CHILD INTERACTIONS

Effective teaching about diversity, as in all other areas, *is a continuous interaction between adults and children.* On the one hand, teachers are responsible for brainstorming, planning and initiating diversity topics, based on their analyses of children's needs and life experiences. On the other hand, careful attention to children's thinking and behavior, and to "teachable moments," leads educators to modify initial plans.

Find ways to engage children in critical thinking and the planning and carrying out of "activism" activities appropriate to their developmental levels, cultural backgrounds and interests.

Critical thinking and activism activities should rise out of real life situations that are of interest to children. The purpose of such activities is to provide opportunities for children, 4 years old and up, to build their empathy, skills and confidence and to encourage their sense of responsibility for both themselves and for others. Consequently, activities should reflect *their* ideas and issues, not the teacher's. The following two examples are appropriate activism activities.

In the first situation, the children's school did not have a "handicapped" parking space in their parking lot. After a parent was unable to attend open school night because of this lack, the teacher told the class of 4- and 5-year-olds what had happened and why. They then visited other places in their neighborhood that had "handicapped" parking and decided to make one in their school lot. After they did so, they then noticed that teachers were inappropriately parking in the "handicapped" spot (their classroom overlooked the parking lot), so they decided to make tickets. The children dictated their messages, which their teacher faithfully took down, and drew pictures to accompany their words. They then ticketed those cars that did not have "handicapped parking" plaques in their windows.

In the second example, a class of 1st- through 3rd-graders visited a homeless shelter and talked to the director to find out what people needed. They started a toy and blanket collection drive, which they promoted using posters and flyers. They visited several classrooms to talk about what they were doing. They also wrote to the Mayor and the City Council to say that homeless people needed more houses and jobs.

PARENTS AND FAMILY INVOLVEMENT

Find ways to involve parents and other adult family members in all aspects of anti-bias education. Education and collaboration with parents is *essential*. Educators have to be creative and ingenious to make this happen. Parents can help plan, implement and evaluate environmental adaptations and curricular activities. They can serve on advisory/planning committees with staff, provide information about their lifestyles and beliefs, participate in classroom activities and serve as community liaisons. Teachers can send home regular short newsletters to share ongoing plans and classroom activities, and elicit parent advice and resources. Parent meetings on child-rearing and education issues should also incorporate relevant diversity topics.

When a family member disagrees with an aspect of the curriculum, it is essential that the teachers listen carefully and sensitively to the issues underlying the disagreement. Objections may include: 1) family's belief that learning about differences will "make the children prejudiced" ("color-blind" view), 2) parent's belief that teaching about stereotyping and such values belongs in the home, not at school, 3) family members' strong prejudices against specific groups.

Staff need to find out all they can about the cultural and other issues that influence the family's concerns, and then work with family members to find ways to meet their needs while also maintaining the goals of anti-bias education. The techniques for working with parents on anti-bias issues are generally the same as those used for other child development and education topics. The difference, however, lies in the teachers' level of comfort about addressing such topics with other adults.

TEACHER EDUCATION AND PROFESSIONAL DEVELOPMENT

Teacher training must incorporate liberating pedagogical techniques that:

- engage students on cognitive, emotional and behavioral levels
- use storytelling to enable students to both name and identify the ways that various identity contexts and bias have affected their lives
- use experiential activities that engage learners in discovering the dynamics of cultural differences and the various "isms"
- provide new information and analysis that give deeper meaning to what is learned through storytelling and experiential activities
- create a balance between supporting and challenging students in an environment of safety, not necessarily comfort.

The most useful way to work on our own development is to join with others (staff, or staff and parents) in support groups that meet regularly over a long period of time. By collaborating, sharing resources and providing encouragement, we can work on our self-awareness issues, build and improve our practices, strengthen our courage and determination and maintain the joy and excitement of education.

In sum, children of the 21st century will not be able to function if they are psychologically bound by outdated and narrow assumptions about their neighbors. To thrive, even to survive, in this more complicated world, children need to learn how to function in many different cultural contexts, to recognize and respect different histories and perspectives, and to know how to work together to create a more just world that can take care of all its people, its living creatures, its land.

Let's remember the African American novelist Alice Walker's call to "Keep in mind always the present you are constructing. It should be the future you want" (Walker, 1989, p. 238).

REFERENCES

Walker, A. (1989). *The temple of my familiar.* New York: Pocket Books.
Weikart, D. (1975). *Young children in action.* Ypsilanti, MI: High Scope Press.

16.2 JAMES A. BANKS

Transforming the Mainstream Curriculum

James A. Banks is a professor in and director of the Center for Multicultural Education at the University of Washington. As a world-renowned scholar in the field of multicultural education, he has received a number of honors and awards, including the Distinguished Career Contribution Award from the American Educational Research Association's Committee on the Role and Status of Minorities in Educational Research and Development. He has also received fellowships from the National Academy of Education, the Kellogg Foundation, and the Rockefeller Foundation. While he writes on virtually all areas related to multicultural education, much of Banks's work focuses on teaching strategies and curriculum development for multicultural education and for social studies.

The following selection is from "Transforming the Mainstream Curriculum," *Educational Leadership* (May 1994). In it, Banks describes five popular dimensions of a multicultural classroom, then provides a different dimension that he recommends for helping students to better understand the complexities of a multicultural society. In the five dimensions of multicultural education that already exist, Banks expresses concern that the curriculum remains dominated by mainstream perspectives. Thus, he recommends a different dimension of instruction for the multicultural classroom: the *transformation approach*. The basic assumptions of the curriculum under this approach are changed to include the perspectives of many groups. To demonstrate this approach, Banks presents a lesson in which the Montgomery bus boycott, which followed Rosa Parks's refusal to give up her seat on the bus, is reinterpreted. In this way he shows how the transformation approach can result in a much greater and deeper understanding of an event in history by including different perspectives on the event, often the perspectives that have been left out of the traditional interpretation of that event.

Key Concept: approaches to making the curriculum more multicultural

*S*chools today are rich in student diversity. A growing number of American classrooms and schools contain a complex mix of races, cultures, languages, and religious affiliations.

Two other sources of diversity are becoming increasingly prominent as well. The widening gap between rich and poor students is creating more social class diversity, and an increasing number of gay students and teachers are publicly proclaiming their sexual orientations.

TOWARD AN AUTHENTIC *UNUM*

The increasing recognition of diversity within American society poses a significant challenge: how to create a cohesive and democratic society while at the same time allowing citizens to maintain their ethnic, cultural, socioeconomic, and primordial identities.

Our ideal as a nation has been and continues to be *e pluribus unum*—out of many, one. In the past, Americans have tried to reach this goal by eradicating diversity and forcing all citizens into a white Anglo-Saxon Protestant culture (Higham 1972).

This coerced assimilation does not work very well. An imposed *unum* is not authentic, is not perceived as legitimate by nonmainstream populations, does not have moral authority, and is inconsistent with democratic ideals. To create an authentic, democratic *unum* with moral authority and perceived legitimacy, the *pluribus* (diverse peoples) must negotiate and share power.

Even with its shortcomings, the United States has done better in this regard than most nations. Still, citizen expectations for a just *unum* are far outpacing the nation's progress toward its ideal. Many citizens of color, people with low incomes, or speakers of languages other than English feel alienated, left out, abandoned, and forgotten.

Our society has a lot to gain by restructuring institutions in ways that incorporate all citizens. People who now feel disenfranchised will become more effective and productive citizens, and new perspectives will be added to the nation's mainstream institutions. The institutions themselves will then be transformed and enriched.

In the past two decades, multicultural education has emerged as a vehicle for including diverse groups and transforming the nation's educational institutions (Banks 1994a, Banks and Banks 1992). Multicultural education tries to create equal educational opportunities for all students by ensuring that the total school environment reflects the diversity of groups in classrooms, schools, and the society as a whole.

CONSIDERING THE DIMENSIONS OF MULTICULTURAL EDUCATION

The following five dimensions of multicultural education can help educators implement and assess programs that respond to student diversity (Banks 1993, 1994b).

1. The first dimension, *content integration*, deals with the extent to which teachers illuminate key points of instruction with content reflecting diversity. Typically, teachers integrate such content into curriculum in several different ways (Banks 1991b). One common approach is the recognition of contributions —that is, teachers work into the curriculum various isolated facts about heroes from diverse groups. Otherwise, lesson plans and units are unchanged. With the additive approach, on the other hand, the curriculum remains unchanged, but teachers add special units on topics like the Women's Rights Movement, African Americans in the West, and Famous Americans with Disabilities. While an improvement over the passing mention of contributions, the additive approach still relegates groups like women, African Americans, and disabled people to the periphery of the curriculum.

2. A second dimension of multicultural education is *knowledge construction*, or the extent to which teachers help students understand how perspectives of people within a discipline influence the conclusions reached within that discipline. This dimension is also concerned with whether students learn to form knowledge for themselves.

3. The *prejudice reduction* dimension has to do with efforts to help students to develop positive attitudes about different groups. Research has revealed a need for this kind of education and the efficacy of it. For example, researchers have shown that while children enter school with many negative attitudes and misconceptions about different racial and ethnic groups (Phinney and Rotheram 1987), education can help students develop more positive intergroup attitudes, provided that certain conditions exist. Two such conditions are instructional materials with positive images of diverse groups and the use of such materials in consistent and sustained ways (Banks 1991a).

4. The *equitable pedagogy* dimension concerns ways to modify teaching so as to facilitate academic achievement among students from diverse groups. Research indicates, for example, that the academic achievement of African-American and Mexican-American students improves when teachers use cooperative (rather than competitive) teaching activities and strategies (Aronson and Gonzalez 1988).

5. The *empowering school culture and social structure* dimension concerns the extent to which a school's culture and organization ensure educational equality and cultural empowerment for students from diverse groups. Some of the variables considered are grouping practices, social climate, assessment practices, participation in extracurricular activities, and staff expectations and responses to diversity.

KNOWLEDGE CONSTRUCTION AND TRANSFORMATION

I would like to suggest an alternative to the contributions and additive approaches that are used in the content integration dimension. This alternative, the *transformation approach,* changes the structure, assumptions, and perspectives of the curriculum so that subject matter is viewed from the perspectives and experiences of a range of groups. The transformation approach changes instructional materials, teaching techniques, and student learning.

This approach can be used to teach about our differences as well as our similarities. Teachers can help students understand that, while Americans have a variety of viewpoints, we share many cultural traditions, values, and political ideals that cement us together as a nation.

The transformation approach has several advantages. It brings content about currently marginalized groups to the center of the curriculum. It helps students understand that how people construct knowledge depends on their experiences, values, and perspectives. It helps students learn to construct knowledge themselves. And it helps students grasp the complex group interactions that have produced the American culture and civilization.

REINTERPRETING THE MONTGOMERY BUS BOYCOTT

The history of the Montgomery (Alabama) bus boycott, which began on December 5, 1955, can be used to illustrate how the transformation approach works. Viewing this event from different perspectives shows how historians construct interpretations, how central figures can be omitted from historical records, how history can be rewritten, and how students can create their own interpretations.

Textbook accounts of the Montgomery bus boycott generally conclude that: (1) when a bus driver asked Rosa Parks to give up her seat to a white person, she refused because she was tired from working hard all day, and (2) the arrest of Rosa Parks triggered the planning and execution of the boycott.

Two important accounts by women who played key roles in the boycott contradict important aspects of the textbook conclusions. The two memoirs are those of Rosa Parks (with Haskins 1992) and Jo Ann Gibson Robinson (Garrow 1987). Robinson was an Alabama State College English professor and president of the Women's Political Council.

Students can compare mainstream accounts of the events (such as those in textbooks) with transformative accounts (such as those by Robinson and Parks). This activity presents an excellent opportunity both to learn content about diverse groups and to gain insights about the construction of knowledge.

According to Robinson, professional African-American women in Montgomery founded the Women's Political Council in 1946 to provide leadership, support, and improvement in the black community and to work for voting rights for African Americans. Many council members were Alabama State College professors. Others were black public school teachers.

In 1953, the council received more than 30 complaints concerning bus driver offenses against African Americans. For instance, black people (even when seated in the "Negro" section of the bus) were asked to give up their seats to whites. Further, blacks often had to pay their fares in the front of the bus, exit, and reenter through the back door—and sometimes when they stepped off the bus, the driver left them.

Robinson and other council members worked with city leaders to improve the treatment of black bus riders, but to no avail. African Americans continued to experience intimidating, demeaning, and hostile encounters with bus drivers.

As the negative pattern of incidents persisted, the council concluded that only a boycott against the bus system would end the abuse of black bus riders and bus segregation. A boycott was thought to have good potential for success because about 70 percent of Montgomery's bus riders were African American. The council planned the boycott and then waited for the right time to launch it.

The year 1955 presented three choices for the "right time." On March 2, 1955, Claudette Colvin, a 15-year-old high school student seated in the "Negro" section of a bus, was arrested after refusing to give up her seat to a white rider. Next, Robinson said:

> They dragged her, kicking and screaming hysterically, off the bus. Still half-dragging, half-pushing, they forced her into a patrol car that had been summoned, put handcuffs on her wrists so she would do no physical harm to the arresting police, and drove her to jail. There she was charged with misconduct, resisting arrest, and violating the city segregation laws (Garrow 1987).

Claudette Colvin was later found guilty and released on probation. The conviction enraged the African-American community. Six months after the Colvin incident, Mary Louise Smith, 18, was arrested on a similar charge. Smith was fined.

Then, on December 1, Rosa Parks was arrested for refusing to give up her seat. She gives quite a different reason for her intransigence than has commonly been reported:

> People always say that I didn't give up my seat because I was tired, but that isn't true. I was not tired physically, or no more tired than I usually was at the end of a working day. I was not old, although some people have an image of me being old then. I was 42. No, the only tired I was, was tired of giving in.
>
> The driver of the bus saw me still sitting there, and he asked was I going to stand up. I said, "No." He said, "Well, I'm going to have you arrested." Then I said, "You may do that." These were the only words we said to each other.
>
> ... People have asked me if it occurred to me that I could be the test case the NAACP had been looking for. I did not think about that at all. In fact if I had let myself think too deeply about what might happen to me, I might have gotten off the bus. But I chose to remain.

Fed up with mistreatment, the African-American women of Montgomery, led by their council, called for a boycott of city buses. Robinson described the preparations for the boycott:

> I sat down and quickly drafted a message and then called a good friend and colleague, John Cannon, chairman of the business department of the college, who had access to the college's mimeograph equipment. When I told him that the WPC was staging a boycott and needed to run off the notices, he told me that he too had suffered embarrassment on the city buses. Like myself, he had been hurt and angry. He said that he would happily assist me.

Along with two of my most trusted students, we quickly agreed to meet almost immediately, in the middle of the night, at the college's duplicating room. We were able to get three messages to a page, greatly reducing the number of pages that had to be mimeographed in order to produce the tens of thousands of leaflets we knew would be needed. By 4 a. m. on Friday, the sheets had been duplicated, cut in thirds, and bundled (Garrow 1987).

Part of Robinson's leaflets read:

Another Negro woman has been arrested and thrown in jail because she refused to get up out of her seat on the bus for a white person to sit down.... This has to be stopped. Negroes have rights, too, for if Negroes did not ride the buses, they could not operate. Three-fourths of the riders are Negroes, yet we are arrested, or have to stand over empty seats. If we do not do something to stop the arrests, they will continue. The next time it may be you, your daughter, or mother. This woman's case will come up on Monday. We are, therefore, asking every Negro to stay off the buses Monday in protest of the arrest and trial. Don't ride the buses to work, to town, to school, or anywhere else on Monday (Garrow 1987).

REINTERPRETING THE PAST

Robinson's and Parks' accounts of the Montgomery bus boycott reveal that significant players in historical events can be virtually ignored in written history. For instance, most textbook accounts of the Montgomery bus boycott emphasize the work of men (like Martin Luther King Jr. and Ralph D. Abernathy) or organizations headed by men. The work of women like Robinson and her female colleagues in the Women's Political Council simply cannot be found in most textbooks.

Further, Rosa Parks' stated reason for refusing to give up her seat helps students understand that recorded history can be wrong. Students can also see that when people who have been excluded from the construction of historical knowledge begin to play active roles in interpreting history, the resulting accounts can be strikingly different and much more accurate. As Robert Merton (1972) observed, insiders and outsiders often have different perspectives on the same events, and both perspectives are needed to give the total picture of social and historical reality.

INCORPORATING NEW SCHOLARSHIP

Since the 1970s, people of color—who have historically been outsiders and transformative scholars—have produced a prodigious amount of scholarship on multicultural education. Their thoughtful and informative works include Ronald Takaki's *A Different Mirror: A History of Multicultural America* (1993); John Hope Franklin's *The Color Line: Legacy for the Twenty-First Century* (1993); Gloria Anzaldua's *Borderlands: La Frontera* (1987); Patricia Hill Collins's *Black*

Because men of color have often been as silent on women's issues as white men have been (hooks [*sic*] and West 1991), a special effort should be made to include works by women (such as those by Anzaldua, Collins, and Allen). Two important new books edited by women are Carol Dubois and Vicki Ruiz's *Unequal Sisters: A Multicultural Reader in U. S. Women's History* (1990) and Darlene Clark Hine and her colleagues' *Black Women in America: A Historical Encyclopedia* (1993).

TEACHING CIVIC ACTION

One of multicultural education's important goals is to help students acquire the knowledge and commitment needed to think, decide, and take personal, social, and civic action. Activism helps students apply what they have learned and develop a sense of personal and civic efficacy (Banks with Clegg 1990).

Action activities and projects should be practical, feasible, and attuned to the developmental levels of students. For instance, students in the primary grades can take action by refusing to laugh at ethnic jokes. Students in the early and middle grades can read about and make friends with people from other racial, ethnic, and cultural groups. Upper-grade students can participate in community projects that help people with special needs. Lewis (1991) has written a helpful guide that describes ways to plan and initiate social action activities and projects for students.

When content, concepts, and events are studied from many points of view, all of our students will be ready to play their roles in the life of the nation. They can help to transform the United States from what it is to what it could and should be—many groups working together to build a strong nation that celebrates its diversity.

REFERENCES

Aronson E., and A. Gonzalez. (1988). "Desegregation, Jigsaw, and the Mexican-American Experience." In *Eliminating Racism: Profiles in Controversy*, edited by P. A. Katz and D. A. Taylor. New York: Plenum Press.

Banks, J. A. (1991a). "Multicultural Education: Its Effects on Students' Racial and Gender Role Attitudes." In *Handbook of Research on Social Teaching and Learning*, edited by J. P. Shaver. New York: Macmillan.

Banks, J. A. (1991b). *Teaching Strategies for Ethnic Studies.* 5th ed. Boston: Allyn and Bacon.

Banks, J. A. (1993). "Multicultural Education: Historical Development, Dimensions and Practice." In *Review of Research in Education*, vol. 19, edited by L. Darling-Hammond. Washington, D. C.: American Educational Research Association.

Banks, J. A. (1994b). *Multiethnic Education: Theory and Practice.* 3rd ed. Boston: Allyn and Bacon.

Banks, J. A., with A. A. Clegg Jr. (1990). *Teaching Strategies for the Social Studies: Inquiry, Valuing, and Decision-Making.* 4th ed. New York: Longman.

Banks, J. A., and C. A. McGee Banks, eds. (1992). *Multicultural Education: Issues and Perspectives.* 2nd ed. Boston: Allyn and Bacon.

Garrow, D. J., ed. (1987). *The Montgomery Bus Boycott and the Women Who Started It: The Memoir of Jo Ann Gibson Robinson.* Knoxville: The University of Tennessee Press.

Higham, J. (1972). *Strangers in the Land: Patterns of American Nativism 1860–1925.* New York: Atheneum.

hooks, b., and West, C. (1991). *Breaking Bread: Insurgent Black Intellectual Life.* Boston: South End Press.

Lewis, B. A. (1991). *The Kid's Guide to Social Action.* Minneapolis: Free Spirit Publishing.

Merton, R. K. (1972). "Insiders and Outsiders: A Chapter in the Sociology of Knowledge." *The American Journal of Sociology* 78, 1:9–47.

Parks, R., with J. Haskins. (1992). *Rosa Parks: My Story.* New York: Dial Books.

Phinney, J. S., and M. J. Rotheram, eds. (1987). *Children's Ethnic Socialization: Pluralism and Development.* Beverly Hills, Calif.: Sage Publications.

CHAPTER 17 Multicultural Schools

17.1 SONIA NIETO

Multicultural Education and School Reform

Sonia Nieto puts multicultural education in a sociopolitical context. She encourages educators to make multicultural education a comprehensive education that is schoolwide and that is good education for all students. According to Nieto, a comprehensive, schoolwide multicultural education would be antiracist education, basic education, important for all students, pervasive, education for social justice, a process, and critical pedagogy.

Nieto is a professor in the Cultural Diversity and Curriculum Reform Program at the University of Massachusetts, Amherst. She taught in public schools in Brooklyn, New York, and the Bronx before moving to the college level. She writes on multicultural education and curriculum and is probably best known for her studies of and writing on Puerto Rican education and communities. Nieto has served on many boards of organizations that focus on educational equity and social justice. She has also received numerous awards, including the Human and Civil Rights Award from the Massachusetts Teachers Association in 1989 and the Outstanding Accomplishment in Higher Education Award from the Hispanic Caucus of the American Association for Higher Education in 1991. The following selection is from her textbook *Affirming Diversity: The Sociopolitical Context of Multicultural Education,* 2d ed. (Longman, 1998).

Key Concept: characteristics of a comprehensive multicultural education

A DEFINITION OF
MULTICULTURAL EDUCATION

I define *multicultural education* in a sociopolitical context as follows:

> Multicultural education is a process of comprehensive school reform and basic education for all students. It challenges and rejects racism and other forms of discrimination in schools and society and accepts and affirms the pluralism (ethnic, racial, linguistic, religious, economic, and gender, among others) that students, their communities, and teachers represent. Multicultural education permeates the curriculum and instructional strategies used in schools, as well as the interactions among teachers, students, and parents, and the very way that schools conceptualize the nature of teaching and learning. Because it uses critical pedagogy as its underlying philosophy and focuses on knowledge, reflection, and action (praxis) as the basis for social change, multicultural education promotes the democratic principles of social justice.

The seven basic characteristics of multicultural education in this definition are:

- Multicultural education is *antiracist education.*
- Multicultural education is *basic education.*
- Multicultural education is *important for* all *students.*
- Multicultural education is *pervasive.*
- Multicultural education is *education for social justice.*
- Multicultural education is a *process.*
- Multicultural education is *critical pedagogy.*

Multicultural Education Is Antiracist Education

Antiracism, indeed antidiscrimination in general, is at the very core of a multicultural perspective. This is especially important to keep in mind when we consider that only the most superficial aspects of multicultural education are apparent in many schools, even those that espouse a multicultural philosophy. Celebrations of ethnic festivals are as far as it goes in some places. In others, sincere attempts to decorate bulletin boards or purchase materials with what is thought to be a multicultural perspective end up perpetuating the worst kind of stereotypes. And even where there are serious attempts to develop a truly pluralistic environment, it is not unusual to find incongruencies, such as the children of color as overwhelmingly visible in the lowest academic tracks and invisible in the highest. All of these are examples of multicultural education *without* an explicitly antiracist perspective.

It is important to stress multicultural education as antiracist because many people may believe that a multicultural program *automatically* takes care of racism. Unfortunately this is not always true....

Confronting in an honest and direct way both the positive and negative aspects of history, the arts, and science is avoided in too many schools. Michelle Fine calls this the "fear of naming," and it is part of the system of silencing in public schools.[1] To name might become too messy, or so the thinking goes. Teachers often refuse to engage their students in discussions about racism because it might "demoralize" them. Too dangerous a topic, it is best left untouched....

To be antiracist also means to work affirmatively to combat racism. It means making antiracism and antidiscrimination an explicit part of the curriculum and teaching young people skills in confronting racism. It also means that students must not be isolated, alienated, or punished for naming it when they see it. If developing productive and critical citizens for a democratic society is one of the important goals of public education, antiracist behaviors can help to meet that objective....

Multicultural education is also antiracist because it exposes the racist and discriminatory practices in schools.... A school truly committed to a multicultural philosophy will closely examine its policies and the attitudes and behaviors of its staff to determine how these might be discriminating against some students. How teachers react to their students, whether native language use is permitted in the school, how sorting takes place, and the way in which classroom organization might hurt some students and help others are questions to be considered. In addition, individual teachers will reflect on their own attitudes and practices in the classroom and how they are influenced by their background as well as by their ignorance of students' backgrounds. Although such soul-searching is often difficult, it is a necessary step in becoming a teacher committed to an antiracist multicultural philosophy....

Multicultural Education Is Basic Education

Given the recurring concern for the "basics" in education, it is absolutely essential that multicultural education be understood as *basic* education. Multicultural literacy is as indispensable for living in today's world as are reading, writing, arithmetic, and computer literacy. When multicultural education is unrelated to the core curriculum, it is perceived as unimportant to basic education.

One of the major stumbling blocks to implementing a broadly conceptualized multicultural education is the ossification of the "canon" in our schools. The canon, as used in contemporary U.S. education, assumes that the knowledge that is most worthy is already in place. According to this rather narrow view, the basics have in effect already been defined. Knowledge, in this context, is inevitably European, male, and upper class in origin and conception, especially in the arts and social sciences. In art history, courses rarely leave France, Italy, and sometimes England in considering the "great masters." What is called "classical" music is classical only in Europe, not in Africa, Asia, or Latin America. This same ethnocentrism is found in our history books, which places Europeans and European Americans as the actors and all others as the recipients, bystanders, or bit players of history.

It is unrealistic, for a number of reasons, to expect a perfectly "equal treatment" in the curriculum. A force-fit, which tries to equalize the number of African Americans, women, Jewish Americans, and so on in the curriculum, is not what multicultural education is all about. A great many groups have in effect been denied access in the actual making of history. Their participation therefore has not been equal, at least if we consider history in the traditional sense of great movers and shakers, monarchs and despots, and makers of war and peace. The participation of diverse groups, even within this somewhat narrow view of history, has been appreciable. It therefore deserves to be included. The point is that those who *have* been present in our history, arts, literature, and science should be made visible. More recent literature anthologies are a good example of the inclusion of more voices and perspectives than ever before. Did these become "great writers" overnight, or was it simply that they had been buried for too long?

However, we are not talking here simply of the "contributions" approach to history, literature, and the arts. Such an approach may consider some small contributions from usually excluded groups and can easily become patronizing by looking for contributions to a preconceived canon. Rather, the way in which generally excluded groups have made history and affected the arts, literature, geography, science, and philosophy *on their own terms* is what is missing.

The "canon" is unrealistic and incomplete because history is never as one-sided as it appears in most of our schools' curricula. What is needed is the expansion of what we define as basic by opening up the curriculum to a variety of perspectives and experiences. The problem that a canon tries to address is a real one: Modern-day knowledge is so dispersed and compartmentalized that our young people learn very little that is common. There is no *core* to the knowledge to which they are exposed.[2] However, proposing a static list of terms, almost exclusively with European and European American referents, does little to expand our common culture.

The alternative to multicultural education is *monocultural education.* Education reflective of only one reality and biased toward the dominant group, monocultural education is the order of the day in most of our schools. What students learn represents only a fraction of what is available knowledge, and those who decide what is most important make choices that are of necessity influenced by their own limited background, education, and experiences. Because the viewpoints of so many are left out, monocultural education is at best a partial education. It deprives all students of the diversity that is part of our world.

No school can consider that it is doing a proper or complete job unless its students develop multicultural literacy. What such a conception might mean in practice would no doubt differ from school to school. At the very least, we would expect all students to be fluent in a language other than their own; aware of the literature and arts of many different peoples; and conversant with the history and geography not only of the United States but also of African, Asian, Latin American, and European countries. Through such an education, we would expect our students to develop the social skills to understand and empathize with a wide diversity of people. Nothing can be more basic than this.

Sonia Nieto

There is a widespread perception that multicultural education is only for students of color, or for urban students, or for so-called disadvantaged students. This belief is probably based on the roots of multicultural education, which grew out of the civil rights and equal education movements of the 1960s. The primary objective of multicultural education was defined as addressing the needs of students who historically had been most neglected or miseducated by the schools, primarily students of color. In trying to strike more of a balance, it was felt that attention should be paid to developing curriculum and materials that reflect the reality of these students' history, culture, and experience and that this curriculum should be destined particularly for inner-city schools populated primarily by children of color. This thinking was historically necessary and is understandable even today, given the great curricular imbalance that continues to exist in most schools....

Multicultural education is by definition expansive. Because it is *about* all people, it is also *for* all people, regardless of their ethnicity, language, religion, gender, race, or class. It can even be convincingly argued that students from the dominant culture need multicultural education more than others, for they are often the most miseducated about diversity in our society. In fact, European American youths often feel that they do not even *have* a culture, at least not in the same sense that clearly culturally identifiable youths do. At the same time, they feel that their way of living, of doing things, of believing, and of acting are simply the only possibilities. Anything else is ethnic and exotic.

Feeling as they do, these children are prone to develop an unrealistic view of the world and of their place in it. They learn to think of themselves and their group as the norm and of all others as a deviation. These are the children who learn not to question, for example, the name of "flesh-colored" adhesive strips even though they are not the flesh color of three-quarters of humanity. They do not even have to think about the fact that everyone, Christian or not, gets holidays at Christmas and Easter and that other religious holidays are given little attention in our calendars and school schedules. Whereas children from dominated groups may develop feelings of inferiority based on their school experiences, dominant group children may develop feelings of superiority. Both responses are based on incomplete and inaccurate information about the complexity and diversity of the world, and both are harmful.

... A broadly conceptualized multicultural education focusing on school reform represents a substantive way of changing the curriculum, the environment, the structure of schools, and instructional strategies so that all students can benefit.

Multicultural Education Is Pervasive

Multicultural education is sometimes thought of as something that happens at a set period of the day, yet another subject area to be covered. Some school systems even have a "multicultural teacher" who goes from class to class in the same way as the music or art teacher. Although the intent of this approach may be to formalize a multicultural perspective in the standard curriculum, it is in the long run self-defeating because it tends to isolate the multicultural philosophy from everything else that happens in the classroom. By letting classroom teachers avoid responsibility for creating a multicultural approach, this strategy often alienates them by presenting multicultural knowledge as somehow contradictory to all other knowledge. The schism between what is "regular" and what is "multicultural" widens. In this kind of arrangement, classroom teachers are not encouraged, through either formal in-service programs or alternative opportunities, to develop expertise in multicultural education. It becomes exotic knowledge that is external to the real work that goes on in most classrooms. Given this conception of multicultural education, it is no wonder that teachers sometimes feel that it is a frill they cannot afford.

A true multicultural approach to education is pervasive. It permeates everything: the school climate, physical environment, curriculum, and relationships among teachers and students and community. It can be seen in every lesson, curriculum guide, unit, bulletin board, and letter that is sent home; it can be seen in the process by which books and audiovisual aids are acquired for the library, in the games played during recess, and in the lunch that is served. Thus, multicultural education is a philosophy, a way of looking at the world, not simply a program or a class or a teacher. In this comprehensive way, multicultural education helps us rethink school reform.

... In summary, the school would be a learning environment in which curriculum, pedagogy, and outreach are all consistent with a broadly conceptualized multicultural philosophy.

Multicultural Education Is Education for Social Justice

All good education connects theory with reflection and action, which is what Paulo Freire defines as *praxis*.[3] In particular, developing a multicultural perspective means learning how to think in more inclusive and expansive ways, reflecting on what we learn, and putting our learning into action. Multicultural education invites students and teachers to put their learning into action for social justice. Whether debating an issue, developing a community newspaper, starting a collaborative program at a local senior center, or beginning a petition for the removal of a potentially dangerous waste treatment plant in the neighborhood, students learn that they have power, collectively and individually, to make change....

The fact that social structures and power are rarely discussed in school should come as no surprise. Schools are organizations fundamentally concerned with maintaining the status quo and not exposing contradictions that make people uncomfortable in a society that has democratic ideals but wherein democratic realities are not always apparent. Such contradictions include the many manifestations of inequality. Yet schools are also supposed to wipe out these inequalities. To admit that inequality exists and that it is even perpetuated by the very institutions charged with doing away with it are topics far too dangerous to discuss. Nevertheless, such issues are at the heart of a broadly conceptualized multicultural perspective because the subject matter of schooling is society, with all its wrinkles and warts and contradictions. And because society is concerned with ethics and with the distribution of power, status, and rewards, education must focus on these concerns as well.

Although the connection of multicultural education with students' rights and responsibilities in a democracy is unmistakable, many young people do not learn about these responsibilities, the challenges of democracy, or the important role of citizens in ensuring and maintaining the privileges of democracy. A major study on adolescents found, for example, that most youths know little about the political process and do not make connections between the actions of government and the actions of citizens.[4] This is precisely where multicultural education can have a great impact. Not only should classrooms *allow* discussions that focus on social justice, but they should in fact *welcome* them. These discussions might center on concerns that heavily affect culturally diverse communities—poverty, discrimination, war, the national budget—and what students can do to change them. Schools cannot be separated from social justice. Because all of these concerns are pluralistic, education must of necessity be multicultural.

Multicultural Education Is a Process

Curriculum and materials represent the *content* of multicultural education, but multicultural education is above all a *process*. First, it is ongoing and dynamic. No one ever stops becoming a multicultural person, and knowledge is never complete. Thus, there is no established canon, frozen in cement. Second, it is a process because it involves relationships among people. The sensitivity and understanding teachers show their students are often more important than the facts and figures they may know about different ethnic and cultural groups. Third, and most important, multicultural education is a process because it focuses on such intangibles as teachers' expectations, learning environments, students' learning styles, and other cultural variables that are absolutely essential for schools to understand how to be successful with all of their students....

Multicultural education must be accompanied by unlearning conventional wisdom as well as dismantling policies and practices that are disadvantageous for some students at the expense of others. Teacher education programs, for example, need to be reconceptualized to include awareness of the influence of culture and language on learning, the persistence of racism and discrimination in schools and society, and instructional and curricular strategies that encourage learning among a wide variety of students. Teachers' roles in the school also need to be redefined, because empowered teachers help to empower students. The role of parents needs to be expanded so that the insights and values of the community could be more faithfully reflected in the school. A complete restructuring of curriculum and of the organization of schools is called for. The process is complex, problematic, controversial, and time-consuming, but it is one in which teachers and schools must engage to make their schools truly multicultural.

... What does critical pedagogy mean in terms of multicultural education? Critical pedagogy acknowledges rather than suppresses cultural and linguistic diversity. According to Cummins, because transmission models exclude and deny students' experiences, they cannot be multicultural: "A genuine multicultural orientation that promotes minority student empowerment is impossible within a transmission model of pedagogy."[5] ...

Critical pedagogy is also an exploder of myths. It helps to expose and demystify as well as demythologize some of the truths that we have been taught to take for granted and to analyze them critically and carefully. Justice for all, equal treatment under the law, and equal educational opportunity, although certainly ideals worth believing in and striving for, are not always a reality. The problem is that we teach them as if they were always real, always true, with no exceptions. Critical pedagogy allows us to have faith in these ideals without uncritically accepting their reality.

Critical pedagogy is based on the experiences and viewpoints of students rather than on an imposed culture. It is therefore multicultural as well because the most successful education is that which begins with the learner. Students themselves are the foundation for the curriculum. Nevertheless, a liberating education takes students beyond their own particular and therefore limited experiences, no matter what their background....

This discussion leads us to an important consideration: *In the final analysis, multicultural education as defined here is simply good pedagogy.* That is, all good education takes students seriously, uses their experiences as a basis for further learning, and helps them to develop into critical and empowered citizens. What is multicultural about this? To put it simply, in our multicultural society, all good education needs to take into account the diversity of our student body. That is, multicultural education is good education for a larger number of students.

Is multicultural education just as necessary in a monocultural society? We might legitimately ask whether even the most ethnically homogeneous society is truly monocultural, given the diversity of social class, language, sexual preference, physical ability, and other human and social differences present in all societies. Furthermore, our world is becoming increasingly interdependent, and all students need to understand their role in a global society and not simply in a nation. Multicultural education, therefore, is a process that goes beyond the changing demographics in a particular country. It is more effective education for a changing world.

NOTES

1. Michelle Fine, *Framing Dropouts: Notes on the Politics of an Urban Public High School* (Albany: State University of New York Press, 1991).

2. E. D. Hirsch, *Cultural Literacy* (Boston: Houghton Mifflin, 1987).

3. Paulo Freire, *Pedagogy of the Oppressed* (New York: Seabury Press, 1970).

4. S. Shirley Feldman and Glen R. Elliott, *At the Threshold: The Developing Adolescent* (Cambridge, MA: Harvard University Press, 1990).

5. Jim Cummins, "The Sanitized Curriculum: Educational Disempowerment in a Nation at Risk." In *Richness in Writing: Empowering ESL Students*, edited by Donna M. Johnson and Duane H. Roen (White Plains, NY: Longman, 1989).

The Multicultural Education Program Evaluation Checklist

Prepared by the National Council for the Social Studies (NCSS) Task Force on Ethnic Studies Curriculum Guidelines, the following selection comprises a series of guidelines that can be used by teachers and administrators to determine a school's level of commitment to multicultural education. The guidelines are presented in checklist form to give a quick way to initially evaluate the total school practices and policies for the purpose of creating a curriculum and an environment that recognizes and respects the cultural diversity of our society. The checklist includes guidelines dealing with the total school environment, such as teaching strategies, personnel, curriculum, library materials, and school policies, among others.

Members of the NCSS task force include James A. Banks, Carlos Cortes, Geneva Gay, Ricardo Garcia, and Anna Ochoa. In the complete article in which the guidelines were presented, the authors give a full discussion of each checklist item, the history of how each item was created, and the importance of each guideline. The complete article, "Curriculum Guidelines for Multicultural Education," can be found in *Social Education* (September 1992).

Key Concept: checklist of guidelines for multicultural education

GUIDELINES

1.0   Does ethnic and cultural diversity permeate the total school environment?

    1.1 Are ethnic content and perspectives incorporated into all aspects of the curriculum, preschool through 12th grade and beyond?

    1.2 Do instructional materials treat racial and ethnic differences and groups honestly, realistically, and sensitively?

1.3 Do school libraries and resource centers offer a variety of materials on the histories, experiences, and cultures of many racial, ethnic, and cultural groups?

1.4 Do school assemblies, decorations, speakers, holidays, and heroes reflect racial, ethnic, and cultural group differences?

1.5 Are extracurricular activities multiethnic and multicultural?

2.0 Do school policies and procedures foster positive interactions among the various racial, ethnic, and cultural group members of the school?

2.1 Do school policies accommodate the behavioral patterns, learning styles, and orientations of those ethnic and cultural group members actually in the school?

2.2 Does the school provide a variety of instruments and techniques for teaching and counseling students of various ethnic and cultural groups?

2.3 Do school policies recognize the holidays and festivities of various ethnic groups?

2.4 Do school policies avoid instructional and guidance practices based on stereotyped and ethnocentric perceptions?

2.5 Do school policies respect the dignity and worth of students as individuals *and* as members of racial, ethnic, and cultural groups?

3.0 Is the school staff (administrators, instructors, counselors, and support staff) multiethnic and multiracial?

3.1 Has the school established and enforced policies for recruiting and maintaining a staff made up of individuals from various racial and ethnic groups?

4.0 Does the school have systematic, comprehensive, mandatory, and continuing multicultural staff development programs?

4.1 Are teachers, librarians, counselors, administrators, and support staff included in the staff development programs?

4.2 Do the staff development programs include a variety of experiences (such as lectures, field experiences, and curriculum projects)?

4.3 Do the staff development programs provide opportunities to gain knowledge and understanding about various racial, ethnic, and cultural groups?

4.4 Do the staff development programs provide opportunities for participants to explore their attitudes and feelings about their own ethnicity and others'?

4.5 Do the staff development programs examine the verbal and nonverbal patterns of interethnic group interactions?

4.6 Do the staff development programs provide opportunities for learning how to create and select multiethnic instructional materials and how to incorporate multicultural content into curriculum materials?

5.0 Does the curriculum reflect the ethnic learning styles of students within the school?

    5.1 Is the curriculum designed to help students learn how to function effectively in various cultural environments and learn more than one cognitive style?

    5.2 Do the objectives, instructional strategies, and learning materials reflect the cultures and cognitive styles of the various ethnic and cultural groups within the school?

6.0 Does the curriculum provide continuous opportunities for students to develop a better sense of self?

    6.1 Does the curriculum help students strengthen their self-identities?

    6.2 Is the curriculum designed to help students develop greater self-understanding?

    6.3 Does the curriculum help students improve their self-concepts?

    6.4 Does the curriculum help students to better understand themselves in light of their ethnic and cultural heritages?

7.0 Does the curriculum help students understand the wholeness of the experiences of ethnic and cultural groups?

    7.1 Does the curriculum include the study of societal problems some ethnic and cultural group members experience, such as racism, prejudice, discrimination, and exploitation?

    7.2 Does the curriculum include the study of historical experiences, cultural patterns, and social problems of various ethnic and cultural groups?

    7.3 Does the curriculum include both positive and negative aspects of ethnic and cultural group experiences?

    7.4 Does the curriculum present people of color both as active participants in society and as subjects of oppression and exploitation?

    7.5 Does the curriculum examine the diversity within each group's experience?

    7.6 Does the curriculum present group experiences as dynamic and continuously changing?

    7.7 Does the curriculum examine the total experiences of groups instead of focusing exclusively on the "heroes"?

8.0 Does the curriculum help students identify and understand the ever-present conflict between ideals and realities in human societies?

    8.1 Does the curriculum help students identify and understand the value conflicts inherent in a multicultural society?

    8.2 Does the curriculum examine differing views of ideals and realities among ethnic and cultural groups?

9.0 Does the curriculum explore and clarify ethnic alternatives and options within U.S. society?

9.1 Does the teacher create a classroom atmosphere reflecting an acceptance of and respect for ethnic and cultural differences?

9.2 Does the teacher create a classroom atmosphere allowing realistic consideration of alternatives and options for members of ethnic and cultural groups?

10.0 Does the curriculum promote values, attitudes, and behaviors that support ethnic and cultural diversity?

10.1 Does the curriculum help students examine differences within and among ethnic and cultural groups?

10.2 Does the curriculum foster attitudes supportive of cultural democracy and other unifying democratic ideals and values?

10.3 Does the curriculum reflect ethnic and cultural diversity?

10.4 Does the curriculum present diversity as a vital societal force that encompasses both potential strength and potential conflict?

11.0 Does the curriculum help students develop decision-making abilities, social participation skills, and a sense of political efficacy necessary for effective citizenship?

11.1 Does the curriculum help students develop the ability to distinguish facts from interpretations and opinions?

11.2 Does the curriculum help students develop skills in finding and processing information?

11.3 Does the curriculum help students develop sound knowledge, concepts, generalizations, and theories about issues related to ethnicity and cultural identity?

11.4 Does the curriculum help students develop sound methods of thinking about issues related to ethnic and cultural groups?

11.5 Does the curriculum help students develop skills in clarifying and reconsidering their values and relating them to their understanding of ethnicity and cultural identity?

11.6 Does the curriculum include opportunities to use knowledge, valuing, and thinking in decision making on issues related to race, ethnicity, and culture?

11.7 Does the curriculum provide opportunities for students to take action on social problems affecting racial, ethnic, and cultural groups?

11.8 Does the curriculum help students develop a sense of efficacy?

12.0 Does the curriculum help students develop skills necessary for effective interpersonal and intercultural group interactions?

12.1 Does the curriculum help students understand ethnic and cultural reference points that influence communication?
12.2 Does the curriculum help students participate in cross-ethnic and cross-cultural experiences and reflect upon them?

13.0 Is the multicultural curriculum comprehensive in scope and sequence, presenting holistic views of ethnic and cultural groups, and an integral part of the total school curriculum?

13.1 Does the curriculum introduce students to the experiences of persons of widely varying backgrounds in the study of each ethnic and cultural group?
13.2 Does the curriculum discuss the successes and contributions of group members within the context of that group's values?
13.3 Does the curriculum include the role of ethnicity and culture in the local community as well as in the nation?
13.4 Does content related to ethnic and cultural groups extend beyond special units, courses, occasions, and holidays?
13.5 Are materials written by and about ethnic and cultural groups used in teaching fundamental skills?
13.6 Does the curriculum provide for the development of progressively more complex concepts, abilities, and values?
13.7 Is the study of ethnicity and culture incorporated into instructional plans rather than being supplementary or additive?

14.0 Does the curriculum include the continuous study of the cultures, historical experiences, social realities, and existential conditions of ethnic groups with a variety of racial compositions?

14.1 Does the curriculum include study of several ethnic and cultural groups?
14.2 Does the curriculum include studies of both white ethnic groups and ethnic groups of color?
14.3 Does the curriculum provide for continuity in the examination of aspects of experience affected by race?

15.0 Are interdisciplinary and multidisciplinary approaches used in designing and implementing the curriculum?

15.1 Are interdisciplinary and multidisciplinary perspectives used in the study of ethnic and cultural groups and related issues?
15.2 Are approaches used authentic and comprehensive explanations of ethnic and cultural issues, events, and problems?

16.0 Does the curriculum use comparative approaches in the study of racial, ethnic, and cultural groups?

16.1 Does the curriculum focus on the similarities and differences among and between ethnic and cultural groups?

16.2 Are matters examined from comparative perspectives with fairness to all?

17.0 Does the curriculum help students view and interpret events, situations, and conflict from diverse ethnic and cultural perspectives and points of view?

17.1 Are the perspectives of various ethnic and cultural groups represented in the instructional program?

17.2 Are students taught why different ethnic and cultural groups often perceive the same historical event or contemporary situation differently?

17.3 Are the perspectives of each ethnic and cultural group presented as valid ways to perceive the past and the present?

18.0 Does the curriculum conceptualize and describe the development of the United States as a multidirectional society?

18.1 Does the curriculum view the territorial and cultural growth of the United States as flowing from several directions?

18.2 Does the curriculum include a parallel study of the various societies that developed in the geo-cultural United States?

19.0 Does the school provide opportunities for students to participate in the aesthetic experiences of various ethnic and cultural groups?

19.1 Are multiethnic literature and art used to promote empathy and understanding of people from various ethnic and cultural groups?

19.2 Are multiethnic literature and art used to promote self-examination and self-understanding?

19.3 Do students read and hear the poetry, short stories, novels, folklore, plays, essays, and autobiographies of a variety of ethnic and cultural groups?

19.4 Do students examine the music, art, architecture, and dance of a variety of ethnic and cultural groups?

19.5 Do students have available the artistic, musical, and literary expression of the local ethnic and cultural communities?

19.6 Are opportunities provided for students to develop their own artistic, literary, and musical expression?

20.0 Does the curriculum provide opportunities for students to develop full literacy in at least two languages?

20.1 Are students taught to communicate (speaking, reading, and writing) in a second language?

20.2 Are students taught about the culture of the people who use the second language?

20.3 Are second language speakers provided opportunities to develop full literacy in their native language?
20.4 Are students for whom English is a second language taught in their native languages as needed?

21.0 Does the curriculum make maximum use of local community resources?

21.1 Are students involved in the continuous study of the local community?
21.2 Are members of the local ethnic and cultural communities continually used as classroom resources?
21.3 Are field trips to the various local ethnic and cultural communities provided for students?

22.0 Do the assessment procedures used with students reflect their ethnic and community cultures?

22.1 Do teachers use a variety of assessment procedures that reflect the ethnic and cultural diversity of students?
22.2 Do teachers' day-to-day assessment techniques take into account the ethnic and cultural diversity of their students?

23.0 Does the school conduct ongoing, systematic evaluations of the goals, methods, and instructional materials used in teaching about ethnicity and culture?

23.1 Do assessment procedures draw on many sources of evidence from many sorts of people?
23.2 Does the evaluation program examine school policies and procedures?
23.3 Does the evaluation program examine the everyday climate of the school?
23.4 Does the evaluation program examine the effectiveness of curricular programs, both academic and nonacademic?
23.5 Are the results of evaluation used to improve the school program?

ACKNOWLEDGMENTS

1.1 From Ronald T. Takaki, *A Different Mirror: A History of Multicultural America* (Little, Brown, 1993). Copyright © 1993 by Ronald T. Takaki. Reprinted by permission of Little, Brown and Company, Inc. Notes omitted.

1.2 From Joel Spring, *Deculturalization and the Struggle for Equality: A Brief History of the Education of Dominated Cultures in the United States*, 2d ed. (McGraw-Hill, 1993). Copyright © 1993 by Joel Spring. Reprinted by permission of The McGraw-Hill Companies, Inc.

2.1 From Booker T. Washington, a Speech During the Atlanta Exposition, Atlanta, Georgia (September 18, 1895).

2.2 From W. E. B. Du Bois, *The Souls of Black Folk* (Vintage Books, 1990).

3.1 From Kenneth R. Howe, "Liberal Democracy, Equal Educational Opportunity, and the Challenge of Multiculturalism," *American Educational Research Journal*, vol. 29, no. 3 (Fall 1992). Copyright © 1992 by The American Educational Research Association. Adapted by permission of the publisher.

3.2 From Maxine Greene, "The Passions of Pluralism: Multiculturalism and the Expanding Community," *Educational Researcher*, vol. 22, no. 1 (January–February 1993). Copyright © 1993 by The American Educational Research Association. Adapted by permission of the publisher.

4.1 From Samuel Bowles, "Unequal Education and the Reproduction of the Social Division of Labor," in Martin Carnoy, ed., *Schooling in a Corporate Society: The Political Economy of Education in America*, 2d ed. (David McKay, 1975). Copyright © 1971 by Samuel Bowles. Reprinted by permission of the author.

4.2 From John U. Ogbu, "Adaptation to Minority Status and Impact on School Success," *Theory into Practice*, vol. 31, no. 4 (Autumn 1992). Copyright © 1992 by The College of Education, Ohio State University. Reprinted by permission.

5.1 From Jonathan Kozol, *Savage Inequalities: Children in America's Schools* (Crown, 1991). Copyright © 1991 by Jonathan Kozol. Reprinted by permission of Crown Publishers, Inc.

5.2 From Penelope Eckert, *Jocks and Burnouts: Social Categories and Identity in the High School* (Teachers College Press, 1989), pp. 1, 3–4, 36–40, 45–48. Copyright © 1989 by Teachers College, Columbia University. Reprinted by permission. Notes omitted.

6.1 From Edward T. Hall, *The Silent Language* (Doubleday, 1981). Copyright © 1959, 1981 by Edward T. Hall. Reprinted by permission of Doubleday, a division of Random House, Inc.

6.2 From Henry T. Trueba, "The Dynamics of Cultural Transmission," in Henry T. Trueba, Cirenio Rodriguez, Yali Zou, and Jose Cintron, *Healing Multicultural America: Mexican Immigrants Rise to Power in Rural California* (Falmer Press, 1993). Copyright © 1993 by Henry T. Trueba, Cirenio Rodriguez, Yali Zou, and Jose Cintron. Reprinted by permission of Taylor & Francis, Inc. Notes omitted.

7.1 From Gordon W. Allport, *The Nature of Prejudice* (Doubleday Anchor, 1958). Copyright © 1954, 1958, 1979 by Gordon W. Allport. Reprinted by permission of Perseus Books Publishers, a member of Perseus Books, LLC.

7.2 From Glenn S. Pate, "Research on Prejudice Reduction," *Educational Leadership* (January 1981). Copyright © 1981 by The Association for Supervision and Curriculum Development. Reprinted by permission of The Association for Supervision and Curriculum Development.

13.3   From Alicia Paredes Scribner, "Advocating for Hispanic High School Students: Research-Based Educational Practices," *The High School Journal*, vol. 78, no. 4 (April/May 1995). Copyright © 1995 by University of North Carolina Press. Reprinted by permission. References omitted.

13.4   From Valerie Ooka Pang, "Asian-American Children: A Diverse Population," *The Educational Forum*, vol. 55, no. 1 (Fall 1990). Copyright © 1990 by Kappa Delta Pi, an International Honor Society in Education. Reprinted by permission of *The Educational Forum*.

14.1   From Jim Cummins, *Empowering Minority Students* (California Association for Bilingual Education, 1989). Copyright © 1989 by The California Association for Bilingual Education. Reprinted by permission of The California Association for Bilingual Education; permission conveyed through The Copyright Clearance Center, Inc.

14.2   From Lily Wong Fillmore and Concepción Valadez, "Teaching Bilingual Learners," in Merlin C. Wittrock, ed., *Handbook of Research on Teaching*, 3rd ed. (Macmillan, 1986). Copyright © 1986 by Macmillan Publishing Company.

15.1   From Jean Anyon, "Social Class and School Knowledge," *Curriculum Inquiry*, vol. 11, no. 1 (1981). Copyright © 1981 by The Ontario Institute for Studies in Education. Reprinted by permission of Blackwell Publishers.

15.2   From Joe L. Kincheloe and Shirley R. Steinberg, *Changing Multiculturalism* (Taylor & Francis, 1997). Copyright © 1997 by Joe L. Kincheloe and Shirley R. Steinberg. Reprinted by permission of Taylor & Francis, Inc.

16.1   From Louise Derman-Sparks, "Empowering Children to Create a Caring Culture in a World of Differences," *Childhood Education* (Winter 1993/1994). Copyright © 1993 by The Association for Childhood Education International. Reprinted by permission of Louise Derman-Sparks and The Association for Childhood Education International.

16.2   From James A. Banks, "Transforming the Mainstream Curriculum," *Educational Leadership*, vol. 51, no. 8 (May 1994). Copyright © 1994 by The Association for Supervision and Curriculum Development. Reprinted by permission of The Association for Supervision and Curriculum Development.

17.1   Abridged from Sonia Nieto, *Affirming Diversity: The Sociopolitical Context of Multicultural Education*, 2d ed. (Longman, 1992). Copyright © 1992, 1996 by Longman Publishers, USA. Reprinted by permission of Addison-Wesley Educational Publishers, Inc.

17.2   From NCSS Task Force on Ethnic Studies Curriculum Guidelines, "Curriculum Guidelines for Multicultural Education," *Social Education* (September 1992). Copyright © 1992 by The National Council for the Social Studies. Reprinted by permission.

Index